City–County Consolidation

Selected Titles in the American Governance and Public Policy Series

Series Editors: Gerard W. Boychuk, Karen Mossberger, and Mark C. Rom

Branching Out, Digging In: Environmental Advocacy and Agenda Setting
Sarah Pralle

Brussels Versus the Beltway: Advocacy in the United States and the European Union
Christine Mahoney

Collaborative Public Management: New Strategies for Local Governments
Robert Agranoff and Michael McGuire

Controlling Technocracy: Citizen Rationality and the NIMBY Syndrome
Gregory E. McAvoy

Custodians of Place: Governing the Growth and Development of Cities
Paul G. Lewis and Max Neiman

The Education Mayor: Improving America's Schools
Kenneth K. Wong, Francis X. Shen, Dorothea Anagnostopoulos, and Stacey Rutledge

Fenced Off: The Suburbanization of American Politics
Juliet F. Gainsborough

From Revenue Sharing to Deficit Sharing: General Revenue Sharing and the Cities
Bruce A. Wallin

Globalization and the Politics of Pay: Policy Choices in the American States
Susan B. Hansen

Healthy Voices, Unhealthy Silence: Advocacy and Health Policy for the Poor
Colleen M. Grogan and Michael K. Gusmano

Improving Governance: A New Logic for Empirical Research
Laurence E. Lynn Jr., Carolyn J. Heinrich, and Carolyn J. Hill

Investing in the Disadvantaged: Assessing the Benefits and Costs of Social Policies
David L. Weimer and Aidan R. Vining, Editors

Lessons of Disaster: Policy Change after Catastrophic Events
Thomas Birkland

Metropolitan Governance: Conflict, Competition, and Cooperation
Richard C. Feiock, Editor

National Health Insurance in the United States and Canada: Race, Territory, and the Roots of Difference
Gerard W. Boychuk

The Politics of Ideas and the Spread of Enterprise Zones
Karen Mossberger

The Shadowlands of Conduct: Ethics and State Politics
Beth A. Rosenson

Ten Thousand Democracies: Politics and Public Opinion in America's School Districts
Michael B. Berkman and Eric Plutzer

Terra Incognita: Vacant Land and Urban Strategies
Ann O'M. Bowman and Michael A. Pagano

Virtual Inequality: Beyond the Digital Divide
Karen Mossberger, Caroline J. Tolbert, and Mary Stansbury

City–County Consolidation

Promises Made, Promises Kept?

Suzanne M. Leland and Kurt Thurmaier, Editors

Georgetown University Press
Washington, DC

Georgetown University Press, Washington, D.C. www.press.georgetown.edu

Library of Congress Cataloging-in-Publication Data

City–county consolidation : promises made, promises kept? / Suzanne M. Leland and Kurt Thurmaier, editors.
p. cm. (American Governance and Public Policy Series)
Includes bibliographical references and index.
ISBN 978-1-58901-628-6 (pbk. : alk. paper)
1. Metropolitan government—United States. I. Leland, Suzanne M., 1971– II. Thurmaier, Kurt M., 1957–
JS422.C54 2010
320.8'590973—dc22
2009035777

This book is printed on acid-free paper meeting the requirements of the American National Standard for Permanence in Paper for Printed Library Materials.

15 14 13 12 11 10 9 8 7 6 5 4 3 2

First printing

Printed in the United States of America

We dedicate this book to

Daniel Brandenburg and Jeanette Leland Dias

Anna Thurmaier and Emily Thurmaier

and the authors of each chapter, who tirelessly searched for data

Contents

→ Preface ←

In our previous book, *Reshaping the Local Government Landscape: Case Studies of City–County Consolidation*, we organized a team of scholars to evaluate a set of city–county consolidation efforts to determine what factors accounted for the success of some cases and the failure of others. Using a rigorous comparative case study research design, we analyzed a sample in which about half the cases were successful and the other half were failures. Our analysis revealed that successful city–county consolidation campaigns were based on promises of improved economic development performance. Conversely, campaigns based on promises of increasing government efficiency uniformly lost.

Reshaping the Local Government Landscape has generated many inquiries about cost savings and economic development from around the country. Many people—proponents, opponents, and neutral observers alike—have asked us whether consolidated local governments live up to the promises made for them in consolidation campaigns. We could not answer this question, however, because there have not been any comprehensive empirical studies that compare findings across several cases—until now.

This volume is an ambitious attempt to apply a rigorous comparative research design to a large enough sample of city–county consolidation cases so that we can more conclusively determine whether those who undertook these efforts kept the promises they made in their campaigns for successful consolidation referenda. There are two keys to a successful comparative research design. First, one needs a rigorous methodology that enables one to identify the critical variables that measure "success" and to analyze each case in the sample with the same measures. The second key is using robust comparison cases to control for internal threats to validity. As you will find in reading this book, a comparative research design of this rigor is much stronger in theory than in practice. Both the selection of usable comparison cases and the collection of comparable data were much more challenging than even the worst case that one could imagine. Although some case studies were "textbook" examples for selection and collection, others were nightmares for the chapter authors and editors alike—and so we were sometimes haunted by the threats to internal validity of "not quite" the exact selection we desired, and of the "not available" data that we wanted to use across all cases.

Yet we remained undaunted throughout the project. Countless e-mails, phone calls, and chats in the corridors of conferences mixed prodding for "more and better" with encouragement and understanding for the challenges. Throughout this project, our goal was always the most rigorous comparative research we could muster; to the extent that we fall short of the standards inherent in a classic quasi-experimental design, it is not for lack of effort. Sometimes we simply could not gather the data we desired; or if it exists, we could not find it. That said, we are very proud of the data we present in this volume—one of the most extensive collections of data on the effects of city–county consolidations in the United States. Although the conclusions in some chapters are more certain than those in others, we are quite confident about the overall value of the conclusions reached from our analysis of the data across the broad sample of the book's city–county consolidation cases.

These nine cases, explored in detail in chapters 2 through 10, portray a great variety of intriguing city–county consolidation promises—ranging from improving service delivery in Nashville/Davidson County and Athens/Clarke County, to throwing "the rascals out" of office in Jacksonville/Duvall and Butte/Silverbow County, to improving the overall efficiency of government in Carson City/Ormsby County and thwarting aggressive annexation attempts by nearby municipalities in Lexington/Fayetteville and Virginia Beach/Princess Anne County to rescuing the economic base in Lynchburg/Moore and improving economic development in Wyandotte County/Kansas City, Kansas, by landing a NASCAR track.

Chapter 11 concludes by considering the nine cases together with respect to each hypothesis. We reach a summary judgment about whether consolidations achieve the promises of their proponents, and we identify the factors that contribute to the success of consolidation efforts. Our analyses indicate that economic gains are more likely than efficiency gains. This is an interesting result given that our previous examination of successful consolidation campaigns revealed that voters typically do not believe consolidation will deliver a more efficient government but are sometimes convinced that economic development can be improved under a unified governing structure.

This book will appeal to those interested in urban affairs, economic development, local government management, and general public administration. Community leaders such as members of the League of Women Voters, the staffs of both proconsolidation and anticonsolidation groups, mayors, city council members, county commission members, sheriffs, and city administrators will find the book valuable. The book provides theoretical and empirical contributions that will be useful for scholars of urban policy, public administration, geography, political science, criminal justice, and sociology. We trust that it will also be useful for students working on master's degrees in public administration and in urban planning, and on doctorates in public administration, public policy, political science, sociology, and geography.

We now realize that there is a very good reason why a research project of this nature and scope has not been done before—even though there has been strong demand and enduring interest. It is really hard work. On behalf of the entire research team, we hope you, the reader, will enjoy the fruits of our collective labors.

Acknowledgments

We first and foremost owe a great debt of gratitude to our research team. These chapter authors have gone way above and beyond the normal expectations for contributors to an edited volume. They have spent, literally, hundreds of hours rooting through archival boxes of budgets and other data in the basements of county courthouses, talking with local officials (many now retired or in other positions), searching the Web for alternative sources of comparable information, and revising numerous tables and figures to reflect the latest data "find" to increase the accuracy of chapter conclusions. We are thankful for the sacrifices they made to see this project through. Everyone who reads this book and uses this information owes them their gratitude as well. These types of projects simply are not possible without the generous and eager collaboration of scholars who are willing to work together for goals that cannot be achieved by a single author, or even a pair of authors.

In addition to the chapter authors and the graduate students who helped them, we also thank the countless local and federal officials who went out of their way to help authors find the data they were seeking. In particular, we appreciate the staff at the U.S. Bureau of the Census who dug into the archives to find some of the data we sought. We also appreciate the encouragement of Ed Benton, Beth Honadle, Esther McKee, and other colleagues who appreciated the project's ambitiousness and kept us from becoming discouraged when we met setbacks.

We wish to thank Don Jacobs and the staff of Georgetown University Press for their encouragement and helpful advice. We appreciate the external reviews and the series editor's comments; they greatly improved the book.

Finally, we appreciate beyond measure the love and support of our families, who encouraged us during this lengthy and challenging endeavor.

1

A Research Design for Evaluating Consolidation Performance

Suzanne M. Leland and Kurt Thurmaier

Efficiency and effectiveness are at the forefront of discussions about local government management across the United States. Local government's role in providing who gets what from government has increased greatly in the devolution era as we begin a new century. Governments face cutbacks in state and federal assistance on the one hand, and taxpayer revolts on the other. Public administrators are under pressure to find new ways to improve service delivery more efficiently and effectively.

Although city–county consolidation is a frequently discussed local government reform, structurally merging a major municipality and county to form a unified government is often unsuccessful; about 80 percent of merger referenda fail (Leland and Thurmaier 2006). Rosenbaum and Kammerer (1974) note that consolidation proponents work against long odds to win the referendum vote. One cause for the low success rate may be that there is little evidence to convince voters that consolidated governments are more efficient than separate cities and counties. Many promises have been made in successful consolidation campaigns, but have they been kept? In this book, we present a careful study of the promises made in successful referenda campaigns, and we analyze the extent to which the promises have been kept. This chapter first reviews what previous studies have demonstrated, and it then presents a research design to empirically explore whether consolidated governments are more efficient, lead to improved economic development, and keep other promises made to voters.

City–County Consolidation

Consolidated city–county governments only make up slightly more than 1 percent of the 3,043 county governments in the United States and about 1.5 percent of the 19,371 city governments (Durning 2003; Leland and Thurmaier 2006). City–county consolidation occurs when a county and one or more of the cities within a county merge to form a single government entity. The boundary lines of the jurisdictions become coterminous. In most cases, smaller towns, school districts, and city- or county-owned utilities are excluded from consolidations (Leland and Thurmaier 2004), although water and sewer services are usually included in the new government. Political considerations typically dictate exempting smaller suburban towns from initial consolidation, giving them the option of joining the unified government at a later time (Glendening and Atkins 1980). Consolidation is distinctive from other forms of metropolitan cooperation because it involves the most visible and comprehensive change local governments can undertake (Carr and Sneed 2004). Currently there are forty consolidated governments in the United States (table 1.1), including Greeley County and the city of Tribune, Kansas, which voted to consolidate in 2007.

The first consolidated government was adopted in 1805, with New Orleans and Orleans Parish, Louisiana. Some noteworthy city–county consolidations include Jacksonville/Duval County, Florida, which was adopted in 1967; Indianapolis/Marion County, Indiana (UNIGOV), adopted in 1969; and the recently consolidated government of Louisville/Jefferson, Kentucky, adopted in 2001. Consolidated governments are located in every region of the country except the Northeast. They range from very small rural communities, such as Butte/Silver Bow County, Montana, to medium-sized urban areas such as Nashville/Davidson County, Tennessee.

Every year several communities consider the issue, and in the words of Dan Durning, consolidation is "an evergreen issue." At the time we are writing this, reformers in several major cities are contemplating consolidation, including in Cleveland, Pittsburgh, Buffalo, and Orlando. Despite this persistent interest in city–county consolidation, reformers are simply unable to point to successful implementation elsewhere that have overwhelming evidence of cost savings.

In Walker's (1969) classic study of the diffusion of innovation of state policies, he notes that opposition to a particular policy can be overcome if the proponent of change can point to successful implementation elsewhere. We believe this situation is also applicable to the diffusion of innovation among local governments and provides one explanation for why few consolidations are adopted. Local government reformers often advocate consolidation on the basis of cost savings, yet they are unable to point to a particular case that would convince elected officials and voters to adopt such a radical reform (Leland and Thurmaier 2004).

The Structural Effectiveness of a Unified Voice versus the Technical Efficiency Argument

In most cases, if proconsolidation reformers are lucky enough to get consolidation on the ballot, a successful campaign is difficult. In our previous book, *Reshaping the Local Government Landscape: Case Studies of City–County Consolidation* (Leland and Thurmaier 2004), we argue that economic development is the primary catalyst for successful city–county consolidation. Through a careful, multicase study of modern consolidation referenda that passed and failed, we find that the underlying rationale common to the successful cases is that reformers argue for city–county consolidation to improve economic development.

The reformers, mainly the civic elite, develop a vision for the economic development of the community—a countywide vision larger than the city. Civic elites are largely led and funded by the local business community and are often motivated by the central and enduring issue of whether the community as a whole faces economic decline or economic growth. The economic conditions do not need to be in "crisis," as previous studies have argued (Rosenbaum and Kammerer 1974). The more important concern of these civic leaders is whether the current government structure of multiple, competing jurisdictions is capable of supporting and nurturing their economic vision (Leland and Thurmaier 2004, 2005).

The essential elements of a successful consolidation attempt, then, are civic elites who are able to define the economic development vision for the community, determine that the existing political structure is inadequate to support and implement that vision, and then successfully convince the average voter that consolidation is the solution to the economic development that will benefit the whole community, not just the elites, through a unified voice (Leland and Thurmaier 2004, 2005). We believe that the reason for this success lies in the fact that citizens and civic leaders believe a consolidated city–county government will achieve *structural effectiveness* in the area of economic development, which in turn creates a more unified vision and voice for the county. A unified voice can only be achieved by structural consolidation, merging the two elected bodies of the city and the county, and not simply through an interlocal government agreement.

Creating a unified voice is one of the reasons behind the successful ballot to merge Wyandotte County and Kansas City, Kansas, a newly consolidated government (1997) that many in the metropolitan region deem an economic success. Reformers ran a successful campaign based on the arguement that

Table 1.1 Forty City–County Consolidations in the United States

Year	City/County	Vote in Favor (%)
1805	New Orleans/Orleans Parish, Louisiana	N.A.
1821	Boston/Suffolk County, Massachusetts	N.A.
1821	Nantucket Town/Nantucket County, Massachusetts	N.A.
1854	Philadelphia/Philadelphia County, Pennsylvania	N.A.
1856	San Francisco/San Francisco County, California	N.A.
1874	New York City (5 counties), New York	N.A.
1902	Denver/Denver County, Colorado	N.A.
1907	Honolulu/Honolulu County, Hawaii	N.A.
1947	Baton Rouge/East Baton Rouge Parish, Louisiana	55.1
1952	Hampton and Phoebus/Elizabeth City County, Virginia	88.1
1957	Newport News/Warwick County, Virginia	66.9
1962	Nashville/Davidson County, Tennessee	56.8
1962	South Norfolk/Norfolk County, Virginia	66.0
1962	Virginia Beach/Princess Anne County, Virginia	81.9
1967	Jacksonville/Duval County, Florida	64.7
1969	Carson City/Ormsby County, Nevada	65.1
1969	Indianapolis/Marion County, Indiana	N.A.
1969	Juneau and Douglas/Greater Juneau Borough, Alaska	54.1
1970	Columbus/Muscogee County, Georgia	80.7
1971	Holland and Whaleyville/Nansemond County, Virginia	N.A.
1971	Sitka/Greater Sitka Borough, Alaska	77.2
1972	Lexington/Fayette County, Kentucky	69.4
1972	Suffolk/Nansemond County, Virginia	75.7
1975	Anchorage, Glen Alps, and Girdwood/Greater Anchorage Area Borough, Alaska	62.0

Table 1.1 (Continued)

1976	Anaconda/Deer Lodge County, Montana	56.0
1976	Butte/Silver Bow County, Montana	62.0
1981	Houma/Terrebonne Parish, Louisiana	53.8
1987	Lynchburg/Moore County, Tennessee	52.0
1990	Athens/Clarke County, Georgia	59.2
1992	Lafayette/Lafayette Parish, Louisiana	60.0
1995	Augusta/Richmond County, Georgia	66.7
1997	Wyandotte County/Kansas City, Kansas	60.0
1998	Broomfield/Broomfield, Colorado	NA
2000	Louisville/Jefferson County, Kentucky	54.0
2000	Hartsville/Trousdale County, Tennessee	52.0
2002	Haines City/Haines Borough, Alaska	51.0
2003	Cusseta City/Chattahoochee County, Georgia	69.0
2006	Georgetown/Quitman County, Georgia	68.0
2006	Camden/Camden County, North Carolina	54.0
2007	Tribune/Greeley County, Kansas	73.0

Sources: Glendening and Atkins 1980, 70; with additional information provided by Jackie Byers from the National Association of Counties, Suzanne Leland, Dan Durning, and Terrell Blodgett.

Note: N.A. = consolidation was created by state legislation, not a referendum by the people in the affected area.

consolidation would lead to improved economic development for the region and would end the county's efforts to woo the same businesses that the city was trying to lure. Many thought that combining the unreformed county with the professionalized city would end the periodic scandals and corruption and make the new unified government a credible force that could have more clout at the state capital as well as with prospective developers. After structural consolidation, they then could work together to bring about large capital projects that would be located in the same jurisdiction, a benefit for all.

According to Leland and Wood (chapter 10 of this volume), structural consolidation has indeed allowed the unified government to lure new economic development projects that the area needed to keep taxes from rising. Consolidation allowed the unified government to work together and attract a new NASCAR track and the surrounding development of Village West, a 400-acre retail and entertainment destination district that includes Cabella's Outfitters, Nebraska Furniture Mart, the Kansas City T-Bones Minor League Baseball Park, a destination hotel, a family destination resort, and a shopping center. All have contributed significantly to the revitalization of Wyandotte County/Kansas City. The NASCAR race track and Village West development have led to rising home values and a housing boom, increased sales and property tax revenue, and attracted millions of tourists each year. The Homebuilders Association of Greater Kansas City ranked Kansas City, sixth out of sixty-eight metro communities in the number of new housing starts (Dornbrook 2006).

However, we certainly should not ignore the technical efficiency effects of consolidation. Technical efficiency, often measured as increased productivity, can be achieved over the long run by a combination of factors. First, economies of scale can be achieved for select services that both the city and county provide, including combining benefit plans, vehicle maintenance, and select areas of administration. There is potential to cut costs if the two governments are both conducting a similar function and paying separately for capital expenses; for example, both a city and county can have separate parks departments and each maintain their own equipment (e.g., trucks, lawnmowers). Combining these functions and sharing equipment may reduce costs.

Although consolidation could lead to this type of efficiency, most cities and counties serve very different purposes, and there may be few or no overlapping services and therefore little potential to achieve cost savings. Other governments may already achieve such levels of efficiency by using an interlocal agreement with neighboring governments. In rare cases, some functions that were overlapping, such as law enforcement, fire, and poor relief services, still remain separate even after structural consolidation (Crawford and Swindell 1999, 159).

Technical efficiency can be also be improved indirectly with the increased accountability produced by a professional management structure, especially a city–county manager with day-to-day administrative powers, a personnel system based on merit rather than patronage, and improved budgetary transparency that fosters opportunities to reallocate resources (positions and dollars) for more effective uses (Leland and Thurmaier 2000). Whether the unified government is more efficient overall is an open question. Our previous research suggests that reform arguments emphasizing the values of technical efficiency, where one government is seen as more efficient than two, are still likely to fail. They do not pass muster with voters in referenda because the claims lack credible evidence to support them (Leland and Thurmaier 2006).

Previous Studies

There has been considerable controversy in the urban policy literature about the debate over new regionalism versus fragmentation. Although the regionalists' perspective advocates consolidation to reduce governmental fragmentation and take advantage of economies of scale, public choice theorists (with the exception of Treisman 2007) argue that this approach will fail to achieve any efficiency with regard to the use of scarce resources (Tiebout 1956; Ostrom, Tiebout, and Warren 1961). Indeed, from the public choice perspective, single-unit governments are more likely to behave as monopolists and reduce the quality of services while prices (taxes) rise (Leland and Rosentraub 2007).

Because consolidated governments are compromises that usually reduce the number of jurisdictions by one less government when several other governments in a region remain, it does not necessarily end local governmental fragmentation. Therefore this is not a particularly useful way to characterize the current literature or debate. In most cases of consolidation, minor municipalities and school districts are left out. Metropolitan areas also span more than one county, and therefore even if all these other governments were to be included, the result would still be fragmentation. Consolidation of a city and county is simply not necessarily a "regional approach" to government. For example, when Wyandotte County and Kansas City, consolidated, it still meant that three municipalities and fifteen special districts (including school districts, cemetery districts, community college districts, and utility districts) were left out of the consolidation. Even if the consolidation encompassed all these jurisdictions, the Kansas City metropolitan statistical area comprises four other counties and their special districts and cities. A more relevant way for our study to contribute to our understanding of urban governance is by examining whether or not consolidated governments yield any technical efficiency or economic development gains, or live up to the other promises made to voters.

Few empirical studies have examined whether consolidation produces improves economic growth and technical efficiency.[1] As indicated in table 1.2, the majority of studies involve single case studies (e.g., Benton and Gamble 1984; Honadle 1998; Selden and Campbell 2000; Carr, Bae, and Lu 2006; Swanson 1996). Others focus on multiple cases and their longer-term results (Carr and Feiock 1999; Feiock and Carr 1997; Lyons and Lowery 1989; and Reese 2004). Of particular interest to our work is Benton and Gamble's (1984) time-series study of Jacksonville/Duval

Table 1.2 Select Consolidation Studies of Economic and Efficiency Effects

Consolidated Difference	Single Case/Comparative Case	"Large" *N*
Yes	Seldon and Campbell Durning	Nelson and Foster[a] Vojnovic
No	Benton and Gamble Carr, Bae, and Lu Honadle Feiock and Carr	Carr and Feiock

[a] This study provides an indirect test of consolidation performance.

County (consolidated) and Tampa/Hillsborough County (unconsolidated) in Florida. They find that city–county consolidation has no measurable impact on technical efficiency. In fact, both taxes and expenditures increased as a result of consolidation in Jacksonville. We include this pair of cases in our analysis.

The second case study of note is Athens/Clarke County, Georgia, where Selden and Campbell (2000) find cost savings in some departments and in real operating expenditures, but overall find an increase in real and per capita expenditures (given one-time transition costs). Interviews with department heads point to the importance of individual decision making within the new government and not necessarily consolidation itself as leading to cost savings.

Moore, Nolan, and Segal (2005) analyze forty-six large U.S. cities and eleven public services and find that city size is not an important determinant of technical efficiency. This contradicts Bunch and Strauss (1992), who argue that the size of the city plays an important role in achieving economies of scale and the reduction of operating deficits, based on a simulation of the consolidation of nine fiscally distressed cities in the Pittsburgh area.

After examining the literature on whether consolidation leads to a more technically efficient government and more effective economic growth, one study concluded: "The overriding finding of these few studies is that significant gains in efficiency are unlikely and that context matters. Because salaries and benefits are often standardized at the highest level, consolidated governments' operating costs often increase. Gains in efficiency are also dependent on the actions of government officials and local characteristics that may limit efficiency gains" (Staley et al. 2005, 1). What is missing from this debate on technical efficiency gains is a comparative assessment of U.S. consolidations that test the root of the technical efficiency hypothesis:

H1: The consolidated governments operate more efficiently than unconsolidated governments, due to technical efficiency gains in selective functional service consolidations.

Finding consistent evidence to support or refute this hypothesis is something of a challenge, however. One of the challenges is that proponents may use the term "efficiency" to mean something other than the academic definition of improving the input/output ratio. In the case of consolidation referenda, politicians and proponents typically define efficiency as the reduction of government expenditures or lowering the cost of government. It can also mean slowing the growth of expenditures, or, most important, reducing taxes. They believe there is "waste" in government (i.e., duplication of services in the city and county operations) and that a merger will allow their taxes either to be reduced or slowed in growth. If duplicated services are eliminated, they argue, then the cost of government (inputs = taxes) will be less for the same level of services. Because we are assessing these problems, we adopt their definition of efficiency to assess the success of consolidation. Throughout this book, therefore, we refer to the reduction of such costs discussed by politicians and proponents as our definition of efficiency.

If one accepts expenditure growth as a proxy for the efficiencies implied in slower growth, then one can measure the relative growth in expenditures of a consolidated government and the expenditure growth in a comparable city–county pair that is not merged as a test of the efficiency (economizing) hypothesis. That is the avenue we pursue in this book. We also use multiple measures of expenditure growth to hedge the risk of a single measure being distorted by the peculiar way in which a single local government might account for spending. Thus, in addition to using total direct general government expenditures, we also assess expenditure growth for public works (or highways), public safety, and fire services (other than public safety expenditures).

In assessing the pair of cases within a specific state, we ensure that the same expenditure measures are used in both cases. Finally, we seek consistent patterns across all three or four measures in each pair and across all pairs. We do not base our conclusion on any one of the four measures alone.

Technical Efficiency Expectations

Aside from the confounding issue of efficiency and economizing, another aspect of the efficiency hypothesis deserves more careful treatment. Put simply, how much one should expect to gain in efficiency from a city–county consolidation will depend both on the level of consolidated services *before* the political merger and the level of consolidated services *after* the merger.

For city–county consolidation to be adopted, it is not unusual to have many departments of the city and county remain independent even though they are governed by a unified elected body. This is because the process of adopting consolidation is politically charged and the end product is typically developed as a result of years of bargaining at both the state and local levels. This means that consolidated governments are not uniform when compared with one another. Each one varies greatly in the level of consolidation of services between the city and county.

Table 1.3 presents a matrix with three groups of cases, based on the relative levels of functional consolidation, both premerger and postmerger. The only group where we would expect to see large efficiency gains from merging city and county governments is when there are completely separate city and county services before the merger and all the services are merged postconsolidation (group A). We would expect consolidating cities and counties to have the greatest opportunity to realize efficiencies when the major services (e.g., police, fire, public works) previously were operated separately by both the city and county but were merged after consolidation. In these cases, there are opportunities to streamline operations by ridding the governments of duplication and taking advantage of economies of scale.

In group B, functional consolidation is already present before the adoption of the consolidated government, and few functions (if any) are left to be merged; that is, the efficiency gains are already achieved before merger. The efficiency gains in group C are also small, but for a different reason; the city–county consolidation that results still retains separated service jurisdictions, with small efficiency gains, if any.

The cases in our sample populate all three hypothesized relationships represented in table 1.3. Our analyses across these cases in chapter 11 will also allow us to draw conclusions about each of the different types of cases to test the root technical efficiency hypothesis.

Table 1.3 Variable Expectations of Efficiency Gains

	Premerger Level	
Postmerger Level	**Low Consolidation**	**High Consolidation**
High	Large Efficiency Gains A	Small Efficiency Gains B
Low	C Small Efficiency Gains	

Economic Development as Effectiveness

There have been even fewer studies that systematically assess whether city–county consolidation is effective in improving economic development. Again, the evidence is mixed. In a case study of UNIGOV, Rosentraub (2000) finds that much of Indianapolis's national reputation and downtown revitalization is attributable to the consolidation of core development services under a unified Department of Metropolitan Development. Feiock and Carr (1997) study job growth after consolidation in Jacksonville and find a positive but statistically insignificant relationship between consolidation and job growth in the manufacturing, retail, and service sectors. Finally, Carr and Feiock (1999) analyze the attraction of manufacturing and service firms to nine cities, preconsolidation and postconsolidation, from 1950 to 1993. They do find some indication that consolidation leads to improved economic development. However, once they compare it with other cities' economic development progress in the state, the (causal) statistical significance disappears.

Academics see some benefits and some costs of city–county consolidation but, like practitioners and citizens, are largely undecided on the issue. Staley and his colleagues (2005) conducted a study of twenty-eight academics who publish and conduct research on city–county consolidation to better understand their views of "structural consolidation," or consolidating government services across the board as a general reform. These questions essentially asked whether local government would be more or less efficient, responsive, or effective if the region were governed by a single unified government. The academic experts surveyed were near consensus on their belief that consolidating local government would improve technical efficiency of services delivered, improve economic development for the region, reduce urban/suburban inequalities, and encourage uniform service provision (Staley et al. 2005). They also agree that consolidating local governments would not reduce taxes or reduce public employee satisfaction. Finally, Staley and his colleagues find that a consensus also exists among the experts surveyed that fragmented local government is an inefficient way to organize local governments.

The mixed evidence regarding economic development effectiveness leads us to test the basic hypothesis:

> H2: The consolidated governments will have higher economic growth rates than similar nonconsolidated governments due to structural effectiveness gains.

Other Consolidation Promises

The third group of promises addressed by consolidation proponents is usually particular to the circumstances of the community. Sometimes the promises relate to improving water or fire services to unincorporated areas that will be included in the unified government; others relate to issues of increased accountability and professionalization of the city or county (or both) governments. There is virtually no empirical evidence to test whether the new unified governments have satisfied these claims. Staley and his colleagues observe that much less agreement exists among academic experts on whether consolidating local governments would increase or reduce accountability. Only 21 percent of the academics "strongly" agree that consolidating governments would increase the accountability of elected officials, although 36 percent "agree" that consolidation would lead to an increase in accountability. A little less than half disagree (32 percent) or strongly disagree (11 percent), indicating that they believe consolidation might well reduce accountability of elected officials. Academics are evenly split (36 percent agreed, and 36 percent disagreed) on whether consolidating governments increased or decreased citizen participation and involvement. They also generally disagree on whether consolidating governments would lead to a decrease in the diversity of elected officials. Half believe it would increase diversity, and half say it would reduce it (Staley et al. 2005). We include all the other promises not related to technical efficiency or economic development effectiveness in one broad hypothesis to test across our sample of cases:

> H3: The consolidated government delivered on the other promises made in the proconsolidation campaign.

The comparative case study design for this project provides us with a robust means for testing these hypotheses using a set of cases that span more than fifty years of data.

Research Design and Methods

The comparative case study of governmental consolidations in the United States is a classic problem of many potential explanatory variables and a relatively small *N*. For this reason, we plan to study the effects of city–county consolidation using a comparative, multiple-case-study design. Lijphart (1975,

172–73) defends the comparative case methodology against three major criticisms. The first criticism relates to overdetermination of the sample. Although the number of differences among similar cases may be limited, it will often be sufficiently large to overdetermine the dependent phenomenon. That is, it may be difficult to find a sufficient number of similar cases.

Second, the comparative method is criticized for leading to no more than partial generalizations when the search is for more universal generalizations. Finally, the comparative case method is criticized because the rarity of comparable cases forces the researcher to design hypotheses to fit the sample rather than some general model. Lijphart agrees that these issues can be problems, but he counters that the methodology requires a careful selection of cases, that even partial generalizations are a step toward building a useful theory, and that dysfunctional formation of hypotheses is no more likely in the comparative case methodology as in any statistical methodology.

As demonstrated in *Reshaping the Local Government Landscape: Cases Studies of City–County Consolidation*, we believe that a carefully designed systematic comparative case study of consolidation cases can substantially increase our understanding of local government reforms. We also agree with Bailey (1992, 53) that the development of a rigorous case methodology offers the potential for enriching the public administration theory literature and strengthening the theory–practice linkage that is fundamental to the field. Case studies are rich in details, and the nuances of a specific case enrich the exposition of the reform effort in that particular place at that particular time. They allow us to investigate a contemporary phenomenon within its real-life context when the boundaries between the phenomenon and context are not clearly evident (Bailey 1992, 50; Yin 1990, 4). Consolidation case studies contribute to regional governance model building because they help scholars "understand the fiscal and service dynamics of preconsolidation and the aftermath of consolidation in ways statistical research cannot" (Honadle 1998, 41).

We agree "most useful social science theories are valid under particular conditions. . . or in particular settings" (King, Keohane, and Verba 1994, 103). Our research design can measure each case against the testable (i.e., falsifiable) hypotheses embedded in the causal model. From each "unique" case one seeks to extract the systematic component hypothesized in the model to lead to a predictable outcome. Each case that contradicts a given hypothesis forces the model to be reevaluated and modified. Each consolidation case selected into the sample for this project probes the boundaries of the causal model's legitimacy, leading us to better specify the bounds of applicability of the theory or hypothesis (Leland and Thurmaier 2004).

Each of the case studies in the sample must address each of the three hypotheses, using uniform measures adopted by the editors in consultation with the chapter authors (ten years before consolidation, the year of the consolidation, and ten years after consolidation). These measures include expenditures per capita to test the efficiency hypotheses. We use multiple measures of expenditure growth to hedge the risk of a single measure being distorted by the peculiar way in which a single local government might account for spending. Thus, in addition to using total direct general government expenditures, we also assess expenditure growth for public works (or highways), public safety, and fire services (other than public safety expenditures). Public works and public safety expenditures are particularly well suited for comparative analysis because they are core functions of cities and counties across the nation.[2] The 2002 Census of Governments, for example, indicates that transportation (mainly highways) accounts for almost 10 percent of county and 15 percent of municipal general fund expenditures. Similarly, public safety spending (police and fire combined) accounts for more than 16 percent of county and almost 30 percent of municipal general fund expenditures. Combined, these core functional areas account for more than 25 percent of county and more than 43 percent of municipal general fund spending. Some case authors have been able to collect other types of supplementary data to test the efficiency hypothesis, but we focus our final chapter analysis on these core measures. Regardless, in assessing the pair of cases within a specific state, we ensure that the same expenditure measures are used in both cases.

The economic development hypothesis is tested by several measures, with the key measures including

- population and rate of population change in both the cities and counties—ten years before and ten years after;
- economic data often available only at the county level, including housing growth, manufacturing and retail employment, and retail sales (ten years before the consolidation and ten years after the consolidation); and
- data specific to the promises of each case (e.g., stemming the population decline, no new property tax increases, not laying off any workers due to merger) are gathered from newspapers, previous academic analyses, and other sources.

We use a classic comparative case study design (figure 1.1) to assess these questions. This assessment required the author(s) to collect preconsolidation and postconsolidation data on one consolidated government and a comparable city/county in the same state that did not consolidate. One of the greatest benefits of a comparative case design is that one gains valuable information from a systematic analysis without losing the rich variation of data obtainable from a case analysis. To test our hypotheses, the author(s) in each case chapter need to compare several sets of observations (figure 1.1). The first comparison is of the specific efficiency and economic development measures of each city and county, preconsolidation and postconsolidation (Ob_{t11} to Ob_{t12} and Ob_{t21} to Ob_{t22}). Next, the author(s) compare these measures of both the counties ten years before consolidation (Ob_{t11} and Ob_{t21}) and ten years after consolidation (Ob_{t12} and Ob_{t22}) to identify the relative cost savings and economic development effectiveness produced by the merger—if any. Finally, the editors compare the measures across both groups, both preconsolidation and postconsolidation.

Criteria for Case Selection

The population frame for our sample of consolidation cases includes consolidations created by referenda since 1960. We do not include consolidations created through state legislation, such as Indiana's UNIGOV.

Consolidation Cases

Case selection for this study creates a sample with high external validity. It is representative in terms of geographic distribution, contains large and small city consolidations, and includes older (from the 1960s) and newer (from the 1980s and 1990s) consolidation cases. The sample of our eighteen paired sets of cities and counties (including comparison cases) includes a natural and inherent weight of more cases in the Southeast and no cases from the Northeast. This results because modern city–county consolidation has been primarily a Southern phenomenon due to state and local government law and the diffusion of innovation. Although several cities such as Buffalo, Pittsburgh, and Erie have frequently discussed the idea of consolidation, they have not yet progressed to referenda. As Glendening and Atkins (1980, 68) observe, "For a variety of reasons, the mature city of the North Central and Northeast regions continues to be the odd man out of consolidation referenda." There has not been a merger in the Northeast since 1874, when what we know as New York City was formed with the merger of what are now its five boroughs. State law is prohibitive in this

Experimental Group (unified government)	$\mathbf{Ob_{t11}}$	$\mathbf{C^3}$	$\mathbf{Ob_{t12}}$
Comparison Group (unconsolidated)	$\mathbf{Ob_{t21}}$		$\mathbf{Ob_{t22}}$

Figure 1.1 Research Design
Note: C^3 = City–County Consolidation.

region because unlike the South, northeastern states typically do not allow local governments to reform their structures and forms of government (Leland and Thurmaier 2006). Instead, many opt for functional transfer rather than attempt to pass the insurmountable barriers to structural consolidation (Glendening and Atkins 1980).

We have eight different states represented in our sample (table 1.4). Sixteen of the 26 city–county consolidation cases (62 percent) that have occurred since 1960 via referendum are located in the Southeast, and 66 percent of our sample is from the Southeast. We also include cases from the Midwest (Kansas) and the West (Montana and Nevada). Since 1960, city–county consolidation has only occurred in small and medium-sized cities. The largest city to consolidate has been Louisville/Jefferson County, which has a population of just under 700,000. We have selected consolidation cities ranging from 4,700 (Lynchburg) to 528,000 (Jacksonville) at the time of consolidation.

Comparison Cases

The most significant challenge for the project was choosing the comparative cases. For example, Carson City/Ormsby County, Nevada, lacks an obvious comparison county. Lukemeyer (2005) proposes a multicity/county comparison instead. One of the main issues is the impact of Reno on the case city. The potential comparison cases lack a comparable "neighboring influence." Conversely, this type of difficulty also points to the value of using a qualitative, comparative case study design instead of a strictly quantitative approach, because it allows the field research to probe and discuss the nuances of each case. Although each chapter author carefully explains how the comparative case was selected, we provided general guidelines within the comparative case study design structure. The design sought cases matched on demographic and economic variables at the time of the consolidation. The key to the research design is comparing the cases *with respect to the point of departure* as a consolidated government structure.

Population size is the most important demographic variable. Size of government is related to population, including the number of local government employees and the opportunities for efficiency gains from economies of scale. There also are many economic development implications for city size, including levels and types of retail activity and manufacturing infrastructure. The chapter authors also have tried to match cases based on other demographic variables, including age and educational structures, and (where available) median income levels.

Table 1.4 Case Selection, with Population in Year of Consolidation

State	Case	C^3 Year	Population in C^3 Year	Region
	Consolidation Case			
Tennessee	Nashville/Davidson County	1963	399,743	Southeast
Virginia	Virginia Beach/Princess Anne County	1963	84,215	Southeast
Florida	Jacksonville/Duval County	1967	528,865	Southeast
Nevada	Carson City/Ormsby County	1969	15,468	West
Kentucky	Lexington/Fayette County	1972	174,323	Southeast
Montana	Butte/Silver Bow County	1976	38,092	West
Tennessee	Lynchburg/Moore County	1988	4,696	Southeast
Georgia	Athens/Clarke County	1990	87,594	Southeast
Kansas	Wyandotte County/ Kansas City	1997	155,072	Midwest
	Comparison Case			
Tennessee	Knoxville/Knox County	1963	250,523	Southeast
Virginia	Richmond/Henrico County	1963	337,297	Southeast
Florida	Tampa/Hillsborough County	1967	490,265	Southeast
Nevada	Sparks /Washoe County	1969	48,513	West
Kentucky	Louisville/Jefferson County	1972	695,055	Southeast
Montana	Bozeman/Gallatin County	1976	42,865	West
Tennessee	Decatur/Meigs County	1988	9,394	Southeast
Georgia	Gainesville/Hall County	1990	95,428	Southeast
Kansas	Topeka/Shawnee County	1997	165,122	Midwest

Note: Population data are from census or local government documents.

Economic variables provide a secondary set of factors for comparative case selection. The goal has been to find two cases with similar economies in the year of consolidation, given similar populations. This has been challenging. For example, Athens/Clarke County is home to the University of Georgia, a large and stable employer that heavily influences the economic development of the county. The comparison county has been much more heavily influenced by exurban growth and urban sprawl from Atlanta.

An important constraint on case selection imposed by the research design is that the comparison county must be in the same state. This allows each author to control for the fiscal, legal (constitutional and statutory), and political constraints and influences on cities, counties, and consolidated governments. As these factors changed during the twenty-year study period in each state, both the consolidated and comparison cases should have been affected in a similar way, though not always to the same degree.

The case selection criteria in the research design permit us to compare across the states because our analysis searches for *patterns of differences between the pairs of cases* as the starting point for testing the overall hypotheses.

Case Analysis

The test of the three root hypotheses within each chapter follows the research design closely. The advantages of the comparative case design over a standard regression analysis are several. First, as readers will quickly note, all consolidations are not necessarily promoted to increase efficiency and economic development performance. Although these points can be included in the referendum campaign rhetoric, in some cases, the most important issue is related to annexation wars and preservation of community identity (e.g., Virginia Beach, Lynchburg, and Lexington). These cases would dilute efficiency gains as "success" measures in a standard regression.

Second, regression analyses require uniform data on the prescribed set of variables. An important consequence has been the limited ability to use regression analysis to study consolidation performance—mainly because there is not a source of standard data for all the key measures scholars would like to use to evaluate consolidation performance.[3] This is particularly true of efforts to use data from ten years before consolidations in the 1960s, and for small population cities and counties. The Census of Governments neglects surveys of small cities, and only began to do surveys for counties in 1957. Hence, scholars need to poke in basements of courthouses, library archives, and so on to find basic data. Finally, it is wrong to assume that the information we seek is available even in the basements of courthouses or library archives. One of the startling revelations of our collective research project across eight states is how far we have come in local government transparency and information management. States did not require local governments to collect or retain much of the information we seek until very recently. Open records acts did not become part of routine local government business until the 1980s for most states. Florida led the states in "sunshine laws" only in the 1970s. Even then, there has been wide variation in requirements and practice among local governments regarding management of their financial data and records. Thus, it is not very feasible for someone using a standard regression technique; and even then, the found data are unlikely to meet the standardization requirements of regression assumptions.

Third, there are a limited number of consolidation efforts and successes to begin with. With only 120 attempts and 40 referenda successes, the inability to collect uniform data quickly shrinks the sample selection to a small-*N* study. The comparative case approach can overcome the small-*N* limitation as long as rigorous attention is paid to internal validity in the research design. For this reason, we have an overall assessment of the evidence from each chapter for each of the three key hypotheses, presented in a summary table similar to table 1.5. In some cases, the data are not available to reach a conclusion on a hypothesis. In some cases, the data are available, but there is no evidence to reject the null hypothesis. However, in most cases, there are enough data available to allow the case researcher(s) to conclude that there is weak, moderate, or strong evidence to support a particular hypothesis. *Weak* evidence indicates that one or two of the economic or efficiency indicators showed improvement, or only a small part of the promises were kept. An assessment of *moderate* would indicate that several measures showed improvement, and the evidence indicates that, so far, most promises were kept. A rating of *strong* is reserved for cases that indicate that all measures showed improvement and promises were kept. The assessment is primarily by the case author(s), based on the evidence

Table 1.5 Overall Chapter Assessment Template

Overall Assessment of Evidence	H1: Efficiency	H2: Economic Development	H3: Other Promises
Not enough data available	☑		
No evidence		☑	
Weak			
Moderate			
Strong			☑

presented in each case, comparing the consolidated government with the companion case before and after consolidation, and in consultation with the editors.

Fourth, the analysis in a comparative case design allows the researcher to use the qualitative data in a pair of cases from the same state to put the quantitative data into context. Hence, the comparison of Jacksonville and Tampa in economic performance needs to account for the different economic development strategies and trajectories that condition their overall economic development performance. Tampa has blossomed in retail development, while Jacksonville has been stronger in manufacturing. The blending of the qualitative and quantitative data permits the researcher to draw causal inferences with more confidence than a purely quantitative regression allows. Our incorporation of multiple measures into the analysis permits us to see a more complete picture of the two cases, even when we are not looking at exactly the same data in each pair of cases. Finally, the pairing of cases from the same state allows us to control for state institutional and legal structures that can affect economic development, revenue and expenditure options, and the feasibility of assorted other campaign promises (Honadle 1998, 41).

Conclusion

This chapter has set the stage to answer three empirical questions that both practitioners and academics are asking. Are consolidated governments more efficient than similar nonconsolidated governments? Are they more effective in terms of economic development? And finally, are the other promises made to voters kept? This study is designed to answer these questions by comparatively and systematically examining nine in-depth experimental case studies compared with nine comparison cases. Each of the next nine chapters tests the hypotheses with respect to each case of consolidation and its companion case. The final chapter analyzes these questions and related hypotheses at an aggregated level.

Our analysis provides detailed insight into whether consolidation improves the efficiency of service delivery. It also informs other communities that are interested in consolidation about its potential benefits and costs. Finally, our study provides public administrators, elected officials, and citizens with further insights into consolidation as a local government service delivery innovation.

Notes

1. Studies that evaluate the electoral impacts of consolidations are not part of our current project, although they are important. See, e.g., Clarke 2006; and Savitch and Vogel 2004.
2. We acknowledge that a few states do not have counties.
3. One of the editors has been reviewing city and county budgets for the Government Finance Officers Association for nearly two decades and can attest to the overwhelming lack of reported data on output measures in local governments. Even if most cities and counties are collecting such data (a strong assumption), they are not reporting the data publicly.

References

Benton, Edwin, and Darwin Gamble. 1984. City/County Consolidation and Economies of Scale: Evidence from a Time-Series Analysis in Jacksonville, Florida. *Social Science Quarterly* 65:190–98.

Bailey, Mary Timney. 1992. Do Physicists Use Case Studies? *Public Administration Review* 52, no. 1:47–54.

Bunch, Beverly, and R. P. Strauss. 1992. Municipal Consolidation. *Urban Affairs Quarterly* 27, no. 4:615–30.

Carr, Jered, Sang-Seok Bae, and Wenjue Lu. 2006. City–County Government and Promises of Economic Development: A Tale of Two Cities. *State and Local Government Review* 38, no. 3:131–41.

Carr, Jered, and Richard Feiock. 1999. Metropolitan Government and Economic Development. *Urban Affairs Review* 34, no. 3:476–89.

Carr, Jered, and Bethany Sneed. 2004. The Politics of City–County Consolidation: Findings from a National Survey. In *City–County Consolidation and Its Alternatives: Reshaping the Local Government Landscape*, ed. Jered Carr and Richard Feiock. Armonk, NY: M. E. Sharpe.

Clarke, Kristin. 2006. Voting Rights and City–County Consolidations. *Houston Law Review* 43, no. 3 (Summer): 621–99.

Crawford, Sue, and David Swindell. 1999. Local Politics Is State Politics: Urban Government in the State's Capital. In *Indiana Politics and Public Policy*, ed. Maurice Eisenstein. Boston, MA: Pearson Custom.

Dornbrook, James. 2006. Pole Position: Kansas Speedway Transforms Wyandotte County's Economy, Reputation. Kansas City Business Journal. Available at www.kansascity.bizjournals.com.
Durning, Dan. 2003. Consolidated Governments. In *Encyclopedia of Public Administration and Public Policy*. New York: Marcel Dekker.
Feiock, Richard C., and Jered B. Carr. 1997. A Reassessment of City/County Consolidation: Economic Development Impacts. *State and Local Government Review* 29, no. 3:166–71.
Glendening, Parris N., and Patricia Atkins. 1980. City–County Consolidations: New Views for the Eighties. In *The Municipal Yearbook, 1980*. Washington, DC: International City/County Management Association.
Honadle, Beth. 1998. Projecting the Public Services and Finance Implications of Municipal Consolidation: Evidence from a Small-City Consolidation Study. *The Regionalist* 3 (Fall): 41–53.
King, Gary, Robert Keohane, and Sidney Verba. 1994. *Designing Social Inquiry: Scientific Inference in Qualitative Research*. Princeton, NJ: Princeton University Press.
Leland, Suzanne, and Mark Rosentraub. 2007. Consolidated and Fragmented Governments and Regional Cooperation: Surprising Lessons from Charlotte, Cleveland, Indianapolis, and Wyandotte County/Kansas City, Kansas. Paper presented at 2008 Urban Affairs Association Conference, Baltimore.
Leland, Suzanne, and Kurt Thurmaier. 2000. Metropolitan Consolidation Success: Returning to the Roots of Local Government Reform. *Public Administration Quarterly* 24, no. 2:202–21.
———, eds. 2004. *Reshaping the Local Government Landscape: Case Studies of City–County Consolidation*. Armonk, NY: M. E. Sharpe.
——— 2005. When Efficiency Is Unbelievable: Normative Lessons from 30 Years of City–County Consolidations. *Public Administration Review* 65, no. 4:475–89.
———. 2006. Lessons from 35 Years of City–County Consolidation Attempts. In *Municipal Yearbook*. Washington, DC: International City/County Management Association.
Lijphart, Arend. 1975. The Comparable-Cases Strategy in Comparative Research. *Comparative Political Studies* 8, no. 2:158–77.
Lukemeyer, Anna. City–County Consolidation: A Case Study of Carson City, Nevada. Paper presented at meeting of Association for Budgeting and Financial Management, Washington, November 11–12, 2005.
Lyons, W. E., and David Lowery. 1989. Governmental Fragmentation versus Consolidation: Five Public-Choice Myths about How to Create

Informed, Involved, and Happy Citizens. *Public Administration Review* 49, no. 6:533–43.

Moore, Adrian, James Nolan, and Geoffrey Segal. 2005. Putting Out the Trash: Measuring Municipal Service Efficiency in U.S. Cities. *Urban Affairs Review* 41:237–59.

Ostrom, Vincent, Charles Tiebout, and R. Warren. 1961. The Organization of Government in Metropolitan Areas: A Theoretical Inquiry. *American Political Science Review* 55:831–42.

Reese, L. 2004. Sane Governance, Different Day: Does Metropolitan Reorganization Make a Difference? *Review of Policy Research* 21, no. 4:595–611.

Rosenbaum, W. A., and Gladys Kammerer. 1974. *Against Long Odds: The Theory and Practice of Successful Governmental Consolidation.* Administrative and Policy Studies Series 03-022, vol. 2. Beverly Hills, CA: Sage.

Rosentraub, Mark. 2000. City–County Consolidation and the Rebuilding of Image: The Fiscal Lessons from Indianapolis's UNIGOV Program. *State and Local Government Review* 32:180–91.

Savitch, Hank, and Ron Vogel. 2004. Suburbs without Cities: Power and City–County Consolidation. *Urban Affairs Review* 39:758–90.

Selden, Sally C., and Richard W. Campbell. 2000. The Expenditure Impacts of Unification on a Small Georgia County: A Contingency Perspective of City–County Consolidation. *Public Administration Quarterly* 24, no. 2 :169–201.

Staley, S., D. Faulk, S. Leland, and D. E. Schansburg. 2005. *The Effects of City–County Consolidation : A Review of the Recent Academic Literature.* Report Prepared for Indiana General Assembly. Fort Wayne: Policy Review Foundation.

Swanson, B. 1996. Jacksonville, Consolidation, and Regional Governance. In *Regional Politics in a Post-City Age*, ed. H. V. Savitch. Thousand Oaks, CA: Sage.

Tiebout, 1956. A Pure Theory of Local Government Expenditures. *Journal of Political Economy* 44:416–24.

Treisman, Daniel. 2007. *The Architecture of Government: Rethinking Political Decentralization.* University of California, Los Angeles.

Walker, Jack. 1969. The Diffusion of Innovation among the American States. *American Political Science Review* 63:880–99.

Yin, Robert. 1990. *Case Study Research: Design and Methods.* Newbury Park, CA: Sage.

⇢ 2 ⇠

An Assessment of the City–County Consolidation of Nashville and Davidson County, Tennessee

Anthony J. Nownes, David J. Houston, and Marc Schwerdt

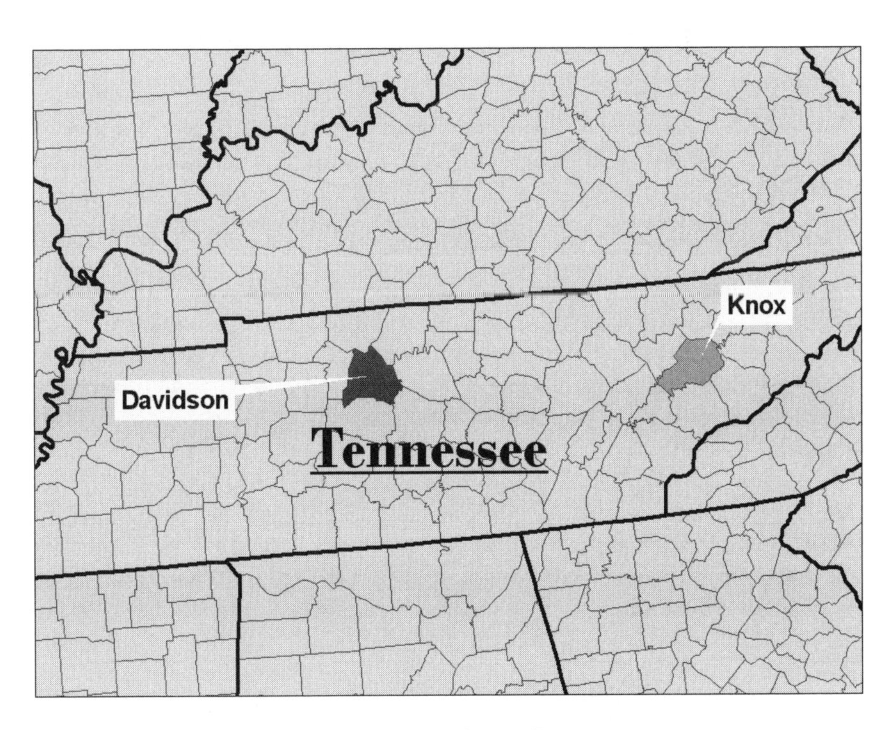

Map 2 Locations of Davidson County and Knox County, Tennessee
Source: U.S. Bureau of the Census.

City–county consolidation is a rare event. But it does happen. In fact, some of the largest and best-known metropolises in the country are governed by consolidated governments, including Boston, Denver, Honolulu, Philadelphia, and San Francisco. This chapter examines the case of Nashville/Davidson County, Tennessee (map 2), a large locality that has been governed by a consolidated government for forty-five years. To evaluate the performance of the consolidated government of Nashville/Davidson County, we compare it with that of the fragmented governments of Knox County, Tennessee, and the City of Knoxville. We begin with a brief background on the consolidation effort, highlighting the promises made by consolidation supporters. From here, we discuss our methodology. Finally, we evaluate the performance of the consolidated government of Nashville/Davidson County. In the end, we conclude that there is substantial evidence that consolidation has been good for Nashville/Davidson County.

The Consolidation Effort

The Nashville/Davidson County metropolitan government opened for business on April 1, 1963, replacing the separate governments of the City of Nashville and of Davidson County. This event was merely the culmination of a decades-long effort to address the problems that had come to plague metropolitan Nashville.

In the two decades before consolidation, the forces of suburbanization pushed beyond the Nashville city limits out into surrounding counties, creating an urban fringe that strained the resources and government outside the city limits. Because the city itself did not grow in size during this preconsolidation period, its population in 1960 was only 2.1 percent larger than it had been in 1940. In contrast, during the same twenty-year period the population of Davidson County outside Nashville grew from 89,865 to 228,869—an increase of 155 percent (Hawkins 1966). No longer did the political boundaries of the city match up with the urbanized area. Additionally, the county government was not equipped to provide the urban-type services needed by people living in a densely populated area (Booth 1963). In short, by 1960 it was clear that the governments of Davidson County and Nashville were having trouble providing necessary services to citizens.

The First Election

In 1951, a group of local government officials requested that the Tennessee state legislature authorize a formal examination of the problems facing metropolitan Nashville. The resulting Community Services Act authorized the establishment of a Nashville/Davidson County joint Community Services Commission that produced a set of recommendations to address the metropolitan problems. The report, titled *A Future for Nashville,* was produced by the commission the following year (Greene and Grant 1952). The report recommended that the city annex 69 square miles of suburban land outside its limits, and that the governments of Nashville and Davidson County consider the functional consolidation of certain areawide services. As a result of the report, both the city's health department and juvenile court were transferred to the county. However, competition between the city and the county in other areas (including schools and law enforcement) precluded further functional consolidation. Moreover, the Tennessee legislature failed to act on the annexation recommendation (Hawkins 1966). In the end, the commission's report led to only minor changes. However, it succeeded in stimulating widespread interest in the problems facing metropolitan Nashville. Although annexation and the functional consolidation of specific services were regarded as the most feasible responses to these problems, many local actors believed that the commission's recommendations went only part of the way toward addressing existing problems.

During the next few years, two legal changes paved the way for additional efforts to address the problems of metropolitan Nashville. First, the state legislature amended the state Constitution in 1953 to vest in the General Assembly the authority to provide for the consolidation of city and county governments in the state provided that consolidation is approved by separate majorities of voters both in the city and the county outside the city (Hawkins 1966). Second, in 1955 the Tennessee Municipal League convinced the General Assembly to relax annexation laws. Specifically, the state legislature changed the law to allow the annexation by cities of contiguous areas without the approval of those residing in the areas being annexed (Hawkins 1966).

The Plan for Metropolitan Government

These changes led local leaders in 1956 to request that the City of Nashville and Davidson County planning commissions jointly examine the ongoing problems facing metropolitan Nashville. In October of that year, the joint commission produced a watershed document titled *Plan of Metropolitan Government for Nashville and Davidson County* that detailed the problems facing the area, and recommended the creation of a single government to address them. The report stated: "The root of our metropolitan problem is found in the fact that during the past twenty-five years metropolitan Nashville has outgrown both its City and County governments. *It has outgrown the City government geographically, and it has outgrown the County government in its ability to meet the needs of a modern, expanding urban community*" (Nashville and Davidson County Planning Commission 1956, 4–5; emphasis in the original).

According to the commission, this "metropolitan problem" manifested itself most visibly in a lack of adequate services in densely populated areas beyond the city's boundaries. For example, the commission noted that areas outside the city limits lacked a sanitary sewer system. This "septic tank" problem was the result of terrain that often featured rock below only a few inches of soil. This made the construction of sewers expensive. It also meant that the entire area was poorly suited for the absorption of sewage (Hawkins 1966). All this raised public health concerns. The commission also noted that residents outside the city had to rely on substandard private fire and police protection, as well as pay higher fire insurance rates (Booth 1963). The commission identified a number of other service problems facing the suburbs, including a lack of adequate street lighting, a paucity of fire hydrants, and high water rates (in some places outside the city, water rates were double what they were inside the city). Overall, the commission concluded that the "metropolitan problem" that faced Nashville and its immediate environs led to wasteful duplicate spending, government's inability to address areawide problems, and low citizen control over government, stemming from a complicated local government structure (Booth 1963; Grant 1965a; Nashville and Davidson County Planning Commission 1956).

In short, the joint commission concluded that the fragmented governments of Davidson County and Nashville were failing to provide adequate services to citizens. The commission also implied that this failure was hurting the local economy (as citizens were paying relatively high fire insurance and water rates) and leading to citizen dissatisfaction with local government. Later, consolidation boosters would draw upon the commission's report to argue that consolidation would not only improve government performance but also help the community overall by creating "a progressive-community image" for Nashville (Grant 1965a, 37). This, they believed, would attract citizens and businesses, thereby leading to enhanced economic growth.

The existence of separate school systems (one operated by Nashville and one operated by Davidson County) highlighted duplicative and wasteful spending, especially given that city schools had vacant classrooms and county schools suffered from overcrowding (Elazar 1961; Booth 1963). Although tension and competition existed between the two school systems, the problems surrounding education were not a driving force toward the first consolidation effort.

On the basis of the commission's report, the local delegation to the Tennessee General Assembly drafted and obtained passage of legislation permitting the creation of a charter commission in 1957. The charter commission had ten members, five each appointed by the mayor of Nashville and the county judge. It set out to craft a consolidated local government with a single elected chief executive, and to eliminate wasteful spending by merging duplicative city and county agencies.

The proposed consolidated government was a mayor–council government with a strong mayor and a representative metropolitan council of twenty-one elected officials. The consolidation plan called for the merging of duplicative agencies. It also called for the creation of two taxing districts. A general services district would encompass the entire county and would be responsible for fire protection, hospitals, streets and roads, parks and recreation, fairgrounds, public housing, urban redevelopment, electricity, housing codes, police, courts, jails, health, welfare, traffic control, schools, libraries, airports, zoning, and planning. An urban services district would correspond to the old city boundaries and annexed areas (but could be expanded by annexing areas via a simple ordinance), and would be responsible for providing enhanced levels of police and fire protection, water, sewers, street lighting, refuse collection and disposal, wine and whiskey regulation, and taxicab regulation (Hawkins 1966). Other incorporated areas in the county (six in all) would have the choice of joining the metropolitan government.

In drafting the proposed charter the commission openly addressed the issue of African American vote dilution. The initial reaction of African Americans and their leadership to the idea of a consolidated government was negative (Elazar 1961). Suspicion of consolidation was understandable, given that before 1950, gerrymandering, changes to the electoral process, and even a disappearing "crucial ballot box" kept African Americans from electoral success in Nashville (Elazar 1961; Hawkins 1966).

Yet by 1958 African Americans held two of the twenty-one city council positions and "under the present system, [African Americans] could elect one-third of the city council in the very near future and, given the rate at which their proportion of the city's population is increasing, even think about electing [an African American] mayor within a generation" (Elazar 1961, 65). This political influence was perceived to be threatened by consolidation because, although African Americans made up an estimated 45 percent of the Nashville population in 1958, they accounted for no more than 8 percent of the population in the rest of the county (Elazar 1961). Thus, it was clear that African American political influence was endangered by the merger. To address these concerns about vote dilution, the council districts were drawn to ensure that African Americans would control the electoral outcome in two districts.

The charter was endorsed by the Nashville mayor Ben West, County Judge C. Beverly Briley, both Nashville daily newspapers, the planning commission, the Tennessee Municipal League, and many business and civic groups (Hawkins 1966). To drum up support for the referendum, consolidation supporters relied primarily upon speaking engagements (by consolidation boosters) and newspaper editorials (Booth 1963; Hawkins 1966).

Opposition to Metro Government

There was, however, considerable opposition to consolidation. Specifically, politicians and businesses tied to local communities outside the city, many county schoolteachers, employees and owners of private police and fire companies, and garbage collectors in the suburbs came out in opposition to consolidation (Hawkins 1966). Private police and fire companies feared losing their service subscriptions in the more densely populated portions of the county beyond the city that would be contained in the proposed urban services district and served directly by the metropolitan government (Elazar 1961; Booth 1963; Hawkins 1966). County teachers were wary of consolidation because they were afraid that their superintendent would not be appointed to head the new metropolitan system (Elazar 1961).

However, all this opposition remained relatively silent and hidden until the last days of the campaign (Elazar 1961; Booth 1963). In the two weeks immediately before the consolidation vote, opposition forces made a concerted effort to influence voters, focusing primarily on areas in the county outside the city limits. They distributed leaflets, sent out mailings, and even created a radio jingle. The opposition campaign was based on the premise that city–county consolidation would result in bigger government and higher taxes without better services. Opponents also maintained that suburban voters would be saddled with the city's debt and would be the subjects of a strong mayor who would take over the county. The opposition attempted to exploit county voters' distrust of Mayor West and his political machine, central city leaders, and daily newspapers (Hawkins 1966).

The Outcome

On June 17, 1958, the charter was submitted to a referendum of the voters in Nashville and Davidson County. On Election Day, the charter was approved by 61.9 percent of the voters in the city. However, it received only 41.8 percent of the vote outside the city. Turnout was low—22.2 percent in the city, and 43.8 percent in the county (Elazar 1961). Observers concluded that the defeat was the result of a failure to communicate with county voters and to speak to their fears regarding unified government. For instance, the public meetings that were convened to inform citizens about the proposed charter generally were attended only by consolidation supporters. Thus, the campaign for metropolitan government reached only a small portion of the voting public (Elazar 1961). As Grubbs (1961, 353) explained: "A grassroots, door-to-door, neighborhood procharter campaign was lacking."

Elazar (1961) concludes that attitudes toward consolidation reflected distinct individual identities. A "cosmopolitan" identity reflected urban and suburban residents that actively participated in the economic and social activities of the city. In contrast, a "local" identity was held by those who confined their activities of their small, local communities. This latter group did not want to be associated with the city. Elazar indicates that a cosmopolitan identity led to support of consolidation, whereas a local orientation was consistent with opposition. Similarly, Booth (1963) reports that proponents of consolidation held urban values (e.g., desire for good municipal services, closeness to work, big stores, and professional services), while opponents tended to hold suburban values (e.g., desire for lower taxes and family-friendly neighborhoods).

Some observers speculated that County Judge C. Beverly Briley's support for consolidation waned considerably before the referendum was submitted to the voters amid concerns that he might not be elected the new metro mayor (Hawkins 1966). It is also worth pointing out that although there were service delivery concerns—especially for those in densely populated areas just outside the city boundaries—there was no focusing event or crisis that motivated voters in rural county areas to support a change in governmental structure. This may explain the lack of interest in metro government among many suburbanites.

The Second Election

After the defeat of the 1958 charter, both city and county governments struggled to address the service needs of their citizens. Almost immediately the county raised taxes, and during the next two years it increased spending on bridges, highways, and sewers in the most densely populated areas of the county (Booth 1963). However, schools remained overcrowded and teachers still were underpaid. Overall, the county government found it difficult to provide urban service levels.

Because of a declining tax base, the city wrestled with its own financial problems. Analysts at the time estimated that 40 percent of property in the city was tax exempt—that is, owned and operated for governmental, religious, or charitable purposes. Furthermore, low-income residents were a growing part of the city population (Booth 1963). To generate more revenue for the city, within one month of the defeat of the metro government, Mayor West annexed 7 square miles of industrial territory (population, 4,587) without the consent of residents or property owners (Booth 1963; Hawkins 1966). Later, in April 1960, the city annexed an additional 42.46 square miles of densely populated land (population, 82,512), more than doubling the city's area, again without the approval of residents (Booth 1963).

Taxes and Trouble

In another bid to increase revenue, the city government levied a tax on all vehicles that used the streets of Nashville "more than 30 days per year" (Hawkins 1966). The city argued that the tax was justified because maintaining city roads was expensive and unfairly burdened city residents. After the tax was levied, motorists were expected to display green stickers on their windshields. Although many motorists at first failed to comply with the new law, Mayor West cracked down, first by ordering the police to issue tickets to violators, and then to arrest violators. Compliance increased after heightened police enforcement, as did resentment toward Mayor West among suburban residents (Hawkins 1966).

Schools became a much larger issue during the second charter campaign. As a part of city annexation, twenty-two county schools were now inside the Nashville city limits. Government officials disagreed about three issues related to schools. First, city and county officials disagreed about the amount of money the city would pay the county for the schools in the annexed areas. Second, the county wanted to continue to operate four of these schools, including a high school, because a large portion of the students who attended still resided outside the city. Third, the county announced that it intended to cease bus service to the schools in the annexed areas (Hawkins 1966).

In the end, the mayor's aggressive annexations and the "green sticker" program once again created the impetus to pursue the cause of metropolitan government. This time around consolidation did not have the support of either Mayor West or the *Nashville Banner* (Hawkins 1966). The city council also proved to be an obstacle. Although the County Quarterly Court voted in favor of creating a second charter commission, the state Constitution also required the Nashville City Council to support the creation of a charter commission, which it did not.

To bypass the city council's opposition, the Davidson County delegation sponsored and secured passage in the Tennessee General Assembly of an amendment to the general act that created a second avenue for establishing a charter commission (March 9, 1961). This alternative avenue permitted the establishment of a charter commission by a private act legislated by the General Assembly (Hawkins 1966). However, this mechanism required a public referendum on the formation of a charter commission that had to receive a majority of "yes" votes in both areas (inside the city and in the county beyond the city). This issue was placed before the voters of Davidson

County on August 17, 1961. Although turnout was light (only 14,826 voters in the city and 11,172 voters in the remaining county), the formation of a new charter commission was supported by 58.8 percent of city voters and 65.5 percent of voters in the surrounding county (Hawkins 1966).

The second charter commission was made up of nearly the same membership as the previous commission and produced a similar proposal for a metro government. There were, however, a few significant differences. First, the size of the metropolitan council was increased from twenty-one to forty, a response to public opinion in favor of a larger representative body (Hawkins 1966). Of these council members, thirty-five would be elected from districts and five would be at-large members. Second, in response to African American fears, the councilmanic district lines were drawn to ensure that African Americans would determine the selection of council members in six districts. Third, also in response to African American concerns, an automatic reapportionment and representation provision was included in the charter that required the metropolitan council to adjust district lines every ten years based on population, not area (Hawkins 1966).

Another provision reflected disagreement among charter commission members over how best to obtain a "good" school board: election versus appointment. It was finally resolved that school board members would be elected in nine districts. Additionally, the commission's proposal provided for a public referendum on the school budget if two-thirds of the Board of Education judged the final budget adopted by the Metropolitan Council to be inadequate (Hawkins 1966).

The Second Campaign

This time the campaign was different. Mayor West's controversial practices led many to see the new vote as a referendum on West's performance (Booth 1963). Residents in the suburban areas of the county were no longer choosing between consolidation and the status quo. Now they were choosing between annexation and consolidation. And at least under a consolidated government county residents would have some say in government decisions (Booth 1963). Additionally, support for Metro surprisingly came from providers of subscriptions services. As the City of Nashville expanded the delivery of police and fire services into recently annexed areas, some subscription services lost revenue and ceased operations. However, the remaining fire subscription service providers "began to champion the cause of Metro government since they now believed that they would be incorporated into an overall fire protection system" (Booth 1963, 78).

The second campaign was marked by a much more extensive and effective grassroots campaign by consolidation supporters (Hawkins 1966).

The campaign worked. The charter passed in both the city and the rest of the county. Specifically, the charter received 57.5 percent of the vote within the city and 56 percent in the county beyond the city (Booth 1963). However, support for the new charter was the opposite of that from the first charter campaign. In 1962, residents of the old city narrowly voted down consolidation, perhaps an indication of the strength of Mayor West's political machine (Booth 1963). But residents in recently annexed areas, whose votes were now added to the city vote total, voted in support of consolidated government by a margin of six to one. In the end, city residents voted in favor of consolidation, 21,064 to 15,599. Voters in the remainder of the county voted in favor of consolidation, 15,914 to 12,514, no doubt due to an effective procharter campaign, worries over annexation, and fear of continued taxation without representation (Booth 1963).

In November 1962, elections were held to select the officers of the new Metropolitan Government of Nashville/Davidson County. The new Legislative Council comprised forty members—thirty-five from single-member districts and five selected at large. The new mayor was C. Beverly Briley, the former county judge. Ben West did not run for mayor. The officials were inaugurated on April 1, 1963, and the new government began to function.

Summary

In sum, after a decade of turmoil the voters of the greater Nashville area turned to consolidated government. Supporters of consolidation argued that it would improve government efficiency. Specifically, they argued that consolidation would improve government services, eliminate duplicative spending, and keep taxes under control. Supporters of consolidation also argued that it would foster economic development. Specifically, they believed that consolidation would bolster Nashville/Davidson County's image as a progressive community, and would attract new citizens and new businesses. In addition, supporters of consolidation believed that consolidation would increase citizen satisfaction with local government. The complicated and fragmented governments of Nashville and Davidson County, consolidation supporters argued, hurt government responsiveness to citizens, and had the potential to undermine citizen trust in local government.

In sum, consolidation supporters believed that consolidation would improve government efficiency, foster economic growth, and increase citizen satisfaction with government. This was not all, however. Consolidation supporters also argued during the course of the campaign that consolidation would bring with it a number of other benefits. Specifically, they argued that consolidation would (1) eliminate city–county "buck-passing," by making it very clear who was responsible for government decisions; (2) eliminate city–

county financial inequities; (3) eliminate "double taxation," that is, the practice of levying both city and county taxes on certain residents while providing only city services to them, and "free riding," the practice of out-of-city residents using city facilities without paying for them; (4) equalize city and county services; and (5) make local government more professional.

Did consolidation lead to more efficient government in Nashville/Davidson County? Did it foster economic growth? Did it lead to greater citizen satisfaction with local government?[1] Did the creation of the new government solve the myriad problems that faced the city and county in the 1950s and early 1960s? These are the questions we address in the remainder of this chapter. Before we do, however, we describe our basic approach to answering them.

Data, Methods, and Background of the Comparison Case

In the remainder of this chapter, we test four hypotheses. In testing these hypotheses we hope to assess the overall impact of city–county consolidation on Nashville/Davidson County. Like the authors of the other chapters in this book, we use a comparative case study design to test our hypotheses. Specifically, we evaluate and assess data on one consolidated government (Nashville/Davidson County) and a comparable city/county (Knoxville/Knox County) combination within the state of Tennessee that did not consolidate.

Hypothesis 1: Government Efficiency

Our first substantive hypothesis is:

> H1: The consolidated government of Nashville/Davidson County has operated more efficiently than the unconsolidated governments of Knox County and Knoxville.

We test this hypothesis against data on government spending. Our original intention was to test Hypothesis 1 against data on government spending for the years 1953 (ten years before consolidation), 1963 (the year of consolidation), and 1973 (ten years after consolidation). But we could not locate reliable data for these years.[2] Thus, we test Hypothesis 1 against data for 1957, 1962, and 1977 because they are years for which we have reliable data from an internal U.S. Bureau of the Census file on city and county government spending. Although the data are quite reliable, they are rather limited in detail. In particular, they lack information on spending for several specific purposes (including education). Thus, in testing Hypothesis 1 we do not present a full breakdown of government spending for the years under study, but instead present a truncated picture that shows only overall spending, spending on fire protection, spending on highways, and spending on police protection. As a secondary test of Hypothesis 1, we examine property tax rates over time. We obtained data on property tax rates from the governments of Nashville/Davidson County, the City of Knoxville, and Knox County.

Hypothesis 2: Economic Growth

One of the most noteworthy promises made by consolidation boosters was that consolidation would "create a progressive-community image" for Nashville (Grant 1965a, 37), thereby attracting citizens and businesses, and thereby leading to strong economic growth in Nashville/Davidson County. Thus, we test the following hypothesis:

> H2: The consolidated government of Nashville/Davidson County has been more successful at fostering economic growth than the unconsolidated governments of Knox County and Knoxville.

To test this hypothesis, we examine trends in population growth and economic growth over time. In our assessment of economic growth we examine data on retail sales, manufacturing employment, number of housing units, and per capita income. The population and economic growth data come primarily from one source—the periodic volume *Tennessee Statistical Abstract* (*TSA*). Unfortunately, the *TSA* was only published periodically during the years under study. Moreover, the data in the various volumes of the *TSA* are in many cases incomplete. Thus, we do not have data for all indicators for all years. In the end, due to data limitations we were forced to use different years for different indicators. Overall, however, we believe that the data allow for a reasonable test of Hypothesis 2 because we can measure changes over the same relative period in both counties.

Hypothesis 3: Citizen Satisfaction

Consolidation boosters in Nashville and Davidson County also argued that consolidation would lead to higher levels of citizen satisfaction with government. Thus, we also test the following hypothesis:

H3: Consolidation in Nashville/Davidson County increased citizen satisfaction with local government.

We test this hypothesis against survey data gathered in the immediate aftermath of the Nashville/Davidson County consolidation.

Hypothesis 4: Promises Made

Finally, we test the following general, overarching hypothesis:

H4: The consolidated government of Nashville/Davidson County delivered on its promises.

Consolidation boosters in Nashville/Davidson County promised greater government efficiency, enhanced economic growth, and greater citizen satisfaction with government. They also argued that consolidation would eliminate city–county "buck-passing," eliminate city–county financial inequities, eliminate double taxation and "free riding," equalize city and county services, and make local government more professional. The data we bring to bear on Hypotheses 1 through 4 will allow us to determine the extent to which the consolidated government of Nashville/Davidson County delivered on its promises to voters.

Background of Comparison City–County: Knoxville/Knox County

As we mention above, we test our hypotheses using a comparative case study design in which the two cases are Nashville/Davidson County, and Knoxville/Knox County. We selected Knoxville/Knox County as our comparison case for several reasons. First, Knoxville/Knox County is a fascinating case in and of itself. As we noted in our previous work (see Nownes and Houston 2004), Knoxville and Knox County have a long history of rejecting government consolidation (attempts failed in 1959, 1978, 1983, and 1996). It would be interesting, we thought, to gather empirical evidence concerning the wisdom of these repeated rejections. Second, Knoxville/Knox County are in Tennessee, and thus are under the same local government constraints as Nashville/Davidson County. Third, demographically the cities and counties are (and have been) similar. Knoxville and Nashville are both medium-sized cities, and Knox County and Davidson County are both medium-sized counties.[3]

As table 2.1 shows, before consolidation, Davidson County and Nashville were marginally larger than Knox County and Knoxville, respectively.[4]

Table 2.1 Population of Davidson County, Knox County, Nashville, and Knoxville, 1950 and 1960 (Preconsolidation), and Rate of Change

Jurisdiction	1950	1960	% Change, 1950–60
Davidson County	321,758	399,743	+24
Knox County	223,007	250,523	+12
Nashville	174,307	170,874	–2
Knoxville	124,769	111,827	–12

Source: Tennessee Statistical Abstract (hereafter *TSA*) *1969,* 536, 537, 549.

During the period 1950–60 (again, before consolidation), Davidson County was gaining population, while the city of Nashville was losing population. During the same period, Knox County was gaining population (though not at the same rate as Davidson County), and Knoxville was losing population (though at a higher rate than Nashville). Fourth, the two cases are similar in other ways.

As table 2.2 shows, unemployment rates in the two places were comparable, though Knox County's was 1.2 percentage points higher in 1960.[5] On other measures the counties were quite similar. In per capita income, for example, both counties were relatively affluent. Davidson County ranked second in the state, whereas Knox County ranked seventh. The median age was close to identical. As for housing units, Davidson County ranked second in the state in 1960, whereas Knox County ranked third. Reflecting the fact that Knox County was slightly poorer in 1960 than Davidson County, Knox County reported a higher number of families receiving Aid to Families with Dependent Children payments (the county ranked second in the state), though the two counties were quite comparable on this measure as well (Davidson County ranked fourth in the state). Table 2.2 also shows that Davidson County ranked second in the state in total retail sales in 1960, whereas Knox County ranked fourth.

We are the first to admit that our two cases are far from identical. Most notably, Davidson County is (and was) larger than Knox County, and Knox County is (and was) poorer than Davidson County. Nonetheless, we believe the two cases allow a reasonable test of our hypotheses.

Table 2.2 Comparison of Knox County and Davidson County, 1960 (Preconsolidation)

Measure	Davidson County	Knox County	Tennessee
Unemployment rate	4.6, for Nashville MSA	5.8, Knoxville MSA	6.3
Per capita income	$2,009 (2nd)	$1,830 (7th)	$1,543
Median age	28.6	29.3	30.3
Number of housing units	120,834 (2nd)	77,187 (3rd)	1,084,340
Number of families receiving AFDC	1,698 (4th)	1,924 (2nd)	27,733
Retail sales (1958; thousands)	$480,913 (2nd)	$272,303 (4th)	$3,199,129
Population	399,743	250,523	3,567,089

Sources: TSA 1969, 126, 127, 159, 162, 163, 387, 395, 396, 447, 448, 532, 536, 537, 540, 541, 590, 591; Coulter and Cecil, n.d., 31.

Notes: AFDC = Aid to Families with Dependent Children. MSA = metropolitan statistical area. Numbers in parentheses refer to the county's ranking among all counties in the state on the variable in question.

Government Efficiency

One of the promises made by consolidation supporters was that consolidation would end the duplication of services and administrative effort, and thus provide for more efficient government (Grant 1965a). To assess this claim (and hence to test Hypothesis 1), we sought out comprehensive budget data for our two test cases. As we mention above, we were not altogether successful. We did, however, find reliable data on government spending for 1957, 1962, and 1972.

Government Spending

Table 2.3 shows that combined Nashville/Davidson County total per capita expenditures were growing faster than those of Knoxville/Knox County in the five years before consolidation. Specifically, in Nashville/Davidson County total per capita expenditures grew by about 54 percent during the period 1957–62, while those for Knoxville/Knox County grew by 45 percent. As for highway spending (a proxy for public works spending), it decreased in Knoxville/Knox County between 1957 and 1962, while it increased by 45 percent in Nashville/Davidson County. The comparison of public safety spending for the period 1957–62 produces mixed results. Although spending on police protection grew slightly more in Knoxville/Knox County than in Nashville/Davidson County, spending on fire protection grew much more in Nashville/Davidson County.

Table 2.3 suggests a significant change after consolidation. Although total expenditures in Nashville/Davidson County grew by 113 percent between 1962 and 1972, they grew in Knoxville/Knox County by 156 percent. As for fire protection expenditures during this period, they grew by 171 percent in Knoxville/Knox County but actually decreased by 4 percent in Nashville/Davidson County. For the period 1962–72, police spending grew

Table 2.3 Government Expenditures Per Capita, 1962, and Rates of Change, Nashville/Davidson County and Knoxville/Knox County

Year or Period[a]	Jurisdiction(s)	Total	Highways	Police	Fire
		Per Capita Expenditures[b]			
1962	Nashville/Davidson County	$365	$27	$24	$29
	Knoxville/Knox County	$311	$17	$19	$16
		% Change			
1957–62	Nashville/Davidson County	+54	+45	+43	+98
	Knoxville/Knox County	+45	–9	+46	+55
1962–72	Nashville/Davidson County	+113	+70	+97	–4
	Knoxville/Knox County	+156	+68	+108	+171

Sources: U.S. Bureau of the Census, *Annual Survey of State and Local Government Finances*; U.S. Bureau of the Census, *Census of Governments*; U.S. Bureau of the Census 2006. Available data for 1957 and 1962 are limited in detail.

[a] No county data were available for 1952, hence the analysis only accounts for five years of preconsolidation spending.

[b] Expenditures are not adjusted for inflation.

in both Nashville/Davidson County and Knoxville/Knox County. But the rate of growth in police protection expenditures was higher in Knoxville/Knox County than it was in Nashville/Davidson County. Finally, during the period 1962–72, highway spending in both cases grew at approximately the same rate.

In the end, although our analysis does not take into account local government spending in many categories (including education), table 2.3 provides considerable support for Hypothesis 1. Police, fire, and public works account for the primary local government functions and budgetary spending outside education, and the patterns in our case comparison are clear. With the exception of comparable spending growth on highways, spending in Nashville/Davidson County grew more slowly than spending in Knoxville/Knox County. The largest efficiency gain is evident in spending on fire services (a key consolidation promise area).

Property Taxes

Another way to assess whether or not a local government is performing efficiently and economically is to look at tax rates. Indeed, among current local government officials (with some of whom we spoke), the conventional wisdom is that the consolidated government of Nashville/Davidson County has been much more successful than other Tennessee governments at keeping property tax rates low. The low tax rate, they maintain, is both a sign of government efficiency and a beacon to new businesses. Because property tax rates loom so large in the minds of Nashville leaders and boosters, we decided to take a closer look at these rates over time. Specifically, we look at property tax rates for the periods 1957–62 and 1963–72.

Table 2.4 contains the results of this analysis. The table shows that in every year we examine, Nashville/Davidson County (within the urban services district) had a lower tax rate than Knoxville/Knox County (within the city of Knoxville). In short, Nashville/Davidson County had a lower property tax rate than Knoxville/Knox County before consolidation, and it continued to have a lower rate in the ten years after consolidation. The data also show that consolidation appears to have slowed the growth in property tax rates in Nashville/Davidson County. We say "appears to" because while property tax rates in Nashville/Davidson County grew at a much lower rate during the period 1963–72 than they did during the period 1953–62, tax rates in Knoxville/Knox County actually decreased during the period 1963–72. This suggests that forces other than consolidation (e.g., changes in education funding) may have been at work in Nashville/Davidson County (and in the state as a whole) during the period 1963–72.

Table 2.4 Property Tax Rates in Nashville/Davidson County and Knoxville/Knox County, Selected Years, and Rates of Change

					% Change	
Jurisdiction(s)	**1953**	**1962**	**1963**	**1972**	**1952–62**	**1963–72**
Nashville/Davidson County combined[a]	4.35	5.32	5.70	6.00	22.2	5.3
Knoxville/Knox County combined (within city of Knoxville)	4.72	6.48	6.48	6.13	37.3	–5.4

Sources: Metropolitan Government of Nashville and Davidson County 1966, 39, 40; City Directory Company of Knoxville 1953, 1962a, 1962b; personal e-mail from the Office of Management and Budget, Department of Finance, Metropolitan Government of Nashville and Davidson County, January 2006; personal communication from Gretchen Beal, Knoxville/ Knox County Metropolitan Planning Commission, Knoxville, December 2006.

[a] This signifies the combined tax rate for city and county in 1953 and 1962, and the Nashville/Davidson County rate in the urban services district for 1963 and 1972.

Overall, table 2.4 presents a mixed picture. On the one hand, the data appear to support Nashville/Davidson County leaders' contention that consolidated government works to keep property tax rates relatively low. The data show that tax rates in Nashville/Davidson County grew much more slowly after consolidation than they did before consolidation. On the other hand, the data show that Nashville/Davidson County had lower property tax rates than Knoxville/Knox County even before consolidation. The data also show that while tax rates in Nashville/Davidson County increased only slightly during the period 1963–72, they actually decreased in Knoxville/Knox County during this period.

Summary for Hypothesis 1

In all, the data presented here provide moderate support for Hypothesis 1. Government spending data suggest that the consolidated government of Nashville/Davidson County has operated more efficiently since 1963 than the fragmented governments of Knoxville/Knox County. The data on property tax rates, however, are mixed.

Economic Growth and Health

As we mention above, one of the arguments made by supporters of consolidation was that it would "create a progressive-community image" for Nashville (Grant 1965a, 37). The hope, of course, was that a progressive community image would draw both citizens and businesses to Nashville. Did this occur? In this section we attempt to address this question by examining data on population growth and economic growth.

Population Trends

Table 2.5 presents data on the population of Davidson County and Knox County over time. The table shows that the population of Davidson County grew by 24 percent during the 1950s (preconsolidation) and by 43 percent between 1960 and 2000. Knox County's population grew by 12 percent in the 1950s and by 53 percent from 1960 to 2000. Between 1950 and 2000, the population of Davidson County grew by 77 percent, and the population of Knox County grew by 71 percent. Overall, the population figures indicate that consolidation did not much affect population growth within Davidson County relative to Knox County. In fact, if we look at population growth by decade, the greatest increase in population in Nashville and Davidson County occurred *before* consolidation, in the 1950s. Although Nashville/Davidson County remains larger than Knoxville/Knox County, the evidence suggests that since consolidation the population of the latter has grown at a higher rate than the population of the former.

Economic Activity

Next we turn to economic activity. Specifically, we present data on retail sales, number of manufacturing employees, number of housing units, and per capita income. We chose these indicators because each is a broad indicator of economic health.

Table 2.6 presents data on retail sales. The table shows that in the fourteen years after consolidation, retail sales grew more in Davidson County than they did in Knox County. However, the difference between the two counties was not large. As for the most recent period (1977–2001), retail sales grew substantially more in Knox County than they did in Davidson County. Overall, the numbers are very similar, and suggest that consolidation did not significantly affect the level of retail sales in Davidson County relative to those in Knoxville/Knox County.

Table 2.5 The Population of Davidson County and Knox County, Selected Years, and Rates of Change

							% Change		
Jurisdiction	**1950**	**1960**	**1970**	**1980**	**1990**	**2000**	**1950–60**	**1960–2000**	**1950–2000**
Davidson County	321,758	399,743	448,003	477,811	510,784	569,891	24	43	77
Knox County	223,007	250,523	276,293	319,694	335,749	382,032	12	53	71

Sources: *TSA 1974*, 547, 548; *TSA 1983/84*, 11, 12; *TSA 1992/93*, 13; *TSA 2003*, 1.9.

Table 2.6 Retail Sales (in thousands of real dollars), Davidson County and Knox County, Selected Years, and Rates of Change

						% Change		
Jurisdiction	**1963**	**1967**	**1977**	**1982**	**2001**	**1963–77**	**1977–2001**	**1963–2001**
Davidson County	560,212	790,174	2,032,062	2,857,756	9,710,259	263	378	1,633
Knox County	346,999	441,370	1,200,366	1,825,894	6,341,600	246	428	1,727

Sources: *TSA 1971*, 162, 163; *TSA 1980*, 254, 256; *TSA 1989*, 278, 280; *TSA 2003*, 7.10.

Table 2.7 contains data on manufacturing in Davidson County and Knoxville/Knox County. Davidson had nearly twice as many manufacturing employees as Knox at the time of consolidation, and it continued to have nearly twice as many as Knox in 2000. The table shows that in the fifteen years immediately following consolidation, manufacturing boomed in Davidson County relative to Knox County. The gains made by Davidson County were, however, ephemeral. During the entire period under study (1963–2000), the number of manufacturing employees in Davidson County shrank by 19 percent, compared with only 5 percent in Knox County.

Table 2.8 presents data on the number of housing units in Davidson County and Knox County over time. The table shows that between 1960 and 1980, the number of housing units grew substantially more in Knox County than in Davidson County. The same is true for the period 1980–2000, though the difference is very small. Overall, the number of housing units grew substantially more in Knox County than in Davidson County during the entire period under study.

We conclude with one additional economic indicator: per capita income. Table 2.9 shows that since 1970, Davidson County has consistently had a higher per capita income than has Knox County. Moreover, table 2.9 shows that per capita income grew more in Davidson County than in Knox County during the period 1960–98. The difference in the growth rate is 18 points. Moreover, per capita income in Knox County was 85 percent of the per capita income in Davidson County in 1970; and in 2000, it was nearly the same ratio (83 percent). Although it rose slightly in 1980 and 1990, the gains were erased by 2000.

Summary for Hypothesis 2

Together, the data presented in tables 2.5 through 2.8 do not provide much support for Hypothesis 2. In short, there is little evidence that Nashville/Davidson County became a magnet for businesses and citizens (at least relative to Knoxville/Knox County) after consolidation, or that the consolidated government of Nashville/Davidson County has done a better job of fostering economic growth than the fragmented governments of Knoxville and Knox County. This does not mean, of course, that consolidation has not had its benefits for Nashville/Davidson County. But it does mean that Nashville/Davidson County did not grow substantially more during the period under study than Knoxville/Knox County.

Table 2.7 Number of Manufacturing Employees (thousands), Davidson County and Knox County, Selected Years, and Rates of Change

No. of Manufacturing Employees	1963	1977	1982	1997	2000	% Change 1963–77	% Change 1977–97	% Change 1963–2000
Davidson County	39.0	50.1	45.5	31.7	31.5	28	–37	–19
Knox County	21.8	25.4	22.9	20.8	16.9	17	–18	–5

Sources: *TSA 1969*, 490, 491; *TSA 1985/86*, 171, 172; *TSA 1988*, 167, 168; *TSA 2003*, 4.17, 4.18.

Table 2.8 Number of Housing Units, Davidson County and Knox County, Selected Years, and Rates of Change

Jurisdiction	1960	1970	1980	1990	2000	% Change 1960–80	% Change 1980–2000	% Change 1960–2000
Davidson County	120,834	147,269	187,430	229,064	252,977	55	35	109
Knox County	77,187	92,757	125,883	143,582	171,439	63	36	122

Sources: *TSA 1969*, 126, 127; *TSA 1971*, 129, 130; *TSA 1984/85*, 220, 221; *TSA 1992/93*, 232, 233. Metropolitan Development and Housing Agency 2005, 9. Knoxville-Knox County Metropolitan Planning Commission 2001, 2.

Table 2.9 Per Capita Income, Davidson County and Knox County, Selected Years, and Rate of Change

Jurisdiction	1970	1980	1990	2000	% Change, 1970–2000
Davidson County	3,962	9,924	20,741	34,008	758
Knox County	3,364	9,106	18,966	28,281	740

Source: *TSA 2003*, 2.14.

Note: The source from which we obtained these data did not indicate whether or not these figures were adjusted for inflation.

Citizen Satisfaction

One way, albeit an indirect way, to determine the success of consolidation is to ask residents whether or not they are satisfied with its results. Implicit in the assurances made by Nashville and Davidson County consolidation boosters in the early 1960s was the promise that citizens would be more satisfied with their new consolidated government than they were with their old fragmented governments. In this section we test Hypothesis 3 that consolidation led to greater satisfaction with local government among residents of Nashville/Davidson County.

Fortunately for us, Daniel R. Grant, a professor at Vanderbilt University in Nashville, conducted a series of surveys in the 1960s to ascertain the attitudes of Nashville residents vis-à-vis consolidation. In one survey conducted in 1964, he and his colleagues asked residents, "Are you generally satisfied or dissatisfied with the way 'Metro' [i.e., unified government] has worked in its first year of operation?" (Grant 1965b, 375). The answers to this question are presented in table 2.10. The results are overwhelmingly favorable to consolidation and provide strong support for Hypothesis 3. As Grant puts it, "By a ratio of two and a half to one, voters expressed satisfaction" (Grant 1965b, 375). Grant compares these results with the voting pattern of the 1962 consolidation election and finds that support for unified government increased once the government was up and running. Specifically, Grant notes that 60 percent of voters were satisfied with the results of Metro government one year after it began, while 57 percent of voters cast their ballots for consolidation in 1962 (Grant 1965b, 376).

Table 2.10 Residents' Opinions about the Metropolitan Government of Nashville/Davidson County One Year after Consolidation (percent)

Question: Are you generally satisfied or dissatisfied with the way 'Metro' has worked in its first year of operation?	
Answer:	
Satisfied	60
Dissatisfied	24
No answer or don't know	16

Source: Adapted from Grant 1965a, 375.

Note: Grant does not report an *N* for his sample. Nor does he tell us precisely whom he sampled. He repeatedly refers to respondents as "voters," but he does not explicitly state that he limited his sample to voters.

In a follow-up study of public opinion conducted in 1972, Nicholar A. Sieveking and Dick Battle found even more support for consolidated government. Table 2.11 presents the results of their survey research. The table shows that a large majority of respondents from Nashville/Davidson County replied that local government had gotten better since consolidation.

Not every observer was impressed with Metro government. In a 1974 study, Bruce Rogers and C. McCurdy Lipsey presented a far different picture. They conducted an ingenious study of public opinion in two jurisdictions—one area (called Woodbine) "located entirely within the jurisdiction of the Metropolitan Government of Nashville–Davidson County," and another (a small city next to Woodbine called Berry Hill) that "provides its own police services, parks services, and contracts for the provision of other urban services." "The major difference between the two communities," Rogers and Lipsey (1974, 25) noted, "is the size of the governmental unit producing the public goods and services." Rogers and Lipsey conducted a survey of residents in both communities and found that the residents of Berry Hill were much happier with their public services than were the residents of Woodbine. Table 2.12 contains the results of their analysis. In the end, Rogers and Lipsey concluded that the citizens of Berry Hill—a "small independent community"—"expressed higher levels of satisfaction with...the level of public services provided," than did residents of Woodbine—a community part and parcel of Metro government (Rogers and Lipsey 1974, 32).

In all, despite Rogers and Lipsey's dissent, the data provide strong support for Hypothesis 3. Consolidation did apparently lead to increased

Table 2.11 Residents' Opinions about the Nashville/Davidson County Metropolitan Government, 1970 (percent)

Question: Do you think Nashville government has gotten better, stayed the same, or is not as good as it was five or ten years ago?			
	Overall (n = 425)	**USD** (n = 284)	**GSD** (n = 141)
Answer:			
The same or better	72	69	76
Not as good	22	24	22
No answer or don't know	6	7	6

Source: Adapted from Coomer and Tyer 1974, 40.

Note: USD = urban services district; GSD = general services district. Coomer and Tyer do not report the actual question wording, so this is an approximation based on the information they provide.

citizen satisfaction with local government. Of course, all of this begs this question: What about the citizens of Knoxville and Knox County? How satisfied are they and have they been with their governments? Unfortunately, we do not have the necessary data to answer these questions, so a comparison is not possible. But the data we do have provide strong support for Hypothesis 3.

Other Promises

As the earlier part of this chapter suggests, backers of consolidation made a number of arguments in support of consolidation. They promised more efficient government, increased economic growth, and increased citizen satisfaction with government. But they also made numerous other promises. Before we reach any final conclusions, we assess how well the consolidated government of Nashville/Davidson County kept these other promises.

In a 1965 study designed to evaluate the impact of consolidated government, Daniel Grant (1965a) assessed the promises and the performance of Metro government. Briefly, we highlight his major findings. First, he concluded that as per the predictions of Metro government supporters, consolidation did indeed eliminate city–county "buck-passing," in which citizens had trouble assigning responsibilities for services. He notes that, by definition, under a single unified government it is easy for citizens to know

Table 2.12 Satisfaction with Public Services, Berry Hill and Woodbine (percent)

Service	Community: Berry Hill (outside consolidated government) ($n = 105$)	Community: Woodbine (within consolidated government) ($n = 97$)
Police		
Good	86	52
Fair	14	25
Poor	0	23
Fire		
Good	58	80
Fair	26	19
Poor	16	1
Garbage Collection		
Good	78	80
Fair	15	7
Poor	7	12
Street Repair		
Good	63	21
Fair	28	14
Poor	9	65
Parks		
Good	62	36
Fair	21	26
Poor	17	38

Source: Adapted from Rogers and Lipsey 1974, 28, table 1.

Note: Rogers and Lipsey do not report the actual question wording. This is an approximation based on the information they provide: "How would you rate ______ services in Woodbine/Berry Hill—good, fair, or poor?" *N*s may vary for individual survey items owing to missing data.

who is responsible for government decisions. There is, he notes, only one government to which to assign responsibility. He also noted that in the immediate aftermath of consolidation (he does not tell us precisely when), "by a ratio of more than two and one-half to one," the citizens of Nashville/ Davidson County "agree that 'under metro it is easier to know who to call or see when you have a problem than it was under separate city and county government'" (Grant 1965a, 38).

Second, Grant concluded that the new government's attempts to eliminate city–county financial inequities were successful early on. Specifically, he notes that the problem of double taxation, in which people paid taxes to both "the city and the county while receiving certain services only from the city;" and "free riding" done by "out-of-city residents who used city facilities without being taxed for them," had been solved by 1965. In addition, he notes that shortly after consolidation, "Several services formerly financed entirely (or almost entirely) by city taxpayers were shifted to a countywide tax base" (Grant 1965a, 44–45).

Third, Grant concludes that the equalization of services had begun to occur by 1965. "Metro," he notes, "was proposed as a method of equalizing core-city and suburban services on a single-community basis." The suburbs, he says, "had been poorly served" for "thirty years prior to 1960" (Grant 1965a, 42). A mere year or so after consolidation, he concluded that the countywide equalization of services had begun in earnest, and that particular strides had been made in the areas of schools and parks.

Fourth, Grant noted that evidence he obtained supported "the prediction" of Metro government backers that "greater specialization and professionalization of personnel" would occur under Metro government (Grant 1965a, 41). Specifically, he notes that the new government undertook a number of ambitious studies between 1962 and 1965 designed to enhance professionalization and specialization. From here, the Metro government did a number of things to improve professionalization and specialization, including hiring "a consultant from outside the state" to run the fire department, hiring a "director of schools from Des Moines after a nationwide search," and employing "a survey team from the International Association of Chiefs of Police" to "replace the rather unsavory image of the old city police department and county sheriff's patrol" (Grant 1965a, 41).

In all, Grant concluded that many of the promises made by the Metro government had been kept. Two and a half years after consolidation, he concluded that "Nashville's metro is living up to most of the predictions of its supporters and is moving in the direction of proving incorrect most of the predictions of its opponents" (Grant 1965a, 54).[6]

Conclusions

Table 2.13 summarizes the results of our various analyses. We begin with the issue of government efficiency. Overall, the data provide moderate support for Hypothesis 1. The government expenditure data indicate that consolidation did indeed lead to more efficient government in Nashville/Davidson County. Per capita spending in Nashville/Davidson County grew more slowly than per capita spending in Knoxville/Knox County, with the largest efficiency gains realized in spending on fire services. The property tax data, however, are mixed.

Turning next to population growth and economic development, the data provide no support for Hypothesis 2. We examine a number of indicators of economic health, and we cannot conclude on the basis of these indicators that the consolidated government of Nashville/Davidson County has done a better job than the fragmented governments of Knoxville and Knox County fostering economic growth and development.

Hypothesis 3 is supported by the data. The survey data we examine indicate that consolidation, at least in the decade following unification, led to greater citizen satisfaction with local government. Specifically, the data show that one year after consolidation, the residents of Nashville/Davidson County were very happy with their local government. Moreover, ten years after consolidation, the vast majority of citizens surveyed reported that the Nashville/Davidson County government was performing "the same or better" than the previous arrangement of fragmented governments. In all, the evidence in support of Hypothesis 3 is quite strong.

Finally, we consider other "promises made." Overall, the evidence in support of Hypothesis 4 is moderate, bordering on strong. First, our brief analysis of *other* promises made by consolidation boosters (i.e., promises unrelated to government efficiency, economic growth, and citizen satisfaction) indicates

Table 2.13 Summary of the Nashville/Davidson County Case

Overall Assessment of Evidence	H1: Efficiency	H2: Economic Development	H3: Other Promises
Not enough data available			
No evidence		☑	
Weak			
Moderate	☑		☑
Strong			

that consolidation delivered. Consolidation also appears to have increased government efficiency and citizen satisfaction with local government. The only thing we can conclude that consolidation did not deliver was enhanced economic and population growth.

Thus, on the basis of all the data we examine for the chapter, our overall assessment is as follows: Unified government has been a success in Nashville/Davidson County, and it has delivered on most promises made. We cannot conclude that it has been a rousing success, because there is little evidence that Nashville/Davidson County has become the "model community"—a model that would draw residents and businesses—that consolidation supporters had hoped. Nonetheless, there is strong evidence that the government of Nashville/Davidson County has become more efficient since consolidation and has had relative success at keeping property tax rates down. There is also evidence that the citizens of Nashville/Davidson County were pleased with the performance of their newly unified local government in the first decade after consolidation. Finally, it appears that many of the problems that consolidation was designed to fix were indeed fixed early on. In the end, our conclusion is that consolidation has been good for Nashville/Davidson County.

Notes

1. Unlike other chapters, Nownes and Houston were able to include data on citizen satsifaction. We believe it is important to include.
2. Here are some specifics on our data search. We managed to find adequate budgetary data for Nashville and Davidson County for almost all years since consolidation. We had a difficult time, however, finding budget data for the 1950s. We had some luck obtaining good data on the Knoxville city budget for the 1950s and beyond, but had much worse luck obtaining budget data for Knox County. In the end, we believed that relying on Census Bureau data—limited as it is—was the best course of action.
3. Memphis is the only truly large city in Tennessee, and Shelby County is the only truly large county. Relative to other jurisdictions in the state, the jurisdictions we study are large.
4. For both tables 2.1 and 2.2, we present data for 1950 and 1960. This is not ideal, because consolidation took place in 1963. However, after searching for data from "off years," we came to believe that relying on

these numbers—which are drawn largely from the U.S. Census—was the wise thing to do.

5. We were unable to obtain unemployment figures for the individual counties, so the data given in table 2.2 compare metropolitan statistical areas.
6. Among the predictions of opponents that Grant stated had not been fulfilled were the following: The new government would be less responsible to the people, there would be a substantial increase in property taxes, rural residents would see increased taxes with no benefits, minority political influence would be diluted, and extensive litigation would follow consolidation. See Grant 1965a, 47–53.

References

Booth, David A. 1963. *Metropolitics: The Nashville Consolidation.* East Lansing: Institute for Community Development and Services, Michigan State University.

City Directory Company of Knoxville. 1953. *Knoxville City Directory, 1953.* Knoxville: City Directory Company of Knoxville.

———. 1962a. *Knoxville City Directory, 1962.* Knoxville: City Directory Company of Knoxville.

———. 1962b. *Knoxville City Directory, 1963.* Knoxville: City Directory Company of Knoxville.

Coomer, James C., and Charlie B. Tyer. 1974. *Nashville Metropolitan Government: The First Decade.* Knoxville: Bureau of Public Administration, University of Tennessee.

Coulter, Steven L., and Bill Cecil. N.d. Tennessee: A White Paper Detail on Conditions and Concerns That Affect and Drive Rising Health Plan Rates. http://209.85.165.104/search?q=cache:eENJiqtq-rAJ:www.bcbst.com/learn/affordability/health_plan_affordability.pdf+%22median+age%22+1960+tennessee&hl=en&gl=us&ct=clnk&cd=23.

Elazar, Daniel J. 1961. A Case Study of Failure in Attempted Metropolitan Integration: Nashville and Davidson County, Tennessee. Chicago: National Opinion Research Center, University of Chicago.

Grant, Daniel R. 1965a. A Comparison of Predictions and Experience with Nashville "Metro." *Urban Affairs Quarterly* 1:34–54.

———. 1965b. Opinions Surveyed on Nashville Metro: Public Support Increases after Year's Operation. *National Civic Review,* July, 375–77.

Greene, Lee S., and Daniel R. Grant. 1952. *A Future for Nashville: A Report of the Community Services Commission for Nashville and Davidson County.* Nashville: Community Services Commission for Davidson County and the City of Nashville.

Grubbs, David. 1961. City–County Consolidation Attempts in Nashville and Knoxville, Tennessee. Ph.D. diss. University of Pennsylvania.

Hawkins, Brett W. 1966. *Nashville Metro: The Politics of City–County Consolidation.* Nashville: Vanderbilt University Press.

Knoxville–Knox County Metropolitan Planning Commission. 2001. *Knox County Demographic Trends.* Knoxville: Knoxville–Knox County Metropolitan Planning Commission. http://cadescoveplanning.com/locldata/demo01.pdf.

Metropolitan Development and Housing Agency. 2005. *Nashville–Davidson County Consolidated Plan, 2005–2010.* Nashville/Davidson County: Metropolitan Development and Housing Agency.

Metropolitan Government of Nashville and Davidson County. 1966. *Local Government: Nashville and Davidson County, Tennessee, Fact Book Series Vol. II.* Nashville: Metropolitan Government of Nashville and Davidson County.

Nashville and Davidson County Planning Commission. 1956. *Plan of Metropolitan Government for Nashville and Davidson County.* Nashville: Nashville and Davidson County Planning Commissions.

Nownes, Anthony J., and David J. Houston. 2004. Knoxville/Knox County, Tennessee, A Predictable Failure: The Knoxville/Knox Experience, 1996. In *Case Studies of City–County Consolidation: Reshaping the Local Government Landscape,* ed. Suzanne M. Leland and Kurt Thurmaier Armonk, NY: M. E. Sharpe.

Rogers, Bruce D., and C. McCurdy Lipsey. 1974. Metropolitan Reform: Citizen Evaluation of Performances in Nashville–Davidson County, Tennessee. *Publius* 4:19–34.

U.S. Bureau of the Census. Multiple years. *Annual Survey of State and Local Government Finances.* Washington, DC: U.S. Government Printing Office.

———. Multiple years. *Census of Governments.* Washington, DC: U.S. Government Printing Office.

———. 2006. *Data Base on Historical Finances of Municipal Governments* (Internal U.S. Bureau of the Census File). Washington, DC: U.S. Government Printing Office.

3

Does Consolidation Make a Difference?

A Comparative Analysis of Richmond and Virginia Beach, Virginia

Nicholas J. Swartz

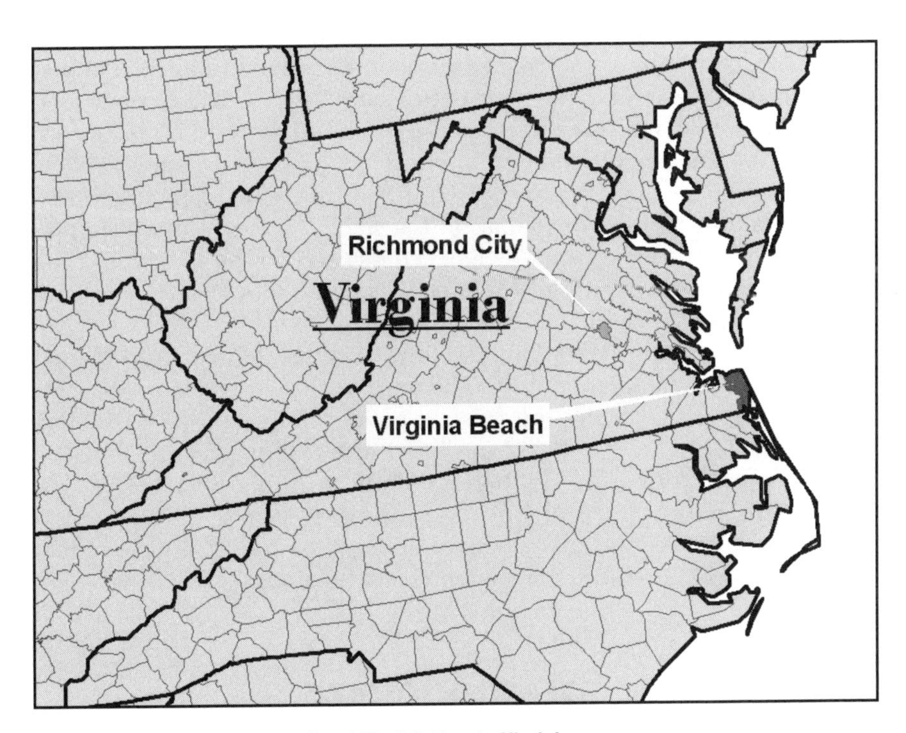

Map 3 Locations of Richmond and Virginia Beach, Virginia
Source: U.S. Bureau of the Census.

Although boundary lines become more and more blurred as a result of urbanization, communities across the United States continue to experiment with the structure of local government. As Vincent Marando stated (1979, 409), "There are serious questions being raised in the recent literature as to whether city–county consolidation is, still, or ever was, a viable reorganization alternative for most of metro America." Now, many years later, municipal scholars, leaders of cities, and officials of counties across the United States are still asking themselves whether or not city–county consolidation is a viable option. Harold Laswell's famous definition that politics is "who gets what, when, and how" is at the forefront of many city and county council agendas, where politicians and managers face the question of how they can better serve their constituency. Issues concerning the use of consolidation, annexation, and interlocal cooperation as strategies to make more efficient use of local fiscal resources are consistent themes in local government.

This chapter attempts to help answer the "how" part of Laswell's definition of politics. This comparative case study analysis examines and compares the consolidated governments of Virginia Beach, Virginia, which consolidated with Princess Anne County in 1963, and the more traditional decentralized system of governance found in Richmond (map 3). Through an analysis of Richmond, the control case, and Virginia Beach, the experimental case, both ten years before and after consolidation, I hope to reveal whether the efficiency arguments often cited as reasons for a merger actually occurred in the tidewater area of Virginia. Although the debate continues on whether consolidation is a viable option for metropolitan America, it is the responsibility of academics to provide insight into the effects of city–county consolidation so that communities seeking alternative structures can have empirical evidence to examine.

The analysis is broken down as follows: The second section presents a brief outline of the methodology. The third section provides a descriptive review of the status of cities, annexation policy, and merger law in Virginia at the time of the merger. The fourth and fifth sections provide historical background information on Richmond and Virginia Beach. The sixth section discusses the results of the findings from the budgetary and economic analysis. And the seventh section wraps up the discussion and provides insight into future research on consolidation.

Methodology

Following the methodology of the previous chapters, a comparative case study analysis is used to determine whether fiscal efficiencies were gained through the merger of Princess Anne County and Virginia Beach as compared with the decentralized system of government found in Richmond. We must perform data collection exercises, which according to King, Keohane, and Verba (1994, 46) "refer to a wide range of methods, including observation, participant observation, intense interviews, large scale sample surveys, history recorded from secondary sources, randomized experiments, ethnography, content analyses, and any other method of collecting reliable evidence." Yin's (2003) convergence of evidence serves as a guide for the case study design (figure 3.1). There are a "portfolio of measures to triangulate" the data obtained for this research. Multiple sources of evidence allow "an investigator to address a broader range of historical, attitudinal and behavioral issues," while at the same time "allowing the development of converging lines of inquiry." Triangulation addresses the problems associated with construct validity because using multiple sources of evidence "essentially provide multiple measures of the same phenomenon" (Yin 2003, 41, 98, 99). Though not all the methods suggested by Yin and by King, Keohane, and Verba were utilized, triangulation was sought by examining archival records, documents, and any previous surveys.

The Experimental Case: Virginia Beach

The governments of Virginia Beach and Princess Anne County consolidated in 1963. At the time of consolidation, Virginia Beach had a population of 172,106 (U.S. Census).

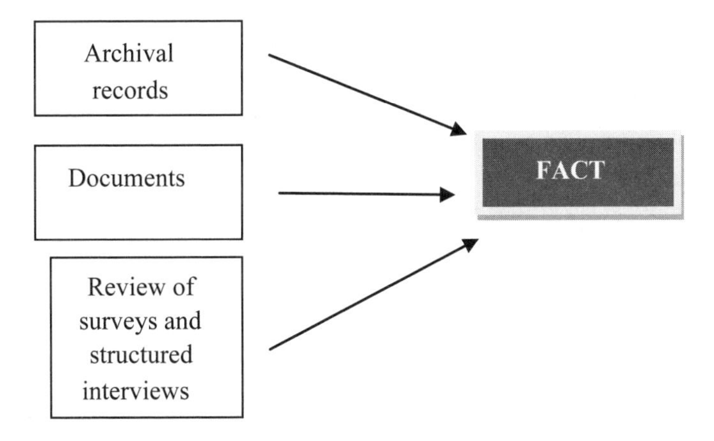

Figure 3.1 Convergence of Evidence
Source: Adapted from Yin 2003.

The Control Case: Richmond

At the time of the consolidation, the City of Richmond (also known as Richmond City) had a population of 219,958 (U.S. Census). The only city in Virginia, other than Richmond, that had a population close to Virginia Beach at the time of consolidation was Norfolk, with a population of 305,872. Norfolk was not selected as the control case because it was already a consolidated government. A city in Virginia was selected as a control case so that both cases were under the same state law at the time of the consolidation.

For the purposes of this analysis, Richmond and Henrico County are combined as if they were a consolidated government. Before consolidation, Princess Anne County's expenditures are combined with the Town of Virginia Beach. To truly test whether the experimental case had any differences when compared with the control case, we must combine Richmond and Henrico County for comparison purposes.

Hypotheses

The following hypotheses are tested:

H1: The consolidated governments of Virginia Beach and Princess Anne County operate more efficiently than the unconsolidated governments of Richmond and Henrico County.

H2: As promised by the supporters of consolidation, the consolidated government protected the residents of Princess Anne County against annexation by Norfolk.

H3: As promised by the supporters of consolidation, the consolidated government appealed to the local pride of Virginia Beach.

H4: As promised by the supporters of consolidation, the consolidated government provided long-term economic progress.

H5: As promised by the supporters of consolidation, the consolidated government provided improvements in metropolitan possibilities.

To test these hypotheses, preconsolidation and postconsolidation data are examined for each case. An examination is provided of specific measures for each case of unified per capita expenditures, per capita general revenue, per capita property taxes, per capita outstanding debt, local employees per 1,000 population, number of wholesale establishments, number of manufacturing establishments, number of retail establishments, and number of building permits issued for housing. Next, these measures are compared in order to identify the relative change or improvement brought about by the consolidation. The design is shown in figure 3.2.

In addition to the budgetary analysis, a description of each case is provided. Rossman and Rallis (2003, 105) suggest that the "application of lessons learned in one case to another population or set of circumstances 'believed to be sufficiently similar to the study sample...apply there as well.'" Despite the small-*N* problem associated with case study analysis, and the study of consolidation in general, hopefully communities interested in consolidation can learn from this analysis based on the experiences of Virginia Beach as compared with Richmond.

The historical analysis of Virginia Beach includes several newspaper articles that portray the socioeconomic climate leading up to the consolidation. As Rossman and Rallis (2003, 64) suggest, individuals providing raw data, or raw information, "often have reasons for providing estimates that are systematically too high or low," a major source of bias.

Experimental Group (Virginia Beach)

Ob_{t11} Ob_{t12} Ob_{t13} Ob_{t14} Ob_{t15} Ob_{t16} Ob_{t17} Ob_{t18} Ob_{t19} Ob_{t20} C Ob_{t21} Ob_{t22} Ob_{t23} Ob_{t24} Ob_{t25} Ob_{t26} Ob_{t27} Ob_{t28} Ob_{t29} Ob_{t30}

Control Group (Richmond)

Ob_{t31} Ob_{t32} Ob_{t33} Ob_{t34} Ob_{t35} Ob_{t36} Ob_{t37} Ob_{t38} Ob_{t39} Ob_{t40} C Ob_{t41} Ob_{t42} Ob_{t43} Ob_{t44} Ob_{t45} Ob_{t46} Ob_{t47} Ob_{t48} Ob_{t49} Ob_{t50}

Figure 3.2 Research Design

Note: Ob_t denotes observation at time t; t represents a fiscal year. C denotes the consolidation in 1963 of Virginia Beach and Princess Anne County. For Ob_{t11} — Ob_{t20} Princess Anne County and Virginia Beach budgets will be combined. For Ob_{t31} — Ob_{t40} Henrico County and Richmond budgets will be combined.

City Status in Virginia, Annexation Policy, and Merger Law

Perhaps the single most distinctive feature of local government in the Commonwealth of Virginia is the principle of city and county separation (Bain 1966, 1967). There are approximately forty-two independent cities in the United States, and thirty-nine of these are located in Virginia.[1] Each Virginia city is politically independent of the county within which it is located; thus, the city only interacts with the Commonwealth of Virginia. Because the city is independent of its surrounding county, city residents do not pay taxes or receive services from the county government. This separation is viewed in the same way as are two counties that are separate entities. County governments in Virginia serve the needs of rural residents and less densely populated areas. Conversely, city governments are viewed as urban governments. As a result of this distinction and separation, duplication of services rarely occurs (Temple 1972, 15).

Table 3.1 reveals Virginia's principle of city and county separation. Only two services in Virginia Beach (culture and public health) were functionally consolidated ten years before the 1963 merger. Public welfare and education were also functionally consolidated one year before the merger, and all services were consolidated ten years after consolidation. Conversely, all services in Richmond were provided separately for all the years under review.

At the time of the consolidation, Virginia had three tiers of municipal corporations:[2]

- city of the first class: population 10,000 or more,
- city of the second class: population 5,000–9,999, and
- city of the third class: population less than 5,000.

At the time of consolidation, Virginia Beach, with a population of 8,091, was a city of the second class. Richmond, with a population of 219,958, was a city of the first class.

Also unique in Virginia is its complex annexation policy. Basically, annexation in Virginia is "quasi-judicial in nature and takes the form of an adversary proceeding between the city and county before a special three-judge annexation court" (Bain 1966, 6). Once a portion of a county has become urban, the city sues the county for that portion of landmass.[3]

Two aspects of Virginia's annexation law are worth noting. First, cases are decided on the basis "of the need for orderly growth and development

Table 3.1 Levels of Functional Consolidation of Services, Before and After 1962

	10 Years before Consolidation		1 Year before Consolidation		10 Years after Consolidation	
Service Function	**Virginia Beach**	**Richmond**	**Virginia Beach**	**Richmond**	**Virginia Beach**	**Richmond**
Department of Law	F	S	F	S	F	S
Judiciary (Courts)	S	S	S	S	F	S
Public safety	S	S	S	S	F	S
Public welfare	S	S	F	S	F	S
Public health	F	S	F	S	F	S
Public works	S	S	S	S	F	S
Parks and recreation	S	S	S	S	F	S
Education	S	S	F	S	F	S

Note: F= functional consolidation (city and county operations combined into single department); S = separately provided by both city and county. The experimental case is Virginia Beach/Princess Anne County, and the comparison case is Richmond/Henrico County.

of the entire area rather than on the wishes of the residents" (Temple 1972, 17). Second, no provision is made for a referendum on annexation. This forces the process to be left entirely in the hands of the annexation court. The annexation court bases its decision on whether or not it feels that county residents need municipal government because of their new urban condition. Between 1901 and 1965, there were 109 annexation proceedings in Virginia. Of these, the court granted annexation to the city on 86 occasions, leading to the conclusion that the courts overwhelming favored the wishes of the city versus that of the county (Bain 1966, 34). This is important in understanding the background leading up to the consolidation of Virginia Beach and Princess Anne County, because the threat of annexation by the City of Norfolk was one of the main factors associated with the successful consolidation campaign.

As we will see, one significant factor associated with the successful consolidation of Princess Anne County and Virginia Beach was Virginia's laws governing consolidation. Three main points are worth noting. First, "Virginia laws controlling local government consolidations are clearly intended to promote merger wherever agreement can be reached by the local participants through negotiation" (Temple 1972, 24). Second, there was a proconsolidation climate within the General Assembly, which took steps to weaken the barriers to state laws so that requirements imposed by statutory law were simple and flexible. Third, local governments in Virginia were active in shaping merger law. Now that we have been provided with the status of cities and laws in Virginia at the time of the merger, we move into a brief description of each case.

The History of Richmond

Richmond, Virginia's current capital, was first settled in 1607. At that time, Williamsburg was the capital, but Richmond became the capital in 1780. During the Civil War, the city was the capital of the Confederate States of America. The town of Richmond consolidated with the city of Manchester in 1910 to form what is now known as the City of Richmond. As with all Virginia cities, Richmond is an independent city having no ties to any county government. Henrico and Chesterfield counties surround Richmond, but geographically Richmond is in the center of Henrico County.

The city's strategic location on the James River historically provided a natural site for the development of commerce. As with many older cities in the United States, Richmond has seen its fair share of loss of population and manufacturing jobs during the last several decades. Richmond falls into the same category as what were historically known as booming manufacturing towns such as Cleveland, Akron, Detroit, and Pittsburgh (Katz and Lang 2003). During the 1980s, Chesterfield and Henrico Counties lost population "in almost one-half and one-quarter of their census tracts, respectively" (Rusk 1999, 294). Richmond's 2000 population was approaching its 1940 level (Rusk 2000).

Before the city's downward population trends began, Henrico County was becoming truly urban. This meant that the services traditionally provided by the county government in Virginia did not meet the demands of its citizens. Voters went to the polls in 1961 to vote on whether they supported the consolidation between the City of Richmond and Henrico County. At a time when mergers in the state seemed politically popular, merger at the polls was not a success in Richmond. During this same period, residents of Virginia Beach and Princess Anne County experienced issues similar to those in Henrico County and Richmond. Voters were much more supportive of merger on the eastern side of the state, where Princess Anne County and Virginia Beach were located.

The History of Virginia Beach and the Path to Merger

The history of Virginia Beach begins with the first landing of English colonists in America on April 26, 1607, at Cape Henry (Virginia Beach Chamber of Commerce, n.d.). Until the late 1880s, when oceanfront resorts began to emerge, the area now known as Virginia Beach remained thinly settled. By the early 1900s the area was becoming a very popular tourist destination. As a result, in 1908 the area was incorporated as the Town of Virginia Beach.

Between 1950 and 1960 the increased urbanization of Princess Anne County, of which the Town of Virginia Beach was part, made the prospective loss of "area, taxable wealth, and population" through annexation a paramount issue for the City of Norfolk, Princess Anne County, and Virginia Beach. During this time, Princess Anne County and the town of Virginia Beach shared certain functions; such as schools, health, welfare, library service, and mosquito control (Temple 1972, 34, 122). Though the two entities shared certain services, continued urbanization required the government of Princess Anne County to undertake expensive urban services—traditionally the job of a city government. Rosenbaum and Henderson (1972) would more than likely agree that the increase in the county's population was an environment-changing event, because the population increase had high visibility and change was necessary given that the demands placed on the county government by its citizens were not being met.

The threat from adjacent Norfolk to annex lands in Princess Anne County interfered with the county's attempts to plan, finance, and develop these urban services. As aforementioned, Norfolk's threat of annexation in Princess Anne County was one of the most significant factors associated with the successful merger. Rosenbaum and Kammerer (1974) argue that a crisis climate must exist for the creation of a consolidation referendum.[4] The fear of the "big bully" annexing lands away from Princess Anne County truly sparked a crisis for residents of both Princess Anne County and Virginia Beach (Blackford 1961). The residents wanted to "immunize the county against further encroachment by the City of Norfolk" (Rusk 1999, 132). Princess Anne County's residents attached themselves to the civic pride of Virginia Beach—not Norfolk. The merger promised protection from annexation, appeals to local pride, continued economic progress, and improvement of "the metro possibilities" (Temple 1972, 76). The promises made were by the most visible merger supporter and popular politician in the area, Sidney Severn Kellam. The role of elites in the electoral outcome of a successful merger was seen in Henderson and Rosenbaum's (1973) comparative case study analysis of Jacksonville and Tampa. They found that the simplest explanation for the success or failure of comprehensive campaigns is that a successful outcome depends upon actively involving a broad spectrum of the community's elite on the side of the proposal. This was certainly the case in what became known as the Kellam Organization in Virginia Beach.

The Kellam Organization, led by Sidney Severn Kellam (who at the time was the Democratic Party National Committeeman for Virginia) controlled the politics of both the City of Virginia Beach and Princess Anne County (Temple 1972, 38). A reporter for the *Virginian Pilot* stated in 1965 that "in each of the booming subdivisions of Virginia Beach, there is generally one resident who is close to the dominant political organization. New residents usually receive a call from the organization neighbor who offers help to expedite any services the local government offers" (Blackford 1965, 39). Kellam and his family had lived in Virginia Beach for years and did not want Norfolk to take away the civic pride that they and the community cherished. He and his supporters were strong advocates of the merger and outlined the suggested schedule for the consolidation campaign, as seen in table 3.2. He was also responsible for convincing Norfolk to pledge a five-year informal moratorium on future annexation against Princess Anne County.

Table 3.2 Timetable for the Virginia Beach/Princess Anne County Consolidation Campaign

Event	Date
Completion of merger agreement and charter in printed form	November 6, 1961
Execution of agreement	November 8
Presentation of petition to Circuit Court of Princess Anne County and entry of order of publication	November 8
Newspaper publication dates	November 9, 16, 23, 30
Completion of legal publication	December 8
Entry of order by Circuit Court of Princess Anne County setting the date for referendum	December 8
Referendum	January 9, 1962
Opening of 1962 session of General Assembly	January 10

Source: Reproduced by the author from a copy obtained at the Virginia Beach Municipal Reference Library.

In January 1963, after 81.9 percent of eligible residents of Princess Anne County and the Town of Virginia Beach had voted to support consolidation, and with the approval from the Virginia General Assembly, the two separate governmental entities became one. The residents' fears of losing their sense of identity and of being bullied by Norfolk were finally put to rest. The new independent city, the City of Virginia Beach, came to life—with the slogan "A Community for a Lifetime."

Since its merger with Princess Anne County, the city has continued to experience a steady rate of growth in population and tourism. The City of Virginia Beach is currently Virginia's most populous city, with a 2000 population of 425,257, ranking thirty-eighth in the United States.

Findings

Budgetary documents and population data were obtained for the City of Richmond, the City of Virginia Beach, Henrico County, and Princess Anne County. For purposes of this analysis, the data from the budgetary documents for the City of Richmond and Henrico County are combined to represent one consolidated government. The data for Princess Anne County are combined with those for the City of Virginia Beach for the years before the merger in 1963.

Figure 3.3 portrays the indexed population (1953 = 100) rates from 1953 to 2000 for the City of Richmond and Henrico County combined, the City of Richmond, the City of Virginia Beach, and the Commonwealth of Virginia. The City of Richmond is shown separately to reveal the population loss over time associated with the flight to the more suburban area of Henrico County. Virginia Beach increased in population at a much higher rate when compared with the Commonwealth of Virginia and Richmond/Henrico County.

Relevant to the current study are the population figures for 1953–73.[5] Table 3.3 reveals population increases for both Richmond (hereafter, "Richmond" refers to data combined for both Richmond and Henrico County) and Virginia Beach, but Virginia Beach's population change was much larger after consolidation. Table 3.3 reveals that the premerger (1953–62) percentage population increases were relatively similar for Richmond (29.2) and Virginia Beach (35.5)—both of which were above the state's percentage change (22.6) during this same period. After consolidation (1963–73), Richmond enjoyed a much smaller percentage increase (2.6) as compared with the years before the merger. Conversely, Virginia Beach

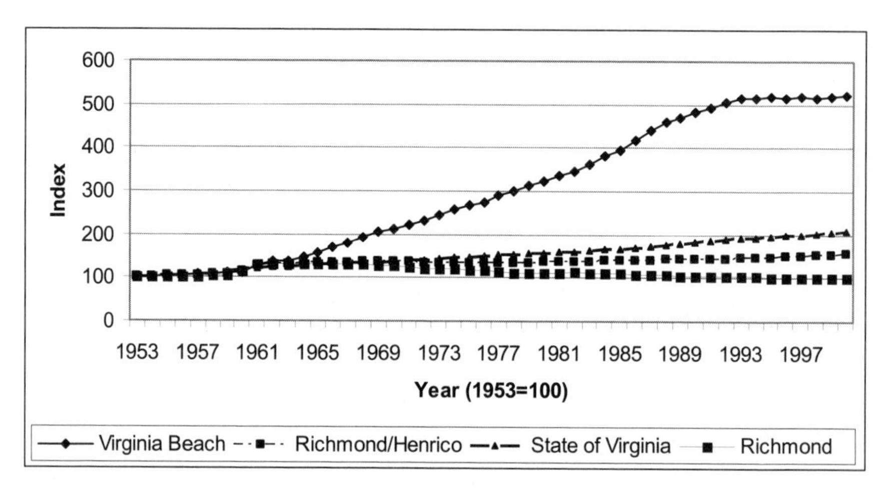

Figure 3.3 Indexed Population Growth, 1953–2000
Source: U.S. Bureau of the Census.

experienced rapid population increases, represented by its 73.7 percent change after the merger. Within this time frame, both cases were above the state's share of 2.3 percent. Examining the entire study period (1953–73), Richmond's proportional change was 35.3 percent, compared with Virginia Beach's 143.9 percent and the state's 43.9 percent. Of even greater interest is the examination of the percentage population changes for the years 1953–2000: Richmond, 55.6; Virginia Beach, 421.1; and the Commonwealth of Virginia, 107.6. Comparing Virginia Beach's percentage population change to Richmond's and the state's from 1953 to 2000 begins to reveal Virginia Beach as the state's most populous city.

These population data can be used to help calculate several government and economic outcomes: expenditures per capita, per capita general

Table 3.3 Population Change Before and After Postconsolidation (percent)

Government	1953–62	1963–73	1953–73	1953–2000
Richmond	29.2	2.62	35.3	55.6
Virginia Beach	35.5	73.7	143.5	421.1
State of Virginia	22.6	2.3	43.9	107.6

Source: U.S. Bureau of the Census.

revenue, per capita property taxes, and per capita outstanding debt. Governmental expenditures per capita were combined for Virginia Beach/ Princess Anne County and the City of Richmond/Henrico County ten years before and ten years after the 1963 consolidation of Princess Anne County and Virginia Beach. Despite numerous attempts, governmental expenditure data for 1957 were not available for either Virginia Beach or Princess Anne County. To capture potential long-term effects, data were also collected for per capita general revenue, per capita property taxes, per capita outstanding debt, and local full-time employees per 1,000 population for 1972, 1977, 1982, 1987, 1992, and 1997.

Figure 3.4 portrays adjusted expenditures per capita for both Richmond and Virginia Beach. We can see that for all the years before the merger, expenditures per capita were much higher in Richmond compared with Virginia Beach. Immediately following the merger (between 1962 and 1963), expenditures per capita nearly doubled in Virginia Beach—mainly due to large increases across the board in all categories as a result of providing urban services to all residents. As mentioned above, before the merger, Princess Anne County served the needs of rural residents and the City of Virginia Beach served the needs of urban residents, and the two entities were independent of one another (as explained above). Duplication of services between the city and the county were not common; therefore, traditional city services expanded across the board to serve county residents who had not been a part of the city government.

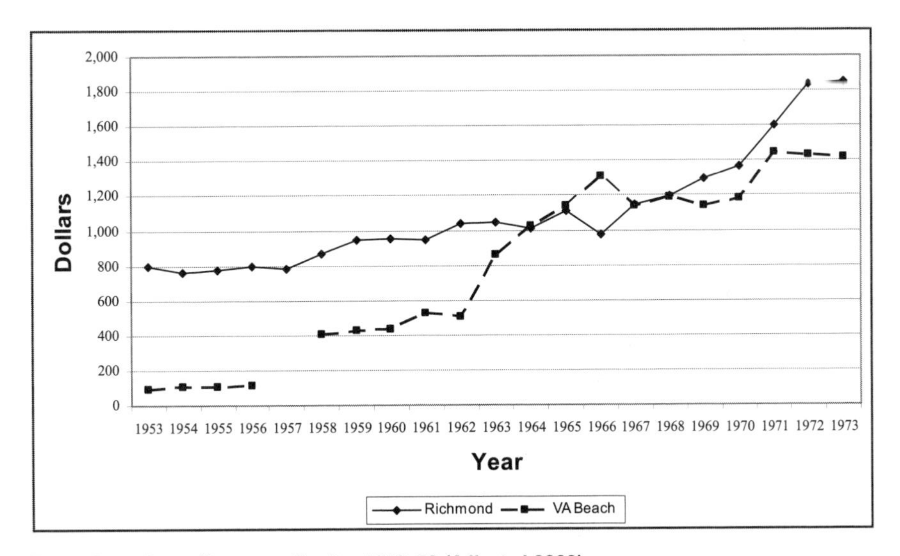

Figure 3.4 Expenditures per Capita, 1953–73 (Adjusted 2000)
Source: U.S. Bureau of the Census.

In addition, expenditures per capita in Virginia Beach rose above Richmond's expenditures per capita in 1963 (the year after the merger) and remained higher until 1967 (four years after the merger). After the merger, Richmond's per capita expenditures continued to rise while Virginia Beach's per capita expenditures remained steady—even declining slightly from 1968 to 1969 and between 1971 and 1973.

Table 3.4 reveals the rate of change for the combined expenditures for Richmond and Virginia Beach and is broken down to show the percentage increase between the premerger (1953–62) and postmerger (1963–73) periods, coupled with an overall percentage increase for the entire study period (1953–73). We can see that before the merger (1953–62), Richmond's rate of change was 30.5 percent while Virginia Beach's was slightly higher, at 32.8 percent. After the merger (1963–73), Richmond had a 78.4 percent increase, which was much lower than Virginia Beach's 181.3 percent increase. For the entire study period (1958–68), we find that Richmond's overall rate of change of 132.4 percent, whereas Virginia Beach's was 442.2 percent.

This reveals that combined total per capita expenditures increased at a much higher rate for Virginia Beach, specifically after the merger, when compared with Richmond. This result paints a gloomy picture for advocates of governmental consolidation, but we must take into account the significant population increases Virginia Beach experienced within this time frame. Referring back to table 3.3, we are reminded that Richmond's population change was 55.6 percent while Virginia Beach's population change was 421 percent. If we calculate the marginal increase (table 3.5) between the change in expenditures per capita and the change in population, a clearer picture of consolidation's potential effects begins to emerge.[6]

Before the merger, the marginal increase for Richmond was 1.04, while the marginal increase for Virginia Beach was 0.92. Thus, a 1 percent increase in the population for the City of Richmond resulted in a 1.04 percent change in per capita expenditures. As such, a 1 percent increase in the population for Virginia Beach resulted in a 0.92 percent

Table 3.4 Rate of Change for Combined Expenditures (percent)

Government	Increase, 1953–62	Increase, 1963–73	Increase, 1953–73
Richmond	30.5	78.4	132.9
Virginia Beach	32.8	181.3	442.2

Sources: Various budget documents obtained for the City of Richmond, the City of Virginia Beach, Henrico County, and Princess Anne County.

Table 3.5 Marginal Increase between the Change in Expenditures per Capita and the Change in Population (percent)

Government	1953–62	1963–73	1953–73
Richmond	1.04	29.93	3.76
Virginia Beach	.92	2.46	3.08

Source: Calculated by the author from various budget documents obtained for the City of Richmond, the City of Virginia Beach, Henrico County, and Princess Anne County.

increase in per capita expenditures. After the merger, the marginal increase for Richmond was 29.9, while the marginal increase for Virginia Beach was much lower, at 2.46. This implies that a 1 percent increase in the population for the City of Richmond resulted in a 29.9 percent change in per capita expenditures, and a 1 percent population change in Virginia Beach resulted in a 2.46 percent change in per capita expenditures. This also may imply that although Virginia Beach's rate of change in per capita expenditures was much higher than Richmond's rate of change, the economies of scale argument (which is usually associated with proconsolidation campaigns) may actually have occurred in Virginia Beach after the merger, when marginal increases and the significant rate of population changes are taken into account.

Changes in expenditure priorities can also be examined before and after consolidation by looking at the changes in expenditures per capita for all governmental functions. Tables 3.6 and 3.7 show priority rankings for both cases. The rankings are based on combined expenditures per capita (a ranking of a 1 means the highest priority) and are calculated by combined expenditures per capita. It is no surprise that expenditures for education ranked 1 for all years for both cases. Richmond's priorities (table 3.6) remained relatively stable during the twenty years examined. The changes made were either a 1 or 2 rank of increase or decrease. The only substantial priority changes were in public welfare (1966) and public works (1964).

Virginia Beach's preconsolidation priority rankings remained relatively stable. Interestingly, expenditures for the Department of Law increased significantly the year before the merger but fell significantly the year of the merger and remained a low priority for the remainder of the study period. Before the merger, public welfare was ranked second or third. After the merger, public welfare decreased in priority, remaining between the sixth or eighth priority (in the last year of examination, it ranked second to last).

(Text continues on p. 76.)

Table 3.6 Expenditures per Capita Ranked by Function, Richmond, by Year

Function	1953	1954	1955	1956	1957	1958	1959	1960	1961	1962	1963
Education	1	1	1	1	1	1	1	1	1	1	1
Public works	2	5	5	5	5	5	2	2	3	3	2
General government	8	7	6	6	6	6	5	3	2	2	3
Public welfare	4	3	2	2	2	3	6	5	4	4	4
Debt service	3	2	3	3	4	4	4	6	6	6	5
Public safety	5	4	4	4	3	2	3	4	5	5	6
Parks and recreation	9	9	8	8	7	7	7	9	7	7	7
Judiciary	10	10	10	10	10	10	9	7	9	8	8
Public health	7	6	7	7	8	8	8	8	8	9	9
Reserve	6	8	9	9	9	9	10	10	10	10	10
Culture	11	12	12	12	11	11	11	11	12	11	11
Department of Law	12	11	11	11	12	12	12	12	11	12	12
City stadium	13	13	13	13	13	13	13	13	13	13	13

Table 3.6 (Continued)

Function	1964	1965	1966	1967	1968	1969	1970	1971	1972	1973
Education	1	1	1	1	1	1	1	1	1	1
Public works	10	4	4	5	3	3	3	4	4	4
General government	2	2	2	6	6	4	5	6	6	6
Public welfare	3	3	9	2	2	2	2	2	2	3
Debt service	4	5	3	3	4	5	4	3	3	2
Public safety	5	6	5	4	5	6	6	5	5	5
Parks and recreation	8	7	8	8	8	7	7	10	7	7
Judiciary	7	8	6	9	7	8	8	8	8	9
Public health	9	9	7	10	9	9	9	7	9	8
Reserve	11	13	10	7	13	11	10	11	12	11
Culture	10	10	11	11	10	10	11	9	10	10
Department of Law	12	12	12	12	11	12	12	12	11	12
City stadium	13	11	13	13	12	13	13	13	13	13

Source: Various budget documents obtained for the City of Richmond and Henrico County

Table 3.7 Expenditures per Capita Ranked by Function, Virginia Beach, by Year

Function	1953	1954	1955	1956	1957	1958	1959	1960	1961	1962	1963
Education	1	1	1	1		1	1	1	1	1	1
Public works	4	4	4	4		4	5	4	5	3	2
Debt service	3	2	2	2	N.A.	2	2	2	2	2	3
Transfer	14	13	12	11		6	6	5	3	5	4
Public safety	5	5	6	3		5	4	6	6	7	5
General government	6	6	7	6		7	7	7	7	7	6
Public welfare	2	3	3	3		3	3	3	4	6	7
Judiciary	9	10	10	10		10	13	8	9	10	8
Parks and recreation	13	11	11	9		8	8	10	8	8	9
Highways, streets, and bridges	12	13	13	13		13	12	13	11	12	10
Reserve	8	8	8	14		12	10	9	10	9	11
Public health	11	9	9	8		11	11	12	14	11	12
Culture	7	7	5	7		9	9	11	12	13	13
Department of Law	10	12	14	12		14	14	14	13	4	14

Table 3.7 (Continued)

Function	1964	1965	1966	1967	1968	1969	1970	1971	1972	1973
Education	1	1	1	1	1	1	1	1	1	1
Public works	3	7	7	3	3	3	3	3	3	5
Debt service	4	4	4	4	5	5	5	5	4	3
Transfer	8	2	3	2	2	2	2	9	7	7
Public safety	6	5	6	6	7	6	10	6	6	6
General government	3	6	5	10	6	14	14	2	2	2
Public welfare	7	8	8	7	8	7	6	7	8	13
Judiciary	10	11	10	8	10	9	7	8	13	8
Parks and recreation	11	9	9	9	9	8	8	10	10	9
Highways, streets, and bridges	2	3	2	5	4	4	4	4	5	4
Reserve	9	10	11	12	11	10	9	12	11	10
Public health	14	12	12	11	13	11	11	11	9	12
Culture	12	13	13	13	12	13	12	13	12	10
Department of Law	13	14	14	14	14	12	13	4	14	14

Source: Various budget documents obtained for the City of Virginia Beach and Princess Anne County.

Note: N.A. = not available.

Also worth noting is the priority shift in the highways, streets, and bridges category. Before the merger, this category remained a low priority. Post merger, it was quite a high priority, ranking between 2 and 5 for all years after the merger (with the exception of the year immediately following the merger). This truly indicates a priority shift, because the newly consolidated Virginia Beach had to provide an adequate transportation system to all residents within its periphery (referring back to city status in Virginia, this is a task that was more than likely left up to the city government and not the county government before the merger).

To capture any long-term effects, several outcomes were examined for 1972, 1977, 1982, 1987, 1992, and 1997: per capita general revenue, per capita property taxes, per capita general expenditures, per capita outstanding debt, local full-time employees per 1,000 population, number of wholesale establishments, number of manufacturing establishments, and number of retail establishments (table 3.8). The number of building permits for housing was also examined for the years 1980–2005.

Table 3.8 reveals that the performance of Virginia Beach outpaced performance in Richmond when one examines the government and economic outcomes. The percentage changes (1972–97) in per capita revenues (all local revenue including taxes and fees, but excluding intergovernmental aid), per capita property taxes, and per capita expenditures were much higher for Virginia Beach when compared with Richmond. Virginia Beach's per capita outstanding debt was much lower (84 percent) than Richmond's (244 percent). Richmond's 1997 per capita outstanding debt was almost 3.5 times more than its 1972 level, whereas Virginia Beach's 1997 per capita outstanding debt was a little less than twice its 1972 level. One explanation for the rapid increase in Richmond's per capita debt is due to the population growth in the county. County government in Viginia provides services to "rural residents." Therefore the county is expected to make significant investments in infrastructure to meet the demands of its new residents. Both Richmond's and Virginia Beach's percentage change in local government employees per 1,000 population decreased during the period 1972–97, though Virginia Beach's decrease was greater than Richmond's.

The last measures (number of wholesale, manufacturing, and retail establishments) show the most significant differences between the two areas under review. It has already been shown that Virginia Beach's population increases have far outpaced those of Richmond. Virginia Beach's large population increase parallels its percentage increases in its number of wholesale, manufacturing, and retail establishments. Richmond experienced population increases, but relatively low growth in the overall percentage increase in the number of establishments. It is worth noting that

Table 3.8 Historical Government Finances and Economics for Richmond (R) and Virginia Beach (VB), 1972–97

Government and Economic Outcome	1972		1977		1982		1987		1992		1997		% Change, 1972–97	
	R	VB	R	VB	R	VB	R	VB	R	VB	R	VB	R	VB
Per capita general revenue	$673	$328	$1,009	$665	$1,362	$1,103	$2,107	$1,104	$2,866	$1,991	$3,019	$2,001	348	510
Per capita property taxes	N.A.	N.A.	$282	$144	$392	$217	$602	$378	$820	$566	$917	$612	225	325
Per capita general expenditures	$751	$311	$1,086	$642	$1,294	$1,108	$2,225	$1,348	$2,969	$1,845	$3,179	$1,963	323	531
Per capita outstanding debt	$1,734	$1,090	$1,989	$1,152	$2,218	$1,285	$2,371	$1,357	$2,754	$1,739	$5,966	$2,012	244	84
Local full-time employees per thousand population	22.7	37.9	20.9	27.74	21.6	29.5	21.7	31.1	20.4	28.2	20.9	28.7	−7.9	−24.3
Wholesale establishments	634	189	650	214	625	276	696	410	696	496	701	529	10.6	180
Manufacturing establishments	398	79	403	85	401	126	428	164	399	210	387	231	−2.76	192.4
Retail establishments	1,994	1,218	2,018	1,373	1,928	1,939	2,256	3,061	2,469	3,580	2,571	3,829	28.9	214.4

Sources: U.S. Bureau of the Census; various budget documents obtained for the City of Richmond, the City of Virginia Beach, Henrico County, and Princess Anne County.

Note: N.A. = not available.

Richmond's proportional change in the number of manufacturing establishments was actually negative, indicating a loss in 2.76 percent of establishments between 1972 and 1997, while Virginia Beach's change was 192.4 percent. All these measures hint at Virginia Beach making and maintaining its promise of long-term economic progress and its improvement of metropolitan possibilities, as was cited throughout the preconsolidation campaign.

Finally, the number of building permits for housing was examined for the years 1980–2005 (figure 3.5). For these data, "Richmond" refers to the number of building permits issued for just the City of Richmond, whereas "Richmond combined" refers to the number of building permits issued for the City of Richmond and Henrico County. The City of Richmond is shown separately to reveal that little to no housing growth occurred within the city limits and that most if not all housing growth occurred in Henrico County. There were several years under review during this period when the City of Richmond issued no building permits.Turning attention to Virginia Beach and Richmond combined, we see that both followed the same general trend, with Virginia Beach outperforming Richmond from 1980 to 1993. Richmond outperformed Virginia Beach for the remainder of the time frame under examination, with the exception of two years.

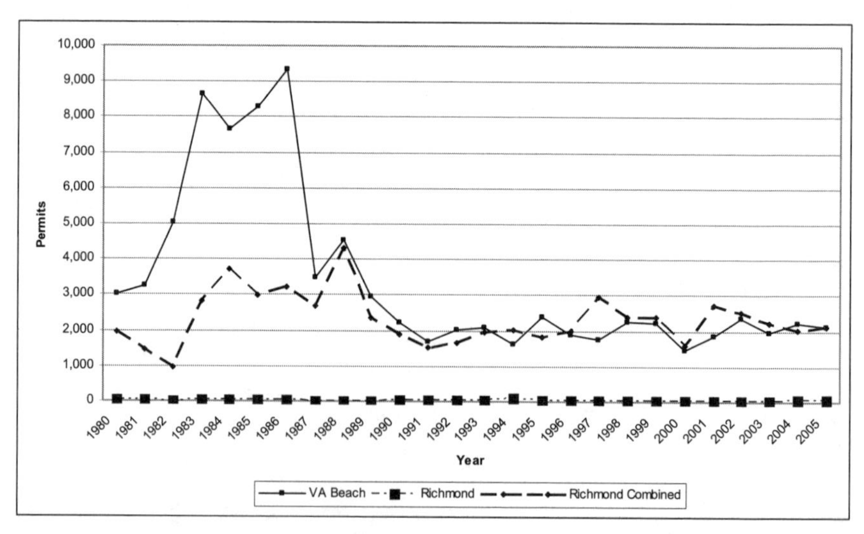

Figure 3.5 Building Permits for Housing
Source: U.S. Bureau of the Census.

Conclusions

It has been many years since Vincent Marando (1979, 409) stated that "there are serious questions being raised . . . as to whether city–county consolidation is still, or ever was, a viable reorganization alternative for most of metro America." This study asks, Do we know any more now?

This analysis has been an attempt to answer the question of whether consolidation yields a more efficient government when compared with the more traditional decentralized form of government, and whether the promises made in the Virginia Beach/Princess Anne County preconsolidation campaign were actually kept. This quasi-experimental case study supports the hypotheses that the consolidated government of Virginia Beach is more efficient and delivered on its campaign promises. Comparing only per capita expenditure data between Richmond and Virginia Beach, however, does not yield findings that bode well for reform advocates. We must take into consideration Virginia Beach's extensive population growth during the years under review. This is taken into account by examining marginal increases, which calculates changes in expenditures per capita by population changes. When this calculation is considered, the efficiency argument associated with economies of scale appears to be true in this instance. Although Virginia Beach's per capita expenditures nearly doubled immediately following consolidation (as a result of expanding services), there was a decrease in per capita expenditures in the last three years of review that hints at possible cost savings in the long run. The results obtained through this analysis of each of the other outcome indicators also bode well for reform advocates when one compares Virginia Beach with Richmond. In addition, reflecting back on the consolidation campaign, the Kellam Organization promised that the merger would result in long-term economic progress, protection from annexation by Norfolk, appeals to local pride, and improvements in metropolitan possibilities. Each of these promises was certainly kept (table 3.9).

All these years later, we are still exploring whether or not consolidation is a viable reorganization alternative for metropolitan America, and we will continue to do so for years to come. The debate as to what effects consolidation has had or will have remains open to continued research and analysis. However, based on this analysis, the consolidated government of Virginia Beach has operated more efficiently and kept the promises made years ago.

Table 3.9 Summary of the Virginia Beach/Princess Anne County Case

Overall Assessment of Evidence	H1: Efficiency	H2: Economic Development	H3: Other Promises
Not enough data available			
No evidence			
Weak			
Moderate	☑	☑	☑
Strong			

Notes

1. According to the Wikipedia website (http://en.wikipedia.org/wiki/Independent_city), the other independent cities include Anchorage; Baltimore (separate from Baltimore County since 1851); Carson City, Nevada; and Saint Louis (separate from Saint Louis County since 1876).
2. For further discussion, see Rush 1941, chap. 21.
3. It should be noted that these annexation policies were in effect at the time of the merger. An examination of Virginia's current annexation policy was not performed for this paper.
4. For an enhanced version of the Rosenbaum and Kammerer model, see Leland and Thurmaier 2004.
5. I was unable to locate data for the intercensal years 1958 and 1959.
6. Marginal increase is calculated as (change in combined expenditures per capita/change in population).

References

Bain, Chester W. 1966. *Annexation in Virginia: The Use of the Judicial Process for Readjusting City–County Boundaries.* Charlottesville: Institute of Government, University of Virginia, and University Press of Virginia.

———. 1967. *"A Body Incorporate": The Evolution of City–County Separation in Virginia.* Charlottesville: Institute of Government, University of Virginia, and University Press of Virginia.

Blackford, Frank R. 1961. Beach–P. A. Merger Move Expected Monday. *Virginian Pilot,* November 4.

———. 1965. A Democrat's Democrat: Sidney Severn Kellman. *Virginian Record,* March.

Henderson, Thomas, and Walter Rosenbaum. 1973. Prospects of Consolidation of Local Government: The Role of Elites in Electoral Outcomes. *American Journal of Political Science* 17, no. 4 (November): 675–719.

Katz, B., and R. Lang. 2003. *Redefining Urban and Suburban American: Evidence from Census 2000.* Washington, DC: Brookings Institution Press.

King, G., R. O. Keohane, and S. Verba. 1994. *Designing Social Inquiry: Scientific Inference in Qualitative Research.* Princeton, NJ: Princeton University Press.

Leland, Suzanne, and Kurt Thurmaier, eds. 2004. *Reshaping the Local Government Landscape: Case Studies of City–County Consolidation.* Armonk, NY: M. E. Sharpe.

Marando, Vincent L. 1979. City–County Consolidation: Reform, Regionalism, Referenda and Requiem. *Western Political Quarterly* 32, no. 4:409–21.

Rosenbaum, Walter, and Thomas Henderson. 1972. Explaining Comprehensive Government Consolidation: Toward a Preliminary Theory. *Journal of Politics* 34, no. 2:428–57.

Rosenbaum, Walter, and Gladys Kammerer. 1974. *Against Long Odds: The Theory and Practice of Successful Governmental Consolidation.* Administrative and Policy Studies Series 03-022, vol. 2. Beverly Hills, CA: Sage.

Rossman, G. B., and S. F. Rallis. 2003. *Learning in the Field: An Introduction to Qualitative Research,* 2nd ed. Thousand Oaks, CA: Sage.

Rush, John A. 1941. *The City–County Consolidated.* Los Angeles: John A. Rush.

Rusk, David. 1999. *Inside Game Outside Game: Winning Strategies for Saving Urban America.* Washington, DC. Brookings Institution Press.

———. 2000. *Cities without Suburbs: A Census 2000 Update.* Washington, DC: Woodrow Wilson Center Press.

Temple, David. 1972. Merger Politics: Local Government Consolidation in Tidewater Virginia. Charlottesville: University Press of Virginia.

Virginia Beach Chamber of Commerce. N.d. *Virginia Beach Facts and Figures.* Virginia Beach: Virginia Beach Chamber of Commerce.

Yin, R. K. 2003. *Case Study Research: Design and Methods,* 3rd ed. Thousand Oaks, CA: Sage.

4

What Difference Does City–County Consolidation Make?

A Historical Analysis of Jacksonville and Tampa, Florida

Milan J. Dluhy

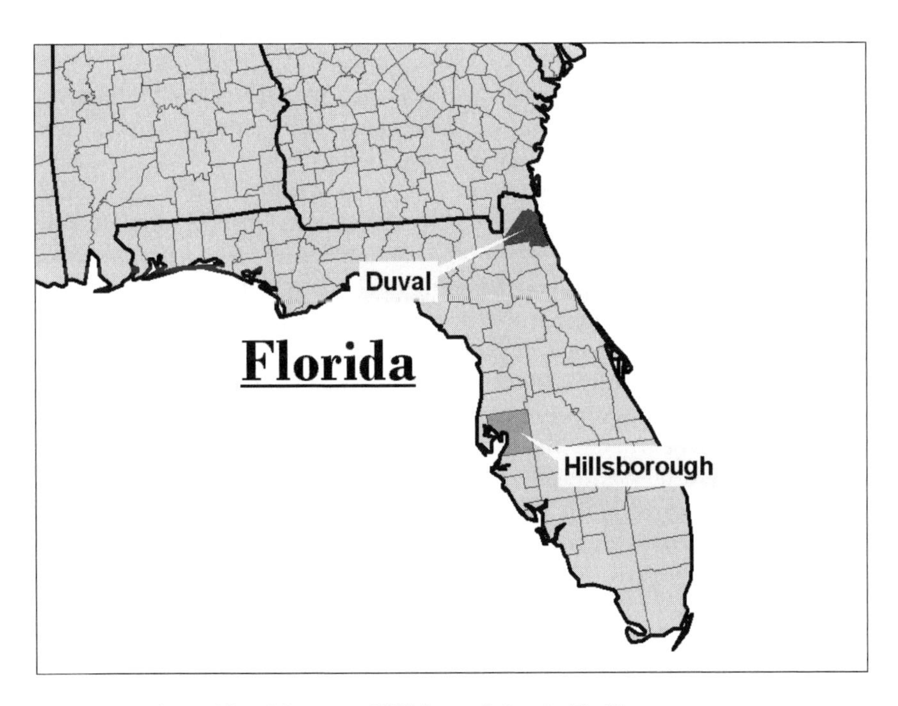

Map 4 Locations of Duval County and Hillsborough County, Florida
Source: U.S. Bureau of the Census.

Reflecting on the last three decades of local government reform literature, it is clear that there is more than one path to regional governance (Feiock 2004). As suburban sprawl has spilled into the areas surrounding our major cities since World War II, there has been an urgent call from many reformers for metropolitan-wide or regionwide governmental structures and governance to deal with the growing metropolitan-wide problems (Peirce 1993).

Historically, there have been at least four different approaches proposed by reformers to improve regional governance in the United States. First, the most traditional approach has been to provide cities with the power to annex surrounding and contiguous areas. If annexations succeed and are aggressive enough, the boundaries of the changed city can come closer to the actual boundaries of the emerging metropolitan area. In this situation, the municipality doing the annexing can expand its customer base to a level that can effectively capture scale economies (Carr 2004). However, the main drawbacks to annexation as a tool are political because the surrounding suburban areas usually fear higher taxes after annexation by the larger central city and/or they fear the loss of their political or decision-making autonomy, especially over their regulatory powers of planning and land use. As a result, most suburbanites vote "no" in public referenda on annexation (Carr 2004). In this analysis, Tampa primarily used the annexation approach in its earliest phases of development from 1950 to 1985.

The second approach that many reformers have pushed since the early 1950s has been the consolidation of city and county governments. In some instances, city–county consolidation has been presented, in part, as a way to stop large-scale annexations by the primary core city in the county or region (Carr 2004). Some of the better-known city–county consolidations historically have been in Baton Rouge (1947), Nashville (1962), Jacksonville (1967), and Indianapolis (1969). There is also a growing body of literature that has concluded that the effects of city–county consolidation have been marginal from an efficiency and economy standpoint (Carr 2004).

As Feiock (2004) and others have pointed out, a review of the empirical evidence regarding the political, economic, and fiscal consequences of consolidation provides only weak support for consolidation arguments. Or put in another way, the evidence with regard to the progressive reform model's predictions that consolidation will reduce costs and enhance efficiency is neither particularly clear nor significant. Part of the reason that there has been so little clear-cut evidence demonstrating the positive effects of consolidation is that most of our knowledge of the history of consolidation comes from the reading of single case studies (Leland and Thurmaier 2004a). The research challenge for those supporting a continuing understanding of city–county consolidation lies in using a careful design of systematic comparative case studies of city–county consolidation that also include nonequivalent control groups whenever possible. This comparative case approach, as discussed below, uses this type of design to further clarify the empirical results of consolidation. The other analyses in this volume also focus on the results found when the comprehensive comparative case design is used.

Despite evidence that consolidations have not led directly to positive economic effects (Benton and Gamble 1984; Feiock and Carr 1997), there still are more qualitative illustrations that consolidation can cause political and leadership changes and even changes in policy visions for a region (Feiock 2004; Swanson 2000). These qualitative changes are explored below in the Jacksonville exemplar.

The third and more common and politically acceptable approach to regionwide governance has been to set up special purpose (single purpose) taxing districts for functions such as transportation, water and sewer, and law enforcement. State legislatures have made this option easy for many urban regions within their states and new special districts are the fastest growing component of local government nationwide (McCabe 2004). For example, the Census of Governments indicates that there are 33,418 special districts (1997) and many of these units are metropolitan in jurisdiction. Because Tampa and Jacksonville are analyzed in this chapter (map 4), it is important to note that Florida is one of the states using special district government the most (i.e., they have 526 special district governments, which ranks them in the top ten states). Both Jacksonville and Tampa have used special purpose districts (i.e., transportation, airport, and port), but county and city governments are still the largest providers of the other basic services in these two regions (the information here is from the websites of Hillsborough County, www.hillsboroughcounty.org; the City of Jacksonville, www.coj.net; and the City of Tampa, www.tampagov.net). This approach has been used in Florida, but it has not been aimed at core urban services:

Duval County Independent Authorities, Boards, and Commissions
School board
Electric authority
Port authority
Airport authority

Hillsborough County Independent Authorities, Boards, and Commissions
School board
Regional transit agency

Aviation authority
Expressway authority
Sports authority
Metropolitan planning organization

The fourth approach to regionwide governance has been to strive for functional consolidation in a region where through cooperation or partnership the county delivers the truly regional services and the cities deliver the others. Miami/Dade County is the most notable example of this approach nationally. The Charlotte/Mecklenburg region has exemplified how a community can use the functional consolidation approach without a complete merger of city and county government. In short, jurisdictions only consolidate the functions where there are clear economies of scale and where there is little political opposition (Carr 2004). The rest of the functions remain with the cities in the region. This approach is very incremental and usually avoids the public referendum or change in government structure required by city–county consolidation or annexation. In the Tampa and Jacksonville areas, functional consolidation has not been an important approach to metropolitan problems. However, the Tampa region has maintained a more traditional split in functions between the city of Tampa and the county, as exemplified in table 4.1.

Regardless of which approach is used, the interest in metropolitan governance has not waned in recent decades, although some researchers point out that there is now more interest in city–county consolidation in the South than in any other region in the United States (Leland and Thurmaier 2004b). What is different today is consideration of the specific approach to be used to increase efficiency, effectiveness, and political equity in metropolitan regions. Largely because most consolidation attempts have failed (73 percent) since 1967, and because most quantitative studies of the economic effects of consolidation have been inconclusive or unclear, decision makers and voters are now more willing to consider alternative paths to metropolitan reform (Carr 2004). In light of this healthy reexamination of alternative paths to metropolitan reform, this analysis emphasizes a longitudinal, comparative, and empirical look at the Tampa and Jacksonville areas. The purpose is to use a more sophisticated methodology to understand the effects of consolidation than the traditional case study approach that has been used in the past. This revised methodology will either confirm the previous findings of the minimal effects of consolidation or will break new ground in our thinking about governmental reform at the local level.

Table 4.1 Level of Functional Consolidation of Services for the Experimental Case (E), Jacksonville/Duval County[a]; and for the Comparison Case (C), Tampa/Hillsborough County[b]

	10 Years before Consolidation		1 Year before Consolidation		10 Years after Consolidation	
Service Function	**E**	**C**	**E**	**C**	**E**	**C**
Fire protection	S	S	S	S	F	S
Social services	S	S	S	S	F	S
Law enforcement	S	S	S	S	F	S
Parks and recreation	S	S	S	S	F	S
Planning	S	S	S	S	F	S
Economic development	S	S	S	S	F	S
Utilities (water/sewer)	S	S	S	S	F	S
Public works	S	S	S	S	F	S
Public health	S	S	S	S	F	S

Key: F = functional consolidation (city and county operations combined into single department); S = separately provided by both city and county.

[a] The cities of Baldwin, Neptune Beach, Atlantic Beach, and Jacksonville Beach in Duval County remained independent and did not join the consolidation. They represented 6 percent of the population in Duval County at the time of consolidation.

[b] Recent figures (2005) indicate that Hillsborough County has three cities, including Plant City, Tampa, and Temple Terrace. In 2005, the cities accounted for 34 percent of the population of the county and the remaining 66 percent lived in unincorporated areas and received both municipal and county services from Hillsborough County. The three cities provided their own municipal services. Thus Hillsborough County was the equivalent of a consolidated government in terms of services for 66 percent of the population. Only 34 percent of the population lived in areas where both the cities and counties overlapped in their service functions. In many unincorporated areas in Florida, the county provides comprehensive municipal services for everyone living in unincorporated areas. Thirty-two identified neighborhoods or subareas in Hillsborough County remain unincorporated.

In keeping with the research design of the book, this chapter examines three hypotheses associated with the Jacksonville/Duval County consolidation:

> H1. The consolidated Jacksonville/Duval County government operates more efficiently than the unconsolidated governments of Tampa and Hillsborough County.

H2. Consolidation resulted in greater economic development in consolidated Jacksonville/Duval County compared with the unconsolidated Tampa and Hillsborough County governments.

H3. The consolidated government delivered on its promises, especially regarding the promise to control property tax increases.

Methodology

Despite the pessimism of many scholars about the viability of city–county consolidation as the preferred option for achieving better metropolitan governance, the story of Jacksonville has continued to interest scholars, and the consolidated government still maintains a national reputation as a comprehensive consolidation of local governments (Swanson 2000; Crooks 2004). Two major empirical studies of Jacksonville have been completed in the last twenty-five years using time-series data. Benton and Gamble (1984) focused on taxes and spending from 1955 to 1981. Later, Feiock and Carr (1997) used time series from 1950 to 1993 focused on the link between consolidation and economic development. Both studies concluded that consolidated Jacksonville has had no particular advantage historically over Hillsborough (Tampa) when it comes to taxes, expenditures, and economic development.

The analysis here tests the three hypotheses using different sources of data and somewhat different measures of impact in an effort to build upon these previous empirical studies. This analysis uses a more comprehensive research design than the other case studies that have already been completed on Tampa (Kerstein 2001) and Jacksonville (Crooks 2004; Martin 1968). Following Benton and Gamble (1984) and Feiock and Carr (1997), effects in this analysis are examined using data from 1959 to 1978. The design is quasi-experimental, with the city of Tampa and Hillsborough County serving as a comparison area (nonequivalent control group). Jacksonville/Duval is the experimental or consolidation case.

Tampa and Hillsborough County have been used by other scholars as a comparison case for Jacksonville/Duval County because they allow for the analysis to control for the effect of state statutes and constitutional provisions on local government structure and policy; Tampa and Hillsborough County come the closest of other Florida cities and counties to matching Jacksonville with respect to key socioeconomic factors that affect policy choices; and the governments had similar forms of government before Jacksonville's consolidation; and, in 1967, the year consolidation passed in Jacksonville, Hillsborough County voters defeated a similar consolidation proposal (Feiock and Carr 1997; Benton and Gamble 1984; Swanson 2004).

Social and Economic Similarities and Differences

Table 4.2 illustrates the historical growth patterns of the two urban areas. Looking back to 1950, the metropolitan statistical areas (MSA) were fairly close in population size, with the Tampa area being about 100,000 larger in 1950. However, fifty years later, in 2000, the Tampa area was well over 2 million people, whereas the Jacksonville area was just over 1 million. In the interim, the Tampa metropolitan region grew by 485.6 percent, compared with 262 percent in Jacksonville. The Tampa area, including the Saint Petersburg/Pinellas area, was the faster grower. The data for Duval and Hillsborough counties follow the same pattern as the larger MSAs, with Duval County (which included Jacksonville from 1970 on) almost tripling in size but Hillsborough quadrupling. The Tampa region is growing at a faster rate, regardless of whether the city, county, or MSA data are used.

Jacksonville City actually lost population between 1950 and 1960 and was experiencing further population and economic decline when the consolidation referendum passed in 1967. Had the census reported for Jacksonville City separately in 1970 (which it did not), the city would have surely declined still further (Crooks 2004). Another important consideration in the story about Jacksonville is that not only was population declining in the city, but also voters had twice rejected annexation attempts in the decade preceding consolidation. At that time, suburbanites opposed annexation and did not want to take on the responsibility for a declining city (Crooks 2004).

Tampa's experience was very different. Although Hillsborough County defeated city-consolidation proposals in 1967, 1970, and 1972 overwhelmingly with light voter turnout (Crooks 2004), Tampa completed two major annexations in 1953 and 1961. Large parcels of land were annexed successfully in 1953, in 1961, and then much later in 1985. Consequently, Tampa went from 19 square miles in 1950 to 85 square miles in 1960 and then to 08.7 square miles in 1990. These annexations allowed Tampa City to grow accordingly, as table 4.3 shows. During the study period, Tampa increase its

Table 4.2 Population Growth, 1950–2004

Year	Jacksonville	Duval County	Jacksonville MSA	Tampa City	Hillsborough County	Tampa MSA
1950	204,517	304,029	304,029	124,681	249,894	409,143
1960	201,030	455,411	455,411	274,970	397,788	772,453
1970		528,865	621,827	277,767	490,265	1,012,594
1980		571,003	737,541	271,523	646,960	1,613,600
1990		672,971	906,727	280,015	834,054	2,067,959
2000		778,879	1,100,049	303,447	998,948	2,395,997
2004		821,338		321,772	1,101,261	
% change, 1950–2004	–1.7	170.2	262	158.1	340.7	485.6

Source: U.S. Bureau of the Census, *County and City Data Book*, selected years.

Note: MSA = metropolitan statistical area.

land area by five times and its population by 158.1 percent from 1950 to 2004. Thus a strategy of aggressive annexations has been the major approach adopted for the metropolitan governance issue in the Tampa region (Kerstein 2001). As table 4.3 further reveals, since 1980, Tampa City has become less than a majority in Hillsborough County, making it very difficult for the Tampa voters who supported 1967, 1970, and 1972 attempts to win a countywide vote as long as suburbanites consistently opposed consolidation (which they did). Kerstein's (2001) analysis reveals how the City of Tampa's voters have supported consolidation but suburbanites surrounding the city have consistently opposed any consolidation.

In addition, Hillsborough County set up a metropolitan services taxing unit (MSTU) for the unincorporated areas of the county in 1977. The MSTU district allowed the county to provide urban services in unincorporated areas, and this resulted in suburban citizens being less interested in receiving urban services from a consolidated government dominated by Tampa (Kerstein 2001). MSTU districts were also used in other parts of Florida to compensate for the lack of urban services in the unincorporated suburbs. The more efficient and effective the MSTU district was in providing urban services in the Tampa area, the less need there was to create a consolidated government. As the suburban portion of Hillsborough grew to 70 to 80 percent of the countywide population and as the MSTU district took on

Table 4.3 Population Share of Principal Cities in Each County

Year	Cities in Duval County (percent)	Cities in Hillsborough County (percent)
1950	72.9	54.9
1960	49.7	74.2
1970		72.9
1980		47.1
1990		38.7
2000		35.5
2004		34.3

Source: U.S. Bureau of the Census, *County and City Data Book*, selected years.

Note: Duval County includes Atlantic Beach, Baldwin, Jacksonville City, Jacksonville Beach, and Neptune Beach. Hillsborough County includes Plant City, Tampa City, and Temple Terrace. These cities chose to remain independent and not join the new Consolidated Government in 1967. However, Jacksonville, the largest independent city in the county, joined the Consolidated Government.

the responsibility for urban service provision, voters in the suburban areas showed little interest in consolidated government. In contrast, in Jacksonville, when the vote on consolidation was taken in 1967, there was political parity between the city voters and the suburban voters. Table 4.4 shows some important additional comparisons between the Tampa and Jacksonville areas in the 1957–70 period. At the time of consolidation, these areas were similar in population, median household income, home ownership, median home value, and percent employed in wholesale and retail. Among the larger differences in 1970, Duval County had less land area, a higher population density, a younger population, and almost twice the number of blacks as Hillsborough County. Interestingly, Duval County had considerably less manufacturing in 1970.

Other Historical Differences between the Two Areas

Jacksonville in the 1950s and 1960s struggled with the typical urban problems of inner-city decay and decline, serious water pollution in the Saint Johns River, unaccredited schools, political corruption and patronage, minimal government, and domination by an old guard (Crooks 2004). However, what emerged in the mid-1960s and later resulted in passage of city–county consolidation (in 1967) was the emergence of a new consensual elite. This elite promoted a new economic vision for the community, the eradication of political corruption and patronage, the correction of serious environmental problems, and the utilization of professional management in government (Swanson 2000). Swanson (1996) calls this the "progrowth machine" and traces how this elite replaced the good old boys of the past, labeling it regime change (Swanson 2000). Jacksonville was growing, and economic development became the new goal of the community. It also brought new actors into power.

In fact, looking at the very successful consolidation movement, there were a number of major arguments or promises put forth by the growth machine and others. They believed consolidation would accelerate and promote the growth of a progressive community that was competitive economically—especially with Tampa. Among other things, they wanted new industry and businesses, lower taxes and a more equitable tax burden, and more efficiently and effectively delivered services. In short, they wanted government to work and they wanted to give the appearance to others, especially business and industry, that Jacksonville was a great place to live and to bring their businesses. These goals and commitments to the future development of the area were the promises made to the electorate, and the electorate bought those promises by a wide margin in the election (Crooks 2004).

The vote in favor of consolidation was overwhelming (65 percent) and included all major segments of the Jacksonville community—the media,

Table 4.4 Historical Demographic and Economic Characteristics of Duval County (D) and Hillsborough County (H), 1957–70

Demographic Characteristic	County	1957	1960	1970
Population	D		455,411	528,865
	H		397,788	490,265
Land area	D		766	766
	H		1038	1038
Density	D		595	690
	H		383	472
Population 65 years and older (%)	D		6.2	7.5
	H		9.8	10.5
African American (%)	D		23.2	22.4
	H		14.0	13.6
Foreign stock (%)	D		6.3	6.5
	H		14.6	13.5
Median household income	D		$5,345	$8,669
	H		$4,616	$8,161
			(1959)	(1969)
Home ownership (%)	D		66.2	67.6
	H		71.0	73.0
Median value of home	D		$10,900	$12,154
	H		$9,300	$12,078
Employed in manufacturing (%)	D	12.6		12.3
	H	17.4		17.5
Employed in wholesale and retail (%)	D	22.0		25.2
	H	22.9		25.9

Source: U.S. Bureau of the Census, *County and City Data Book*, 1957, 1962, 1967, 1972.

Note: Actual figures to measure changes before and after the city–county consolidation in Duval are for 1960 and 1970. Interim figures for 1967, the actual year the vote was successful, were not available. The 1962 and 1967 *County and City Data Book* both used 1960 data, and the 1972 *County and City Data Book* used 1970 data.

the Chamber of Commerce and business leaders, the very influential and well-financed reform group Citizens for Better Government, the governor, the state delegation to the Florida legislature, and a plethora of community groups. Opposition to consolidation came only from city and county employees, the city and county Democratic leaders, and the elected officials for the old city council and county commission (Crooks 2004).

In contrast, Kerstein (2001) indicates that in Tampa no cohesive regime supporting economic development emerged until the late 1970s and 1980s. During the 1950s and 1960s, as indicated above, consolidation failed at the ballot box three times because of the lack of suburban support and the failure to galvanize civic and business leaders or develop a viable reform group in the area. The media also played a more passive role in reform efforts, in contrast to the very strong leadership role by the media in Jacksonville (Martin 1968). The alternative of annexation was used by the city instead of consolidation, as indicated above. In the Tampa area there was not widespread support for consolidation from the media, the business community, or the local political leaders during the 1950s and 1960s. In short, Jacksonville followed the economic development model for successful consolidation developed by Leland and Thurmaier (2004a). Conversely, Tampa lacked the preconditions for reform such as institutional support, interest group advocacy, and the effective referendum campaigns found in communities that have supported consolidation around the country (Leland and Thurmaier 2004a, 2004b).

Finally, in the late 1970s and 1980s, the Tampa area began to experience its own "urban renaissance," with skyscrapers, a new skyline, corporate headquarters, and financial towers in the downtown area. In total, more than $800 million was spent on fifty-five major projects in the downtown area. What was different here is that it was the City of Tampa government in partnership with other entities that jump-started the renaissance. The area apparently did not need or use a consolidated government. It stayed with its old government structure and its existing power structure, whereby aggressive mayors and city council supporters courted outside business interests in the region (Mormino 1983). In addition to these developments within Hillsborough County, one needs to also note the economic development growth effects of Saint Petersburg and Pinellas County on Tampa. Although these effects are beyond the scope of this research design, one cannot ignore the rapid and substantial growth in tourism and other development associated with Tampa's sister city on the other side of Tampa Bay.

Testing Hypotheses about the Jacksonville and Tampa Areas

The first hypothesis is that consolidation led to more efficient government, measured as lower rates of expenditure growth. Benton and Gamble (1984) find that total expenditure growth in the two cases was comparable before and after consolidation. Although total expenditures increased in the postconsolidation period (compared with a decline in growth rates before consolidation), the same was true in the Tampa/Hillsborough case.

Thus the change in total expenditures does not support the hypothesis that consolidation made Jacksonville/Duval more efficient. Similarly, they find that public safety expenditures before consolidation were declining in both cases but that these expenditures grew faster in Jacksonville/Duval in the postconsolidation period than in Tampa/Hillsborough (Benton and Gamble 1984, 195–96).

Table 4.5 looks at government spending in the study areas for two periods, 1957–68 and 1969–78. The second period represents the postconsolidation period and more clearly tests the hypotheses about the impact of consolidation on government spending. Spending includes combined Tampa and Hillsborough per capita expenditures and combined Jacksonville and Duval expenditures until consolidation took place. After that only one jurisdiction is used for Jacksonville/Duval. Percent changes represent the changes in per capita spending for both periods. In this analysis, I look at per capita spending for total government, public works, fire, and law enforcement to identify patterns. The hypothesis is that Jacksonville/Duval should have been able to keep its government spending more under control than Tampa, been able to take advantage of economies of scale, and been able to eliminate the duplication of government services between the city and county. This is the classical argument for why a unified government is the most efficient.

For the period 1959–68, in three of four service areas, Tampa's spending per capita grew faster than in Jacksonville. But the more interesting comparison is for the period after consolidation. Table 4.5 shows that with total overall spending, Jacksonville actually grew about 30 percent faster than Tampa in the decade after consolidation. However, Tampa grew faster, by far, when expenditures focus on public works and fire, an argument in favor of the hypothesis. Law enforcement changes have been about the same. The data provide mixed

Table 4.5 Spending Changes per Capita in Duval County (D) and Hillsborough County (H), 1959–1978 (percent)

Period	County	Total Government Spending per Capita	Public Works Spending per Capita	Fire Spending per Capita	Law Enforcement Spending per Capita
1959–68	D	61.6	74.5	51.0	69.5
	H	250.2	93.7	126.1	150.7
1969–78	D	137.5	99.2	137.5	308.1
	H	107.7	215.2	318.5	313.3

Source: U.S. Bureau of the Census, *County and City Data Book*, selected years.

support for the efficiency hypothesis; there is some support in three specific functions, but not with respect to overall spending.

A second hypothesis is that consolidated governments have a better ability to coordinate and centralize functions and thus are better able to accelerate and stimulate economic growth faster because of this capacity.

Feiock and Carr (1997), using a limited five-year postconsolidation research design, find no statistically significant differences in manufacturing, retail, or service establishments in the five-year postconsolidation period—either in Jacksonville/Duval or in Tampa/Hillsborough. In another study, Carr and Feiock (1999), using a very limited five-year post-consolidation (noncomparison case) research design, find no postconsolidation increase in manufacturing in Jacksonville/Duval but do find an increase in growth in retail establishments after consolidation. However, the Jacksonville/Duval case was not compared with the comparable Tampa/Hillsborough case in their analysis.

Although the Carr and Feiock studies raise doubts about the short-term economic impact of the Jacksonville/Duval consolidation, the longer-term effects seem clearer in table 4.5. First, one can see that these two metropolitan areas have taken different economic development paths. Jacksonville/Duval has maintained its relative strength in manufacturing by value added (although growth in the number of manufacturing establishments is slower than in Tampa/Hillsborough), whereas Tampa/Hillsborough has outperformed Jacksonville/Duval in retail sales and wholesale growth. Such a result is consistent with the development effects of Saint Petersburg and the larger Saint Petersburg–Tampa MSA (although it is difficult to isolate those effects from Tampa/Hillsborough developments).

As seen in table 4.6, Hillsborough County was growing value added in manufacturing faster than Duval County before consolidation (1957–67). However, Jacksonville/Duval grew more value added by manufacturing in the fifteen years following consolidation, despite the fact that Tampa was able to grow more manufacturing establishments in the 1967–82 period. Tampa's retail sales and number of wholesale establishments also grew faster than Jacksonville/Duval in the postconsolidation period. The number of establishments means jobs, taxes, and more development, but additional value added demonstrates the ability to get the more successful and profitable businesses and industries to locate in the region. Each area demonstrates robust economic growth. Table 4.6 shows somesupport for Hypothesis 2, but it depends on the actual economic measure used; both areas demonstrated healthy and robust economic growth.

One of the other major promises made by the consolidation movement was that taxes would become more equitable, especially by moving away from the property tax and drawing more heavily on the sales tax. Hypothesis 3 is that the property tax burden would be lower in the consolidated government

Table 4.6 Historical Differences in Government and Economics in Duval County (D) and Hillsborough County (H), 1967–82

Economic Outcome	County	1957	1967	% Change, 1958–67	1982	% Change, 1967–82
Value added by manufacturing	D	$176,641,000	$331,200,000	87	$1,516,500,000	358
	H	$172,659,000	$367,900,000	113	$1,267,200,000	244
Retail sales	D	$522,591,000	$836,054,000	60	$6,150,000,000	636
	H	$444,134,000	$739,921,000	67	$7,860,000,000	962
Manufacturing establishments	D	510	577	13	683	18
	H	591	626	6	889	42
Wholesale establishments	D	856	995	16	1,327	33
	H	811	1,006	24	1,736	73

Source: U.S. Bureau of the Census, *County and City Data Book*, selected years.

than in Tampa/Hillsborough. Benton and Gamble's (1984) analysis supports Hypothesis 3. They analyzed the Jacksonville/Duval consolidation performance relative to Tampa/Hillsborough on several measures, including property tax revenues. Using interrupted time-series analysis for 1955 through 1981, they find that the rate of property tax growth in both cases was declining, and that the declining growth rate was steeper in Jacksonville/Duval than Tampa/Hillsborough on an annual basis during the period. Although they find the short-term effect of consolidation in Jacksonville/Duval is higher property tax growth relative to Tampa/Hillsborough, the long-term effect of consolidation was that the Jacksonville/Duval 1.6 percent growth in property tax revenues was lower than the 1.8 percent increase in the Tampa/Hillsborough property tax revenue increase (Benton and Gamble 1984, 193–94).

In summary, the reformers in Jacksonville advocating consolidation promised that something would be done about property taxes, economic development, and government efficiency. The data analyzed above lend mixed support for two of these three promises, and stronger support for the efficiency hypothesis. A more qualitative analysis can shed further light on the relative performance of these two metropolitan areas.

Qualitative Effects of Consolidation in Jacksonville

Different analysts of the Jacksonville consolidation have also focused on the more qualitative effects of the consolidation. For example, Swanson (2000) has argued that the consolidation has led to substantial instability and multiple changes in the community power structure. Business leaders replaced the "good old boys" of the Democratic Party as the dominant partner. Business professionals wanted "good government," less corruption, and the elimination of patronage. In subsequent years, progrowth mayors were elected, and the community promoted economic development, the growth of manufacturing, cleaning up the river and the environment, and the revitalization of downtown. Eventually Jacksonville became the insurance headquarters for the Southeast, and it also attracted a new state university, an NFL franchise, and a $2.2 million infrastructure investment (Swanson 2000).

Can we attribute some of this to consolidation? The economic data presented above show some support for the economic development part. As another historian of Jacksonville has pointed out, ten years after consolidation, Jacksonville was emphasizing the "growth machine." Tampa's business leaders also began their own partnership with the city government to push for economic growth (Crooks 2004). Among other things, the civic and business leaders pushed for bay front development, the development of an industrial park, and the recruitment of Schlitz and Anheuser-Bush. Whereas Tampa began a broad-based urban renaissance and began recruiting professional NFL and NHL teams in the 1970s, Jacksonville and Miami had done those things a decade earlier.

Questions of political representation and political equity and of government structure can make a qualitative difference. At about the time of the 1967 consolidation vote in Jacksonville, the black community was about ready to compete for control of the city council and to elect a mayor. Before the merger, 40 percent of the population in the inner city was black, but in the new consolidated government only 25 percent of the population was black, thus diluting the vote of the black population (Swanson 2000). In the new consolidated government, suburban whites continued to dominate politically. As Duval County has grown, the black population has stabilized at about 30 percent, which is still considerably less than this population group would need for more political parity. However, the consolidated government did use a combination of district and at-large representatives, which at least guaranteed blacks four out of nineteen district council members in 1968 when the new government formed (Crooks 2004). The black community has been denied the election of a black majority on the council and/or a black mayor like other cities in the South that did not consolidate (e.g., Atlanta, Richmond, Birmingham, and New Orleans).

Citizen Satisfaction

So far this analysis has focused on the city and county governments in the Tampa and Jacksonville areas. But there are also other boards, commissions, and authorities in both areas whereby citizens can participate and provide input. However, when one hears about or talks about Jacksonville or Tampa, we rarely pay attention to their accomplishments. Yet some of these are important to testing the hypotheses on consolidation in this analysis. For Jacksonville, with the broad mandate of economic development, the electric authority, port authority, and airport authority all contribute to the financing and pushing of "the big economic growth machine." With Tampa, the transit agency, aviation authority, and expressway authority also contribute to the area of economic development.

Besides these other government entities, the satisfaction of citizens with governments is always critical. With the Jacksonville consolidation, one measure of success or effectiveness of reform is what the citizen thinks about the changes and the government. People in Jacksonville are proud of the attention their city has received nationally (Crooks 2004). Jacksonville's image as a good government organization has lasted all these years, and national discussions about consolidation always include Jacksonville as one of the early success stories.

Citizens reflecting on their hometown of Jacksonville frequently refer to the quality of public services, including water and sewers, schools, libraries, police, and fire (Crooks 2004). The region's success in creating racially and economically inclusive neighborhoods along with protected natural environments is frequently noted on websites for Jacksonville area businesses and organizations. It is always noted that to achieve this urban quality of life, it is necessary to have an engaged citizenry that is willing to pay the cost and also with pride enjoy the benefits.

As Crooks (2004) also notes, the citizens of Jacksonville continued to support their government as they cleaned up the Saint Johns River and completed other public facility and public works projects by supporting sales tax increases on a number of occasions. The long-range positive impact of the consolidated government is that it continues to keep the support and trust of citizens. There have been no movements to disband the government since 1967, and on a number of occasions citizens have supported taxes to implement the goals of the community. There have been no antitax movements connected to the consolidated government. There also have not been any candidates running against the consolidated government or any political organizations seeking to eliminate or challenge the consolidated government. Expanding growth and developing the region's economy have required not only leadership and an organizational structure but also, and most important, a confident and supportive citizenry.

Conclusion

This analysis of Jacksonville and Tampa has shown both similarities and differences. Although Jacksonville has functioned with a consolidated government, Tampa has used aggressive annexation. Both areas, like other urban regions in Florida, have used special districts to help with metropolitan problems. Despite those differences, both have accomplished much economic development generally. Both have shown growth—Jacksonville in manufacturing and downtown, and Tampa in the wholesale and retail sector. Both have also followed aggressive and well-thought-out downtown and economic development strategies. Whether consolidated government stands out in facilitating the development of these strategies is questionable.

It seems that cities throughout the South were pursuing a similar agenda. Success in broader economic development has not been limited to just consolidated governments, but consolidated governments can get a jump start on the process and strategies to use.

More specifically, this comparative and longitudinal analysis has enhanced the literature on Jacksonville. Up to this point, the literature has concluded that consolidated government has made little difference in government finance and public policy. But this analysis, by using different data sets and measures and different time periods, has demonstrated that Jacksonville has kept property taxes low, been able to attract high-value-added manufacturing, and reduced government spending in areas like public works and fire services. In addition, Jacksonville has invested considerable resources in infrastructure development, and largely as a result of this investment, it has been able to maintain steady and significant growth in the value added by manufacturing over time to the local economy (table 4.7).

From a more qualitative standpoint, case study materials have argued that the consolidation diluted black political power, suppressed electoral participation, and reduced administrative effectiveness. These more negative consequences may serve as a caution to the more positive effects reported in this analysis. In the end, consolidation continues to thrive while more quantitative and qualitative evidence on outcomes are analyzed. For the future, comparative and longitudinal research designs are recommended for thosewho want to continue to look for empirical evidence to support their arguments for governmental reform.

On balance, the question of what effects consolidation can have on an urban region's economy, efficiency, political equity, and economic development remains open to research and analysis. The Jacksonville/Duval County consolidation has not been a "wash," as some contend, and it continues to offer promise as a model for other metropolitan areas.

Table 4.7 Summary of the Jacksonville/Duval County Case

Overall Assessment of Evidence	H1: Efficiency	H2: Economic Development	H3: Other Promises
Not enough data available			
No evidence			
Weak	☑	☑	
Moderate			☑
Strong			

Although the type of governmental reform adopted in Jacksonville is not a panacea for all metropolitan areas, it can serve as a focus for the emergence of a new regime in local politics with different values and policy goals (Swanson 2000).

References

Benton, Edwin, and D. Gamble. 1984. City–County Consolidation and Economies of Scale: Evidence from a Time-Series Analysis in Jacksonville, Florida. *Social Science Quarterly*, March, 193–96.

Carr, Jered. 2004. Perspectives on City–County Consolidation and Its Alternatives. In *City–County Consolidation and Its Alternatives*, ed. J. B. Carr and Richard Feiock. Armonk, NY: M. E. Sharpe.

Carr, Jered, and Richard Feiock. 1999. Metropolitan Government and Economic Development. *Urban Affairs Review* 34, no. 3:476–89.

———, eds. 2004. *City –County Consolidation and Its Alternatives: Reshaping the Local Government Landscape.* Armonk, NY: M. E. Sharpe.

Crooks, J. B. 2004. *Jacksonville: The Consolidation Story from Civil Rights to the Jaguars.* Gainesville: University Press of Florida.

Feiock, Richard. 2004. Do Consolidation Entrepreneurs Make a Deal with the Devil? In *City–County Consolidation and Its Alternatives*, ed. J. B. Carr and Richard Feiock. Armonk, NY: M. E. Sharpe.

Feiock, Richard, and Jered Carr. 1997. A Reassessment of City–County Consolidation: Economic Development Impacts. *State and Local Government Review* 29, no. 3 (Fall):166–71.

Kerstein, R. 2001. *Politics and Growth in Twentieth-Century Tampa.* Gainesville: University Press of Florida.

Leland, Suzanne, and Kurt Thurmaier, eds. 2004a. *Case Studies of City–County Consolidation: Reshaping the Local Government Landscape.* Armonk, NY: M. E. Sharpe.

———. 2004b. Introduction. In *Case Studies of City–County Consolidation: Reshaping the Local Government Landscape.* Armonk, NY: M. E. Sharpe.

Martin, R. C. 1968. *Consolidation: The Dynamics of Urban Political Reform.* Jacksonville: Crawford.

McCabe, B. C. 2004. Special Districts. In *City–County Consolidation and Its Alternatives*, ed. J. B. Carr and Richard Feiock. Armonk, NY: M. E. Sharpe.

Mormino, G. R. 1983. From Hell Hole to the Good Life. In *Sunbelt Cities: Politics and Growth since World War II*, ed. R. M. Bernard and Bradley Rice. Austin: University of Texas Press.

Peirce, N. 1993. *Citistates: How Urban America Can Prosper in a Competitive World.* Washington, DC: Seven Locks Press.

Swanson, Burt. 1996. Jacksonville, Consolidation and Regional Governance. In *Regional Politics in a Post City Age,* ed. H. V. Savitch and Ronald K. Vogel. Thousand Oaks, CA: Sage.

———. 2000. Quandaries of Pragmatic Reform: A Reassessment of the Jacksonville Experience. *State and Local Government Review* 32, no. 3 (Fall):227–38.

———. 2004. Alternative Explanations for the Adoption of City–County Consolidation in Jacksonville/Duval, Florida. In *Case Studies of City–County Consolidation: Reshaping the Local Government Landscape,* ed. Suzanne Leland and Kurt Thurmaier. Armonk, NY: M. E. Sharpe.

5

City–County Consolidation

A Case Study of Carson City, Nevada

Anna Lukemeyer

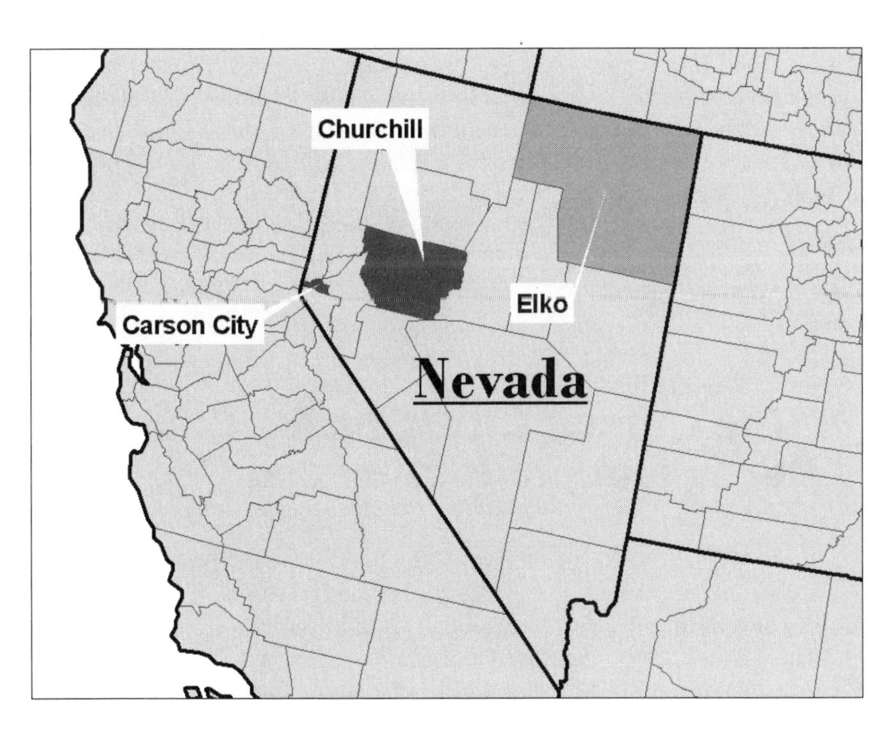

Map 5 Locations of Carson City, Churchill County, and Elko County, Nevada
Source: U.S. Bureau of the Census.

City–county consolidation—that is, the structural consolidation of city and county governments into one government—has been characterized as "a reform idea that does not die" (Leland and Johnson 2004, 27). This characterization seems to reflect two factors. First, reformers continue to pursue consolidation, despite the fact that the voters rarely accept consolidation proposals. Second, scholars have increasingly questioned whether the expected benefits of consolidation have been realized in practice (Feiock 2004; Campbell and Durning 2000). Recent scholarship suggests that the impact of consolidation varies according to the characteristics of the consolidating governments and their environments, the structure of the consolidated government, and decisions made during implementation (Campbell and Durning 2000; Selden and Campbell 2000). Thus, as is often the case for public policy, "the devil is in the details" (Sawhill and Smith 1998).

This chapter seeks to contribute to our understanding of whether, and under what circumstances, consolidation results in the expected benefits, by examining the 1969 consolidation of Carson City and Ormsby County, Nevada (map 5). The first section that follows describes the context surrounding the Carson City/Ormsby County merger. It highlights not only proponents' claims concerning consolidation's benefits but also the structural decisions likely to influence whether those benefits were realized in practice. The second section presents research questions and identifies three specific hypotheses. The third section presents an overview of the research design—a comparative case analysis—and discusses the selection of comparison cases. The fourth section is organized by hypothesis, in turn presenting specific research methods and findings for each hypothesis. The fifth section presents conclusions.

The Carson City/Ormsby County Consolidation: History and Context

Carson City, the capital of Nevada, and the surrounding Ormsby County consolidated into one "municipal" government on July 1, 1969. Ormsby County was a small county, located near Reno in northern Nevada. Before the merger, in 1960, Ormsby County's population was 8,063 (State of Nevada 1977). The population was largely white (almost 85 percent). At about 13 percent of the county's population, Native Americans made up the largest minority group (Gordon 1972).[1]

At the time of consolidation, Carson City dominated Ormsby County in a way that was unusual in Nevada. Ormsby County, at 157 square miles, was the smallest county in Nevada. Rugged mountain ranges occupied almost 74 percent of its territory, and 7.4 percent was under the waters of Lake Tahoe. This left only about 18,700 acres suitable for residential, economic, or agricultural development. At the time of consolidation, Carson City occupied 2,570 acres, or almost 14 percent of the land suitable for development (Gordon 1972). More than 60 percent of the county residents (5,163 people) lived in Carson City. There were no other population centers of more than 1,000 people or incorporated cities in Ormsby County (State of Nevada 1977).

The Formal Process

The Carson City board of trustees and the Ormsby County commissioners were interested in consolidating as early as 1951, when they requested an attorney general's opinion concerning the constitutionality of a proposed consolidation plan. The attorney general responded that any plan abolishing or converting the offices of the county commissioners would require a constitutional amendment (Attorney General Opinion 51-26, 1951). In response, the local governments pursued various functional consolidation measures. By 1968, the year before consolidation, the city and county shared fire and engineering departments, as well as, among other positions, a city–county manager and clerk.

In the 1960s, government officials began the formal process of amending the Constitution. Article 16, Section 1, of the Nevada Constitution describes one process for amending the Constitution. The text of the proposed amendment must be approved by joint resolution of both houses of the Nevada legislature at two succeeding legislative sessions. Then the amendment must be approved by a majority of the state's qualified voters.

In 1965 and 1967, the Nevada Assembly and Senate approved Assembly Joint Resolution 27, proposing a constitutional amendment allowing the consolidation of Carson City and its surrounding county. The state's voters approved the amendment in November 1968, and Section 37(A) was added to Article 4 of the Nevada Constitution.[2] In April 1969, the state legislature approved the charter creating the consolidated Carson City municipal government, and Carson City and Ormsby County merged into one unit effective July 1, 1969.

Charter Provisions

The legislature enacted the Carson City charter as Chapter 213 of the Statutes of Nevada 1969. This act defines Carson City as a "municipal government" (Section 2) with the powers of, and subject to the laws controlling, both a city and a county (Article 1, Section 1.010[2]). A five-member board of supervisors governed the city, one representing each of four wards and a mayor representing the city at large (Article 2, Section 2.010). Despite the ward structure, all supervisors were "voted upon by the registered voters of Carson City at large" (Article 5).

In addition to presiding over board meetings, the charter also charged the mayor with being the ceremonial head of the Carson City government, with heading the government for purposes of military law, and with performing necessary duties in an emergency (Section 3.010). The charter allowed the board to appoint a manager to perform delegated administrative duties (Section 3.020). The charter also created a number of positions—such as clerk, recorder, auditor, assessor, sheriff, and district attorney—that are typically county officials and specified that these positions were governed by the laws applicable to these county officials (Sections 3.030–070). At the time of consolidation, the charter contained no other significant provisions concerning public employees.[3]

The charter divided the newly created Carson City into two tax districts: an "urban district" that corresponded to the area within the boundaries of Carson City before the consolidation, and an Ormsby district consisting of the rest of the county (Article 1, Section 1.050). The supervisors could transfer territories between the two districts by following the statutory procedures for municipal annexation or detachment of territory (Article 1, Section 1.050[3]).

The Political Process: Supporters, Opponents, and Claims

The mayor and board of trustees of Carson City and the Ormsby County commissioners unanimously supported the 1969 consolidation (Minutes of March 20, 1968). Other supporters also included the local newspaper and the League of Women Voters. Proponents presented the consolidation as a "logical and legal conclusion to the de facto consolidation that has taken place over a number of years" and "a natural direction" for a city that someday may "occupy the entire county" (*Nevada Appeal* 1969; Minutes of March 20, 1968). Local government officials also stressed that the plan would result in some cost savings and efficiencies. Consolidating the five-member city council and the three county commissioners into a five-member "board of supervisors" would save $7,200 in salaries, and there would be some additional savings from combining bookkeeping and other procedures ("Senate Hearings," February 21, 1969).

Proponents emphasized that the consolidation would not result in a tax increase for either city or county residents. The proposed charter divided the consolidated area into an urban services district and a general services district, with tax rates corresponding to those currently in effect in the city and the county. Thus, residents of county would continue to pay lower taxes. County residents might eventually experience an increase in taxes, but this would be due to development rather than the consolidation as such ("Senate Hearing," 1969; "City County Consolidation," 1969; Minutes of March 20, 1968).

Some individuals, primarily county residents, and a former Carson City mayor expressed opposition, suggesting that they were being railroaded into an arrangement where county residents would be "more shortchanged than ever" (Senate Hearing, 1969). Nevertheless, there appears to have been little or no organized opposition.[4] Indeed, the primary local concern seemed to be the loss of historic "Ormsby" County as an identifiable entity ("Senate Hearing," 1969).

In general, the archival records reveal relatively little discussion of the details of the consolidation and the likely cost savings, either in the media, at public hearings, or at city council or county commissioner meetings, at least in the years immediately preceding the merger.[5] In the months preceding the merger, the implementation topic most often addressed at city council and county commissioner meetings was consolidating the two sets of ordinances into one code. Beyond this and a brief comment that the bond attorneys had reviewed the proposed charter, the minutes of city council and county commissioner meetings reveal only the following two entries:

> Mayor Robertson asked about the timing on the budget. Manager Etchemendy advised . . . that within two weeks [after January 10] he would have something to present . . . . The mayor asked if the County Pay Ordinance was in line with that of the City. Discussion was held on working hours and laws governing this. The mayor suggested that we should increase everyone's salary 3½–4 percent while working on the budget. This was agreeable. (Minutes of Meeting of Carson City Board of Trustees, January 4, 1968)

> Manager Etchemendy advised there will be a public hearing . . . on the 1969–70 budget, as a joint meeting with the county . . . . The Mayor suggested we should plan for combining the Street Dept. and the County Road Dept. to be done as fast as possible for the sake of efficiency. A good site would be near the sewer plant. Mr. Rankin suggested an area

> near the Airport as an alternate, and also brought up the use of prison labor, which is a problem with respect to picking them up and bringing them back in. The manager suggested working with Jack Butti on this problem. Mr. Rankin was requested to have suggestions by the 21st meeting as to how to physically construct the department and how much money it will take if buildings have to be moved. (Minutes of Meeting of Carson City Board of Trustees, April 7, 1969)

In short, proponents portrayed the consolidation as a relatively minor step leading to more efficient and rational government, likely to result in few immediate changes for city or county residents and no increases in taxes. It was simply a measure to bring formal government structures in line with the existing functional consolidation and the prospect of future growth of the urban area. In terms of economic benefits, consolidation was presented as likely to result in modest cost savings, due primarily to the net loss of two elected officials. Beyond this, there appears to be little public concern or discussion about the details of implementing the consolidation or the likely source of cost savings.[6]

Research Questions and Hypotheses

This case study addresses three hypotheses:

H1. The consolidated government operates more efficiently than unconsolidated governments.

H2. Consolidation resulted in increased economic development in counties with consolidated as compared with unconsolidated governments.

H3. The consolidated government delivered on its promises. In the case of Carson City/Ormsby County, the promises were relatively few:

a. No increases in taxes *initially*.

b. Cost savings of $7,200 due to reduction of number of elected officials from seven to five.

c. Unspecified cost savings due to reduced duplication of services in areas such as bookkeeping and auditing.

Research Design: Overview and Selection of Control Cases

This study uses a comparative, before and after design to test these hypotheses. Because consolidation occurred in July 1969, that year is considered the baseline for comparison. Relevant characteristics of Carson City and Ormsby County are measured several years before and again several years after consolidation. Where possible, I report measures for nine years before consolidation (fiscal year 1960) and nine years after (fiscal year 1978). Because records from this period were sometimes incomplete, however, the specific number of years before and after consolidation varies with the hypothesis being tested and the characteristic being measured. Data from the years before and after consolidation are compared with each other and with corresponding observations from other Nevada cities and counties selected as control cases.

The purpose of the control cases is to provide a rough measure of the counterfactual: What would Carson City and Ormsby county be like if they had not consolidated? Therefore, the controls should be as similar to Carson City and Ormsby County as possible. Because the selection of a control case presents particular challenges here, this section addresses this issue in some detail.

Nevada consists of seventeen counties. Ormsby County (now Carson City) is one of four small counties clustered on the middle west side of Nevada, close to Lake Tahoe. In area, at 153 square miles, it is the smallest county, and it is one of only three that are smaller than 2,000 square miles. In 1960, Ormsby County had by far the highest population density. At 52.7 persons per square mile, it was more than three times denser than its nearest rival, Clark County, which had 15.7 persons per square mile.[7] With a few exceptions, Nevada counties were, and are, large and sparsely populated.

In 1960, there were two population centers in the state, the Reno/Sparks area in the north (combined population 68,088), and Las Vegas and the surrounding communities in the south (combined population

95,352).[8] Gaming and tourism made up a large part of the economic base in these population centers. In the sparsely populated areas outside these centers (i.e., in the "cow counties"), Nevada's economy centered on ranching, agriculture, and mining (Gordon 1972).

Because Carson City was the state capital, government was the primary employer in the city and in Ormsby County. Although it was close to Reno and Lake Tahoe, tourism and gambling were a relatively small part of the county's economic base at that time. Nor did it have any significant agriculture, ranching, or mining (Gordon 1972). Thus, in terms of size, population density, and economic base, Carson City and Ormsby County were different from the other cities and counties in Nevada, and there appears to be no one set of city–county governments sufficiently similar to Carson City/Ormsby County to allow a valid comparison. Therefore, this study proposes a comparison with multiple city/county combinations, each similar to Carson City/Ormsby County in important ways.

Three city/county combinations seem likely control cases: Sparks/Washoe County, Elko/Elko County, and Fallon/Churchill County. Table 5.1 summarizes these counties' relevant geographic, demographic, and political characteristics. Perhaps because it was the seat of state government, Ormsby County had the most highly educated population in the state at the time of consolidation. It was higher than all the other counties in median education level (12.6 years), percentage of high school graduates (73.9), and percentage of college graduates (15.1).

Of the potential control cases, Washoe County came closest to Ormsby County on these measures of educational achievement.[9] In addition, like Ormsby County, Washoe County is located in northwestern Nevada and borders Lake Tahoe. Although Sparks and Washoe County both have much larger populations than Carson City and Ormsby County, Washoe is the closest of the control cases to Ormsby County in population density and in the trajectory of population growth. Further, Sparks, like Carson City, incorporated under special rather than general law, and it had a similar governmental structure.[10] Sparks differs from Carson City in one important respect, however. Unlike Carson City, which dominated Ormsby County, Reno rather than Sparks dominated Washoe County.

Two other potential control cases, Elko/Elko County, and Fallon/Churchill County, are smaller cities in sparsely populated, predominantly agricultural counties. Both have a smaller percentage of high school graduates and a smaller percentage of managerial and professional workers than Carson City/Ormsby County. Beyond this, each of these potential controls appears to balance the other in terms of similarities to and differences from Carson City and Ormsby County. In terms of per capita income, population, and population growth (1960–70), Elko/Elko County

Table 5.1 Characteristics of Experimental and Control Cases

Characteristic	Carson City	Ormsby County	Fallon	Churchill County	Sparks	Washoe County	Elko	Elko County
Population								
1960	5,163	8,063	2,734	8,452	16,618	84,743	6,298	12,011
1970	15,468	15,468	2,959	10,513	24,187	121,068	7,621	13,958
2000	52,457	52,457	7,536	23,982	66,346	339,486	16,708	45,291
Area (square miles)		153		4,913		6,608		17,181
Population density								
1960		52.7		1.7		12.8		0.7
1970		101.1		2.1		18.3		.8
% high school, 1970		73.9		58.6		68.7		57.7
% professional and managerial		35.8		22.5		26.6		26.7
Per capita income		4,019		3,027		4,637		4,172
Per capita assessed value		3272.24		3100.64		4485.86		6048.14
Type of city	Charter		General law		Charter		Charter	
Governing structure	Council–manager		Mayor–council		Council–manager		Council–manager	

Source: U.S. Bureau of the Census.

is closer to Carson City/Ormsby County. It also displays the same governmental structure. Nevertheless, Elko County is a large, sparsely populated, rural county in northeastern Nevada, and Elko County's assessed property value per capita was almost twice that of Ormsby County. In contrast, Fallon and Churchill County are smaller in area and geographically close to Carson City and Ormsby County, and Churchill County's per capita assessed valuation was closest to Ormsby County's at the time of consolidation. Unlike Elko and Carson City, Fallon incorporated under general law, with a mayor–council form of government. Neither Fallon nor Churchill County's population grew at the pace of Carson City and Ormsby County, and its citizens were considerably poorer.

Hypothesis Testing: Data, Research Methods, and Findings

As the previous section shows, at the time of consolidation, Carson City was a small city in a sparsely populated western state, as were two of the three control cities. Therefore, finding data to test the three hypotheses represented a significant challenge for this research, and the availability of data greatly shaped the analysis. Because each hypothesis required somewhat different data, and therefore presented different challenges, this section is organized by hypotheses, presenting a discussion of data, research methods, and findings for each hypothesis in turn.

The Efficiency Hypothesis

With respect to the data and research methods, this hypothesis was assessed by comparing preconsolidation and postconsolidation trends in expenditures for Carson City/Ormsby County with trends in the control city/counties during the same period. Data concerning city and county government expenditures for each government were gathered for fiscal years 1960 (nine years before consolidation), 1965 (four years before consolidation), 1969 (the last year before consolidation), 1970 (the first year of consolidation) 1973 (four years after consolidation), and 1978 (nine years after consolidation). As is explained in more detail below, data for county expenditures were obtained from county auditors' financial statements for the relevant years. Data for city government expenditures were obtained from Census of Governments reports. Because of problems obtaining and interpreting data, Sparks/Washoe County is omitted as a comparison case in analyzing this hypothesis.

The study examines expenditures in four core governmental service areas: basic administrative services, police services, fire services, and roads and highways. The specific expenditures assigned to each category are based on the definitions used by the Census of Governments.[11] To allow valid comparisons across years and across cases, expenditure categories used in auditors' reports were examined and adjusted as necessary for consistency with the Census of Governments' category definitions.[12] Expenditures were converted to constant 1969 dollars using the U.S. Department of Commerce's Implicit Price Deflator for State and Local Governments. To adjust for population differences across cases, per capita expenditures are used.[13]

County auditors' annual reports for the relevant years provided data on county expenditures by functional category. Unfortunately, the county auditors' reports provided very limited data about municipal expenditures, and no other state or local documents reporting municipal expenditures for these years were available.[14] As a result, city expenditures were estimated using reports from the U.S. Department of Commerce's Census of Governments.[15] The cities examined to test this hypothesis were too small for the Census of Governments to report expenditure data for each individual city throughout the relevant period. The census reports did, however, include expenditure data for cities of each state, grouped according to population size. I used these reports to estimate expenditures for each of the cities for the relevant years. As a result, expenditure estimates for each of the individual cities are actually average expenditures for Nevada cities of the appropriate population size group.[16]

Actual per capita county expenditures in each functional category (from auditors' reports) were added to estimated per capita city expenditures in each functional category (from Census of Governments reports) to obtain total expenditures in each functional category for each city–county unit.[17] For the control cases, estimates of city expenditures were added to county expenditures for each of the years examined. Because Carson City existed as a separate entity with a separate budget until 1969, I added estimated expenditures for Carson City to those of Ormsby County until 1969. After 1969, however, Carson City no longer existed as a municipal entity, and the consolidated Carson City budget subsumed both county and city expenses. So, for the years following 1969, Carson City expenditures consisted only of those reported in the Carson City auditor's report.[18]

With respect to trends in expenditures by functional category, for the period 1960–78 and the police, figure 5.1 presents trends in real per capita expenditures for police services in Carson City/Ormsby County and the control cases before and after consolidation in 1959. As figure 5.1 shows, Carson City/Ormsby County's expenditures for police services increased

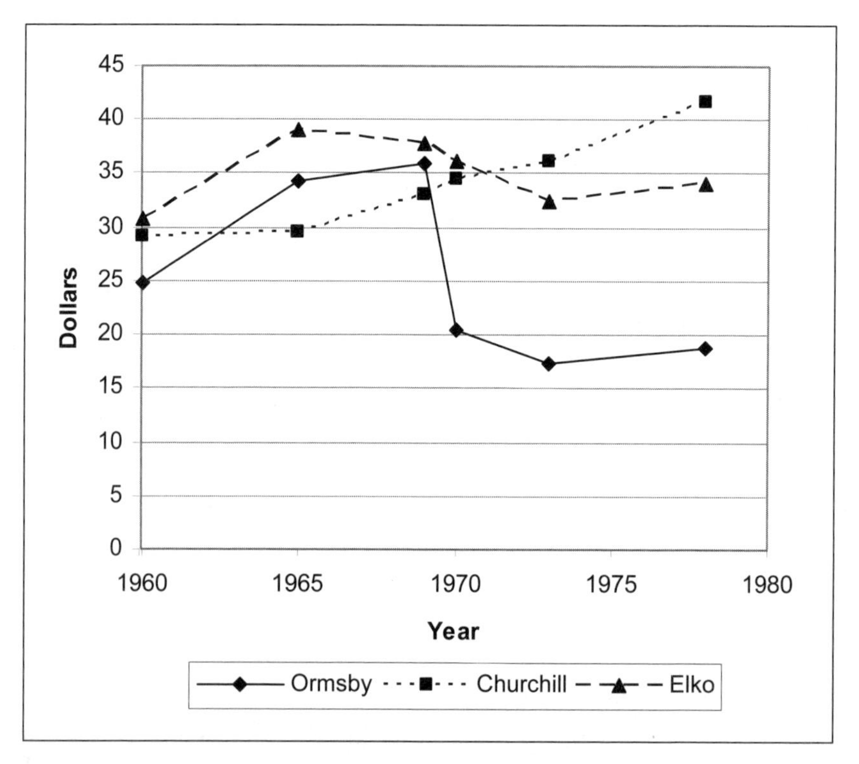

Figure 5.1 Police Expenditures per Capita (constant 1969 dollars)
Sources: Author's calculations from data reported in *County Auditors Annual Reports* for 1960, 1965, 1969, 1970, 1973, and 1978 for Churchill, Elko, and Ormsby/Carson City Counties; and 1962, 1967, 1972, 1977, and 1982 Census of Governments.

dramatically, from $24.81 per resident in 1960 to $34.32 per resident in 1965. Expenditures continued to increase, but more moderately, to $35.85 in 1969.[19] In the year following consolidation, however, Carson City residents experienced a dramatic drop in expenditures, to $20.34 per resident. Expenditures continued to fall through 1973 ($17.30 per resident) and remained low through 1978 ($18.70).

Figure 5.1 shows that Elko/Elko County exhibited a similar—but more moderate—trend in police expenditures. Like Ormsby, Elko experienced a dramatic increase in expenditures from 1960 ($30.69 per resident) to 1965 ($39.08). From there, expenditures declined moderately until reaching $32.44 per resident in 1973. By 1978, they had increased slightly, to $34.04. Churchill, in contrast, showed a pattern of consistent but moderate growth in real police expenditures, from $29.11 per capita in 1960 to $41.66 in 1978.

With respect to fire, figure 5.2 reveals a similar pattern with respect to real per capita expenditures for fire services for Carson City/Ormsby County and the comparison city/counties. Carson City/Ormsby County experienced a dramatic increase in expenditures, from $8.20 per resident in 1960 to $21.40 in 1965 and $22.22 in 1969.[20] This was followed by a precipitous decline to $14.04 in 1970, the first year after consolidation. Expenditures were even lower in 1973 ($11.29). By 1978, real per capita expenditures had again increased, but only slightly, to $13.85. Elko/Elko County also experienced a dramatic increase in real expenditures for fire services, from $7.47 per resident in 1960 to $19.66 in 1969, followed by a moderate decline to $15.48 per resident in 1978. Expenditures in Fallon/Churchill County remained relatively stable, fluctuating around $9.00 to $10.00 per resident throughout this period.

With respect to highways, before consolidation, Ormsby County, Churchill County, and Elko County presented a similar pattern of consistent, moderate increases in real expenditures per capita for highways and roads

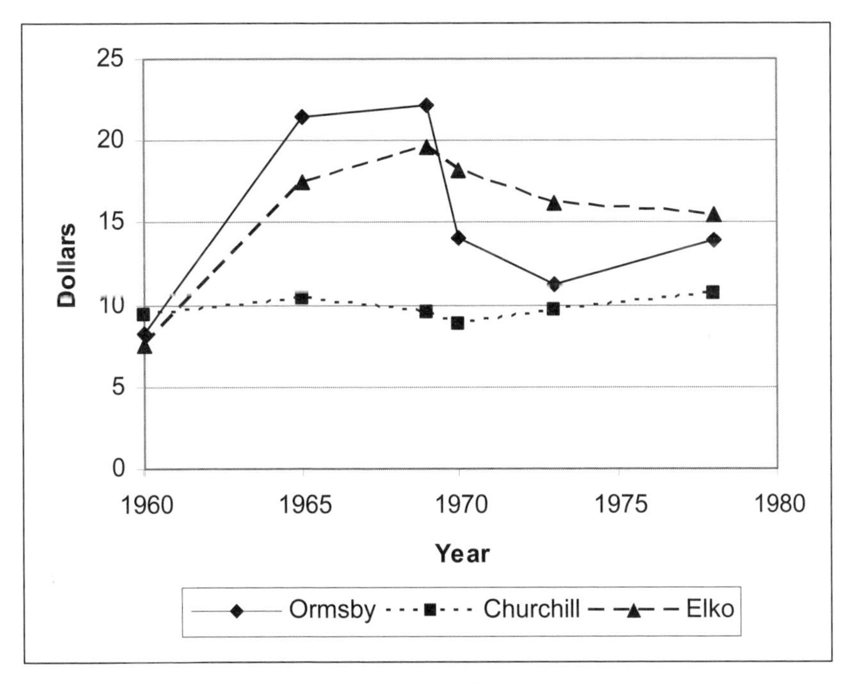

Figure 5.2 Fire Expenditures per Capita (constant 1969 dollars)

Sources: Author's calculations from data reported in *County Auditors Annual Reports* for 1960, 1965, 1969, 1970, 1973, and 1978 for Churchill, Elko, and Ormsby/Carson City Counties; and 1962, 1967, 1972, 1977, and 1982 Census of Governments.

(figure 5.3). After 1969, expenditures in Churchill County remained relatively stable. They declined in Elko County and the newly consolidated Carson City. The decline in Carson City was, once again, substantially greater.[21]

With respect to basic administrative services, figure 5.4 presents trends in real per capita expenditures for administrative services. Again, all three city/counties experienced increasing expenditures leading up to 1969. Following 1969, the comparison counties experienced fluctuating but relatively stable expenditures (Churchill) or moderately increasing expenditures (Elko). Carson City, conversely, exhibited a sharp decline in expenditures in the year following expenditures, followed by a moderate increase.[22]

With respect to the impact of consolidation on expenditures, as figures 5.1 through 5.4 show, in each of these functional categories, Carson City shows a substantial decline in expenditures following consolidation. None of the comparison city/counties show a similar decline. Unfortunately, the lack of specific expenditure data for Carson City and the control cities in

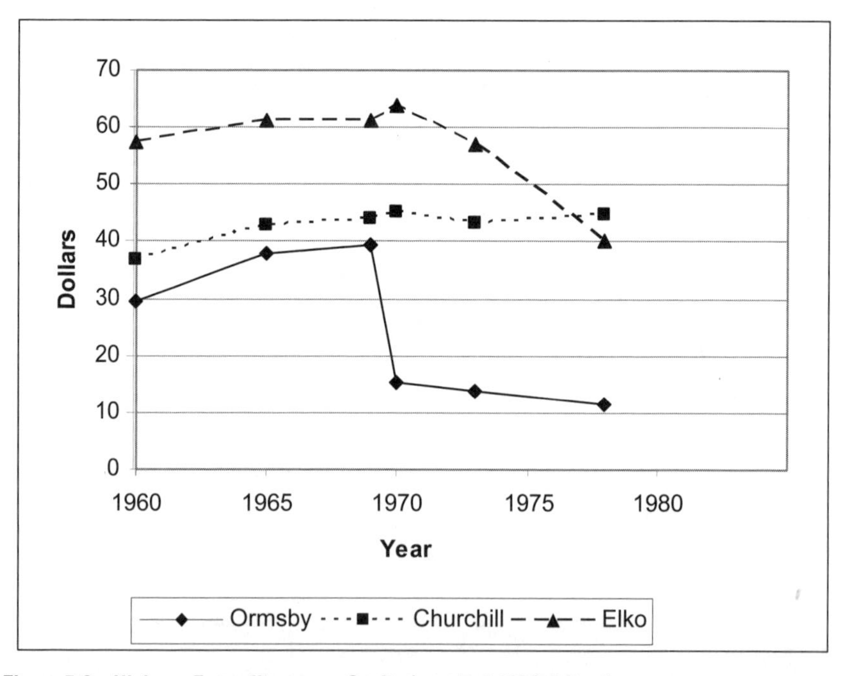

Figure 5.3 Highway Expenditures per Capita (constant 1969 dollars)

Sources: Author's calculations from data reported in *County Auditors Annual Reports* for 1960, 1965, 1969, 1970, 1973, and 1978 for Churchill, Elko, and Ormsby/Carson City Counties; and 1962, 1967, 1972, 1977, and 1982 Census of Governments.

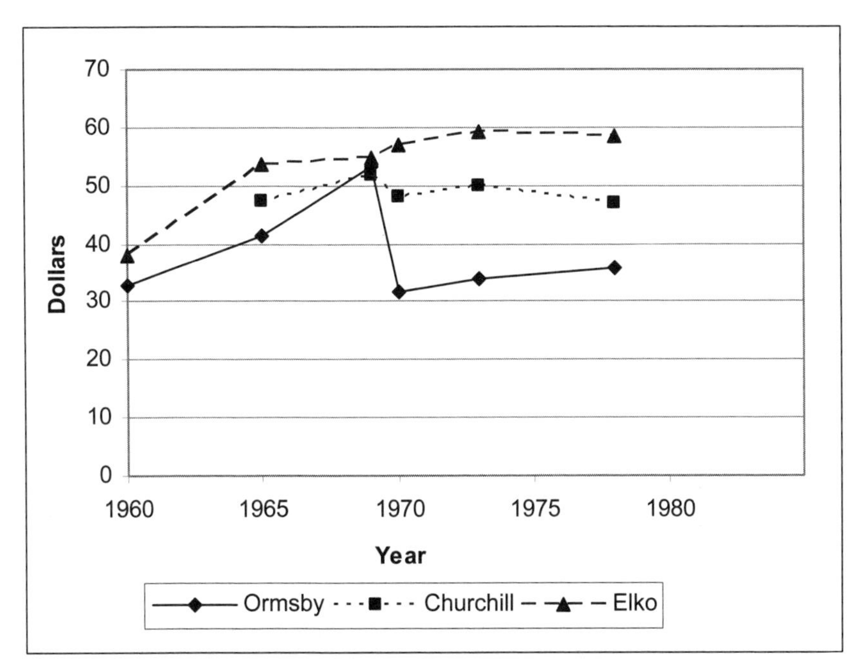

Figure 5.4 Administrative Expenditures per Capita (constant 1969 dollars)
Sources: Author's calculations from data reported in *County Auditors Annual Reports* for 1960, 1965, 1969, 1970, 1973, and 1978 for Churchill, Elko, and Ormsby/Carson City Counties; and 1962, 1967, 1972, 1977, and 1982 Census of Governments.

the years before consolidation makes it impossible to conclude with any certainty that all (or even any) of this decline is a result of consolidation.

As was explained above, I added estimated city expenditure data to actual county expenditure data to estimate expenditures for each city/county unit. This procedure was used both before and after consolidation for the control cases, but only before consolidation for Carson City/Ormsby County. After consolidation, Carson City's entire expenses were reflected in the county auditor's reports, and adding estimated municipal expenses would have been inappropriate. The consistent, dramatic decline in Carson City's post-1969 expenditures across categories and the concentration of the decline in 1970 raise the suspicion that the decline was, at least in part, a product of the method used to estimate expenditures for the city/county unit. The addition of estimated municipal expenditures may have overstated Carson City/Ormsby County's expenditures (and possibly those of the control cases). With consolidation, the method of estimating expenses removed this potential upward bias for Carson City but not for the control cases. Thus, though it is possible that some or all of the decline in Carson City's expenditures between 1969 and 1970 was a result of consolidation, it seems equally possible that some or all of that decline was a result of the removal of upward bias in estimating expenditures. Unfortunately, data limitations make it difficult to sort out how much of this decline is attributable to each cause.

Table 5.2 compares changes in expenditures in each of the functional categories for Carson City/Ormsby County and the comparison cases for the periods before and after consolidation. To control for the potential bias introduced by the precipitous decline in Carson City's expenditures between 1969 and 1970, that year is omitted from the analysis. The three columns on the left present short-term comparisons (1965–69 and 1970–73), and the columns on the right present longer-term comparisons (1960–69 and 1970–78).[23]

Looking first at expenditures for police services, table 5.2 indicates that Carson City/Ormsby County residents experienced a substantial (44 percent) rise in the real per capita cost of providing police protection during the nine years preceding consolidation. Even omitting the precipitous decline of 1970, this pattern was reversed following consolidation. Per capita costs of providing police services decreased almost 15 percent in the short term. The decline was moderated, but expenditures remained 8 percent lower in 1978. Thus, in the years following consolidation, Carson City residents saw a short-term reversal and a longer-term moderation or reversal of the trend of increasing police expenditures that had characterized the 1960s, even when the impact of the 1970 decline is excluded from the analysis.

Further, table 5.2 shows that, even when 1970 is excluded from the analysis, the pattern of increasing expenses before consolidation and a substantial reversal of this pattern following consolidation also holds for Carson City's fire and highway expenditures.[24] Fire expenditures increased almost 171 percent from 1960 to 1969 but declined almost 20 percent during the period from 1970 to 1973 and remained slightly lower in 1978. Similarly, road and highway expenditures increased 33 percent between 1960 and 1969 but declined 24 percent from 1970 to 1978. With respect to basic administrative services, though expenditures did not decline (if 1970 is excluded from the postconsolidation analysis), the rate of increase did slow—an increase of 61 percent from 1960 to 1969, compared with an increase of less than 13 percent from 1970 to 1978.

In short, even controlling for the impact of the 1970 decline, expenditure patterns for Carson City in police services, fire services, and roads and highways look decidedly different for the nine-year period after consolidation in comparison with the preceding nine years. Of the control cases, Fallon/Churchill County exhibits a very different pattern in expenditures

Table 5.2 Comparative Change in Real Expenditures across Time, Combined City and County Expenditures in Selected Functional Categories (percent change in expenditures)

Expenditures on Police						
	Shorter Term			Longer Term		
County	1965–69	1970–73	Difference	1960–69	1970–78	Difference
Ormsby	4.45	–14.93	–19.37	44.46	–8.05	–52.50
Churchill	12.01	4.39	–7.618	13.30	20.67	7.37
Elko	–3.44	–10.00	–6.556	22.97	–5.53	–28.50

Expenditures on Fire						
	Shorter Term			Longer Term		
County	1965–69	1970–73	Difference	1960–69	1970–78	Difference
Ormsby	3.87	–19.59	23.45	170.88	–1.30	–1.72
Churchill	–8.62	8.48	–17.09	1.17	19.84	0.19
Elko	12.84	–10.89	23.73	163.18	–14.98	–1.78

Expenditures on Highway						
	Shorter Term			Longer Term		
County	1965–69	1970–73	Difference	1960–69	1970–78	Difference
Ormsby	4.47	–10.79	15.26	33.33	–24.10	–57.43
Churchill	2.38	–4.03	6.42	20.11	–0.27	–20.38
Elko	0.05	–11.25	11.30	6.27	–37.36	–43.63

Expenditures on Administration						
	Shorter Term			Longer Term		
County	1965–69	1970–73	Difference	1960–69	1970–78	Difference
Ormsby	28.38	6.29	22.09	61.63	12.65	–48.98
Churchill	10.01	3.98	6.02		–9.85	
Elko	2.16	4.27	–2.11	44.72	6.39	–38.32

Sources: Author's calculations from data reported in *County Auditors Annual Report* for 1960, 1965, 1969, 1970, 1973, and 1978 for Churchill, Elko, and Ormsby/Carson City counties; and 1957, 1962, 1967, 1972, 1977, and 1982 Census of Governments.

(table 5.2). In both police and fire services, at least in the long term, expenditures increased during both periods and at a substantially greater pace during the postconsolidation period 1970–79 (almost 21 percent for police and 20 percent for fire) than during the period 1960–69 (13 percent for police and 1 percent for fire). Road and highway expenditures for Fallon/Churchill County present a pattern similar to that of Carson City/Ormsby County—increasing expenditures during 1960 to 1969 followed by declining expenditures in 1970 to 1978, but the magnitude of the difference between the two periods is much greater for Carson City/Ormsby County.

Expenditure patterns for police services, fire services, and highways in Elko/Elko County, however, are very similar to those of Carson City/Ormsby County (table 5.2). Like Carson City/Ormsby County, Elko/Elko County experienced an increase in fire and highway expenditures in both the short and longer terms leading up to 1969. For the periods 1970–73 and 1970–79, both Elko/Elko County and the newly consolidated Carson City experienced declining expenditures in these two functional areas. Further, the magnitude of changes is similar for both entities. With respect to police services, Elko/Elko County's expenditures reveal a longer-term pattern similar to Carson City/Ormsby County. In the short term, though Carson City experienced increasing police expenditures before 1969 (44 percent), followed by a substantial decline during the period 1970–73 (–8 percent), Elko/Elko County experienced declining costs both in 1965–69 (–3 percent) and 1970–73 (10 percent). Figure 5.1 suggests that this difference may simply reflect that a trend toward declining police costs began earlier in Elko/Elko County.

In summary, the pattern of expenditures in Carson City/Ormsby County varies dramatically after consolidation from the pattern before. In all four functional categories of expenditures studied here, Carson City experienced a dramatic decline in expenditures in 1970, the year following consolidation. Further, in police services, fire services, and highways, consolidation marked the end of a nine-year period of increasing expenses and the beginning of a trend toward declining expenses. In basic administrative services, a long-term period of increasing expenditures was moderated. Nevertheless, although it did not experience the dramatic decline of 1970, Elko/Elko County experienced a very similar reversal (or moderation) of trends in expenditures during the same period. Moreover, given the limitations of the data here, it is impossible to determine whether some or all of the dramatic 1970 decline is an artifact of the method necessary for estimating expenditures rather than a result of consolidation. For these reasons, the impact of the consolidation of Carson City/Ormsby County on expenditures remains tantalizingly uncertain. Although the data do not conclusively establish that consolidation resulted in no savings, they also do not provide strong evidence that it did.

The Economic Development Hypothesis

With respect to data and research methods, only limited indicators were available to assess this second hypothesis. State tax and budget reports provided two possible measures. First, equalized assessed real property value provided a comparative measure of overall real property wealth in each county. In addition, sales tax collections were used as a rough indicator of retail sales activity. Data for equalized assessed real property value (reported in current dollars) come from Annual Reports of the Nevada Tax Commission for fiscal years 1960 through 1965. The Local Government Redbook: Ad Valorem Tax Rates Budget Summaries for Nevada Local Government, published yearly by the State of Nevada Department of Taxation, provides reports of equalized assessed real property values for later years (1969 through 1980). The Tax Commission's Annual Reports provided data on sales tax collections for fiscal years 1960 through 1978.[25] These numbers were adjusted to constant 1969 dollars using the U.S. Department of Commerce's Implicit Price Deflator for Personal Consumption Expenditures. Again, to adjust for population differences, per capita figures are reported.

With respect to the impact of consolidation on property value, as figure 5.5 shows, Ormsby County and the three comparison counties experienced considerable growth in real property value per capita from 1960 to 1980. Further, although Ormsby County's growth takes place at a lower absolute level, its trajectory appears similar to that of two of the three comparison counties: Washoe and Elko. Table 5.3 divides growth in property values into that occurring before consolidation and growth after. This table reveals that property values in Ormsby County grew from $1,487 per capita in 1960 to $2,876 in 1969—an increase of 93 percent in the nine years before consolidation. In the nine years following consolidation, property values in the consolidated Carson City grew from $2876 per capita to $5,983—a postconsolidation increase of 108 percent. Therefore, following consolidation, the rate of increase accelerated somewhat, so that total growth in the postconsolidation period exceeded total growth in the preconsolidation period by 15 percentage points.

Nevertheless, the patterns in the comparison counties make it unlikely that the increased growth in property values was due to consolidation. As table 5.3 shows, each of those counties also experienced an increase in the rate of growth in the years following 1969. In comparison with Carson City/Ormsby, both Churchill and Elko counties experienced a much slower rate of growth in property values both before and after 1969. Nevertheless, as in Carson City/Ormsby, the growth in property values in Churchill and Elko accelerated considerably during the nine years after 1969 (78 and 65 percent, respectively) in comparison with the preceding nine years (12 and 25 percent). Washoe County presents a pattern very similar to that of

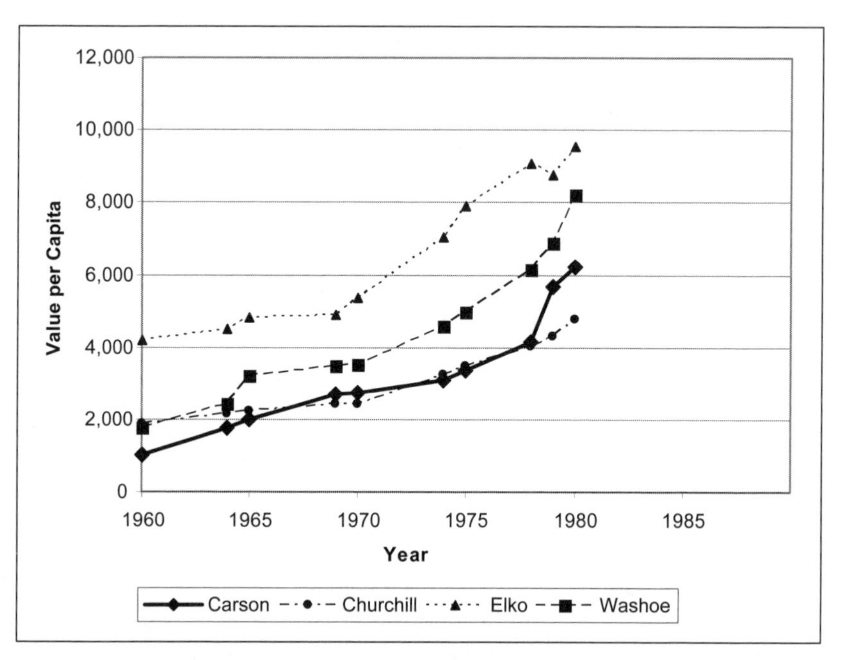

Figure 5.5 Equalized Assessed Real Property Value per Capita (constant 1969 dollars)
Sources: Author's calculations from data reported in the Nevada Tax Commission's *Annual Reports* for 1960–65 and for 1969–80; and *The Local Government Redbook: Ad Valorem Tax Rates Budget Summaries for Nevada Local Government,* published yearly by the State of Nevada Department of Taxation.

Ormsby Carson City. As in Carson City/Ormsby, property values in Washoe grew at a high rate in both periods, with a somewhat higher rate in the later period (84 percent growth from 1960 to 1969; 96 percent growth from 1969 to 1978). Therefore, at least with respect to growth in property values, both figure 5.5 and table 5.3 suggest that Carson City/Ormsby differed little from the comparison counties, and there is little evidence that consolidation had any impact on this measure of economic wealth.

With respect to the impact on retail sales activity, table 5.4 and figure 5.6 present data concerning total sales and use tax collections for the four counties from 1960 through 1969. Because the data are reported on the basis of the state sales tax rate (2 percent), excluding any local options, these figures can be used as a rough indicator of comparative underlying retail activity across the four counties. In contrast to property wealth, Carson City's post-consolidation experience with respect to this measure of economic well-being appears to differ from the comparison counties. During the nine years leading up to consolidation, Ormsby County reported the smallest total growth in sales tax collections of the four counties—a 24 percent increase in

Table 5.3 Change in Assessed Property Value per Capita, Carson City/Ormsby County and Comparison Counties

Jurisdiction	Per Capita Property Value, Fiscal Year 1960 ($)	Per Capita Property Value, Fiscal Year 1969 ($)	Per Capita Property Value, 1978 ($)	% Change in Value, 1960–69	% Change in Value, 1969–78
Carson City/ Ormsby County	1,487.49	2,875.78	5,982.56	93.33	108.03
Churchill County	2,214.13	2,476.99	4,405.63	11.87	77.86
Elko County	4,329.36	5,417.66	8,947.12	25.14	65.15
Washoe County	1,981.12	3,646.05	7,146.98	84.04	96.02

Sources: Author's calculation from total assessed property value reported in State of Nevada Tax Commission, *Annual Report,* 1960; State of Nevada Department of Taxation, *Local Government Redbook: Ad Valorem Tax Rates Budget Summaries for Nevada Local Government,* 1970, 1979.

collections for Ormsby County, compared with increases of 34 to 36 percent for the other counties. Following consolidation, however, the renamed Carson City experienced an 81 percent increase in sales tax collections. That is, in the nine years following consolidation, Carson City's sales tax collections grew at three times the rate of growth in the nine years before consolidation. In contrast, the comparison counties experienced growth in collections ranging from 12 to 23 percent. Thus, unlike in Carson City, in the comparison counties, growth in sales tax collections slowed after 1969.

To the extent that sales tax collections reflect underlying retail sales activity, Carson City appears to have experienced considerably greater growth in retail sales after consolidation than the unconsolidated comparison counties. Given Carson City's unique economic base and its unusually high population density, it is difficult to conclude that this difference is a result of consolidation. For instance, the county auditors' report show that the period following consolidation was one of growth in federal aid for programs such as federal revenue sharing and state and local social programs, and such spending likely stimulated government employment at both the state and local levels. Carson City, as the state capital, may have experienced a greater economic boost from this spending than the comparison cities and counties. Nevertheless, on this measure of economic growth, Carson City's experience was substantially different from and better than that of the comparison counties.

Table 5.4 Change in State 2 Percent Sales and Use Tax Collections per Capita, Carson City/Ormsby County and Comparison Counties (constant 1969 dollars)

Jurisdiction	Per Capita Tax Collections, Fiscal Year 1960 ($)	Per Capita Tax Collections, Fiscal Year 1969 ($)	Per Capita Tax Collections, Fiscal Year 1978 ($)	% Change in Tax Collections, 1960–69	% Change in Tax Collections, 1969–78
Carson City/ Ormsby County	30.95	38.28	69.24	23.69	80.87
Churchill County	26.37	35.05	40.9	36.34	13.78
Elko County	38.42	52.31	58.51	36.17	11.85
Washoe County	49.1	65.84	80.88	34.1	22.84

Sources: Author's calculations from tax collection data reported in State of Nevada Tax Commission, *Annual Report,* 1960, 1969, 1978. Collections reported were adjusted to constant 1969 dollars using the U.S. Department of Commerce's Implicit Price Deflator for Personal Consumption Expenditures.

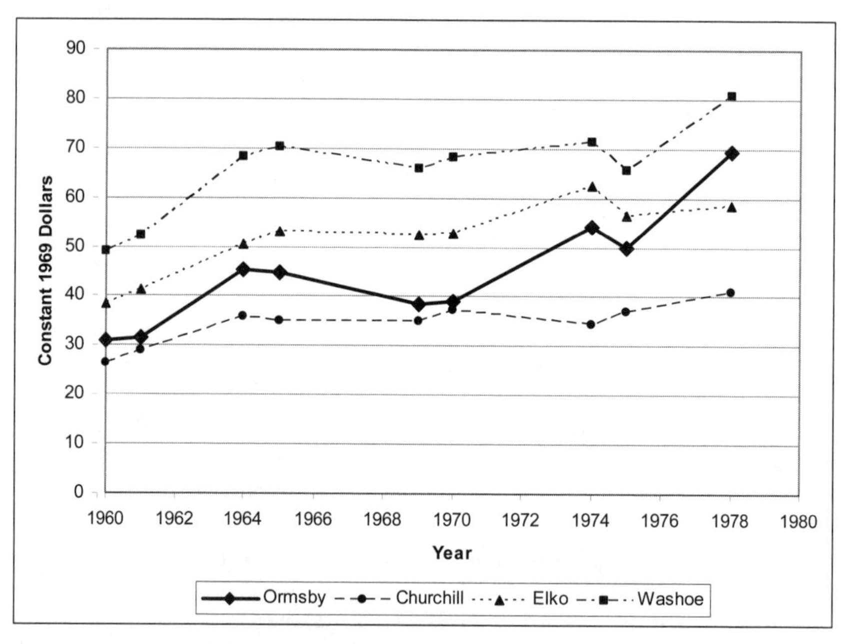

Figure 5.6 Total 2 Percent Sales Tax Collections per Capita, Carson City/Ormsby and Comparison Counties (constant 1969 dollars)
Source: Nevada Tax Commission, *Annual Reports.*

The Other Promises Hypothesis

With respect to the promise of no initial tax increase, proponents promised both city and county residents that consolidation *itself*—as opposed to the forces of continued growth and development—would result in no tax increase. The charter creating Carson City was structured to ensure that this promise was met, at least initially. The charter divided the newly created Carson City into two taxing districts: an "urban district" that corresponded to the area within the boundaries of Carson City before the consolidation, and an Ormsby district consisting of the rest of the county (Statutes of Nevada 1969, Chapter 213, Article 1, Section 1.050, p. 289). This two-taxing-district structure was maintained until 1983, when the Nevada legislature amended Carson City's charter to provide for a single taxing district (Statutes of Nevada 1983, Chapter 425, Section 15.1, p. 1058). By this time, Carson City's population had more than doubled, growing from 15,068 in 1970 to 32,022 in 1980. Thus, it appears that this promise was kept.

With respect to the promise of cost savings of $7,200 due to a reduction of the number of elected officials from seven to five, the lack of detailed and specific data concerning Carson City's expenditures before consolidation make it difficult or impossible to evaluate the precise amount of savings in payments to elected officials. Nevertheless, the charter for the newly consolidated Carson City specified a five-member board of supervisors as the legislative body, suggesting that this promise was kept.

With respect to the promise of unspecified cost savings due to reduced duplication of services in areas such as bookkeeping and auditing, the lack of identified cost savings as well as the limitations of the data available make this promise extremely difficult to evaluate. Given the care that elected officials appear to have taken to limit promises, it seems at least somewhat likely that this one was well founded and kept.

Table 5.5 Summary of the Carson City/Ormsby County Case

Overall Assessment of Evidence	H1: Efficiency	H2: Economic Development	H3: Other Promises
Not enough data available	☑		
No evidence			
Weak		☑	
Moderate			☑
Strong			

Conclusion

The 1969 consolidation of Carson City and Ormsby County seems to have been both relatively uncontroversial and successful (table 5.5). A number of factors likely contributed to its noncontroversial nature: Carson City's unique situation as a geographically small, densely populated county in a state of geographically large, sparsely populated counties; the dominance of Carson City in Ormsby County; the fact that formal consolidation followed—as was presented as primarily formalizing—a series of functional consolidations; and the fact that expectations and promises of benefits were fairly limited. With respect to the light that this case study sheds on whether, and under what circumstances, city/county consolidation more generally results in benefits such as more efficient government or increased economic development, the study provides some evidence that consolidation resulted in increased retail sales, although this is far from conclusive. Unfortunately, due to data limitations, the impact of Carson City's consolidation on governmental expenditures remains uncertain. Nevertheless, proponents presented consolidation as resulting in fairly minor change, and promised benefits were limited to those that could be fairly ensured by structure of the charter. Thus, judged on its own terms, Carson City's consolidation can fairly be considered successful.

Notes

I wish to thank Susie Skarl, research librarian extraordinaire, for her unflagging energy and persistence in the face of scattered documents and archives consisting of warehouses of boxed records. It was only through her efforts that I was able to obtain any financial data at all about Nevada cities and counties in the early 1960s and 1970s. I also owe a debt of gratitude to John Stone and the staff of the Carson City Clerk's Office, who cheerfully and enthusiastically helped me track down handwritten minutes from city and county meetings. I also wish to acknowledge graduate students Renee Martinez, Paul Grimyser, and Mike Herenick for, respectively, slogging through unindexed microfiche copies of old newspaper reports; gathering, sorting and copying old financial records; and converting the data found there into a usable database. Finally, I wish to thank the students of PUA 791–Topics in Administration, who explored the literature concerning city–county consolidation with me. Whatever is right with this paper is due in large part to the help of these individuals. Errors are, of course, entirely my own.

1. Most Native Americans (about 850 of 1,050 Native American people) lived outside Carson City. African Americans and other minorities comprised only about 2 percent of the county's residents (Gordon 1972).
2. Section 37(A) reads: "*Consolidation of city and county containing seat of government into one municipal government; separate taxing districts.* Notwithstanding the general provisions of sections 20, 25, 26, and 36 of this article, the legislature may by law consolidate into one municipal government, with one set of officers, the city designated as the seat of government for this state and the county in which such city is situated. Such consolidated municipality shall be considered as a county for the purpose of representation in the legislature, shall have all of the powers conferred upon counties by this constitution or by general law, and shall have such other powers as may be conferred by its charter. Notwithstanding the general provisions of section 1 of article 10, the legislature may create two or more separate taxing districts within such consolidated municipality."
3. The Nevada legislature amended Carson City's charter in 1979 to establish a merit personnel system. *Statutes of Nevada 1979*, chapter 690, p. 1855.
4. This statement must be viewed with caution. Both state and local legislative histories during this time consisted primarily of abbreviated minutes and summaries of discussions. Issues of the *Nevada Appeal,* the Carson City newspaper, are not indexed during this period, and we did not locate copies of issues for the final quarter of 1968, a key period in the process. Despite the statewide referendum, neither the Reno nor the Las Vegas newspapers provided more than cursory coverage of the consolidation issue. The consolidation process occurred during a period of time. The conclusions here reflect only a review of the available documents from 1968 and 1969.
5. The conclusions in this paragraph are subject to the cautions expressed in note 4.
6. Indeed, because the consolidation required a constitutional amendment and therefore approval of the electorate throughout the state, the primary concern of Carson City and Ormsby County's elected officials seemed to be developing support for the consolidation outside Ormsby County.
7. The cities in Clark County included Las Vegas, North Las Vegas, Henderson, and Boulder City.
8. For example, Henderson and North Las Vegas.

9. The comparable measures for Washoe County were median education level, 12.5 years; percent high school graduates, 68.7; and percent college graduates, 13.6. Reno, the site of the University of Nevada, is in Washoe County.
10. Cities in Nevada may incorporate and operate under general law (NRS 266 and 267) or they may incorporate and operate under individual charters, enacted as special laws by the Nevada legislature (State of Nevada 1977).
11. Although specific definitions of expenditure categories vary somewhat across the years, definitions from the 1967 Census of Governments well represent the categories used in this study: "*Highways:* Streets, highways, and structures necessary for their use, street lighting, snow and ice removal, toll highway and bridge facilities, and ferries" (U.S. Department of Commerce 1967, 51). "*Police Protection:* Preservation of law and order and traffic safety. Includes highway police patrols, crime prevention activities, police communications, detention and custody of persons awaiting trial, traffic safety, vehicular inspection, and the like" (U.S. Department of Commerce 1967, 50).

    Basic administrative service expenditures, as used in this study, includes two categories enumerated in the 1967 Census of Governments: "*Financial Administration:* Officials and agencies concerned with tax assessment and collection, accounting, auditing, budgeting, purchasing, custody of funds, and other central finance activities" (U.S. Department of Commerce 1967, 50). "*General Control:* Governing body, courts, office of the chief executive, and central staff services and agencies concerned with personnel administration, law, recording, planning and zoning, and the like (U.S. Department of Commerce 1967, 50). The report gives no specific definition for fire protection services.
12. Basic administrative, fire, and police expenditures included in this study omit, for the most part, those identified as special district, special purpose, or enterprise funds. This appears to have the greatest impact with respect to Ormsby County/Carson City, which reports expenditures for the Clark-McNary Fire District from 1965 to 1978. Further, distinctions between general and special purpose funds were not always clear before the 1970s, nor were they necessarily consistent across time. Worksheets showing specific expenditure categorizations for each county and each year are available from the author upon request.
13. Census data provided county population figures for 1960, 1970, and 1980. Population figures for intervening years were calculated based on the assumption that population growth was spread evenly across the period.

14. Specifically, the county auditors' reports included only lump sum disbursements to municipal governments, apparently representing their shares of property and (sometimes) gasoline tax revenues.
15. I used Census of Governments expenditure reports for 1957, 1962, 1967, 1972, 1977, and 1982 to interpolate municipal expenditure data for 1960, 1965, 1969, 1970, 1973, and 1978. I assumed that increases or decreases in expenditures were spread evenly across the intervals between the reported years.
16. The 1957 Census of Governments reported separate expenditure data for individual cities with populations of 2,500 or more. Therefore, specific expenditure data were available and were used for Elko and Carson City in 1957. Beginning in 1962, separate expenditure data were reported only for cities with populations of 10,000 or more. Therefore, beginning in 1962, cities' expenditures were estimated based on reports for cities grouped by size of population. Cities, years, and population groupings were:

    Elko 1957: individual report available; 1962: 5,000–9,999 population group; 1967: 5,000–9,999; 1972: 5,000–9,999; 1977: 5,000–9,999; 1982: 5,000–9,999.

    Fallon 1957: 1,000–2,499 population group; 1962: 2,500–4,999; 1967: 2,500–9,999; 1972: 2,500–9,999; 1977: 2,500–9,999; 1982: 2,500–9,999.

    Carson City 1957: individual report available; 1962: 5,000–9,999 population group; 1967: 5,000–9,999; 1972: 5,000–9,999.

    Precise population data for the municipality of Carson City (as opposed to the consolidated Carson City/Ormsby County) are not available after 1960. The 1970 census reports only the population of the consolidated city/county unit. This is unfortunate because the estimate of the number of people living within the municipal boundaries of Carson City in 1969 is crucial. This estimate influences the calculation of per capita government expenditures for 1969, the base year for comparison. Therefore, I analyzed the data using both low and high estimates of population growth. The high estimate placed Carson City in the 10,000–24,999 population group for 1972. The low estimate placed it in the 5,000–9,999 population group.

    Projections based on the previous growth trends in the city and county suggest that the lower population estimate is more accurate for the area within the municipal boundaries. (Details available from the author.) This conclusion is reinforced by the fact that, at the time of consolidation, "there was a substantial segment of the population residing in the County area immediately adjacent to Carson City…in 1969 when amalgamation occurred" (Gordon 1972, 9). This suggests that most of the growth that was occurring was in the area adjacent to, but outside, the municipal boundaries.

Therefore, I report here only the findings based on the low growth analysis. I also report, in these notes, 1969 per capita expenditures based on the high growth estimate so that interested parties may perform there own analyses using these figures. In essence, the results using the high growth assumption are substantively different only for highway expenditures. The results using the high growth assumption are essentially the same for police and fire expenditures. The conclusions are similar but weaker for administration expenditures. Details are available from the author.

17. Both Elko and Churchill County auditors' reports reflect allocations to cities other than those chosen as control cities. Those amounts, where identified, are omitted from the calculation of expenditures here.
18. The consolidated Carson City continued to submit annual county auditors' reports that followed the same format as the other counties.
19. The high population growth assumption yields an estimated expenditure of $36.51 per resident for police services in 1969.
20. Using the high population growth assumption, Carson City/Ormsby County fire service expenditures were approximately $23.59 in 1969.
21. Highway expenditure is the one area in which population growth assumptions make a substantial difference to the findings. Although the low population growth assumption yields a slight but continued increase in expenditures (from approximately $37.78 in 1965 to an estimated $39.47 in 1969), the high population growth assumption results in declining expenditures from 1965 to 1969 (from $37.78 to $29.44). Under this assumption, the decline in Carson City's per capita highway expenditures was well under way before consolidation.
22. The high population growth assumption leads to an estimate of $46.06 for administrative expenditures in 1969, compared to $53.09 for the low population growth assumption. This does not change the shape of the pattern, but it does make both the preconsolidation increase and the postconsolidation decline less dramatic.
23. Due to the omission of 1969–70, the period following consolidation is one year shorter than the period before consolidation. Because this affects both comparison and control cases equally, it should not undermine the conclusions.
24. This statement holds with respect to highway expenditures only if one accepts the low population growth assumption for Carson City.

25. Specifically, this study uses data on equalized assessed real property values for fiscal years 1960, 1965, 1969, 1970, 1971, 1974, 1975, 1978, 1979, and 1980, and data on sales tax collections for fiscal years 1960, 1961, 1964, 1965, 1969, 1970, 1974, 1975, and 1978.

References

Campbell, Richard W., and Dan Durning. 2000. Is City–County Consolidation a Good Policy? A Symposium. *Public Administration Quarterly* 24, no. 2:133–39.

Feiock, Richard C. 2004. Do Consolidation Entrepreneurs Make a Deal with the Devil? In *City–County Consolidation and Its Alternatives: Reshaping the Local Government Landscape*, ed. Jered B. Carr and Richard C. Feiock. Armonk, NY: M. E. Sharpe.

Gordon, Robert A. 1972. *Carson City Master Plan*. Carson City: Office of the City Manager.

Leland, Suzanne M., and Gary A. Johnson. 2004. Consolidation as a Local Reform: Why City–County Consolidation Is an Enduring Issue. In *City–County Consolidation and Its Alternatives: Reshaping the Local Government Landscape*, ed. Jered B. Carr and Richard C. Feiock. Armonk, NY: M. E. Sharpe.

Nevada Appeal. 1969. City–County Consolidation. January 29.

Sawhill, Isabel V., and Shannon L. Smith. 1998. Vouchers for Elementary and Secondary Education. In *Vouchers and the Provision of Public Services*, ed. C. Eugene Steurle, Van Doorn Ooms, George E. Peterson, and Robert D. Reischauer. Washington, DC: Brookings Institution Press, Committee for Economic Development, and Urban Institute Press.

Selden, Sally Coleman, and Richard W. Campbell. 2000. The Expenditure Impacts of Unification in a Small Georgia County: A Contingency Perspective of City–County Consolidation. *Public Administration Quarterly* 24, no. 2:169–201.

State of Nevada, Governor's Office of Planning Coordination. 1977. *Nevada Statistical Abstract 1977*. Carson City: Governor's Office of Planning Coordination.

U.S. Department of Commerce. 1967. *1967 Census of Governments*. Washington, DC: U.S. Government Printing Office.

→ 6 ←

"The Urge to Merge"

The Consolidation of Lexington and Fayette County, Kentucky

Shawn Gillen

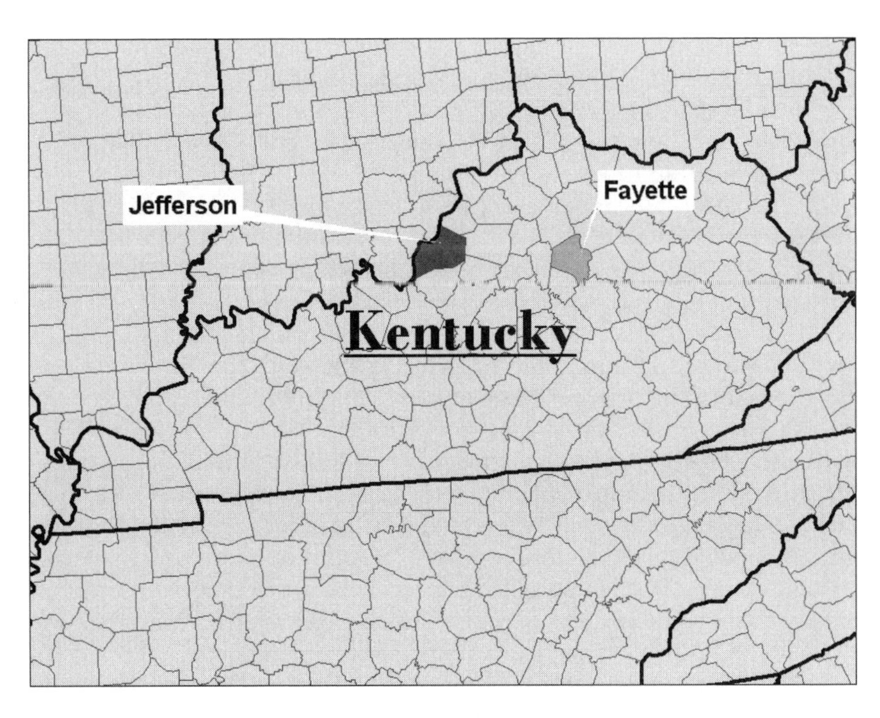

Map 6 Locations of Jefferson County and Fayette County, Kentucky
Source: U.S. Bureau of the Census.

If there is such a thing as a perfect storm when it comes to city–county consolidation, then the Lexington/Fayette County, Kentucky, case is just that (map 6). This chapter looks at the atmosphere in Lexington at the time of the merger proposal and examines some of the driving issues behind the proposal's success. The conditions in Lexington/Fayette County are then compared with Louisville/Jefferson County, a comparable city in Kentucky that did not consolidate during the period under examination.[1] In some cases of city–county consolidation there are arguments made concerning the future economic development of the area, the efficiencies of government services, increasing taxes, and the number of rooftops in the community (Leland and Thurmaier 2004, 2005; Wanamaker and Marando 1972). Sometimes the proponents of consolidation will argue for the improvement of service delivery through the redistribution of tax revenues from fringe areas to central city areas (Kenny and Filer 1980). In the Lexington/Fayette case we see that these efficiencies and economic development arguments were barely mentioned during the drive toward the consolidation referendum. The critical issues that led to the success of the consolidation effort were the inevitable annexation of developed areas in the county, the tax/benefit relationship of municipal services in these areas, and the concern about the dilution of minority group voting power in the city.

The increase in service levels was observed in the examination of the budgetary data, and the changes to the government structure helped alleviate the dilution of minority voting power through codification in the merger charter. A dramatic increase in expenditures occurred in the year following the merger. However, when per capita expenditure data are examined, a temporary decrease is observed in the year following the merger, which in turn was followed by a dramatic increase to levels above that of the premerger years. The temporary decrease may be attributable to the deferral of numerous capital projects and the delay in filling vacant positions until the merger was complete. The rise of per capita expenditures to levels above the premerger years mirrors the expenditure level increases. The demand for service increased when citizens living outside the former Lexington city limits experienced an increase in taxes. The newly formed government responded by expanding service levels to meet the demand. Total expenditures reflect the effort of the Lexington/Fayette Urban County Government (hereafter, Lexington/Fayette County, or Lexington/Fayette) to live up to the promise that service expansion would coincide with the increase in taxes. Thus, rapid increases in police and fire personnel, sanitary and storm sewer expenditures, and the like are seen in the budget data.

The other issue that was a main driver behind the successful merger was the change from at-large council representation to district representation.

This change was codified into the merger charter, thereby eliminating any active resistance from inner-city minority groups. Such groups feared that the forced annexation, which was the inevitable alternative to merger, would dilute their voting power. In addition to this, the proposed voting districts in the merger charter virtually guaranteed that minorities would occupy at least two of the fifteen council seats.

In the case of Lexington/Fayette County, the arguments for the merger were not based on efficiency or economics. The rapid growth and subsequent need to expand services and match the rate of taxation among those who benefited from the services led to a judicially mandated and unpopular annexation plan. This forced annexation, in turn, led to a spontaneous collusion of constituent groups that under normal circumstances would have actively opposed a city–county consolidation.

The C^3 Model

To understand the Lexington/Fayette case and the reasons why there were very few promises made to voters during the campaign leading up to the referendum, we need to conceptualize the factors that led to its success. The City–County Consolidation (or C^3) model proposed by Leland and Thurmaier allows us to do just that. The C^3 Model has two parts; each part consists of several variables that contribute to the success or failure of the consolidation effort. Part 1 models the variables that affect the success of bringing the consolidation issue to a referendum. Part 2 models the variables that affect the outcome of the referendum. There are a total of thirteen independent variables in parts 1 and 2. The dependent variable is the referendum itself, whether the consolidation issue passed or failed (Leland and Thurmaier 2004). This chapter goes beyond the C^3 model to test three hypotheses:

H1: The consolidated government operates more efficiently than unconsolidated governments.

H2: The consolidated government operates more effectively with respect to economic development than a similar nonconsolidated governments due to structural efficiency gains.

H3: The consolidated government delivered on its other promises.

We use a classic comparative case study design (figure 6.1) to try and answer these questions. We assess the impact of consolidation of Lexington / Fayette County with a comparable city–county (Louisville/ Jefferson County) in Kentucky that did not consolidate during the same time frame. This allows us to gain insight from systematic analysis without losing advantages of the depth of the case study.

First we look at the expenditures for Lexington/Fayette before and after the merger: Ob_{t11} and Ob_{t12} and Ob_{t21} and Ob_{t22}. Then we compare the expenditures for Lexington/Fayette with the expenditures of Louisville/Jefferson in the premerger (Ob_{t11} and Ob_{t21}) and postmerger (Ob_{t12} and Ob_{t22}) years. We assess whether or not consolidation brought about service delivery efficiencies through lower combined expenditures and expenditures per capita.

The Lexington/Fayette County Case and the C^3 Model

If we consider the C^3 model, the Lexington/Fayette case is nearly a perfect fit. The variables converged to form the perfect storm as the referendum drew closer, eliminating potential opponents and capsizing the minimal anticonsolidation efforts in place. The consolidation of the Fayette County and City of Lexington governments can be considered unique in the realm of city–county consolidations. At first glance the merger seems rather typical. The total population for the Lexington/Fayette County area was 174,323. This falls well within the average population range for cities and counties that attempted consolidation between World War II and 1970. Lexington is fairly typical when it comes to the number of jurisdictions. Before the merger there were only two local government units, the city and the county (Leland and Thurmaier 2004; Wanamaker and Marando 1972).

The rapid population growth of the area put pressure on local governments to change the status quo. From 1940 to 1970 the metropolitan statistical area's population grew from 79,800 to 174,323 (or 32 percent), making Lexington/Fayette the fourteenth-fastest-growing metropolitan statistical area in the country. In table 6.1 it is apparent that Lexington/Fayette experienced a growth rate greater than that of Louisville/Jefferson County in the six-year period leading up to consolidation. This rapid growth resulted in a "crazy" city/county boundary (Lyons 1977). This growth pattern created a crisis climate and set the foundation for the Lexington/Fayette consolidation effort.

Experimental Group (unified government)	**Ob_{t11}**	**C^3**	**Ob_{t12}**
Comparison Group (unconsolidated)	**Ob_{t21}**		**Ob_{t22}**

Figure 6.1 Research Design

Table 6.1 Comparison of Lexington/Fayette County and Louisville/Jefferson County Population Changes, 1967–85

Jurisdiction	Population 1967	Population 1973	Increase 1967–73 %	Population 1974	Population 1985	Increase 1974–85 %
Lexington/ Fayette Urban County Government	131,906	174,323	32	184,603	210,150	14
Louisville/ Jefferson County	610,947	695,055	14	702,346	682,706	–3

Source: U.S. Bureau of the Census.

The City of Lexington is laid out in a hub-and-spokes pattern. The central business district or downtown has several arterial streets leading into it. At the time of the merger referendum, New Circle Road was the outer edge of the developed areas, but it was not the official jurisdictional boundary of the city and county.[2] The boundary followed an erratic, almost zigzag, pattern caused by incremental annexation over the decades. The political boundaries of the city and county in 1971 were erratic. Pockets of annexed territory are visible along the main arteries.

When we consider the economic development trends before and after the merger, there are clear distinctions between Fayette and Jefferson counties during this period. Fayette County saw significantly higher rates of growth in housing units and retail establishments. These trends are the same before and after the merger of Lexington and Fayette County. These strong growth rates in Fayette County were one of the main thrusts behind the merger movement, which can explain why an enhanced economic development argument was not used during the merger campaign. Instead, the concerns centered on a coordinated countywide response to the rapid rate of growth. This conclusion is supported by the housing data shown in table 6.2.

Recall that the city of Lexington had seen a rather haphazard growth pattern along the corridors into the city. Those citizens living outside the city limits at the time of the merger were in favor of the proposal due to the inevitable city annexation. Additionally, growth in the rural areas of the county has faced increased restrictions due to policy changes instituted by the new government since the merger. For example, there is a restriction on the development of farmland and there are increased impact fees for development outside the urban services area. This is coupled with a "Purchase of Development Rights" program that compensates the rural

Table 6.2 Historic Economic Data for Jefferson and Fayette Counties

Measure	% Change		No.				
	1962–72	1972–82	1960	1970	1980	1990	
Housing units							
Fayette County	48	37	40,263	59,528	81,747	97,942	
Jefferson County	20	17	188,311	226,493	265,930	282,578	
	1962–72	1972–82	1963	1967	1972	1977	1982
Manufacturing establishments							
Fayette County	14	9	145	165	180	216	228
Jefferson County	0	9	764	765	835	911	884
Retail establishments							
Fayette County	8	17	1,228	1,324	1,551	Missing	1,871
Jefferson County	–1	5	5,033	4,962	5,232	Missing	5,282

Source: U.S. Bureau of the Census.

landowners for the loss of development rights of farmland. In this sense, there has been significant follow-through and coordination by the city/ county in response to rapid growth.

One of the more interesting economic outcomes of the Lexington/Fayette merger was the shift in the relative per capita incomes of Jefferson and Fayette counties. In the years before the merger, Fayette County trailed Jefferson County in per capita income. After the merger in 1972, Fayette County per capita income grew at a rate that matched that of Jefferson County, and in 1983 Fayette County surpassed Jefferson County (table 6.3). This seems a logical result of the rapid economic growth causing the labor supply to decline relative to demand, putting upward pressure on wages. This conclusion is borne out when we look at the unemployment data during that period. Table 6.4 shows the unemployment data for the two counties. During the recession of the early 1980s, Jefferson County saw a much greater impact on employment than Fayette County. A rapid growth rate and an increasingly diverse tax base could be the reasons that Fayette County was able to weather this economic storm.

Table 6.3 Historic Per Capita Income Data for Jefferson and Fayette Counties (dollars)

Jurisdiction	1969	1972	1982	1983	1984
Fayette County	3,692	4,444	11,760	12,792	14,386
Jefferson County	3,823	4,766	11,886	12,563	13,800

Source: U.S. Bureau of the Census.

The Annexation Proposal

The vast majority of the development occurred along these main arteries. As the developments grew along the artery, the city would annex in some areas but not others, leaving adjacent neighborhoods with the same type of development in different jurisdictions. That is, some of the neighborhoods would be in the city and others in the county. It was possible to have houses on the same block be in different governmental jurisdictions (Lyons 1977). This issue of spot annexation along the corridors into the city was discussed in an interview with David Stevens, a current member of the Lexington/Fayette County council and a member of the charter commission that drafted the charter for the referendum in 1972. He mentioned an anecdote that came to symbolize the cross-jurisdictional problems arising in these adjacent neighborhoods. On a street perpendicular to one of the corridor streets was a city fire station. Across the street from the city fire station was a county fire station. An apparent inefficiency was occurring here, but one could imagine a developed area that crossed jurisdictional boundaries and was dense enough for both governments to place a fire station in the area.

This jigsaw-like boundary led to service delivery challenges and inefficiencies. It also led to some animosity among the neighborhoods. Garbage collection routes were complicated, and fire and police jurisdictions were

Table 6.4 Historic Unemployment Data for Jefferson and Fayette Counties (percent)

Jurisdiction	1970	1971	1972	1982	1983	1984
Fayette County	2.6	3.2	3.7	5.4	5.2	4.2
Jefferson County	3.3	4.3	5.7	10.6	10.2	8.3

Source: U.S. Bureau of the Census.

difficult to determine without research. These jurisdiction issues provided good banter during the referendum campaign. For example, some alleged that the city had an unofficial "too drunk for jail" policy at the city-owned jail facility. If a severely intoxicated individual was arrested, it increased the chances of personal injury or injury of city correctional staff. In general, intoxicated individuals also bring higher cost of care, whether medical assistance or damage to facilities. To avoid these adverse costs of housing an intoxicated individual, it was alleged that the person would be driven into the county jurisdiction by city officials and dropped off far enough away from the city to not be able to return until they were sober or could be picked up by the county police. The truth of this scenario is questionable, but it did make for interesting conversation during the political debate over the merger. An additional topic of discussion included spillover effects of developed areas in the county jurisdiction, adjacent to annexed territories. These fringe areas were thought to receive the benefit of additional public safety services without having to pay for them.

The annexation of these adjacent developed areas became the catalyst that led to the consolidation proposal. The only option Lexington had in dealing with this issue was annexation. The city began annexation procedures for many of these areas, which prompted the affected residents to file suit against the city. The motivation of the plaintiffs was increased taxes with no guarantee of an increase in services. The city then relaxed its efforts to forcibly annex the properties and instead pursued voluntary annexation. Some developed areas did choose to be annexed, but this only exacerbated the problem because the boundaries became even more disjointed.

In 1968, an independent research commission appointed by the city issued a report recommending that Lexington annex all the developed property surrounding the city. This annexation proposal, if enacted, would have doubled the population and the territory of the city. The city adopted the recommendation as an ordinance. This set off a series of events that moved the city and county toward consolidation (Lyons 1977).

Of all the citizens affected by the 1968 annexation proposal, only about 50 percent filed suit with the city, and the burden of proof was on the citizens to prove that they would suffer irreparable harm as a result of the annexation. The city's officials felt confident that they would win the case, and all indications suggested that they were correct. However, the 1968 city elections changed the political power structure of the city commission. The newly elected commissioners moved quickly to resolve the issue. A compromise was reached, in which the city would rescind the annexation ordinance and agree to voluntary annexation until 1975, when one portion of the area would be annexed. The remainder of the area would not be annexed until 1980, although voluntary annexation was still possible before 1980. After 1980 the residents of the effected areas could not take legal action against the city concerning the annexation.

The city commissioners who opposed the annexation had agreed to the compromise in the hopes of gaining enough political strength to defeat the annexation in 1975 and 1980. However, these commissioners were defeated in the next elections, leaving the door open once again to annexation.[3] It was at this same time that the Kentucky legislature passed a bill that granted local governments in Kentucky the power to consolidate. That meant that the options for Lexington in 1972 were either annexation or consolidation. Those voters that lived on the fringes of the city knew that annexation would lead to immediate tax increases with no promise of additional services. The proposal put forth for consolidation included language that would guarantee these residents no new taxes until the services were provided. The proposal also allowed them to begin receiving services piecemeal as they became available. For example, they would not have to wait for sanitary or storm sewers to be built before they could start receiving garbage collection service. They could also opt out of receiving garbage collection, street light service, and the like, thus avoiding some of the new property taxes.[4]

The other side to this annexation coin was the new city commission's at-large seats. The Lexington/Fayette merger proposal would double the population, just as the annexation proposal would. This was frustrating for the minority community in Lexington because it was nearly impossible for a minority to be elected in a citywide campaign. What political power minorities could muster under the current system faced a serious threat of being diluted even further by the doubling of the city population. However, under the merger proposal, council representatives would be elected by district, guaranteeing minorities at least two and possibly three positions on the council. This fact helped carry the merger effort to fruition because it eliminated opposition from the minority community.

According to W. E. Lyons, who wrote extensively on the Lexington/Fayette merger, one of the merger's most unique factors was the extent to which the social structures in Lexington/Fayette overlapped the existing jurisdictional boundaries. As Lyons (1977,18) put it, "One would be hard pressed to find another setting in which the existing political boundaries cut across social worlds in a more erratic fashion." This statement indirectly refers to the concept that the higher the number of local jurisdictions within the merger area, the more difficult it is to have a successful consolidation effort. Lyons posited that the number of jurisdictions was not as important as the relationship between the boundaries of the social worlds, as he called them, and the official jurisdictional boundaries. He argued that if there were significant overlap of jurisdictional boundaries on the unofficial social boundaries, there would be less opposition from those social groups (Wanamaker and Marando 1972). They would not have as great a fear of losing power after a merger, and in fact might be able to gain voting power (Lowery and Lyons 1989).

The Reclassification Issue

Another issue that added to the crisis climate was the size of Lexington's population. The 1970 census put Lexington's population at 107,944. This population was due to double under the annexation proposal. Cities and counties in Kentucky are separate government entities that do not have overlapping jurisdictions. The cities in Kentucky are classified into six distinct classifications based on population. Table 6.5 presents the city classification categories used in Kentucky. Before the merger, the City of Lexington was a city of the second class; however, the 1970 census showed that Lexington had a population of more than 100,000.

Kentucky law requires that a city with a population greater than 100,000 be classified as a "first class" city. This reclassification would trigger several changes in the existing municipal government structure. First, it would require that the city shift from its current city manager form of government to a strong mayor form of government. With the controversy surrounding the city government corruption charges and increased distrust of the elected city officials, this fact did not play well with the voters. Second, the reclassification would void the city/county merger legislation, which excluded counties containing cities of the first class.[5] Third, the structure of the representation would change from a five-member commission to a twelve-member council. These twelve members would be required to reside

Table 6.5 Kentucky City Classifications

Class	Population
First	100,000 or more
Second	20,000–99,999
Third	8,000–19,999
Fourth	3,000–7,999
Fifth	1,000–2,999
Sixth	999 or less

Source: U.S. Bureau of the Census.

in specific districts; however, they would still be elected at large. Also, the nonpartisan elected officials would be required to run on a partisan ticket (Lyons 1977).

The Promises of Consolidation

Unlike many consolidation efforts, the Lexington/Fayette merger campaign did not tout the efficiencies that would be gained through consolidation—that is, efficiencies defined as lower per capita expenditures. In this case, the positive aspects of consolidation laid out by its proponents during the campaign can be characterized as a single tax/benefit argument. The "threat" of annexation was the main thrust of the campaign, and it is the main issue to analyze to determine if there were follow-through. This is more than looking at a picture of the boundaries before and after to see that the discontinuity of the boundaries disappears after the merger. The annexation issue was at its base a tax/benefit issue. So we can look at the revenue and expenditure patterns to see the impact.

Table 6.6 shows the combined expenditures per capita and the total combined expenditures of both Lexington/Fayette and Louisville/Jefferson from 1967 to 1985. The first year of the merged government was 1974.

Table 6.6 Changes in Combined Expenditures, 1967–85

Jurisdiction	1967	1973	1967–73 % Increase	1974	1975	1985	1975–85 % Increase
Lexington/ Fayette County	$118.91	$164.45	38	$128.74	$273.85	$647.26	136
Louisville/ Jefferson County	$183.05	$259.39	42	$340.47	$359.82	$609.74	69
Total combined expenditures (thousands)							
Lexington/ Fayette County	$15,685	$28,667	82	$23,765	$50,554	$136,022	169
Louisville/ Jefferson County	$111,831	$180,292	61	$239,128	$252,721	$416,276	65

Source: U.S. Bureau of the Census.

In that year we observe a slight decrease in expenditures for Lexington/Fayette followed by a dramatic increase over the next ten years. The slight dip in expenditures could be the result of the delay in fully implementing the merger during the first year. This was due to a lawsuit filed to test the validity of the new government (Lyons 1977). In 1975, there was a dramatic increase in expenditures with a much less dramatic increase in the years 1976 to 1985. This increase in expenditures may indicate that the level of service provision was far below what was needed, and it could also be an indication of the inefficiencies of the government structure before the merger. If the level of service was not sufficient to meet the demand of the voters, then the increase in expenditures could well be the revealed preferences of the citizens of Lexington/Fayette County. This is not to say that, given all possible alternatives, this is the one the voters would have chosen. Rather, the voters were given two alternatives in Lexington/Fayette County: annexation with no guarantee of increases in services with the increase in taxes, or a merger that linked tax increases with service increases. These increased expenditures and increased service levels are likely the revealed preferences of the citizens of Lexington/Fayette County at the new tax level.

The new governmental jurisdiction eliminated the disjointedness of the previous city–county boundary. The merger delivered as promised in this case. There is no longer a spillover of benefits to the county from city services, for example, public safety. As we shall see in the analysis of budget data below, there may have been substantial underprovision of public services to these areas, as evidenced by the dramatic increase in public expenditures after the merger.

Taxes and Benefits

The annexation issue that was the catalyst behind the merger movement in Lexington/Fayette County was essentially a tax/benefit issue. Those residents who were going to have their properties annexed into the City of Lexington faced increased taxes without increased services. The analysis of this issue will focus on the change in budgetary levels of major budget categories before and after the merger as compared with the budget levels for Louisville/Jefferson County during the same period. The merger of the City of Lexington and Fayette County was accompanied by a dramatic rise in budget levels for all the major categories.

Immediately following the merger, Lexington/Fayette County experienced a large shift upward in expenditures. This was due to the nearly doubling in the population receiving urban services. Large increases in expenditures for all urban services were needed to generate services for the developed areas not previously part of the City of Lexington. This meant large capital outlays and increases in manpower, especially in police and fire, which require a large investment in training for new personnel. Figures 6.2 and 6.3 show the spike in general and total expenditures in 1975, respectively, the second year of the merger and the first budget put together by the newly formed council.

If we examine the expenditure increases more closely, we can see why such a large total increase occurred. Figure 6.4 shows the solid waste expenditures per capita from 1967 to 1985. The large increase can be seen in fiscal year 1975, followed by further increases, with a drop in 1983. Solid waste, although not typically the largest portion of a municipal budget, was an urban service that was greatly expanded after the merger. The expansion of solid waste services into the developed areas outside the old city boundary required a larger-than-typical capital outlay and an increase in personnel to cover the new collection routes. Recall that some of the areas could choose not to receive solid waste service, so the expansion of this service may have taken longer. This may be why we see the increase in expenditures spread out over several years. An increase in expenditures was not observed in Louisville/Jefferson County during this same period.

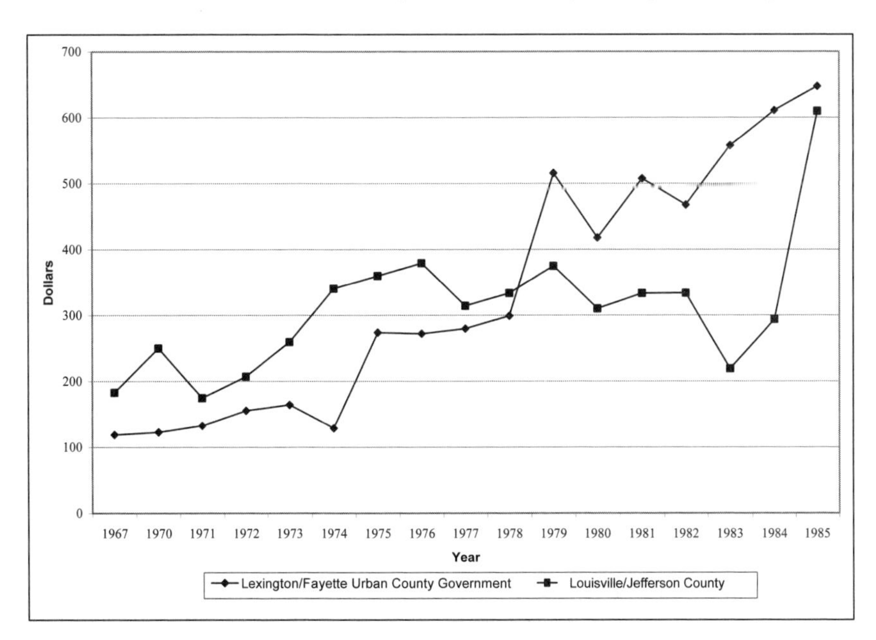

Figure 6.2 Per Capita General Expenditures
Source: U.S. Bureau of the Census.

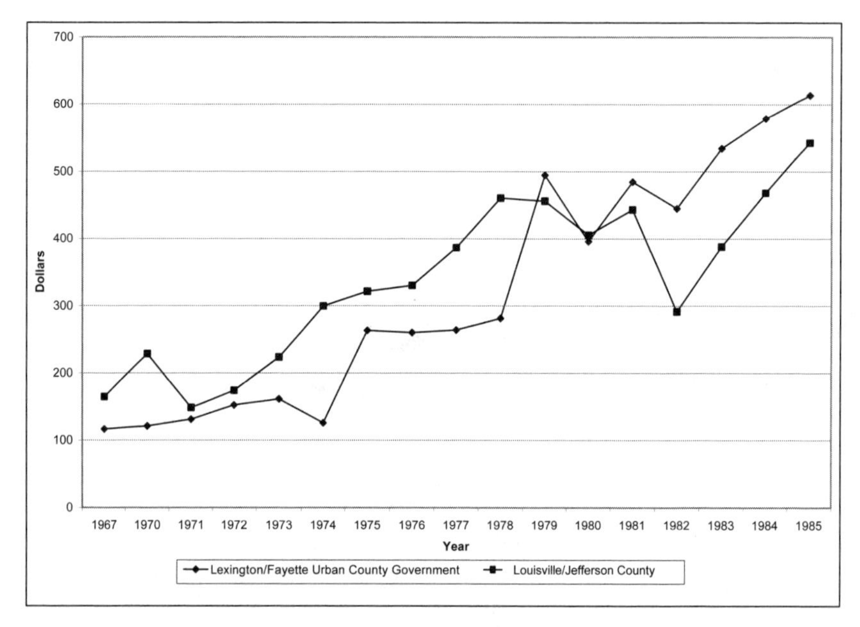

Figure 6.3 Per Capita Total Expenditures
Source: U.S. Bureau of the Census.

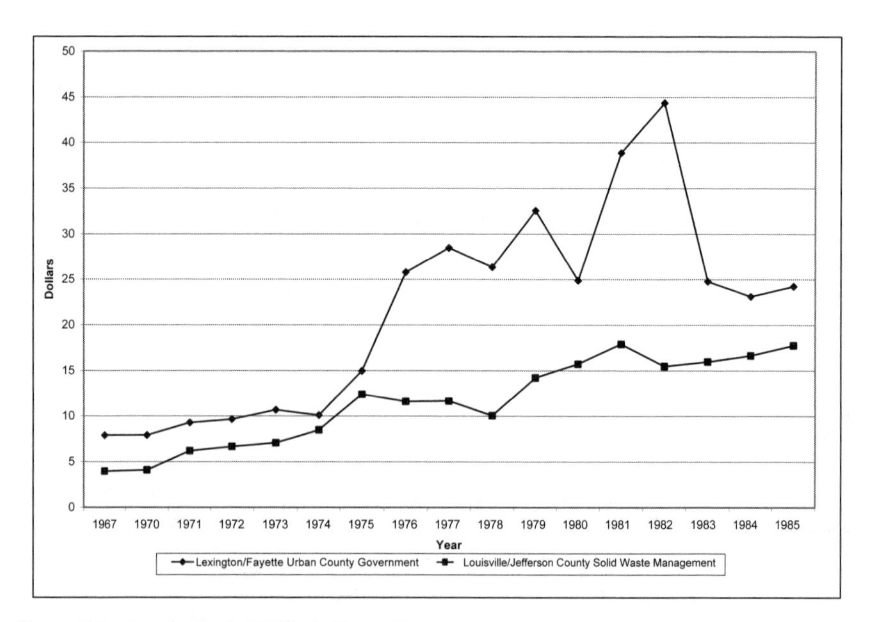

Figure 6.4 Per Capita Solid Waste Expenditures
Source: U.S. Bureau of the Census.

In figure 6.5 there is the initial spike in police expenditures in 1975, but the drop-off in police expenditures after that year is not observed in fire expenditures (figure 6.6). This could have been because the expansion of fire service was extremely capital intensive, causing the city to finance, through borrowing, some or most of the construction of new fire stations and fire apparatus. These new fire stations took time to build, and an increase in manpower would have to accompany the construction of the new stations. This would explain why the initial spike was not as great as with police expenditures but was sustained for a longer period. In fact, this growth in fire expenditures continued on past 1985 due to the rapid growth of the population.

This same scenario explains the same sort of pattern in capital expenditures. As we see in figure 6.7, there is an initial spike in capital outlays following the merger that is sustained over time. The initial increase in capital expenditures lags about two years behind fire expenditures. This can also be explained by the expansion of fire service and its high capitalcosts. Unlike the purchase of additional squad cars, and training for new police officers, fire station and fire apparatus costs would not be borne immediately; the construction and manufacturing time would have to be taken into account.[6] The expenditure pattern in Louisville/Jefferson County seemed to be correlated more directly with federal revenue sharing than in the Lexington/Fayette case.

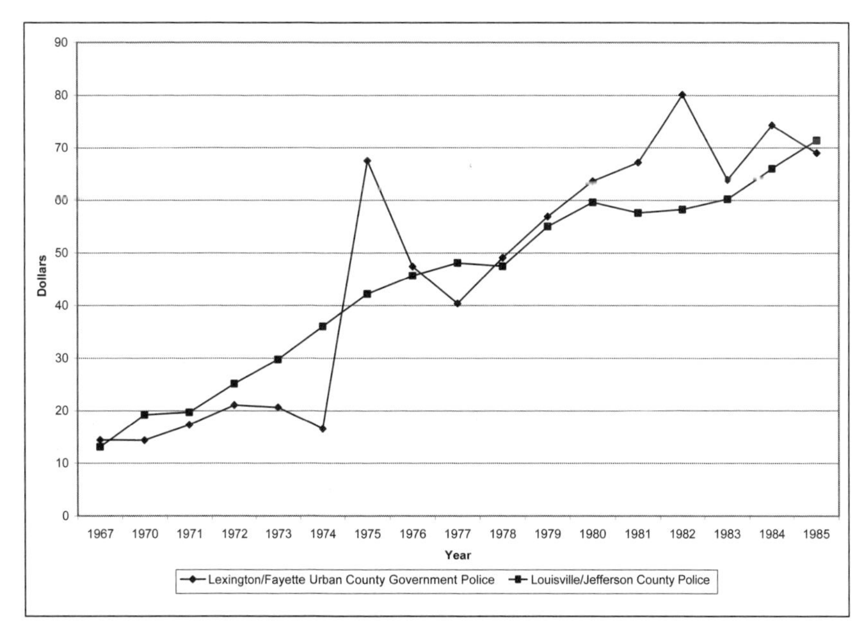

Figure 6.5 Per Capita Police Expenditures
Source: U.S. Bureau of the Census.

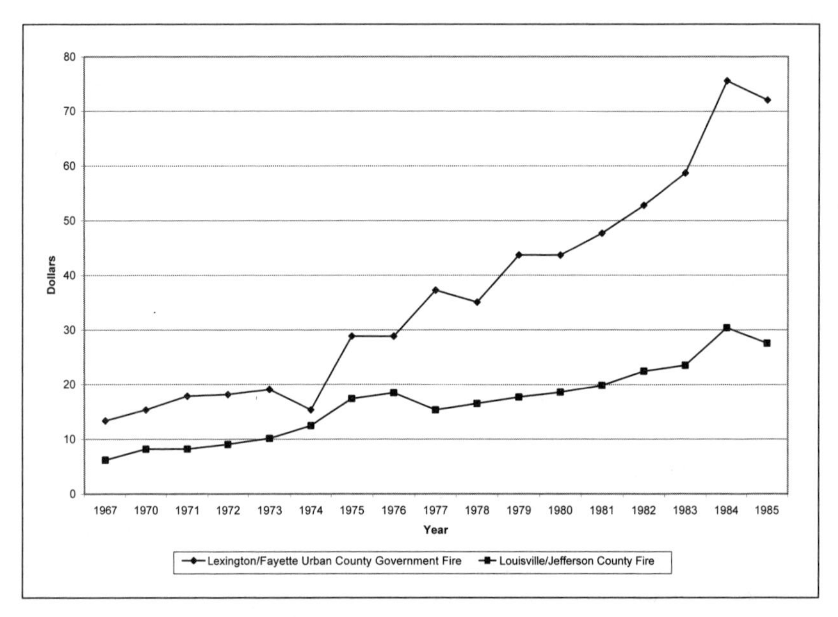

Figure 6.6 Per Capita Fire Expenditures

Source: U.S. Bureau of the Census.

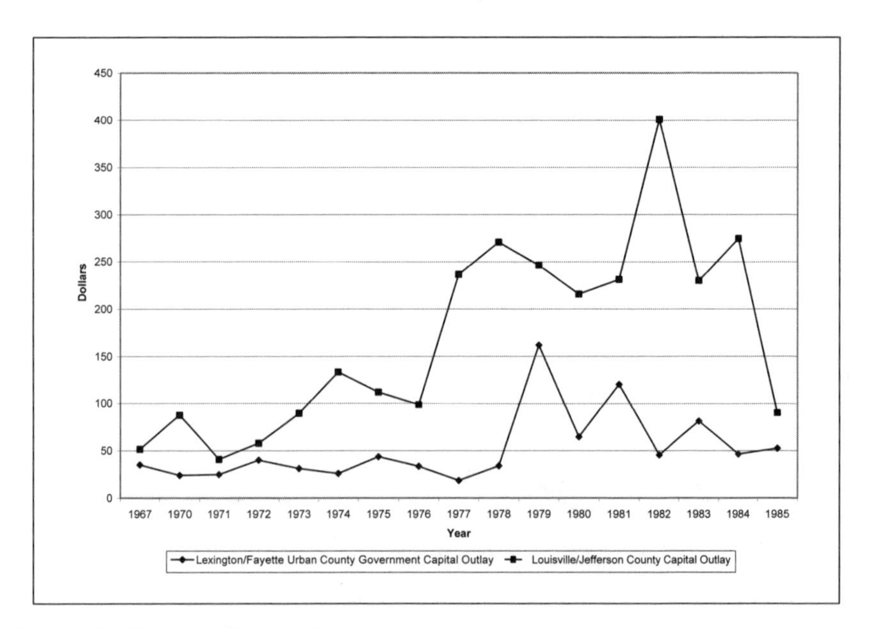

Figure 6.7 Per Capita Capital Outlays

Source: U.S. Bureau of the Census.

In figures 6.8 and 6.9, it is apparent that intergovernmental revenue makes up a much greater proportion of the total revenue in the Louisville/Jefferson case. One of the largest effects on the financial condition of Lexington/Fayette was the change in the tax base. In figure 6.8 the per capita property tax, income tax, and intergovernmental revenue for Louisville/Jefferson are shown as a percentage of total revenue. During the period in question there is little variation in the percentage of total revenue made up by any one source, with the exception of a slight increase in intergovernmental revenues in the mid-1970s. This is not the case for Lexington/Fayette (figure 6.9).

In the seven-year period before the merger, we observe a steady decline of around 10 percent of total revenue from property tax. In the period following the merger, property tax as a proportion of total revenue also saw a reduction to just under 15 percent in 1985. This equated to a 25 percent decrease from the year of the merger to 1985, with the largest portion of that decrease, 20 percent, coming in the first year. This change in the tax base can be explained by the expansion of the occupation license fee (OLF) base. The OLF is often referred to as the local income tax, and it is listed as such in the Census data used for this study. During this period only cities of specific classes were allowed to levy an OLF. Counties did not have this authority, but the city–county merger legislation granted this power to city–county governments. With the inclusion of about 100,000 new residents in the newly formed government, the largest source of revenue more than doubled in just one year. In figure 6.10 the income tax levels are shown for

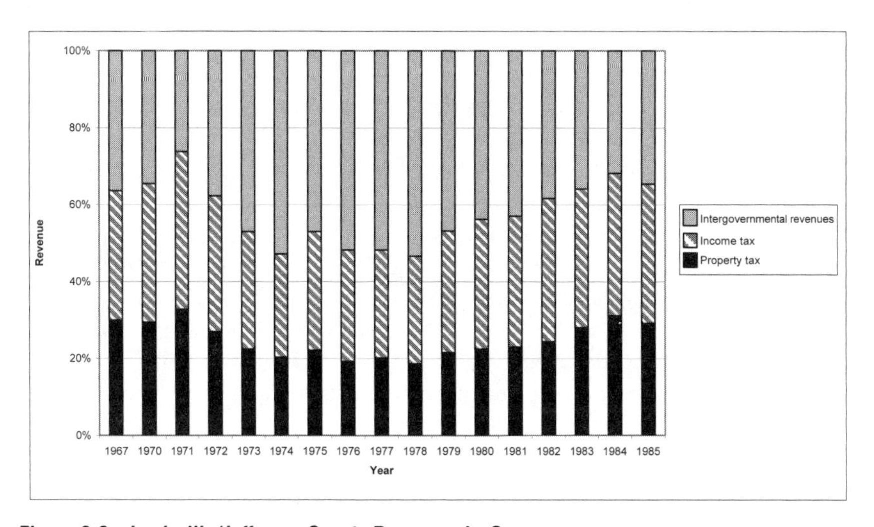

Figure 6.8 Louisville/Jefferson County Revenues by Source
Source: U.S. Bureau of the Census.

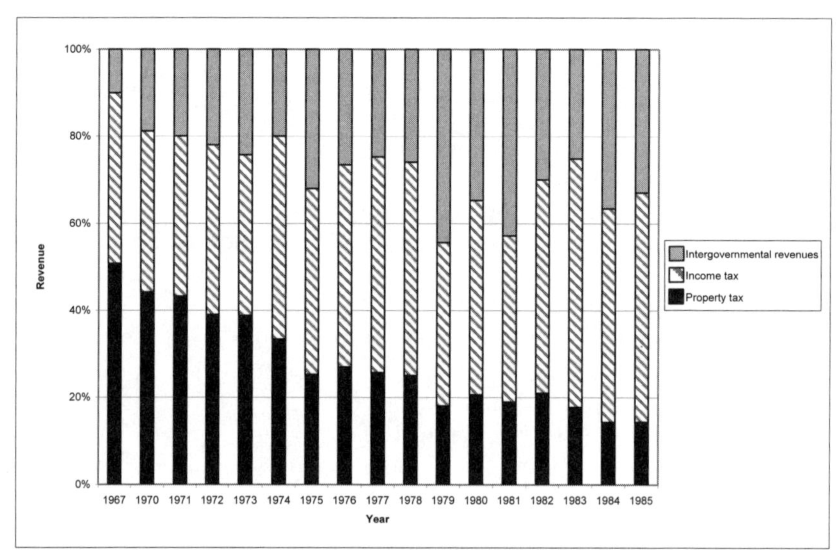

Figure 6.9 Lexington/Fayette Urban County Government Revenue by Source
Source: U.S. Bureau of the Census.

both Louisville/Jefferson County and Lexington/Fayette County. A spike in the level of revenue is observed in 1975 for Lexington/Fayette County. A similar spike in revenue is not seen for Louisville/Jefferson County, which has a smoother (albeit higher) rate of change over the period.

A similar story can be told for Lexington/Fayette County with regard to own source revenues. There should have been a spike in own source revenues attributable to the expansion of the OLF base; however, this spike is not apparent (figure 6.11). Discounting the temporary drop in 1974, the change from 1973 to 1975 is very similar to the increase in Louisville/Jefferson County during the same period. This may be attributable to the influx of general and special revenue sharing dollars that occurred in the same period (figure 6.8). There is not a similar influx in Lexington/Fayette County (figure 6.9).

The question is whether or not the rise in total revenue in Fayette County (figure 6.12) can be attributable to the effects of the merger or to the increase in per capita personal income for both cities (figure 6.13). In both Lexington/Fayette County and Louisville/Jefferson County, there was steady growth in per capita personal income without any anomalies in 1975. Table 6.7 shows various rankings of the per capita expenditures for Louisville/Jefferson County during the study period. Each budget category is ranked from highest to lowest by expenditure. This ranking gives us an idea of the spending priorities of the local governments. It is worth noting that the major changes in the ranking came during the mid-1980s, which was at

(Text continues on p. 157)

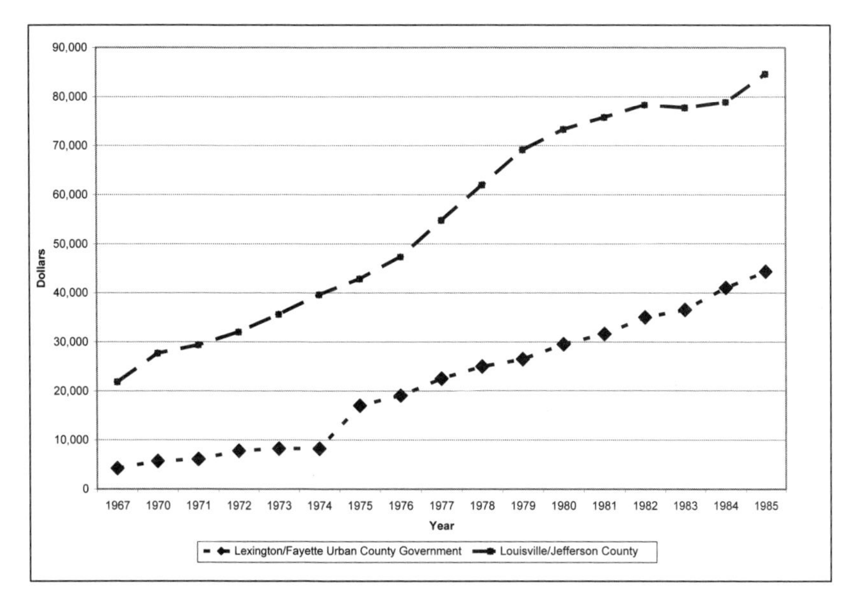

Figure 6.10 Income Tax Revenue
Source: U.S. Bureau of the Census.

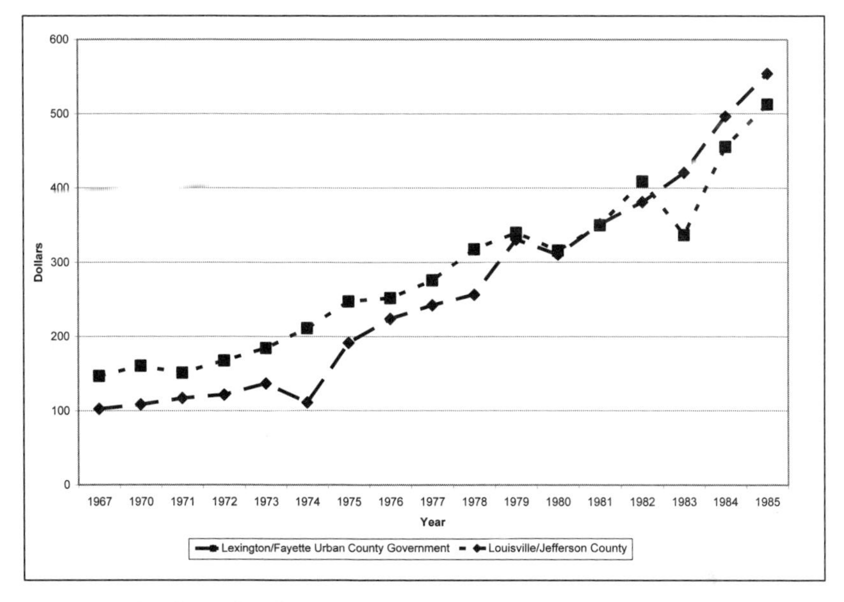

Figure 6.11 Per Capita Own Source Revenue
Source: U.S. Bureau of the Census.

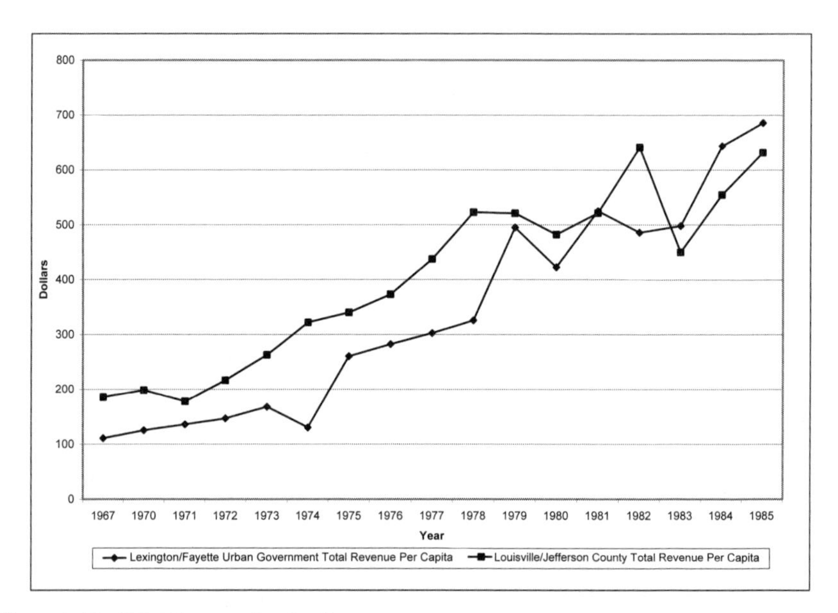

Figure 6.12 Total Revenue Per Capita
Source: U.S. Bureau of the Census.

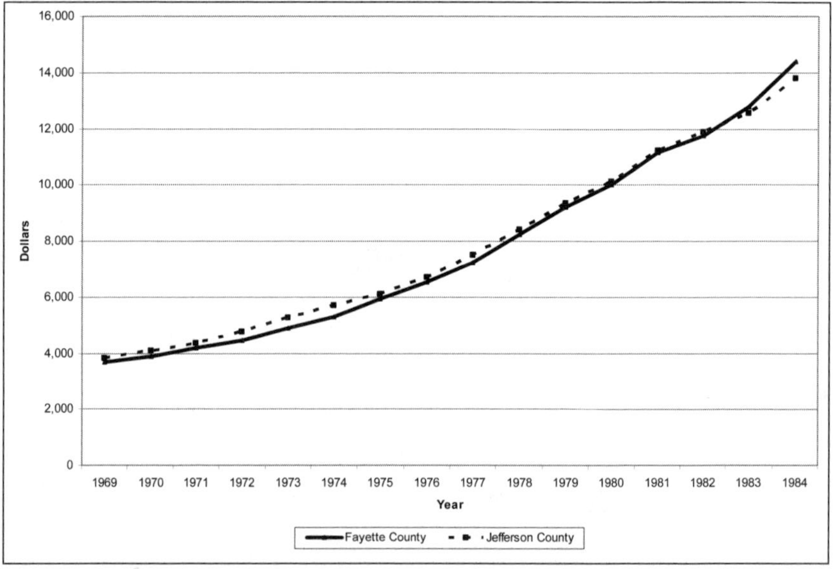

Figure 6.13 Per Capita Personal Income
Source: U.S. Bureau of the Census.

Table 6.7 Expenditures per Capita and Ranking by Function, Louisville/Jefferson County (dollars)

Function	Expenditures, 1967	Ranking, 1967	Expenditures, 1973	Ranking, 1973	Expenditures, 1974	Ranking, 1974	Expenditures, 1985	Ranking, 1985
Total	77.97		154.8		192.69		373.86	
Sewers	11.36	3	36.94	1	48.72	1	0.00	11
Police	13.11	2	29.74	2	36.01	2	71.36	2
Hospitals	13.26	1	21.47	3	25.65	3	9.94	9
Parks and recreation	7.01	5	15.38	4	19.70	4	19.81	7
Debt service	8.74	4	13.63	5	15.55	5	148.32	1
Fire	6.16	6	10.11	6	12.45	6	27.53	3
Solid waste	3.96	9	7.06	7	8.47	8	17.74	8
Central staff	3.70	10	6.27	8	8.76	7	6.28	10
Health	4.62	7	5.74	9	6.77	9	27.99	4
Social services	4.43	8	4.42	10	6.03	10	23.68	5
Corrections	1.62	11	4.04	11	4.58	11	21.21	6

Source: U.S. Bureau of the Census.

Table 6.8 Expenditures per Capita and Ranking by Function, Lexington-Fayette County (dollars)

Function	Expenditures, 1967	Ranking, 1967	Expenditures, 1973	Ranking, 1973	Expenditures, 1974	Ranking, 1974	Expenditures, 1985	Ranking, 1985
Total	75.41		106.76		78.94		386.15	
Police	14.43	2	20.65	1	16.54	2	68.97	2
Fire	13.34	3	19.07	2	15.31	3	72.05	1
Sewers	16.88	1	18.55	3	17.52	1	24.20	8
Solid waste	7.88	4	10.67	4	10.08	4	24.22	7
Debt service	7.66	5	10.31	5	9.59	5	63.45	3
Health	3.59	7	8.31	6	1.33	8	49.90	4
Parks and recreation	4.94	6	7.49	7	4.71	6	30.66	6
Central staff	2.96	9	5.81	8	2.78	7	46.88	5
Social services	3.37	8	4.57	9	1.08	9	14.97	9

Source: U.S. Bureau of the Census.

the end of the study period. Compared with the Lexington/Fayette data during the same period, however, the Louisville/Jefferson ranking seems more unstable. In table 6.8 we can see that the rankings in Lexington/Fayette are more stable during the period, indicating that the extreme increases in expenditures did not bring with it a substantial reshuffling of budget priorities. Police, fire, and sewers remain high priorities (ranked 1–3 during the 1967–85 period), with solid waste, debt service, and parks generally in the next tier of priorities (ranked 4–6).

Conclusions

Some literature on city/county consolidation has found that the success of such an effort relies more on political and social factors than on efficiencies and good government (Wanamaker and Marando 1972). This seems to be the case in Lexington/Fayette County, with the success of the merger having to do with an annexation of developed areas on the fringes of the city boundary. The threat of increased taxes without increased services caused residents in these areas to favor merger over annexation. Merger would bring with it additional taxation—but only when additional services were added. This was the critical tax/benefit argument.

The factors that usually work against a consolidation effort did not have the same effect in the Lexington/Fayette case. Overall, the members of the minority community supported the merger, even though it would dilute their voting power. Unlike the inevitable annexation of nearly 100,000 new residents, however, consolidation would bring with it district representation with the members elected by districts rather than under the previous at-large system. This all but guaranteed minority control of two, and possibly three, seats on the governing council.

As summarized in table 6.9, there is no evidence that the merger led to increased government efficiency (H1), and there is only weak evidence that it led to more effective economic development than its comparison city/county (H2). The most relevant column in table 6.9 is H3, however; the merger fulfilled a host of other promises that were more central to the residents and voters of the city and county.

When a budgetary analysis was done for the years before and after the merger, a dramatic increase in per capita expenditures was observed. If the efficiency of government services is measured in per capita expenditures as compared with another city in the same state, then the newly formed Lexington/Fayette County consolidated government fails in this regard.

Table 6.9 Summary of the Lexington/Fayetteville County Case

Overall Assessment of Evidence	H1: Efficiency	H2: Economic Development	H3: Other Promises
Not enough data available			
No evidence	☑		
Weak		☑	
Moderate			
Strong			☑

Per capita expenditures exceeded those of the comparable city chosen for this study. Because of this, it is fortunate that the efficiency argument was not made during the campaign for the merger. This makes sense because the consolidation movement stemmed from an issue of rapid population growth that had led to a court-ordered annexation of the developed areas outside the city limits. Population was going to increase, requiring expanded services. It was a foregone conclusion that there would have to be an increase in expenditures to accommodate these new residents. What is puzzling is the proportion of this increase. From the year following the merger, 1975 to 1985, there was a 236 percent increase in per capita expenditures. If the year of the merger, 1974, is included in this analysis, then the increase is more than 400 percent. Some of the increase can be accounted for by the need to expand services quickly. This meant purchasing new equipment, constructing new buildings, and the like, which would drive up expenditures in the short run. But the dramatic increase was sustained over the study period.

Perhaps an explanation can be found in the literature on optimal taxation. If we consider Samuelson conditions and the optimum level of public expenditures, we may be able to get at why, in the Lexington/Fayette County case, expenditures increased so dramatically. When it comes to public expenditures, we cannot know the preferences of the median voter in Lexington/Fayette County. We do know that the county's voters approved consolidation and thus essentially agreed to increases in both the property tax and the payroll tax. We do not know the demand function for public goods, however, because the residents who resided outside the old city limits would now be paying taxes for full urban services. We can speculate that the voters' preferences did not change as dramatically as the increased expenditures might suggest. It is more likely that the increased production of public services was supply driven. Sudden windfalls of revenue from consolidation lead to an extraordinary increase in expenditures by the local government (Goodman and Bergstrom 1973).

This did not necessarily mean that the residents of Lexington/Fayette County were subject to a Leviathan local government that robbed them of tax and service package choices that a more fragmented metropolitan government might offer. A study by Lowery and Lyons (1989) found that the variation in taxing districts and the ability of neighborhoods to opt out of certain government services allowed for more choice than was found in Louisville/Jefferson County.[7]

This idea that consolidation brought about overexpenditures on public services warrants further investigation. The literature on consolidation has shown that arguments for efficiency rarely lead to a successful consolidation vote. When we examine the Lexington/Fayette case, we see that all the factors of a successful consolidation came together in near perfect harmony; yet under the standard measures of government service provision efficiency, it failed. It would be interesting to investigate whether or not, in the preconsolidation government structure, the level of public service production was below the optimal and whether or not it was below the desired level of the median voter. This would mean that the median voter's demand for services may have been the driving force behind the consolidation success. That is to say, the new urban service area's residents may have desired services they were not getting before the merger.

Alternatively, it may have been a case of the lesser of two evils—being faced with a forced annexation made it apparent that the marginal tax level was going to increase, causing the median voters to favor consolidation. The increased revenue gave the local government the incentive to increase services beyond what may have been the optimal level, thus making the expenditure increases a supply-driven phenomenon.

Notes

1. Louisville/Jefferson County did merge in 2001.
2. Today the development has pushed out beyond New Circle Road. Man-O-War Boulevard was built as an outer concentric circle but has only been constructed halfway around the city.
3. The leader of this faction on the city commission was involved in much controversy that led to an indictment on charges of accepting bribes and conspiracy to commit bribery. The charges of corruption and mismanagement in the city government accentuated the crisis climate of the time.
4. Residents in these areas could not opt out of nonexcludable services, e.g., public safety.
5. The only other city of the first class was Louisville.

6. Most new fire trucks are made to order and can sometimes take from a year to eighteen months to be delivered from the manufacturer.
7. The Louisville/Jefferson County metropolitan area consists of dozens of incorporated municipalities, each with its own tax and service packages.

References

Goodman, Theodore C., and Robert P. Bergstrom. 1973. Private Demands for Public Goods. *American Economic Review* 63, no. 3:280–96.

Kenny, John E., and Lawrence W. Filer. 1980. Voter Reaction to City–County Consolidation Referenda. *Journal of Law and Economics* 23, no. 1:179–90.

Leland, Suzanne, and Kurt Thurmaier. 2004. Introduction. In *Case Studies of City–County Consolidation*, ed. Suzanne Leland and Kurt Thurmaier. Armonk, NY: M. E. Sharpe.

———. 2005. When Efficiency Is Unbelievable: Normative Lessons from 30 Years of City–County Consolidations. *Public Administration Review* 65, no. 4:475–89.

Lowery, W. E., and David Lyons. 1989. Government Fragmentation versus Consolidation: Five Public Choice Myths about How to Create Informed, Involved, and Happy Citizens. *Public Administration Review* 49, no. 6:533–43.

Lyons, W. E. 1977. *The Politics of City County Merger.* Lexington: University Press of Kentucky.

Wanamaker, Vincent L., and Daniel K. Marando. 1972. Political & Social Variables in City–County Consolidation Referenda. *Polity* 4, no. 4:512–22.

→ 7 ←

From Company Town to Consolidated Government

The Western-Style Consolidation of Butte and Silver Bow County, Montana

Susan Keim and Justin Marlowe

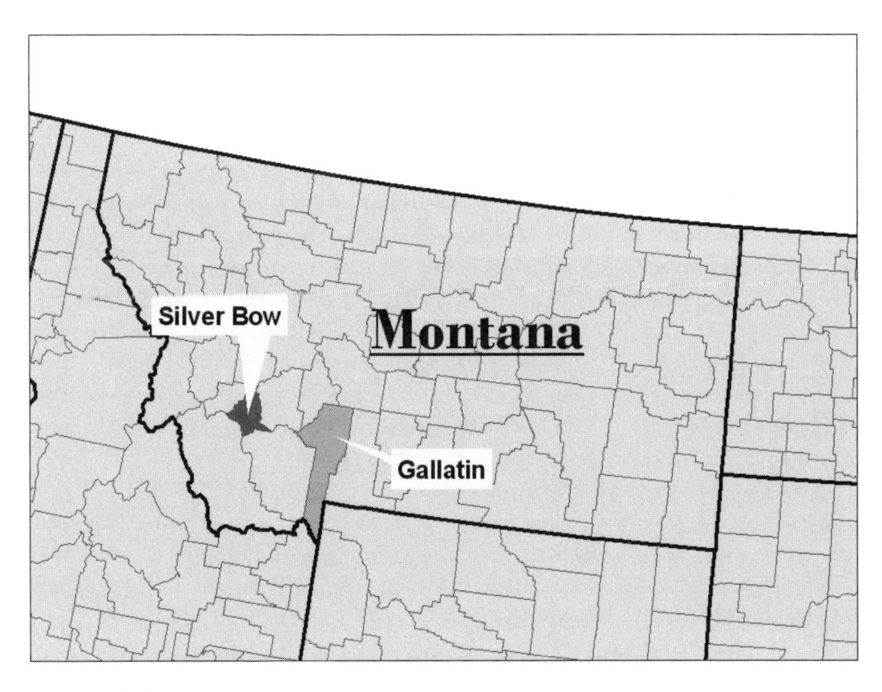

Map 7 Locations of Silver Bow County and Gallatin County, Montana
Source: U.S. Bureau of the Census.

Montana has a reputation as part of the rough-and-tumble Wild West. Its city of Butte certainly fits in this category. After being established by copper and silver miners in the early 1870s, Butte grew overnight into a bustling tent city as word of the miners' discoveries got out. Its booming downtown provided everything the miners and mining companies could need, including saloons and a red light district. This included America's longest-running brothel, in operation from 1890 to 1982 right in the heart of the mining district. The mines actually produced copper, silver, and gold, although copper did not become popular until electricity gained a foothold after World War I. By the 1920s Butte was considered one of the most prosperous cities in the country.

Government and politics in Butte were historically dominated by the mining interests. The mines provided the city's major employment sources and benefits. Other employers merely supported the mines. Needing water for its operation, the mining company even provided the city's water. Until the 1990s there was not a water utility in Butte. The power afforded the mining interests naturally gave rise to ongoing political tensions between the mining elite and everyone else. These political dynamics of populists versus elites enabled a classic form of machine politics to dominate the political scene.

A thorough search of Butte newspaper archives revealed four city–county consolidation elections of Butte and Silver Bow County governments during a period of a little more than fifty years beginning in 1924. Although the issue of finances arose in each election and the opposition used the political machine to scare off voters, the players were not consistent. It was rather like a series of four random elections rather than a concerted push for consolidation during a fifty-year period. Residents interviewed for this study did not actually know how many attempts were made at consolidation, and newspaper stories from the 1960s vaguely elude to one earlier attempt at consolidation, but the exact date was unknown—indicating that consistent reasons and players in consolidation attempts did not carry over through the years.

When the voters finally approved consolidation in 1976, it was actually the State of Montana that had cleared the way for consolidation through a constitutional provision, rather than a homegrown attempt at city–county consolidation. It was a narrow window of opportunity involving the state provision and a county commission kickback scandal that sealed the fate of city–county consolidation for Butte and Silver Bow County. In the end, the power structure shifted only enough to capture the consolidated government rather than the consolidated government reforming the community's political power structure.

Early Consolidation Efforts

All was not rosy in Butte or Silver Bow County. With its legacy of having been founded overnight, Butte was always rumored to have corruption, patronage, and machine politics within its government. In 1924, the *Butte Miner* claimed that the city was infamous for gambling, prostitution, and liquor violations. Reformists at that time pushed for a city–county merger to save the city from financial ruin. The case was taken to the Montana Supreme Court, where on April 27, 1924, the voters' option to consolidate was upheld.

The argument was between the "tax eaters" and the "taxpayers"—or administrative wastefulness versus administrative economy as championed by consolidation proponents. With a tight election turnaround of two weeks, both proconsolidation and anticonsolidation forces were hoping the other side would not gather momentum for an election victory. The mine was not out in front in the election, either as an opponent or proponent. Rather, the political machine worked to subvert the election. On May 13, 1924, the city of Butte passed consolidation but the county defeated it. Thus, overall, it failed.

In the years that followed, things in Butte and Silver Bow County did not get much better. In seven years city–county consolidation was once again on the ballot. This time the forces of the Depression played a great part in the rhetoric of the consolidation campaign. On March 1, 1931, reformers once again began a city–county consolidation plan and a fight for an "honest" election. Once again, the political machine worked against consolidation. The *Montana Standard* (1931c) indicated that voters were worried that fraud would follow the misrepresentation of city–county consolidation to the voters.

Consolidation opponents were skilled in using fear as the election weapon. On March 8, 1931, the *Montana Standard* (1931b) reported:

> Even the destitute in Butte have a vote. And the destitute who have applied for aid in these days of stress and unemployment have felt the pressure of the opponents of consolidation. They have been told that if consolidation is adopted, there will be no more poor funds and no more widow's pensions. And persons in dire extremity have been turned away with the statement that preparations for the election make it impossible to investigate further cases of distress at this time. What a sordid story of deceit and imposition, of knavery and heartlessness! Everybody knows

> that the poor funds and the widow's pension funds are not affected in the remotest degree by the consolidation act.

Voters were frightened by the machine into voting against consolidation and used the country's Depression as the contributing factor to the failure of city–county consolidation.

Consolidationists were sure of victory if the election was fair. What they were not sure of was whether the election would be fair. In the end, they did not feel it was a fair election because opponents used fear of the Depression as a weapon and untruths to counteract the proponents in the election. Once again, opponents claimed victory as county voters came out in force to defeat consolidation while city voters approved it, but without enough votes to carry consolidation. On March 11, 1931, the headlines in the *Montana Standard* (1931a) read: "City–County Merger Proposal Defeated and City Favors Plan but Precincts in County Swamp It."

Opposition to consolidation appeared to gain steam. The difference in the 1924 election was 666 votes, but the difference in the 1931 election was 2,843 votes. Yet was that really the case? Voters could have just been scared into voting "no" by the opponents rather than actually being against consolidation.

The topic of city–county consolidation remained quiet for about thirty years. Until then, reformists could not gather enough momentum to mount another city–county consolidation campaign. On March 20, 1962, a committee of fifty citizens launched another movement for city–county consolidation. The Butte Chamber of Commerce and other civic elites supported consolidation. The chamber was supportive because a reform system of government would provide more opportunities for business to thrive, which they believed would decrease the power of the political machine.

Opponents said consolidation would mean the end of the two-party system, loss of access to elected officials, and "dictatorship" by a manager who would have been appointed by an elected nonpartisan commission. Proponents claimed consolidation would save substantial dollars and that government would be more efficient. Additionally, it was intimated that Butte and Silver Bow County never had a two-party system while the Democrats were in control (Butte–Silver Bow Public Archives).

On March 5, 1963, the voters once again reject consolidation with a tally of 10,359 against and 6,633 for consolidation. Things had not changed much. The *Montana Standard* reported that the consolidation election had aroused more interest than any issue to come before the Silver Bow County public since the 1931 city–county consolidation proposal was defeated (*Montana Standard,* January 5, 1964).

A Successful Attempt

In 1972, a newly passed Montana State Constitutional Provision required each community to revisit the configuration of its local government every ten years. Thus, on November 11, 1974, a Butte and Silver Bow Local Government Study Commission was elected. The elected commissioners could not have any link to local government. The commission was a highly sought after position, with forty-nine individuals vying for election. Fourteen individuals were elected to the commission (City of Butte Local Government Study Commission and the Silver Bow County Local Government Study Commission 1976).

Although members of the Local Government Study Commission were reviewing local government laws, the city of Butte was practically bankrupt. Newspaper reports from the *Montana Standard* continually addressed the city's budget shortfalls. There was a continuing loss of mining interests in Butte, with the decrease in the value of copper greatly affecting the city's coffers. At the same time, the Montana Standard reported that Silver Bow County's commissioners had awarded a paving contract without a bid (*Montana Standard* 1976). The total contract was for more than $10,000, but the county commissioners split the bid so that each of two partial bids fell under $10,000 and within the no-bid guidelines. One split bid was for $2,898 to grade and straighten less than a mile of Vue Road. The other bid was for $9,901 to pave 4.5 miles of that road. With the total bid at $12,799, it was hardly worth jeopardizing the future of the county commission.

Throughout the summer of 1976, the *Montana Standard* not only reported on the Local Government Study Commission but also on the Silver Bow Commission's alleged bid-rigging antics. The Silver Bow commissioners were charged with official misconduct and failing to advertise for bids on two contracts to circumvent statutory bidding requirements. The trial date was set for September 23, 1976, just six weeks before the city–county consolidation election. On October 4, 1976, the commissioners were found guilty, removed from office, and sentenced to $100 fines and one day in jail.

The Butte and Silver Bow County Local Government Study Commission presented its report on July 22, 1976, in the midst of the commission scandal, and it then had little more than three months to campaign for city–county consolidation. On November 2, 1976, voters in a nearly two-to-one margin approved the unification of the governments of the City of Butte and the County of Silver Bow. This created a twelve-member council of commissioners and an elected chief executive officer functioning as a strong mayor, and it retained most elected officials. This particular election was held during the 1976 presidential election, in which then–Georgia governor Jimmy Carter campaigned on a platform of change that likely resonated with proconsolidation voters.

Conversations with two longtime county officials interviewed for this study indicated that the guilty verdict of the commissioners, compounded with the perception of machine politics and a corrupt police and fire department, gave rise to a voter mentality of "Throw the rascals out!" Another official saw the same events as "the stars aligning so the change in the form of government would pass."

These two county executives explained their take on the four additional reasons that city–county consolidation finally passed in Butte and Silver Bow. First, no one who served in local government could serve on the Local Government Study Commission. Therefore, there was no undue influence from elected officials in the process. Second, outsiders to local government were elected as commissioners. They were level-headed and calm while examining options for the commission. Third, the commissioners fought hard to hold on to elected positions within consolidation. Elected positions did not become appointed positions. Finally, the commissioners' scandal and conviction was the icing on the cake for the commission. Voters were eager to get rid of a county commission that was so corrupt.

Both individuals concede that city–county consolidation has been a great thing. The city was small, with no industrial base, and it would have starved without city–county consolidation. Neither felt that the City of Butte or the County of Silver Bow would have survived into the twenty-first century without consolidation.

But was consolidation good for both Butte and Silver Bow? Were the promises made by the Local Government Study Commission kept? The advantages presented by consolidation proponents were (1) unified governmental administration to provide effective leadership for areawide policy and development, (2) simplifying existing governmental structure, (3) achievement of economy and efficiency as a result of a single governmental structure, and (4) a council of part-time commissioners for legislation, with a full-time chief executive for administration (City of Butte Local Government Study Commission and the Silver Bow County Local Government Study Commission 1976).

Methodology: Comparative Context

We selected the City of Bozeman and Gallatin County as our comparison case for several reasons. Perhaps most important, these jurisdictions are less than 90 miles from Butte/Silver Bow—an important consideration, given the distances between Montana's few urban centers. With Montana ranked as the fourth-largest state in the country geographically, it was important to provide regional consistency in this study. Both cases are located in the mountains, with Butte on the western edge of the continental divide and Bozeman at the northern gateway to Yellowstone National Park. Butte's major industry is mining, whereas Bozeman is more diversified, with nearly a hundred technology companies that have grown up over time. The two counties were also similar with respect to key demographic indicators. As shown in table 7.1 and in figures 7.1 and 7.2, both had roughly the same population, taxable property value, property tax mill rates, and total employment in the few years immediately preceding consolidation. Table 7.1 also illustrates that both counties were losing taxable value in the years preceding consolidation. Therefore, these jurisdictions were largely comparable on most typical consolidation-related characteristics.

There were, however, some critical differences. Perhaps most important is the general preconsolidation trajectory of the two communities. Silver Bow County lost population throughout the twenty years preceding consolidation, due largely to the outflow of population, resources, and jobs following the closing of its various mining operations. But Gallatin County's population increased by more than 30 percent during this same period due to the growing enrollment of Montana State University and the attraction of high-technology and manufacturing companies to the area.

Butte/Silver Bow County has an elected chief executive officer (CEO) who serves as the CEO of the city/county. The CEO informs the twelve member council of commissioners, who are elected in partisan district elections. There is no professional management of the city and county. Bozeman, conversely, is a professionally managed city with a five-member nonpartisan commission. The commissioner with the most votes becomes mayor. The city advertises an educated, licensed, and experienced staff as well as its vision, mission, and core values. The Gallatin County administrator's office was created in 2003. The county administrator reports to a three-member nonpartisan commission.

The size and scope of government services is another important distinguishing factor. In 1967 total government expenditures in Butte/Silver Bow County were approximately 30 percent higher than in Bozeman/Gallatin County, even though Silver Bow County's population was only 21 percent larger than Bozeman/Gallatin's. In other words, there is some rough evidence that Butte/Silver Bow County's government was inherently less efficient before consolidation. But despite these differences, we feel Bozeman/Gallatin County provides the best available within-state comparison.

Table 7.1 Countywide Taxable Value, Population, and Total Employment, 1970–2000

Measure and County	1970	1980	1970–80 % Change	1990	1980–90 % Change	2000	1990–2000 % Change
Taxable value							
Silver Bow County	$206,086,405	$122,161,814	–40.72	$62,578,572	–48.77	$74,127,993	18.46
Gallatin County	$145,906,034	$127,474,070	–12.63	$90,859,566	–27.72	$118,593,444	30.52
Population							
Silver Bow County	41,981	38,092	–9.26	33,941	–10.90	34,606	1.96
Gallatin County	32,505	42,865	31.87	50,463	17.73	67,831	34.42
Total employment							
Silver Bow County	16,442	17,238	4.84	16,267	–5.63	18,958	16.54
Gallatin County	13,396	21,797	64.07	31,978	46.71	51,586	61.32

Sources: Gallatin and Silver Bow counties, Montana Department of Commerce.

Note: Taxable value figures are in constant 2000 dollars.

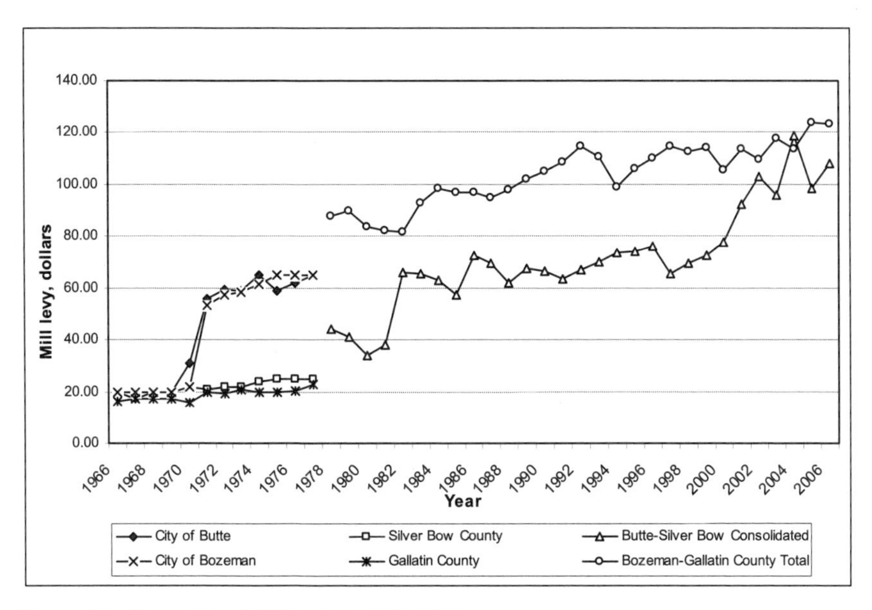

Figure 7.1 General Fund Mill Levies, 1966–2006
Sources: Assorted budget documents for jurisdictions.

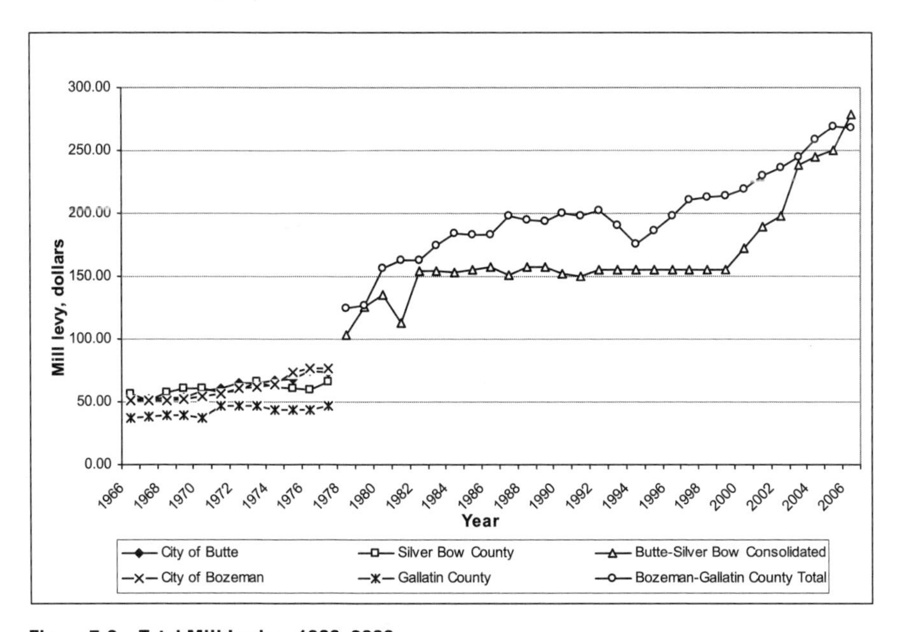

Figure 7.2 Total Mill Levies, 1966–2006
Sources: Assorted budget documents for jurisdictions.

Evaluating the Promises

Next, we evaluate the promises made by the proconsolidation campaign. They are twofold: leadership and government structure, and efficiency and economy.

Leadership and Government Structure

The consolidation of Butte and Silver Bow County did unify governmental administration. In effect there is one-stop shopping for services such as economic development. No longer does a developer, for example, need to get approval from the governmental entities of both the city and county.

Although the governmental structure was consolidated, it was not necessarily simplified. The change in the form of government actually rearranged structure around existing elected offices, keeping the existing partisan elections. No elected offices were eliminated or professionalized. In fact, consolidation most likely was approved because the elected positions were preserved. There are twenty-five local elected partisan positions in Butte/Silver Bow County. These include twelve county commissioners, the CEO, an assessor, a city judge, a clerk and recorder, a clerk of court, a coroner, a county attorney, a district court judge, a justice of the peace, a public administrator, a sheriff, a superintendent of schools, and a treasurer. It almost appears that where professionalism could be eliminated in the consolidated form of government, it was. This was highlighted by the elimination of the position of Butte police chief and the preservation of Silver Bow sheriff, an elected position requiring limited law enforcement expertise.

The structure of government did change for departments that could be functionally consolidated, including social services, planning, economic development, and public health. However, table 7.2 shows these as largely county functions that did not have to be merged during consolidation. Consolidation forced the merger of fire, law enforcement, parks and recreation, and public works. Additionally, there was a unique twist to the consolidation of services for both fire protection and law enforcement. The volunteer fire department in the County of Silver Bow maintained its autonomy because the fire department in Butte was professionalized. Thus today there are more than 150 volunteer firefighters along with 34 full-time firefighters in a consolidated fire department. During consolidation, law enforcement eliminated the police chief and preserved the position of sheriff. Police officers and sheriff's deputies were literally thrown together with no deliberate plan to consolidate or merge staffs. Pay rates for sheriff's deputies were brought up to the level of police officers, adding an immediate increase to law enforcement spending, which stabilized over time. Moreover, at the time of consolidation, water was supplied to the city and county privately by the copper mine, leaving no water utilities to consolidate.

The evidence on leadership concerns is mixed. The position of CEO is selected in a partisan election and has no requirement for professional public management credentials. To the extent that leadership is synonymous with "administrative values" such as efficiency and effectiveness, the consolidated government is no better equipped to lead. One cannot understate the leadership potential of a strong, elected executive, but at the moment there is little evidence of outcomes to that effect. The jurisdiction lacks a comprehensive strategic plan, county mission and/or vision statements, and any evidence of major economic development projects that would suggest the presence of strong and cohesive leadership.

Table 7.2 Level of Functional Consolidation of Services for the Experimental Case (E), Silver Bow County/Butte; and for the Comparison Case (C), Gallatin County/Bozeman

Service Function	10 Years before Consolidation		1 Year before Consolidation		10 Years after Consolidation	
	E	C	E	C	E	C
Fire protection	S	S	S	S	F[a]	S
Social services	CU	CU	CU	CU	F	CU
Law enforcement	S	S	S	S	F	S
Parks and recreation	S	S	S	S	F	S
Planning	CU	CU	CU	CU	F	CU
Economic development	CU	CU	CU	CU	F	CU
Utilities (water)	P	CI	P	CI	P	CI
Public works	S	S	S	S	F	S
Public health	CU	CU	CU	CU	F	CU

Source: Compiled by the authors.

Key: CI = city function only; CU = county function only; F = functional consolidation (city and county operations combined into single department); P = privatized; S = separately provided by both city and county.

[a] The Fire Department is "consolidated"—outlying areas rely on the county volunteer fire department.

Efficiency and Economy

We examined several indicators for evidence of consolidation promises kept in the areas of efficiency and economy. For evidence of improvements in the economy, we examined (1) population growth and (2) growth in taxable property value. For efficiency improvements, we examined (1) trends in property tax mill rates and (2) trends in per capita annual expenditures.

Consolidation appears to have had little impact on trends in total population and total employment in Silver Bow County. Its population declined throughout the 1960s and 1970s and continued to decline for nearly ten years after consolidation. Statewide population growth since the mid-1990s has helped to reverse this trend and restore the countywide population to levels not seen since the peak of its mining operations in the late 1940s. We observed a similar pattern for changes in total employment. But the statewide nature of this growth, along with the lag between consolidation and a reversal in the population trend, indicates that this population growth is largely unrelated to consolidation.

Municipal property tax bases across Montana eroded throughout the 1970s and 1980s. The Butte/Silver Bow consolidation did not mitigate this trend. As shown in table 7.1, in the twelve years following consolidation, countywide taxable value in Silver Bow actually declined at a much faster rate than in Gallatin. And when statewide property values began to appreciate in the early 1990s, they increased nearly 12 percent faster in Gallatin than in Silver Bow. Once again, there is little connection between consolidation and the robustness of the consolidated government's property tax base. Taken together, these provide little (if any) support for the claim that the consolidated government delivered on economy-related promises.

Curbing property tax growth was the main efficiency promise for the consolidation. It then follows that examining longitudinal changes in property tax millage provides the best single indicator of individual property tax burdens in these respective jurisdictions. This comparison is especially important because Montana has no local sales tax or local income tax, and the state government provides little if any support to municipalities. The property tax is the workhorse of Montana local government finance, and mill levies in turn provide a good indicator of overall local tax burdens.

Trends in property tax mill rates provide some evidence that this promise was kept. Figure 7.1 plots the total general fund mill rate for (1) the preconsolidation City of Butte, (2) preconsolidation Silver Bow County, (3) the City of Bozeman, (4) Gallatin County, (5) the sum of the individual levies for the City of Bozeman and Gallatin County, and (6) the Butte/Silver Bow consolidated government. As shown in the figure, both pairs of jurisdictions had nearly identical levies before consolidation. Following consolidation the general fund levy for the Butte/Silver Bow consolidated government increased sharply for six years but then remained generally stable for the next ten years. By 1994 it was 76 mills, 12 more than the 1984 mill rate. By contrast, from 1984 to 1994 the Bozeman/Gallatin combined general fund rate increased roughly 35 mills. Moreover, the consolidated rate was still significantly below the combined Bozeman/Gallatin rate.

Figure 7.2 reports these same trends for the total local government mill levies, which include millage for debt service, roads, and other earmarked purposes outside the general fund. Here the trend is roughly the same. Following an immediate postconsolidation increase, the total levy for the newly consolidated government did not fluctuate more than 7 mills throughout the 1980s and into the early 1990s. By contrast, the total combined levy for Bozeman/Gallatin County increased from 158 mills in 1982 to 202 mills in 1993. In addition, the consolidated rate was still significantly below the combined Bozeman/Gallatin rate.

Caution should be exercised in drawing inferences from these findings because of the previously mentioned trends in population and taxable value. Some of the increasing mill rate in Bozeman/Gallatin County was presumably due to its rapid population growth and the subsequent need for new infrastructure and expansions of municipal services. This inflow of new residents precludes any analysis of whether the consolidated government was more effective than the nonconsolidated government in managing the tax burden on existing residents. Moreover, the fact that mill rates in Butte/Silver Bow County increased even slightly while property values were declining suggests that the tax bill for a typical property owner might have increased throughout the 1980s and early 1990s. How large an increase this might have been is outside the scope of this analysis, but this general trend certainly indicates an absence of property tax relief for most residents under the new Butte/Silver Bow consolidated government. Nonetheless, to the extent that reducing growth in tax rates is evidence of an efficiency promise kept, Butte/Silver Bow was more successful than Bozeman/Gallatin.

It is also important to note that nearly thirty years after consolidation, mill rates in Butte/Silver Bow are now nearly identical to those in Bozeman/Gallatin. This adjustment followed a rapid increase in rates during the late 1990s and early 2000s. During this time rates in Butte/Silver Bow increased much faster than in Bozeman/Gallatin, ultimately resulting in comparable overall rates. This trend seems to indicate that in the long run, efficiency gains are subject to "inertia" and "backsliding."

Our second efficiency indicator is annual expenditures. Table 7.3 presents per capita annual expenditures in six key service areas for selected years from

Table 7.3 Per Capita Annual Expenditures

Jurisdiction and Type of Expenditure	1967 Expenditure ($)	1977 Expenditure ($)	1967–77 % Change	1985 Expenditure ($)	1977–85 % Change
Butte/Silver Bow County					
Debt service	7.77	5.65	–27.31	92.71	1,540.81
General government	60.18	137.71	128.82	7.14	–94.82
Miscellaneous	3.41	47.08	1,280.46	76.61	62.73
Public safety	82.02	169.50	106.65	185.29	9.32
Public works/ service	92.24	117.89	27.81	38.05	–67.72
Social and economic services/ public welfare	141.16	185.85	31.66	14.67	–92.11
Total	407.57	715.75	75.61	437.39	–38.89
Bozeman/Gallatin County					
Debt service	11.94	44.10	269.31	53.21	20.67
General government	49.06	85.19	73.67	101.90	19.61
Miscellaneous	8.27	28.23	241.30	7.23	–74.38
Public safety	58.70	92.18	57.05	123.88	34.38
Public works/ service	104.42	192.17	84.04	77.79	–59.52
Social and economic services/ public welfare	19.82	107.67	443.22	53.86	–49.98
Total	280.51	557.42	98.72	436.05	–21.77

Source: Montana State Examiner's Office and jurisdictions' budget documents. All data are constant 1985 dollars.

1967 through 1985.[1] This analysis identifies two basic trends. First, and perhaps most important, per capita spending in Butte/Silver Bow decreased following consolidation. Total expenditures (in constant 1985 dollars) were $437.39 per capita in 1985, compared with $715.75 per capita in 1977. Much of the spending reduction came from large decreases in spending on general government, public works, and social and economic services. Moreover, the consolidation apparently reversed what was previously a growth trend; total expenditures increased more than 75 percent in the nine years preceding consolidation but then decreased about 39 percent in the eight years after it.

By comparison, general government spending in Bozeman/Gallatin also increased in the years preceding the Butte/Silver Bow consolidation and decreased in the years following it, but the rate of postconsolidation spending reduction was not as great as in Butte/Silver Bow. For instance, the newly consolidated government reduced spending on public works, social and economic services, and total government by, respectively, 68 percent, 91 percent, and 39 percent, whereas Bozeman/Gallatin reduced spending in these same areas by 60 percent, 50 percent, and 22 percent. In addition, where spending did increase (in areas such as public safety, due to immediate increases in pay rates for sheriff's deputies), it increased at a faster rate in Bozeman/Gallatin. And perhaps most important, postconsolidation general fund spending in Butte/Silver Bow decreased about 95 percent but increased in Bozeman/Gallatin by about 20 percent. Some of that increase was likely due to its previously mentioned population growth. Nonetheless, at a glance, there is some evidence that the new consolidated government produced tangible efficiency gains.

However, table 7.3 also shows that this evidence of new efficiencies should be tempered by the fact that the newly consolidated government immediately took on substantial new debt obligations. These new obligations account for much of the previously mentioned increase in the consolidated government's general fund and total mill levies, because new debt must be supported by new millage. They also call into question the long-term efficiency gains, and the long-term changes in government service delivery, resulting from consolidation. Borrowing money to upgrade infrastructure, invest in new plant and equipment, and expand services will certainly produce near-term efficiency gains. But in jurisdictions driven by the property tax such as these, debt service obligations can in some cases simply pass the cost of these near-term efficiencies along to future taxpayers. Long-term growth in the consolidated government's mill levies, as shown in figures 7.1 and 7.2, is certainly consistent with this "buy now/pay later" strategy. So although the consolidated government might have delivered new efficiencies in the near term, those efficiencies were undercut at least in part by long-term mill levy growth.

Conclusion

For Butte/Silver Bow County, the promise of consolidation did not alter basic elected partisan positions but rather rearranged the structure of the government around those positions. It is likely that one of the reasons consolidation was approved in Butte and Silver Bow is because the elected positions were preserved. Although the promise of unified governmental administration was kept, there is little evidence of consistent areawide policy and development. The number of partisan elected positions could be one of the most significant reasons why there is no areawide policy planning and development function.

In the end, there is little evidence of economic gains between consolidation and the robustness of Butte/Silver Bow County's property tax base (table 7.4). There is evidence that the consolidated government delivered on its promises of efficiency and economy in the near and intermediate (ten-year) terms, but it was unable to deliver in the long term because it took on substantial new debt. With time, that debt has undercut long-term efficiency gains. Consolidation did not bring about any true "structural" changes in how services are delivered, or in citizens' demands for services; it simply changed how Butte/Silver Bow collected and spent money in the near term.

However, we cannot discount the importance of short-term gains. The consolidation arguably kept Butte/Silver Bow solvent during a difficult fiscal period. In effect, it bought the jurisdiction enough time to capitalize on the growth in population and capital investment that Montana would soon experience. Consolidation may be one of the reasons that the Butte/Silver Bow community has mitigated a severe erosion of its economic base over the years and has begun to see some recent population and economic development growth. It may have also allowed the political structure to remain as the status quo.

Table 7.4 Summary of the Butte/Silver Bow County Case

Overall Assessment of Evidence	H1: Efficiency	H2: Economic Development	H3: Other Promises
Not enough data available			
No evidence		☑	
Weak			
Moderate	☑		☑
Strong			

Note

1. The accounting, reporting, and formatting requirements for Montana's local government budgets changed substantially during this period. We attempted to respond to those changes by disaggregating each budget into basic line items and then aggregating these items into the categories presented here. Nonetheless, small distortions in individual spending levels are likely, so the data for percentage changes should be interpreted with caution.

References

City of Butte Local Government Study Commission and the Silver Bow County Local Government Study Commission. 1976. *Final Report, Charter for Unification of Butte-Silver Bow Government.* Butte: City of Butte.

Montana Standard. 1931a. City–County Merger Proposal Defeated and City Favors Plan but Precincts in County Swamp It. March 11.

———. 1931b. Fight for Honest Election. March 8.

———. 1931c. Supporters of Consolidation Announce Many Gatherings. March 1.

———. 1976. County Commissioners Awarded Contract without Bid for Paving (Editorial). March 10.

8

The Case of Lynchburg and Moore County, Tennessee, Consolidation

Deborah A. Carroll, Kristin A. Wagers, and Mary Ellen Wiggins

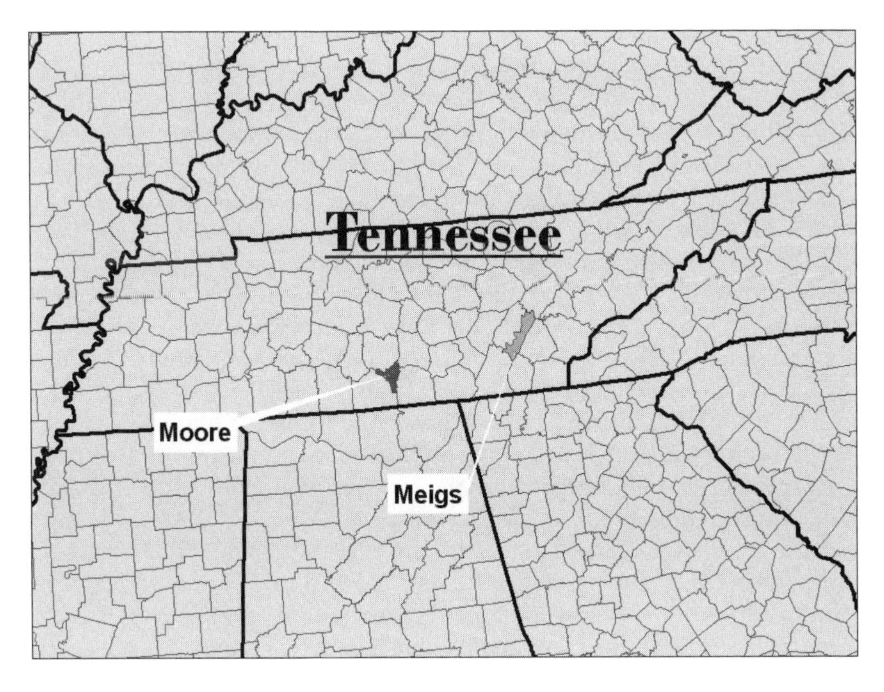

Map 8 Locations of Moore County and Meigs County, Tennessee
Source: U.S. Bureau of the Census.

Visitors to Lynchburg, Tennessee, will find the place to be "so off the beaten path, it's either your destination or you are lost" (Lynchburg/ Moore County Chamber of Commerce website, www.lynchburgtenn.com). Home to the famous Jack Daniel's Distillery and located south of Nashville near the Alabama border, Lynchburg lies in the former Moore County, a diminutive jurisdiction wedged among four larger counties (map 8). Historically, size was a prominent issue for both the City of Lynchburg and Moore County. Anxiety over the potential annexation of portions of the county by the nearby City of Tullahoma propelled their decision to consolidate in 1988. Because Tennessee state law forbids the annexation of one municipal government by another, consolidation was touted as the key to preventing Moore County and its tax base from being chipped away by the larger surrounding governments.

Although apprehension over annexation provided the general impetus for consolidation, proponents advanced several arguments to bolster this premise. First, proponents expressed concern over the loss of tax base and its detrimental impact on funding for local service provision that would likely result from annexation. Second, advocates maintained that both governments were failing to maximize per capita federal aid receipts because their populations were counted separately. These divided lower population counts led to reduced rates of federal aid that translated into diminished service levels. Third, advocates of consolidation argued that, as separate entities, Lynchburg and Moore County used tax dollars inefficiently by duplicating public services. Consolidation of the two governments promised to streamline spending for public service provision.

This chapter examines the build-up to and results of the campaign for consolidation of Lynchburg/Moore County and assesses the efficiency outcomes of consolidation by drawing comparisons with the similar, unconsolidated governments of the Town of Decatur and Meigs County in southeast Tennessee. The following analysis of the Lynchburg/Moore consolidation is guided by two central hypotheses. First, the promises made to the electorate should be delivered. Second, the metropolitan government of Lynchburg/Moore is expected to operate more efficiently than the unconsolidated governments of Decatur and Meigs County. Several factors are examined to test these hypotheses, including changes in the value of the property tax base, revenue and expenditure trends, and demographics variables. Each government entity is examined over a twenty-year period, beginning approximately ten years before the Lynchburg/Moore consolidation and concluding approximately ten years after consolidation, depending upon data availability. All financial data are presented in 1988 constant dollars.

Consolidating Lynchburg/Moore County

Although residents of Moore County voted on the Lynchburg/Moore consolidation proposal for the first time on November 17, 1987, elected officials representing the two governmental entities began to consider the issue more than seven years earlier. The first formal steps in exploring the possibility of consolidation were taken in July 1980, when the county's Board of Commissioners voted unanimously for the county attorney to develop and present a consolidation plan. Three months later, the county attorney's report garnered sufficient interest for the board to create a five-member Metropolitan Government Study Committee. Membership on the committee included the Lynchburg mayor, the Lynchburg recorder, the Moore County executive, and two Moore County commissioners. One year later, the board raised the issue of consolidation again, and it voted to create a committee made up of the chairs of each of the commission's standing committees to conduct further investigation. After six months of study, this committee recommended delaying consideration for an additional six months. This delay would ultimately continue for several years. Despite the interest in consolidation expressed by certain members of the board, the issue did not gain traction with the board as a whole, with city government officials, or with the public for quite some time (Thomas 2007).

Avoiding Annexation

It was not until January 1987 that consolidation efforts were restarted, beginning with the board's appointment of a new five-member committee to again consider the possibility of a consolidated metropolitan government. After four months of additional exploration, the committee's proposal to move forward with consolidation and to create a Metropolitan Government Charter Commission endowed with the legal authority to draft the new metropolitan charter was unanimously adopted by the board in a roll-call vote. This development placed the consolidation decision in the hands of local citizens. Moore County voters approved the measure in November by 1,375 to 95 (a 93.5 percent approval rate), including an unprecedented 112 voters casting absentee ballots—the largest number submitted on a single-issue vote in Moore County history (*Moore County News* 1987a). With 2,668 registered voters, voter turnout reached 55 percent (*Moore County News* 1987b).

What changed that made consolidation so wildly popular in this second attempt? The second consolidation effort unfolded against a backdrop of contention between Moore County and the neighboring City of Tullahoma. Concerns focused around anticipated efforts by Tullahoma to annex portions of Moore County (a suspicion denied by Tullahoma officials) and attempts by the Tullahoma Planning Commission to implement measures with spillover effects expected to cross county lines (*Moore County News* 1987a). Tennessee law permits a municipality to expand its planning and zoning capacity beyond its existing boundaries by 5 miles every two years. After its first encroachment into Moore County, Tullahoma's authority extended to just 5 miles from the city limit of Lynchburg.

The next allowable extension would have usurped Moore County High School, Motlow State Community College, and the Jack Daniel's Distillery, all of which were important fixtures in Moore County, both in terms of identity and economic vitality. Such an extension of planning and zoning power was considered a precursor to formal annexation. If the area including Moore County High School were annexed, the loss of students from the school system would have been paralleled by a loss of tax dollars supporting the county school district. In addition, as the only high school in the county and one of only two schools in the entire Moore County School System, an important piece of the community would have been lost. Motlow State Community College provided a similar source of community identity and increased the prominence of Moore County in the region. Jack Daniel's generated considerable local pride as well as revenue streams from property taxes, local option sales taxes, and alcohol taxes. Although leading city and county officials had resisted consolidation years earlier, the threat of these losses to the county quickly galvanized support for a metropolitan government (Thomas 2007).

Consolidation would also enable the new metropolitan government to receive all revenues from and to control the use of self-imposed special purpose local option sales taxes (SPLOST), which were previously divided between the city and county governments. Although this issue was not formally presented to the public to garner support for consolidation, the added flexibility of having complete discretion over SPLOST funds further heightened the appeal of consolidation among public officials (Thomas 2007).

Eliminating Duplicate Services

Aside from the opportunity to avoid annexation, advocates also presented consolidation as an avenue for using tax dollars more efficiently by eliminating services duplicated by Lynchburg and Moore County. The consolidation united Moore County and the City of Lynchburg into one operational government designated the Metropolitan Government of Lynchburg and Moore County. Under Tennessee state law, both jurisdictions making up the metropolitan government are classified as both counties and municipalities.[1] Practically speaking, however, the consolidation transformed Moore County from a county government to a General Service District and the City of Lynchburg from a municipal government to the Lynchburg Urban Service District (USD).[2] The Lynchburg USD was structured as a municipal corporation and remained an independent taxing district under the authority of the Urban Council, which was composed of the three members of the Metropolitan Council representing the Lynchburg USD. The Lynchburg USD tax district was established to provide funding for services available only to residents of the Lynchburg area and not the remainder of the General Service District.

The potential efficiency gains from eliminating duplicate services through consolidation were most evident in Lynchburg, where the three positions of mayor, recorder, and treasurer could be eliminated and absorbed into the new metropolitan government. When the consolidation occurred, the former Lynchburg mayor's duties were assigned to the new metropolitan executive, and the county trustee (renamed the metropolitan trustee) assumed responsibilities formerly held by the Lynchburg treasurer. The Office of County Clerk assumed responsibility for duties of the Lynchburg recorder under the new title of metropolitan secretary. Likewise, fire and police responsibilities were consolidated into single metropolitan departments. The small size of Lynchburg's city government—for example, the city employed a single police officer, and the fire department was staffed by volunteer firefighters—simplified the consolidation process and generated little concern over job attrition. Moreover, many city offices, such as the mayor, were part-time positions only.[3]

All county offices, with the exceptions of county commissioners and county executive, were retained under the new metropolitan government and were simply renamed to reflect the metropolitan status. These offices included the assessor of property, county clerk, county register, county trustee, county sheriff, and Circuit Court clerk. Offices of the county commissioners were absorbed into the new Metropolitan Council, and the Office of the County Executive was restructured as the Metropolitan Executive. The city and county maintained their separate budgets through the end of the 1987–88 fiscal year and began operations under an integrated budget in the 1988–89 fiscal year. Table 8.1 compares the division of services between the City of Lynchburg and Moore County that existed ten years before the consolidation and ten years after consolidation. As can be seen from table 8.1, several services were provided by both Lynchburg and

Table 8.1 Division of Services, City of Lynchburg and Moore County, Before and After Consolidation

Service	10 Years before Consolidation	10 Years after Consolidation
Fire protection	Lynchburg and Moore County	Metropolitan government
Law enforcement	Lynchburg and Moore County	Metropolitan government
Parks and recreation	Moore County	Metropolitan government
Historic Commission	Moore County	Metropolitan government
Planning Commission	Moore County	Metropolitan government
Utilities	Lynchburg and Moore County	Metropolitan government
Public works	Moore County	Metropolitan government
Schools	Moore County	Metropolitan government

Source: Lynchburg-Moore Clerk's Office, telephone conversation on June 6, 2006.

Moore County before consolidation; however, the metropolitan government assumed responsibility for all these services after consolidation, thereby eliminating the duplication in public service provision.

Background of Comparison Cases

To determine whether the metropolitan government of Lynchburg/Moore County operates more efficiently than unconsolidated governments, an unconsolidated municipality/county pair was identified to serve as the basis for comparison. Meigs County was selected as the comparison case for Moore County, and the Town of Decatur was used for comparison to the City of Lynchburg. Moore and Meigs offer apt opportunities for comparison because, before the consolidation, they shared the distinction of being, geographically, Tennessee's smallest counties. The two jurisdictions also share similar demographics. In addition, both Moore and Meigs have faced significant challenges with respect to maintaining their economic vitality. Due to these similarities, the Tennessee County Technical Assistance Service regularly uses Meigs County as the basis of comparison for the former Moore County.

Preconsolidation Comparison

Table 8.2 provides a 1980 preconsolidation comparison of Moore and Meigs Counties for several demographic and socioeconomic characteristics. As can be seen from this table, Moore County was home to 4,510 residents, making up 1,534 households, in 1980 while Meigs County boasted 7,431 residents and 2,520 households. The average sizes of these households were very similar between the two counties, at 2.94 for Moore and 2.95 for Meigs, but were noticeably larger than the state's average household size of 2.84. Residents in Moore County were slightly older on average (at 31.7 years) than in Meigs County and in the state of Tennessee, which both had median ages of 30.1 years. Poverty afflicted Moore County residents in 1980 at a rate of 16.3 percent, just under the state individual poverty rate of 16.5 percent.[4] However, poverty among minors in Moore County occurred at a higher rate of 20.5 percent. Poverty was somewhat less problematic in Meigs County, where the rates were 14.3 percent for individuals and 13.5 percent for minors. However, the disparity between the two counties almost disappears when one compares the poverty rate among households. In Moore County, 12.5 percent of families lived in poverty, compared with 12.3 percent in Meigs County. In addition, both of these rates were lower than the state's household poverty rate of 13.1 percent.

Table 8.2 Preconsolidation County Comparison, 1980

Characteristic	Moore County	Meigs County	State of Tennessee
Population	4,510	7,431	4,591,120
Households	1,534	2,520	1,618,505
Average household size (persons)	2.94	2.95	2.84
Average age of residents (years)	31.7	30.1	30.1
Individual poverty rate (%)	16.30	14.30	16.50
Child poverty rate (%)	20.50	13.50	20.50
Household poverty rate (%)	12.50	12.30	13.1
Unemployment rate (%)	4.9	8.9	7.3
High school completion rate (%)	52.0	43.4	56.2
Four years of college completion rate (%)	9.2	5.8	12.6

Source: U.S. Bureau of the Census.

With respect to educational attainment and employment in 1980, Moore County's unemployment rate of 4.9 percent was below the state of Tennessee's at 7.3 percent. Conversely, Meigs County's unemployment rate of 8.9 percent was well above the state's rate. Among residents age twenty-five years and over, 52 percent had earned a high school diploma, and 9.2 percent had completed at least four years of college in Moore County. In Meigs County, 43.4 percent of residents over the age of twenty-five held high school diplomas, while 5.8 percent had finished at least four years of college. In both counties, however, these high school and college attainment rates were well below the level of educational achievement throughout the state of Tennessee.

Table 8.3 provides a 1980 preconsolidation comparison of the City of Lynchburg and the Town of Decatur for selected demographic characteristics. These two municipalities were chosen for comparison because Decatur and Lynchburg represented government centers as the seats of their respective counties. Within Moore County, the City of Lynchburg had a 1980 population of 668 residents, making it home to 14.8 percent of the county population, in 276 housing units. Of these residents, 88.2 percent were white. In Meigs County, the Town of Decatur accounted for 14.4 percent of the population, with 1,069 residents in 417 housing units. Of these total residents, 99.7 percent were white. In addition to housing an almost equivalent proportion of their respective county's residents, both Lynchburg and Decatur exhibited very similar housing values, with the mean values for owner-occupied housing at $36,203 for Lynchburg and $36,980 for Decatur.

Table 8.3 Preconsolidation Municipal Comparison, 1980

Demographic Characteristic	City of Lynchburg	Town of Decatur
Total population	668	1,069
% of county population	14.80	14.40
Racial composition—% white	88.20	99.70
Housing units	276	417
Mean value of owner-occupied housing	$36,203	$36,980

Source: U.S. Bureau of the Census.

Comparison Trends throughout the Postconsolidation Period

The period between 1980 and 2000 encompasses the 1988 Lynchburg/Moore County consolidation and also represents both the preconsolidation and postconsolidation periods. A comparison of Lynchburg/Moore to the unconsolidated governments of Decatur and Meigs County during this period reveals several divergent demographic and socioeconomic trends occurring during and after consolidation.

Figure 8.1 illustrates the combined populations for Lynchburg/Moore County and Decatur/Meigs County between 1980 and 2000. During this period, both Lynchburg/Moore and Decatur/Meigs experienced population growth; however, the growth encountered by Decatur/Meigs outpaced that of Lynchburg/Moore significantly. Between 1980 and 1990, the combined population for Meigs County and the Town of Decatur increased by 10.5 percent, compared with a 9.3 percent decline in population in Lynchburg/Moore. From 1990 to 2000, the Decatur/Meigs population surged upward again, by 32.9 percent, giving the county and town a combined total population increase of 46.8 percent for the two decades. Lynchburg/Moore, however, only experienced population growth at a rate

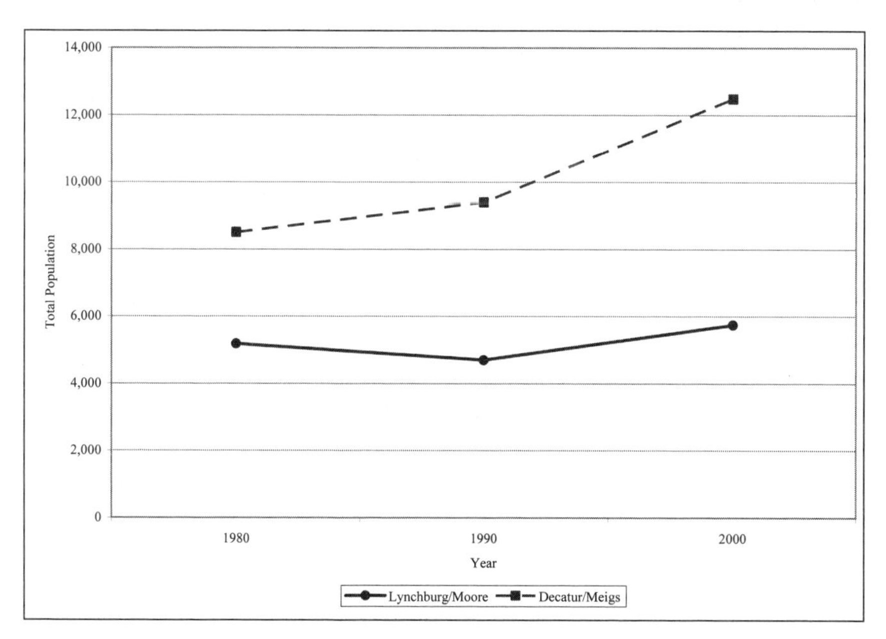

Figure 8.1 Population Growth
Source: U.S. Bureau of the Census.

of 22.2 percent between 1990 and 2000, for a total population growth rate of only 10.9 percent during the 1980–2000 period.

An examination of changes in the number of households during the period reveals a similar trend. Between 1980 and 1990, the combined number of households in Meigs County and the Town of Decatur increased by 20.1 percent, compared with 13.0 percent in Lynchburg/Moore County. This trend was exacerbated further between 1990 and 2000, when Decatur/Meigs County realized a 38.9 percent growth rate in households, while the number of Lynchburg/Moore households only increased by 27.5 percent. This divergence in growth patterns might be partially explained by the less rural character of Meigs County. Although the Lynchburg/Moore Chamber of Commerce touts the area's out-of-the-way location, the Meigs Chamber of Commerce advertises "small town living, big city access" on its website (www.meigscountytnchamber.org) and notes that Meigs County residents live within 50 miles of the economic centers of Chattanooga and Knoxville.

Figure 8.2 illustrates the percentage of residents over the age of twenty-five who attained a high school diploma for both Moore and Meigs counties during the 1980–2000 period.[5] As can be seen from figure 8.2, Moore County maintained higher rates of educational attainment during the period than did Meigs County, although these achievement rates followed no stable pattern over time. Between 1980 and 1990, Moore County went from having more than half of adults over the age twenty-five holding high school diplomas to only 37.2 percent of residents attaining high school diplomas. During the next decade, this attainment rate increased modestly, to 40 percent by 2000, but it failed to reach the 1980 level. High school achievement for Meigs County followed a similar trajectory, though at a slower rate, declining from 43.4 percent in 1980 to 31.5 percent in 1990 and then rising to 36.7 percent by 2000.

A comparison of college attainment rates during the 1980–2000 period seemed to follow an increasing trend before consolidation but then declined for both Moore and Meigs counties in the postconsolidation decade. Although not shown in figure 8.2, about 9 percent of Moore County residents over the age of twenty-five had completed at least four years of college in the year 1980. By 1990, Moore County's rate of college attainment increased to 11.7 percent but then declined to 7.6 percent by 2000.[6] The trend in Meigs County mirrored that of Moore County but on a less dramatic scale. College attainment rates increased from 5.8 percent in 1980 to 6.6 percent in 1990 before declining to 5.1 percent in 2000.

The preceding discussion reveals both congruent and divergent trends in demographic and socioeconomic factors between Lynchburg/Moore and the comparison cases of the Town of Decatur and Meigs County in both the preconsolidation and postconsolidation periods. The next section

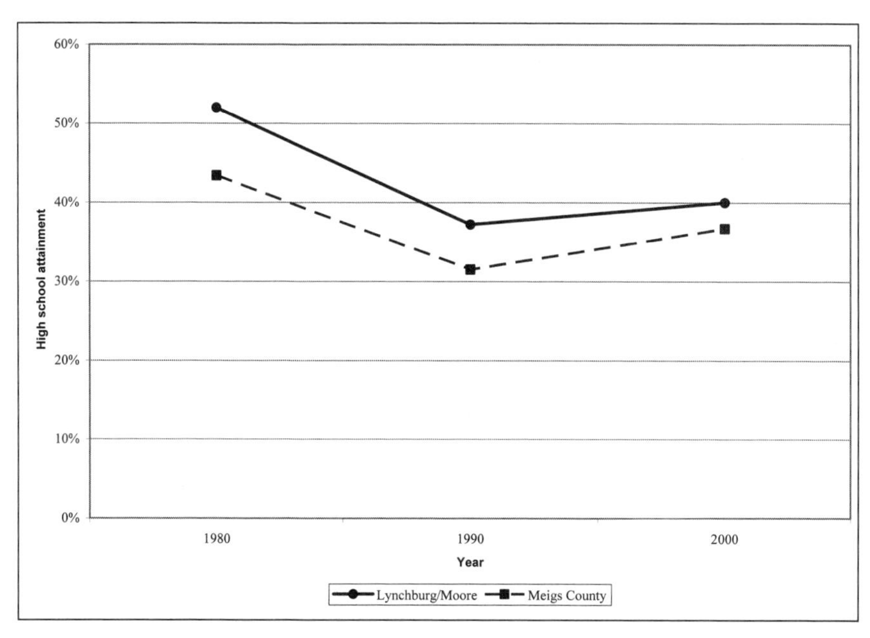

Figure 8.2 High School Attainment
Source: U.S. Bureau of the Census.

provides a fiscal analysis to determine if the divergent trends can be attributed to efforts to keep the promises made to voters during the consolidation pursuit and/or efficiency gains achieved through the consolidation of the City of Lynchburg and Moore County.

Fiscal Comparison and Analysis

This fiscal comparison and analysis are provided to determine whether the promises made to voters during the consolidation campaign were maintained in the postconsolidation era and to assess the extent to which the metropolitan government of Lynchburg/Moore County operates more efficiently than the unconsolidated comparison cases of the Town of Decatur and Meigs County. Several factors are explored in the following subsections to test these hypotheses, including changes to the property tax base as well as revenue and expenditure trends.

The following analysis examines each government entity during a twenty-year period beginning approximately ten years before the Lynchburg/Moore consolidation and concluding approximately ten years after consolidation, depending upon data availability. For the years before consolidation, the information presented is an aggregate of data pertaining to the individual governments of the City of Lynchburg and Moore County. Information covering the years after consolidation pertains directly to the Metropolitan Government of Lynchburg/Moore. Both the preconsolidation and postconsolidation information are referred to as Lynchburg/Moore data. The analysis compares the Lynchburg/Moore data to information that represents an aggregate of data pertaining to the individual and unconsolidated governments of the Town of Decatur and Meigs County for all years under analysis. This information is referred to as Decatur/Meigs data. All financial data are presented in 1988 constant dollars.

Several attempts were made to incorporate actual budgetary information for both Lynchburg/Moore County and Decatur/Meigs County into the fiscal analysis for each year from 1978 to 1998. Unfortunately, much of this information is not available. All these governmental entities are very small, and the Lynchburg/Moore consolidation occurred almost twenty years ago. Many of the individuals who were involved in the consolidation are no longer employed within these governments, which added to the challenge of gathering qualitative information to explain many of the financial trends. For example, former Moore County commissioner and metropolitan executive Billy H. Thomas was quite helpful in providing explanatory information; he is now the proprietor of the Lynchburg Cake and Candy Company.[7] To exacerbate the problem further, the State of Tennessee does not require local governments to keep past copies of budgetary documents or audit reports because these are considered only planning documents. For example, the budgetary data for Meigs County are only available back through 1996, and these data would not be strictly comparable to the available data for Lynchburg/Moore. Therefore, the following fiscal analysis incorporates all available budgetary information for the specified time period. Data obtained from the U.S. Bureau of the Census and the U.S. Department of Education were used for analysis where actual budgetary information was unavailable.

Preserving the Property Tax Base

The consolidation campaign primarily focused on the threat to Moore County of annexation by the larger surrounding governments and particularly by the neighboring City of Tullahoma. The primary concern was that annexation would erode the county's property tax base and lead to a reduction in local public service provision. Consolidation, therefore, was promoted as a strategy for avoiding annexation to preserve the county's property tax base and associated revenue. Because the State of Tennessee forbids annexation of one municipal government by another, the consolidation of Lynchburg and Moore County maintained this promise of avoiding annexation simply through the protection of the law. Consolidation successfully preserved the geographical area of the county's property tax base.

Along with protecting the county's property tax base geographically, the Lynchburg/Moore County consolidation apparently sheltered the value of the property tax base as well. Figure 8.3 illustrates the trends in total assessed property valuation for both Moore and Meigs counties during the 1978–97 period. These assessed value totals include the value of property within the City of Lynchburg and Town of Decatur. In Moore County, revaluations of property occurred preconsolidation in 1984 and postconsolidation in 1994, as evidenced by the two upward shifts in total assessment valuation shown in figure 8.3. In Meigs County, a state-mandated reappraisal of property occurred in 1989, and a cyclical revaluation was conducted in 1995, which can be seen by the increases in assessed value shown in figure 8.3. As required by Tennessee state law, both Meigs County and the Lynchburg/Moore Metropolitan Government now revalue property every six years. Aside from the two revaluations during the

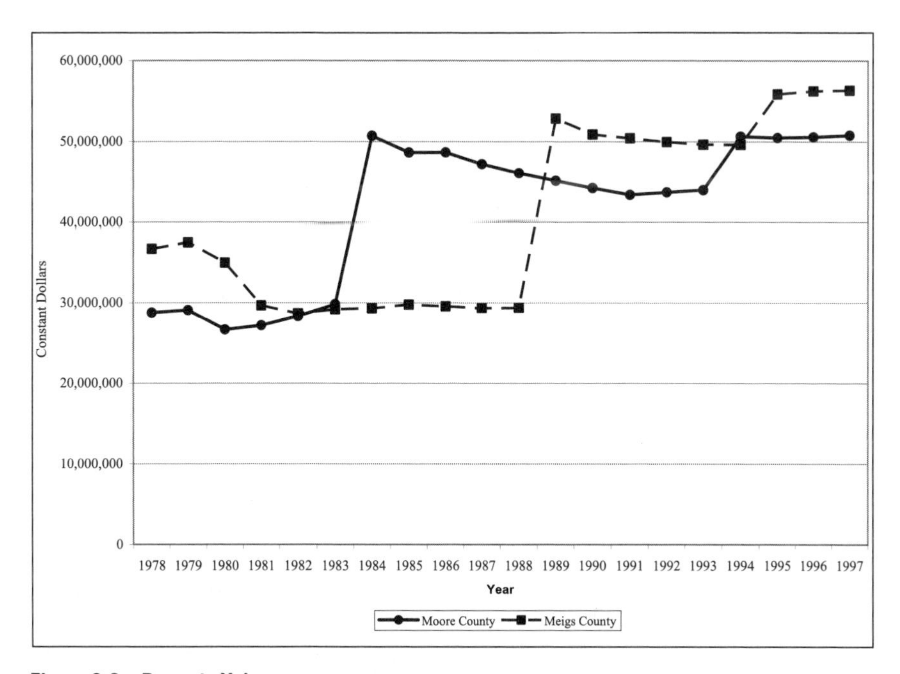

Figure 8.3 Property Values
Source: State of Tennessee.

period, the value of Moore County's property tax base remained relatively stable, with no significant drops in total assessed value that might have occurred if portions of the tax base had been annexed by the larger surrounding governments.

Although local politics often revolve around the issue of property taxes, the Lynchburg/Moore County consolidation effort focused primarily on preserving the existing tax base, with less attention paid to actual tax rates. In a *Moore County News* (1987b) article, the chair of Moore County's Committee on Consolidation underscored this distinction by commenting that "taxes can always be counted on to go up anywhere under any form of government." However, an examination of property tax rates reveals a possible shifting of the tax burden between residents of the Lynchburg USD and the remainder of Moore County in the postconsolidation time period. Some residents experienced a steady reduction in property taxes, despite it not having been advanced as a motive for consolidation (Thomas 2007).

Figure 8.4 illustrates the trends in combined property tax rates for Lynchburg/Moore County and Decatur/Meigs County during the 1980–97 period. In the preconsolidation period, Figure 8.4 highlights a noticeable drop (46.7 percent) in the combined property tax rates for the City of Lynchburg and Moore County between 1983 and 1984. This rate decline coincided with the property revaluation that occurred, and resulted in a 70 percent increase in property value within Moore County. Immediately following the property revaluation, residents of both Moore County and the City of Lynchburg experienced steady increases in property tax rates in the three years leading up to consolidation. Moore County's individual property tax rate (not shown in figure 8.4) increased 14.1 percent, from $2.13 per $100 of assessed value in 1984 to $2.43 in 1987. The City of Lynchburg's individual property tax rate (applied to city residents above the county tax rate) climbed 38.6 percent, from $0.83 per $100 of assessed value in 1984 to $1.15 in 1987.

As can be seen in figure 8.4, the combined property tax rates for Lynchburg/Moore remained fairly stable for several years after the consolidation. However, the property tax rate applied to the Lynchburg USD residents (above the county tax rate for additional USD services) steadily declined throughout the remainder of the period. The USD tax rate (not shown in figure 8.4) decreased 85.7 percent, from $0.70 per $100 of assessed value in 1988 immediately following the consolidation to only $0.10 by 1996. Meanwhile, Moore County's individual property tax rate steadily increased after the consolidation until the rate dropped as a result of the second property revaluation that occurred in 1994. The property tax rate applied to Lynchburg/Moore residents outside the USD increased 19.6 percent, from $2.55 per $100 of assessed value in 1988 to $3.05 by 1993, before dropping to its

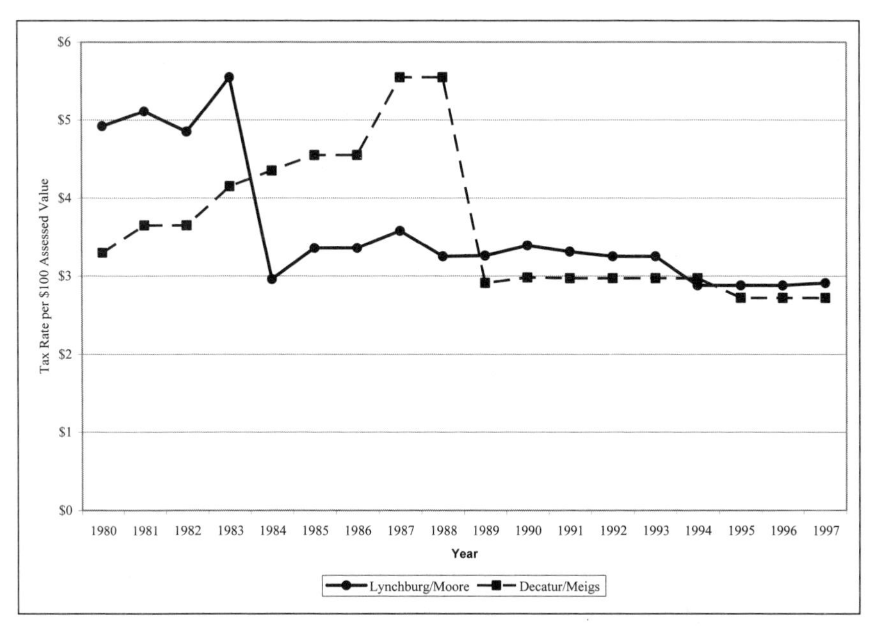

Figure 8.4 Property Tax Rates
Source: State of Tennessee.

lowest rate of $2.73 per $100 of assessed value in 1994. The consistently declining property tax rate applied to USD residents (above the county tax rate) might be attributable to declining service provision for residents within the Lynchburg USD. Without a decline in service provision, however, it appears that the consolidation resulted in a shifting of the tax burden from USD residents to the remainder of Moore County.

Finally, in the postconsolidation period, figure 8.4 shows a significant decline (47.6 percent) in the combined property tax rates for the Town of Decatur and Meigs County between 1988 and 1989, which coincided with a state-mandated property reappraisal resulting in an 80 percent increase in assessed value within Meigs County. For the remainder of the period, the combined property tax rates for Decatur/Meigs remained fairly stable and paralleled the Lynchburg/Moore property tax trend, albeit at a lower rate. However, the individual property tax rates for the Town of Decatur and Meigs County (not shown in figure 8.4) do not evince tax shifting between the two jurisdictions during the postconsolidation period. Immediately following the property revaluation, Meigs County's property tax rate went from $2.33 per $100 of assessed value in 1989 to $2.32 in 1991 and to $2.09 in 1995. At the same time, Decatur's property tax rate (above the county tax rate) went from $0.58 per $100 of assessed value in 1989 to $0.65 in 1990 and to $0.63 in 1995. Unlike the Lynchburg/Moore tax rate trend, there does not appear to be a shifting of the tax burden from Decatur residents to the remainder of Meigs County residents in the postconsolidation period.

Maximizing Federal Aid

Proponents of the consolidation contended that both Moore County and the City of Lynchburg were failing to maximize per capita federal aid receipts as separate governmental entities because their populations were counted separately (Thomas 2007). These divided lower population counts led to reduced rates of federal aid, which were thought to translate into reduced service levels. Therefore, consolidation was touted among government officials as an approach for maximizing federal aid receipts to increase public service provision to residents throughout the Lynchburg/Moore County jurisdiction.

Figure 8.5 illustrates the trends in per capita federal intergovernmental revenue during the 1977–2002 period. As can be seen from the figure, per capita federal aid receipts for both Lynchburg/Moore County and Decatur/Meigs County exhibit inconsistent trends during the period. Lynchburg/Moore only received federal intergovernmental revenue during four of the six fiscal years shown in figure 8.5, and these per capita revenue amounts varied considerably. Although Decatur/Meigs received federal intergovernmental revenue during each of the fiscal years shown, the per capita amounts also followed a rather sporadic trend. At the beginning of the period, the per capita federal intergovernmental revenue received by the Town of Decatur and Meigs County was significantly higher than the amounts received by the City of Lynchburg and Moore County. In 1977 and 1982, the per capita federal intergovernmental revenue for Decatur/Meigs was 4.4 and 3.5 times the amount, respectively, received by Lynchburg/Moore. Immediately preceding the consolidation, however, the 1987 per capita federal aid receipts only differed by $0.58 between the two combined jurisdictions. Lynchburg/Moore did not receive federal intergovernmental revenue in fiscal years 1992 and 1997 following the consolidation. However, the amount of federal aid received by Lynchburg/Moore in 2002 was noticeably greater than the amount received by Decatur/Meigs in that same year.

Figure 8.6 provides a closer examination of Lynchburg/Moore's trends in federal intergovernmental revenue during the postconsolidation period. Total federal intergovernmental revenue is shown in figure 8.6 for each year during the period 1988–98, for both the general fund and the special revenue funds maintained by the metropolitan government.[8] Similar to the trends in figure 8.5, federal aid receipts for each fund remained fairly

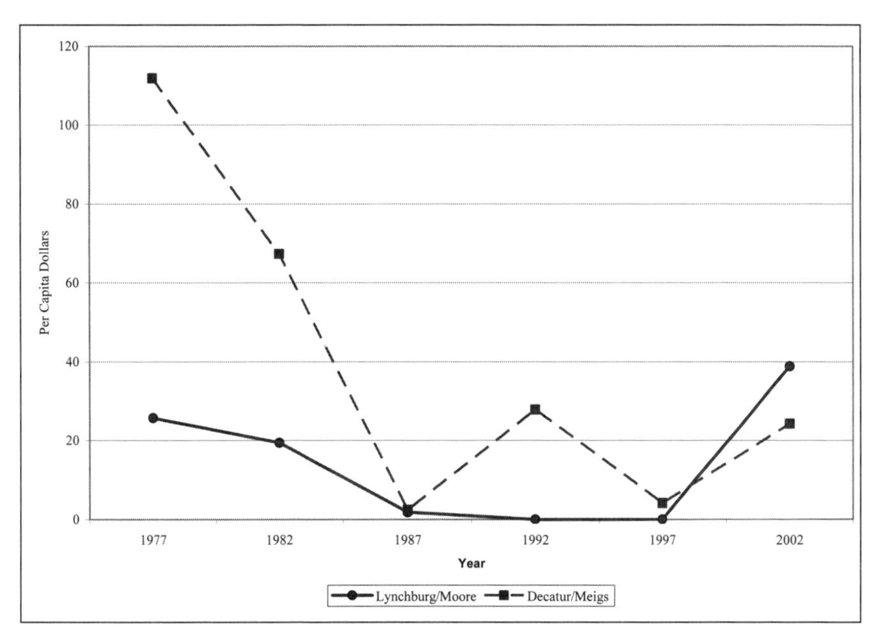

Figure 8.5 Federal Intergovernmental Revenues
Source: U.S. Bureau of the Census.

inconsistent during the period. Figure 8.6 shows that general fund federal aid was received by the metropolitan government in only four of the nine fiscal years, and these revenue amounts were rather volatile. Federal aid receipts for the special revenue funds portrayed a more consistent trend at the beginning of the period but then became more erratic and eventually nonexistent by the end of the period, as Lynchburg/Moore began to receive federal intergovernmental revenue for the general fund. It is possible that Lynchburg/Moore was experiencing a shift from earmarked to general purpose federal aid at this time, which might account for the changes between the two funds. However, even though a somewhat increasing trend in total federal intergovernmental revenue persisted through 1995, federal aid receipts were diminutive by the end of the period.

On the basis of the trends shown in figures 8.5 and 8.6, it appears that the consolidation of Lynchburg and Moore County had little impact on generating additional federal intergovernmental revenue to support expanded public service provision, which was a primary motivation for consolidation. A closer examination of spending for education and highways will help to determine whether the erratic trend in federal intergovernmental revenue had a significant impact on public service provision.

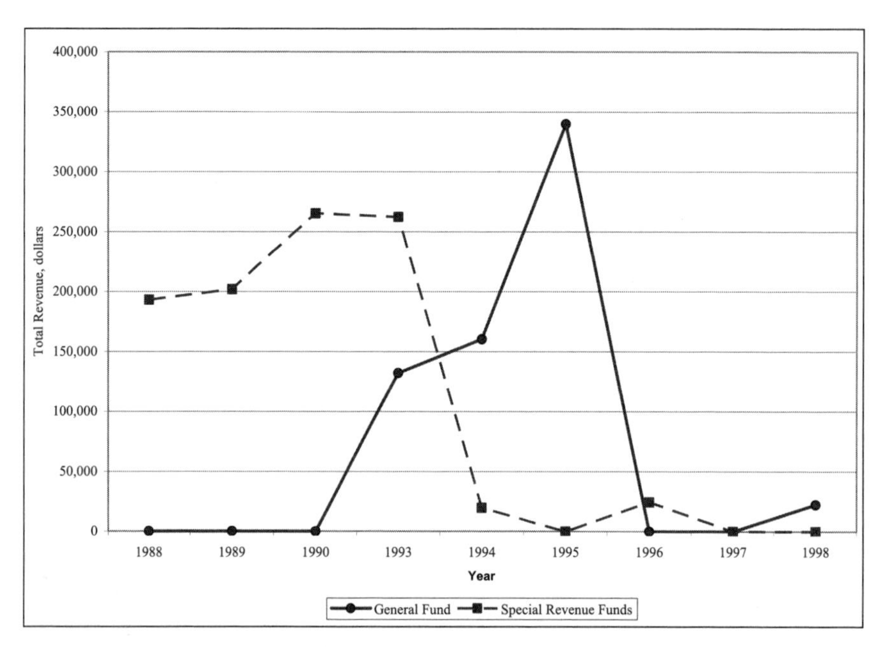

Figure 8.6 Lynchburg-Moore Federal Intergovernmental Revenue
Source: Consolidated Financial Statements for the Metropolitan Government of Lynchburg-Moore.

Figures 8.7 and 8.8 illustrate per capita direct expenditures for Lynchburg/Moore and Decatur/Meigs for highways and education during the 1977–2002 period.[9] These two spending categories are notable because Lynchburg/Moore's federal aid receipts for the special revenue funds portrayed in figure 8.6 were dedicated primarily for education and secondarily for highway and public works purposes. In addition, Moore County had unilateral control over public service provision for these two expenditure categories in the preconsolidation period.

Figure 8.7 shows a 23 percent decline between 1977 and 1982 in highway spending for Lynchburg/Moore County, which coincided with a 24.4 percent decrease in per capita federal intergovernmental revenue received by the City of Lynchburg and Moore County during this same period. After a similar decline between 1977 and 1982, highway spending for Decatur/Meigs County remained fairly stable during the remainder of the period, even amid the erratic trend of federal intergovernmental revenue received by the two governments between 1982 and 2002. Conversely, per capita highway expenditures for Lynchburg/Moore were more volatile during these last two decades. Between 1982 and 1992, Lynchburg/Moore's highway spending increased 66.0 percent before plum-

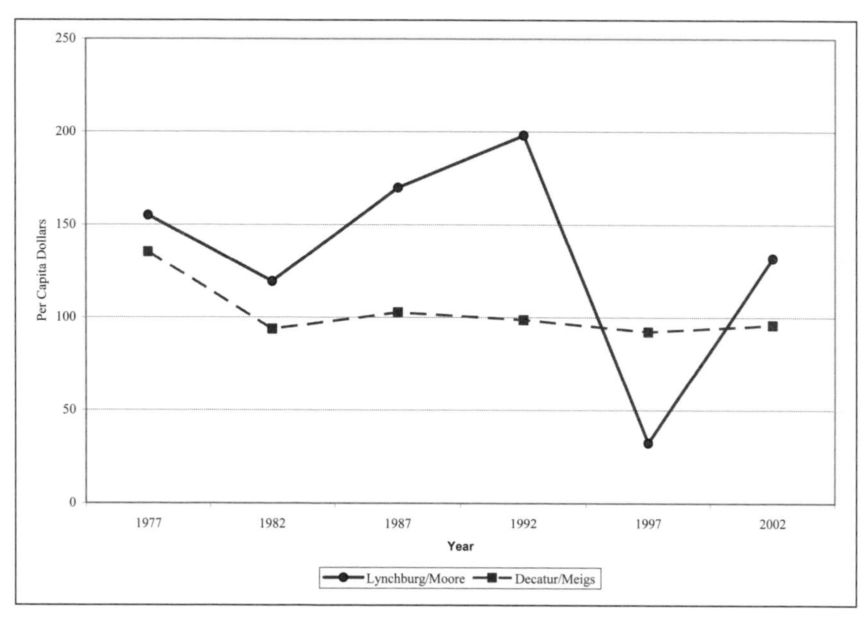

Figure 8.7 Per Capita Highway Expenditures, 1977–2002
Source: U.S. Bureau of the Census.

meting 83.6 percent between 1992 and 1997. This trend coincides with the 92.4 percent decline in federal aid receipts for Lynchburg/Moore's special revenue funds between 1993 and 1994 and the nearly nonexistent federal intergovernmental revenue subsequently received by the special revenue funds through 1997. Moreover, the 305.5 percent increase in Lynchburg/Moore's per capita highway expenditures between 1997 and 2002 paralleled the significant increase in per capita federal intergovernmental revenue received by the metropolitan government during this same time.

The education expenditure data shown in figure 8.8 show spending almost exclusively by Moore and Meigs counties. Except for a minor expenditure by the Town of Decatur in 1987, neither Lynchburg nor Decatur held responsibility for education expenditures during the period under analysis. Figure 8.8 shows a similar trend to highway spending, with a decrease in per capita education expenditures between 1977 and 1982 for both Moore and Meigs counties. The 29.3 percent decline in education spending for Moore County coincided with a 23.0 percent decline in per capita federal intergovernmental revenue received by Moore County between 1977 and 1982. However, both Lynchburg/Moore and Decatur/Meigs maintained consistently increasing per capita education expenditures throughout the remainder of the period, with the exception of Meigs' 2002 decline in

Figure 8.8 Per Capita Education Expenditures, 1977–2002
Source: U.S. Bureau of the Census.

expenditures. Lynchburg-Moore's upward trend in education expenditures includes the years after consolidation, when federal aid receipts for the special purpose funds became nearly nonexistent. Between 1982 and 2002, per capita education expenditures for Lynchburg/Moore increased 115.6 percent compared with only 52.1 percent for Decatur/Meigs. Between 1992 and 2002, Lynchburg/Moore per capita spending for education increased by 39.7 percent, even while federal intergovernmental revenue declined dramatically. Moreover, this decade was the only time that Lynchburg/Moore's per capita education expenditures exceeded spending levels for Decatur/Meigs.

Figures 8.9 and 8.10 offer a closer examination of school district funding during the 1990–2002 postconsolidation period. Figure 8.9 illustrates the amount of per pupil federal intergovernmental revenue received by the Moore County and Meigs County school districts. As can be seen from figure 8.9, the Moore County School District experienced a rather substantial decline in per pupil federal aid in the beginning of the 1990s, with per pupil revenue falling 78 percent, from $1,110 in 1990 to $249 by 1994. For the remainder of the period, per pupil federal intergovernmental revenue remained fairly constant for the Moore County School District and reached its highest level of $286 in 2002. The Meigs County School District received fairly consistent levels of per pupil federal intergovernmental

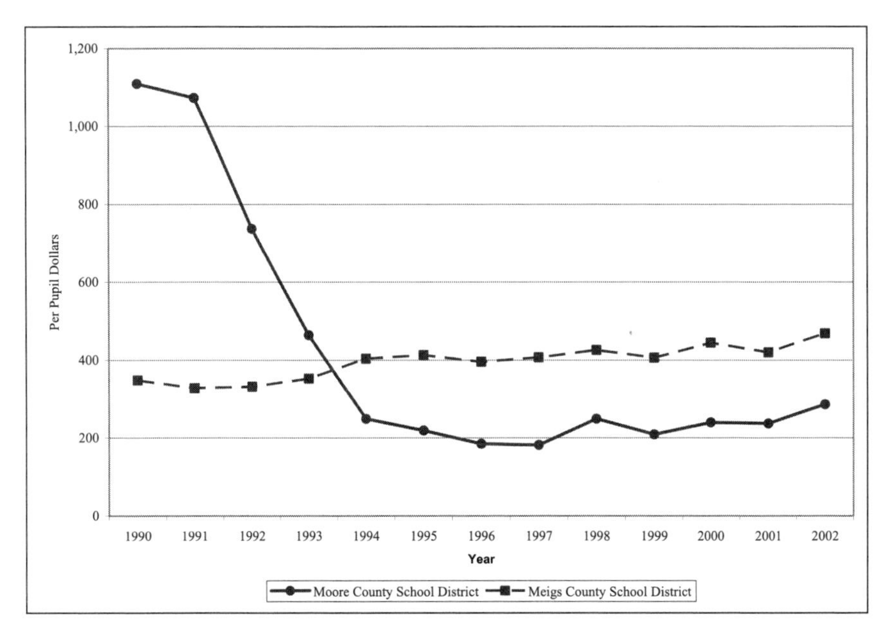

Figure 8.9 School District Federal Intergovernmental Revenue
Source: National Center for Education Statistics, U.S. Department of Education.

revenue throughout the period, with the trend increasing 34 percent, from $348 in 1990 to $468 by 2002.

Figure 8.10 illustrates the amount of per pupil current expenditures for elementary and secondary educational programs for the Moore County and Meigs County school districts.[10] Perhaps most noticeable from the figure is the rather consistent upward trend in education expenditures for both the Moore and Meigs school districts. Even amid the significant decline in per pupil federal intergovernmental revenue between 1990 and 1994, the Moore County School District increased its expenditures nearly every year during this period. Per pupil current expenditures for the Moore County School District increased 13 percent, from $2,520 in 1990 to $2,851 by 1994. Moreover, the Moore County School District maintained this upward trend for the remainder of the period, even while per pupil federal intergovernmental revenue either declined further or only modestly increased. Between 1995 and 2002, the Moore County School District's per pupil expenditures increased 40 percent, from $2,853 to $3,980. This trend compares to Meigs County School District spending, which only increased 15 percent, from $2,892 in 1995 to $3,331 by 2002.

The trends shown in figures 8.7 through 8.10 suggest that Lynchburg/Moore's inability to garner higher levels of federal intergovernmental

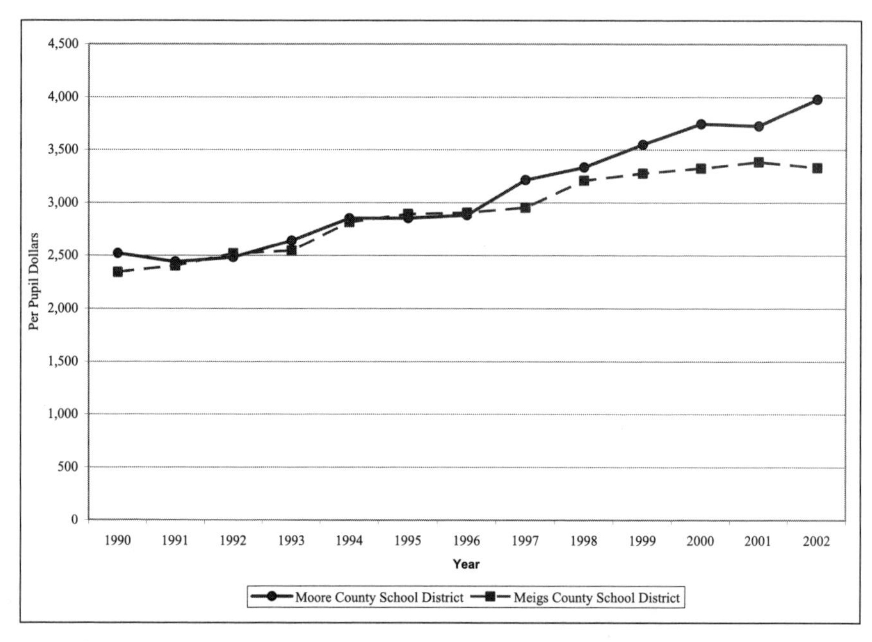

Figure 8.10 Current Expenditures for Elementary and Secondary Education Programs
Source: National Center for Education Statistics, U.S. Department of Education.

revenue as a metropolitan government had a more direct impact upon public service levels for highway-related purposes than educational purposes. The trend in per capita highway expenditures was rather inconsistent and parallel to the erratic trend of federal aid receipts. Conversely, per pupil education expenditures displayed a more stable upward trend throughout the period, even while federal aid receipts were inconsistent. Because public service provision for elementary and secondary education in Lynchburg/Moore appears to have been largely unaffected by federal aid receipts, it is inconsequential whether the consolidation of Lynchburg and Moore County resulted in greater levels of federal intergovernmental revenue to expand public service provision for educational purposes. However, the apparently more direct link between federal intergovernmental revenue and highway spending within Lynchburg/Moore suggests that the metropolitan government may not have fulfilled the promise to generate additional federal aid to expand public service provision.

Using Tax Dollars More Efficiently

The final proconsolidation argument put forth during the campaign—and the issue most closely related to the hypothesis that consolidated governments operate more efficiently than unconsolidated governments—maintained that Lynchburg and Moore County used tax dollars inefficiently by duplicating public services. Consolidating the governments seemed an appropriate approach for streamlining spending for public service provision while protecting the tax base against annexation from surrounding communities. This efficiency outcome is examined in the next two sections by comparing revenue and expenditure trends for the metropolitan government of Lynchburg/Moore to the unconsolidated governments of the Town of Decatur and Meigs County.

Revenue Trends

As noted above, the consolidation focused on avoiding annexation and thereby preserving the property tax base for Moore County. The preceding analysis examined property assessment valuation and tax rate trends in Lynchburg/Moore County compared with Decatur/Meigs County and concluded that the consolidation succeeded in this effort. Moreover, Lynchburg/Moore exemplified stability in both assessed property values and property tax rates throughout the postconsolidation period, which should produce a rather consistent trend in revenue generated from property taxation. Figure 8.11 illustrates the trends in per capita property tax revenue for Lynchburg/Moore and Decatur/Meigs during the 1977–2002 period. As can be seen from the figure, Lynchburg/Moore's per capita property tax revenue consistently followed an upward trend (with the exception of 1997) between 1982 and 2002, which includes both the preconsolidation and postconsolidation periods.[11] Per capita property tax revenue for Lynchburg/Moore increased 63 percent, from $173 in 1982 to $281 in 2002. This suggests again that the Lynchburg/Moore consolidation was successful in protecting the property tax base within the jurisdiction. Meanwhile, Decatur/Meigs generated less per capita revenue from property taxation than Lynchburg/Moore throughout the period as well as followed a more inconsistent trend.

Also embedded in the concern over annexation was a desire to protect the revenue stream generated by the Jack Daniel's Distillery. The distillery acts as a dominant economic force in the metropolitan area, a claim supported by the Lynchburg/Moore Chamber of Commerce website's description of Lynchburg: "It is a tiny little town in a tiny little county with one BIG industry—JACK DANIEL'S DISTILLERY. Granted, most people come to Lynchburg the first time to take the tour of the oldest registered distillery in the United States."

To assess the extent to which the consolidation preserved the sales tax base within the metropolitan area, figure 8.12 illustrates the trends in per

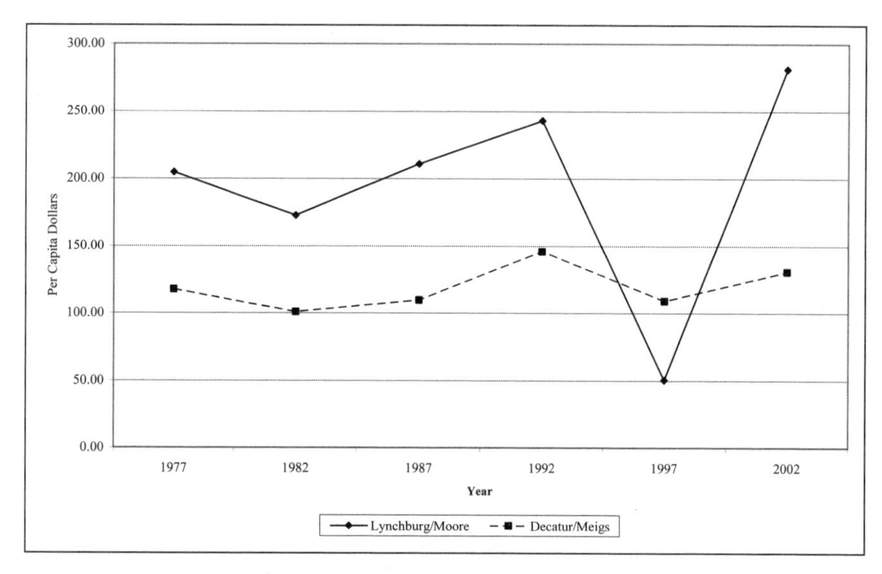

Figure 8.11 Per Capita Property Tax Revenue, 1977–2002
Source: U.S. Bureau of the Census.

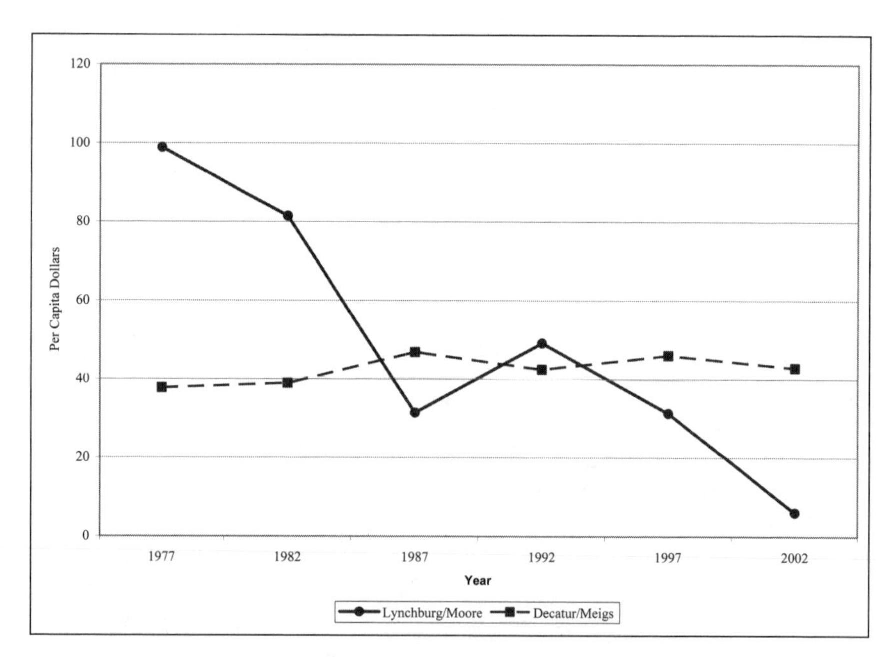

Figure 8.12 Per Capita Sales and Gross Receipts Revenue, 1977–2002
Source: U.S. Bureau of the Census.

capita sales and gross receipts revenue for Lynchburg/Moore County and Decatur/Meigs County from 1977 to 2002. As can be seen from the figure, Lynchburg/Moore experienced fairly consistent declining revenues from sales and gross receipts during the period. Lynchburg/Moore's per capita sales and gross receipts revenue fell from $98.86 in 1977 to $6.08 in 2002. This amounts to a 93.9 percent decline during these twenty-five years. Conversely, per capita sales and gross receipts revenue for Decatur/Meigs fluctuated more modestly, from the lowest level of $37.78 in 1977 to the highest level of $46.83 in 1987 to $42.81 by 2002. It might be the case that the Lynchburg/Moore consolidation provided opportunities for efficiency gains that resulted in a declining need for sales tax revenue within the metropolitan jurisdiction. More likely, however, is a shift for Lynchburg/Moore toward greater reliance on property taxation (evidenced by the consistently upward trend in property tax revenue illustrated in figure 8.11) as a result of the fortification of the property tax base provided by the consolidation. Nonetheless, preserving the sales tax revenue stream from the Jack Daniel's Distillery served as a primary motivation for consolidation. The declining trend in sales and gross receipts revenue also suggests that the consolidation did not achieve the intended outcome of sustaining the sales tax base within the Lynchburg/Moore metropolitan area.

Looking at revenue trends more broadly, figure 8.13 provides a comparison between Lynchburg/Moore and Decatur/Meigs in per capita own source revenue during the 1977–2002 period. Perhaps most notable from the figure is the increase in per capita own source revenue for Lynchburg/Moore immediately following the consolidation between 1987 and 1992, with a subsequent decline back down to the preconsolidation level by 1997. Conversely, per capita own source revenue for the Town of Decatur and Meigs County steadily increased between 1987 and 1997. In Lynchburg/Moore, per capita own source revenue jumped from $348 in 1987 to $425 in 1992 and then fell to $346 in 1997. These changes amount to a 22 percent increase followed by an 18.6 percent decline during the decade. During the same time, per capita own source revenue for Decatur/Meigs increased from $241 in 1987 to $259 in 1992 to $270 by 1997. This amounts to an 11.7 percent increase throughout the decade. These contradictory trends might suggest that the consolidation of Lynchburg and Moore County transpired into greater efficiency, resulting in a declining need for tax revenue. However, the 59.6 percent increase in per capita own source revenue generated by Lynchburg/Moore between 1997 and 2002 suggests that the efficiency issue needs further exploring.

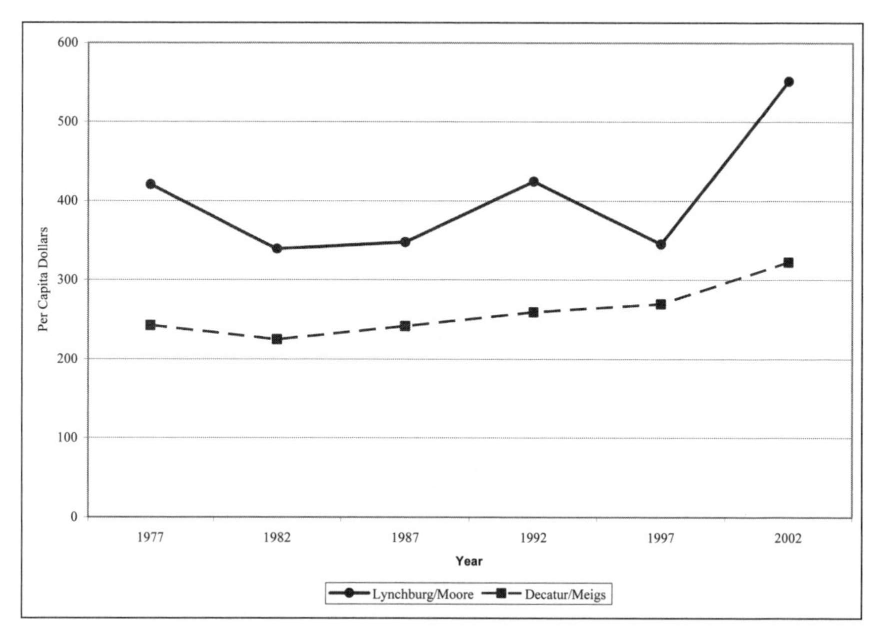

Figure 8.13 Per Capita Own Source Revenue, 1977–2002
Source: U.S. Bureau of the Census.

Expenditure Trends

The potential efficiency outcomes resulting from the elimination of duplicated services from the Lynchburg/Moore County consolidation might be more apparent by examining expenditure trends in the preconsolidation and postconsolidation periods in comparison with the combined expenditure trends for the Town of Decatur and Meigs County. Figure 8.14 illustrates the trends in per capita current expenditures (excluding capital outlay expenditures) for Lynchburg/Moore and Decatur/Meigs during the 1977–2002 period. As can be seen from the figure, the two jurisdictions follow similar trends in per capita spending over the twenty-five years, though the growth rate of expenditures for Lynchburg/Moore noticeably exceeds that of Decatur/Meigs. In 1982, per capita expenditures for Lynchburg/Moore and Decatur/Meigs were nearly equal at $567 and $562, respectively. From that point, per capita expenditures for Decatur/Meigs increased a modest 50 percent, to $842 by 2002, compared with Lynchburg/Moore's 110 percent increase to $1,191 by the end of the period. Lynchburg/Moore's increasing expenditure trend amounts to more than double the rate of increase realized in Decatur/Meigs. This trend seems contrary to what should be expected from a jurisdiction achieving greater efficiency in public service provision by eliminating duplicate services.

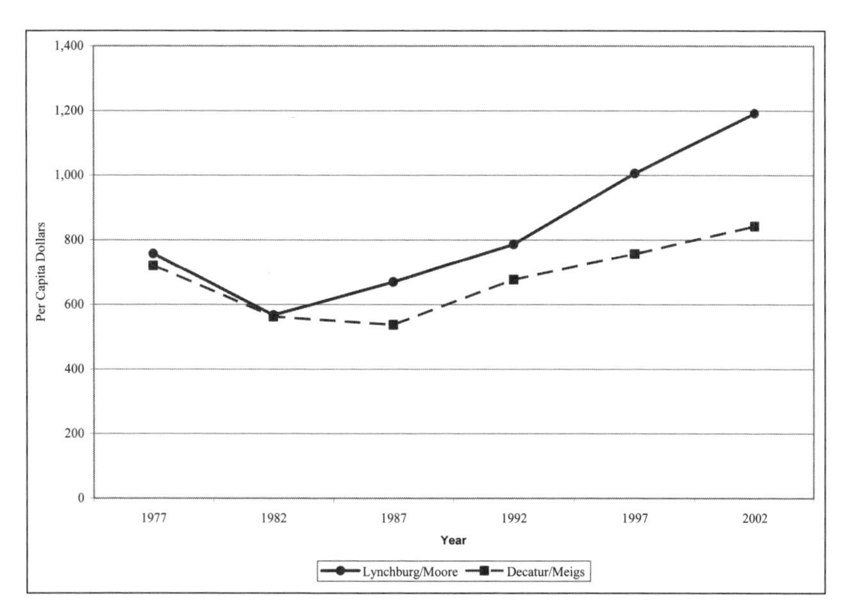

Figure 8.14 Per Capita Current Expenditures, 1977–2002
Source: U.S. Bureau of the Census.

Because local government expenditures are often primarily consumed by spending on wages and salaries, a closer examination of this spending category might offer greater explanation for Lynchburg/Moore County's increasing per capita expenditure trend. Figure 8.15 displays the per capita salaries and wages expenditures for both Lynchburg/Moore and Decatur/Meigs during the 1977–2002 period. The figure shows that after a decline between 1977 and 1982, Decatur/Meigs spending steadily increased throughout the remainder of the period, from $309 in 1982 to $455 in 2002. This amounts to a 47 percent increase throughout the two decades. The City of Lynchburg and Moore County also experienced a decline in per capita spending for salaries and wages between 1977 and 1982, and the decrease was much more pronounced than can be seen in Decatur/Meigs. However, contrary to expectations, per capita expenditures for wages and salaries in Lynchburg/Moore actually increased after the consolidation occurred. The 1987 preconsolidation expenditure level was $402, compared with the postconsolidation expenditure level of $458 in 1992. This amounts to a 14 percent increase in per capita expenditures for salaries and wages following the consolidation. Moreover, although Lynchburg/Moore did experience a fairly substantial decline in per capita salaries and wages expenditures between 1992 and 1997, the subsequent 161 percent increase between 1997 and 2002 from $167 to $435 resulted in a higher spending level than before the governments consolidated.

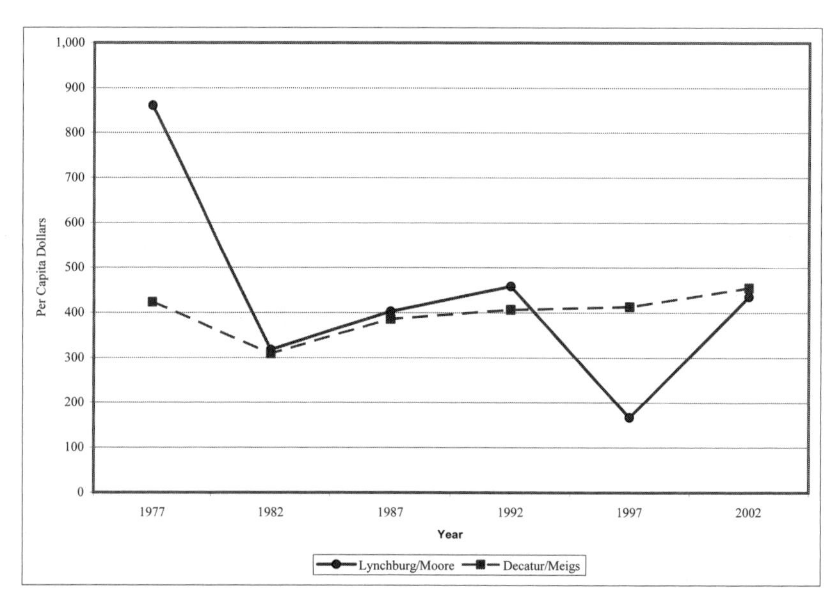

Figure 8.15 Salaries and Wages
Source: U.S. Bureau of the Census.

Because consolidation resulted in the elimination of several positions by streamlining services, at least some of the efficiency gains achieved through consolidation should be apparent through reduced spending levels for salaries and wages. The trends illustrated in figures 8.14 and 8.15 suggest that the consolidation of Lynchburg and Moore County perhaps did not lead to greater efficiency. A closer look at spending related to the specific services in which duplication was eliminated by the consolidation might help to better explain whether greater efficiency was indeed achieved.

As noted in the previous discussion of the Lynchburg/Moore consolidation and shown in table 8.1, three services formerly provided by both the City of Lynchburg and Moore County were transformed by the consolidation into solely metropolitan government functions to eliminate duplication in public service provision. These services included fire, police, and utilities. Figures 8.16, 8.17, and 8.18 illustrate the per capita direct expenditures for both Lynchburg/Moore and Decatur/Meigs for fire, police, and utilities, respectively, during the 1977–2002 period.[12] Unfortunately, however, the expenditure trends for these formerly duplicated services do not clearly reveal the extent to which greater efficiency was achieved through consolidation. Comparisons of Lynchburg/Moore's expenditure trends for these services to expenditures for the Town of Decatur and Meigs County also provide ambiguous evidence regarding this efficiency outcome.

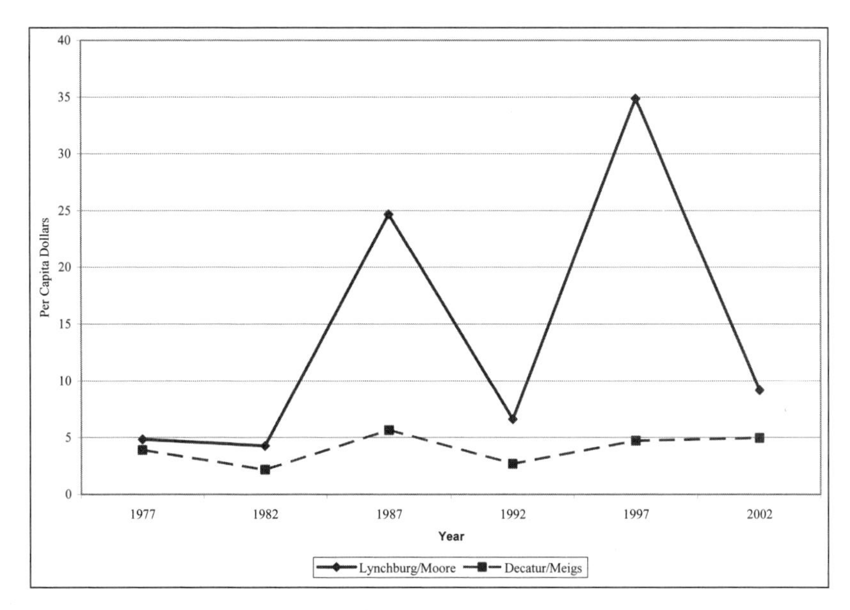

Figure 8.16 Fire Expenditures
Source: U.S. Bureau of the Census.

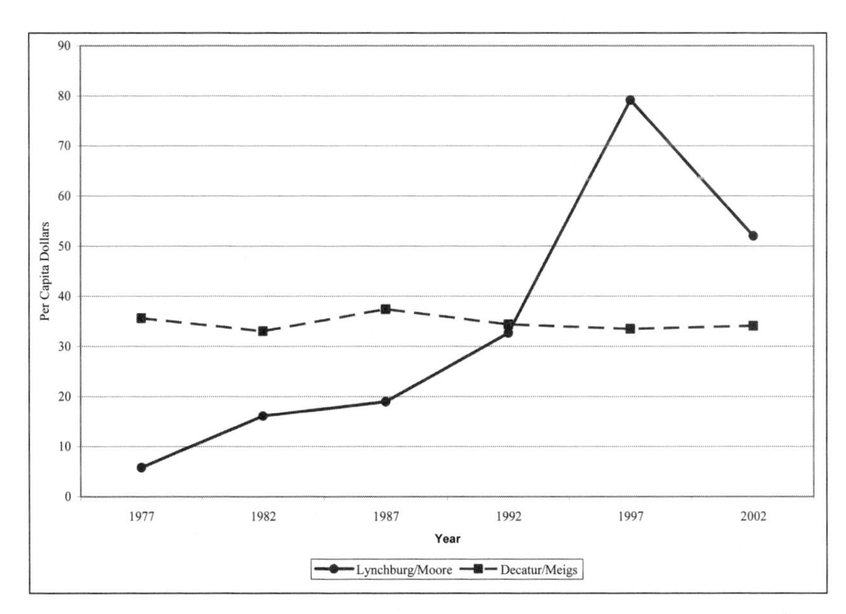

Figure 8.17 Police Expenditures
Source: U.S. Bureau of the Census.

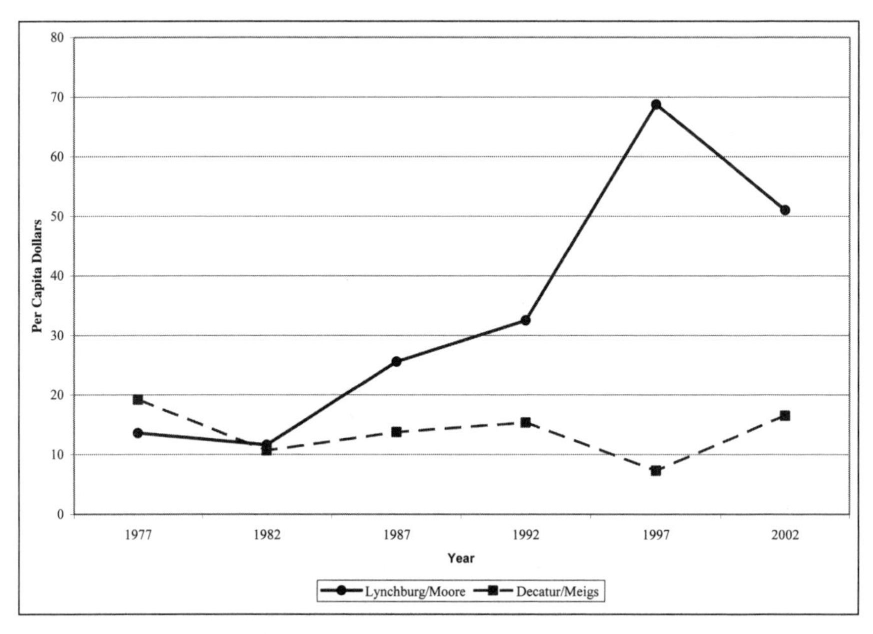

Figure 8.18 Utilities Expenditures
Source: U.S. Bureau of the Census.

Figure 8.16 shows that Lynchburg/Moore's per capita expenditures for fire protection declined after the consolidation from $13.63 in 1987 to $6.61 in 1992. It is difficult to determine, however, if this declining trend could be attributed to efficiency gains from the consolidation because per capita expenditures sharply increased in 1997 before dropping back to $9.17 in 2002. The 1997 expenditure level for Lynchburg/Moore reflects the purchase of a new fire truck. Lynchburg/Moore accounts for capital acquisitions through the metropolitan government's operating budget rather than its capital budget (Thomas 2007). This approach differs from Meigs County, where capital acquisitions like a new fire truck are typically debt financed and recorded through a separate capital outlay rather than within the operating budget. Despite this difference in accounting methods, the expenditure data shown in figure 8.16 is comparable between the two combined jurisdictions because spending for capital outlays is included in the figures for both Lynchburg/Moore and Decatur/Meigs. As seen in figure 8.16, fire expenditures for Decatur/Meigs maintained a more stable trend throughout the period, even if capital outlay expenditures are included in the data. Per capita fire expenditures for Decatur/Meigs ranged from the minimum of $2.16 in 1982 to the maximum of $4.96 in 2002. However, between 1992 and 2002, Decatur/Meigs fire expenditures increased 84.1 percent during the decade. This trend compares to Lynchburg/Moore in which 2002 per capita fire expenditures were only 38.8 percent higher than 1992 expenditures. Moreover, Lynchburg/Moore's 2002 expenditures remained lower than the 1987 preconsolidation spending level for fire protection.

Lynchburg/Moore's per capita expenditures for police protection portray a consistently increasing trend during the period shown in figure 8.17. The county sheriff's office remained intact after the consolidation and became the head of all law enforcement for the metropolitan area. As a result, spending for police protection in Lynchburg/Moore increased from $2.91 in 1977 to $16.39 in 1987 to $52.04 by 2002. Although per capita expenditures in 2002 were significantly lower than in 1997, the 2002 spending level was 59.3 percent higher than the 1992 expenditure level of $32.68. Moreover, the surge in police spending for Lynchburg/Moore in 1997 was likely due to a vehicle or equipment purchase and likely would have been lower without the purchase.[13] Also shown in figure 8.17, Decatur/Meigs per capita police expenditures maintained a more stable trend over the twenty-five-year period, changing only 20.1 percent from the lowest expenditure level of $28.62 in 1997 to the highest level of $34.37 in 1992. Despite this consistency, Lynchburg/Moore's per capita police expenditures were below Decatur/Meigs spending levels between 1977 and 1992, which is the period leading up to and immediately following consolidation. This trend might provide some evidence of efficiency gains from consolidation, which should have eliminated the cost for Lynchburg's duplicate police department staffed with only one officer. However, per capita police expenditures for Lynchburg/Moore in both 1997 and 2002 significantly exceeded Decatur/Meigs spending. In 1997 and 2002, per capita police expenditures for Lynchburg/Moore were 2.77 and 1.53 times, respectively, the level of spending in Decatur/Meigs. This latter trend obscures any indication of efficiency gains achieved through consolidation.

Finally, duplication in utility services was eliminated by the Lynchburg/Moore consolidation when water services were taken over by the metropolitan government. The utilities expenditure data shown in figure 8.18 represent spending exclusively by the City of Lynchburg (before consolidation) and the Town of Decatur. Moreover, these utility expenditures are solely dedicated for water utility services. Similar to the trend for police spending, the figure shows that per capita utility expenditures for Lynchburg/Moore increased rather consistently during the period and therefore also appear to have been unaffected by the consolidation. This trend presents further difficulties in assessing the extent to which the consolidation achieved efficiency gains. Lynchburg/Moore experienced a 26.9 percent increase in per capita utility expenditures in 1992 following consolidation. Between 1992 and 1997, per capita utility expenditures surged up another 111.6 percent due to the metropolitan government's purchase of water lines (Thomas 2007). Although utility spending declined between 1997 and 2002, per capita utility expenditures in 2002 were 57.0 percent higher than the 1992 spending level and 99.3 percent greater than the 1987 preconsolidation spending level for utility services.

Conclusion

The conclusion about the Lynchburg/Moore County consolidation that is most apparent and easiest to gauge is that it indeed fulfilled the promise of fending off annexation and encroachment by surrounding governments, which was an outcome sealed by the act of consolidation itself. As a result of the consolidation, the geographical area of the property tax base within Lynchburg and Moore County was preserved. In addition, the value of the metropolitan property tax base remained relatively stable both during and after consolidation with no significant drops in assessment valuation that might have occurred if portions of the tax base had been annexed by the larger surrounding governments. This annexation issue encompassed powerful implications, both emotionally and economically, for Lynchburg and Moore County and represented the central justification for consolidation. On this basis, the consolidation of Lynchburg/Moore can be deemed an automatic success (H2, in table 8.4).

The impact of consolidation on levels of federal intergovernmental revenue is less straightforward. Although the promise of increased federal intergovernmental revenue was never fulfilled, spending outcomes for

Table 8.4 Summary of the Lynchburg/Moore County Case

Overall Assessment of Evidence	H1: Efficiency	H2: Economic Development	H3: Other Promises
Not enough data available			
No evidence	☑		
Weak			☑
Moderate			
Strong		☑	

public services varied considerably. Although highway-related expenditures appeared to suffer due to fluctuations and declines in federal intergovernmental revenue, these vacillations had no apparent effect on education spending. Consolidation failed to produce evident success in this area, but the tangible implications of consolidation on services funded through federal intergovernmental revenue remain unclear (H3, in table 8.4).

Drawing a conclusion regarding the extent to which the Lynchburg/Moore's consolidation produced efficiency gains is still more difficult. An examination of revenue trends suggests that consolidation was less successful in sustaining the sales tax base within the Lynchburg/Moore metropolitan area. Expenditure trends reveal that the consolidation of Lynchburg and Moore County perhaps did not lead to greater efficiency (H1, in table 8.4), which should have translated into reduced spending levels for salaries and wages from the elimination of several positions related to duplicate services streamlined by the consolidation. Lynchburg/Moore's expenditure trends in the postconsolidation period for the three services in which duplication was directly eliminated by the consolidation reiterate this conclusion. Although the data presented in this chapter suggest that the metropolitan government of Lynchburg/Moore does not operate more efficiently than unconsolidated governments, it is important to recollect that efficiency gains were not at the forefront of the consolidation campaign and were not the primary motivator for creating the metropolitan government.

Regardless of the evidence surrounding the Lynchburg/Moore case, the issue of government consolidation persists within the state of Tennessee. Currently, there is a campaign pursuing the consolidation of the City of Knoxville and Knox County. However, this case is unfolding against a very different backdrop than the Lynchburg/Moore consolidation. In recent years, the city and county have already united to provide several public services, including their school systems, health departments, libraries, and air quality offices (*Knoxville News Sentinel* 2007). This slower progression of events begs the question of whether incremental change would make the final transition to a metropolitan government less controversial for the parties involved and enable spending in critical areas to be streamlined with less infringement on existing city–county power and identity dynamics. Perhaps the Knoxville/Knox County case will shed further light on this question in the near future.

Notes

1. Although metropolitan governments are classified under Tennessee state law as both counties and municipalities, the U.S. Bureau of the Census only counts metropolitan governments once (as municipal governments) for census statistics on governments.
2. The general service district and urban service district are not counted as separate governments by the U.S. Bureau of the Census.
3. Also, Article 1, Section 1.04(c) of the Lynchburg/Moore County Metropolitan Government charter stipulates that the new government may not "impair or diminish the pension, retirement, contract, or civil service rights of persons employed upon the effective date of this Charter by the City of Lynchburg or Moore County; provided that each such employee shall have the option . . . to transfer to the pension, retirement, pay plan, or Civil Service Plan of the Metropolitan Government."
4. The U.S. Bureau of the Census offers the following definition of poverty on its website (www.census.gov/hhes/www/poverty/definitions.html): "Following the Office of Management and Budget's (OMB) Statistical Policy Directive 14, the Census Bureau uses a set of money income thresholds that vary by family size and composition to determine who is in poverty. If a family's total income is less than the family's threshold, then that family and every individual in it is considered in poverty. The official poverty thresholds do not vary geographically, but they are updated for inflation using Consumer Price Index (CPI-U). The official poverty definition uses money income before taxes and does not include capital gains or noncash benefits (such as public housing, Medicaid, and food stamps)."
5. The U.S. Bureau of the Census does not report educational attainment data for places with less than 2,500 population. Therefore, high school and college attainment data for the Town of Decatur and City of Lynchburg were unavailable.
6. The difference in measures between 1980 and 1990 is due to a change in the measure employed by the U.S. Bureau of the Census.
7. The Lynchburg Whiskey Cake comes highly recommended from this chapter's authors.
8. Federal intergovernmental revenue data for fiscal years 1991 and 1992 were unavailable.
9. Direct expenditures include spending for current operations and capital outlays and excludes intergovernmental expenditures.
10. Current expenditures exclude capital outlay expenditures.

11. The fiscal analysis of revenue and expenditure trends using Census data revealed several anomalies in the data pertaining to the year 1997. The information in this chapter accurately presents the data as reported by the U.S. Bureau of the Census. We have made several attempts to obtain information to qualitatively explain the 1997 discrepancies in the data. In some instances, we are able to offer explanations with the analysis but are unable to do so in other instances. We believe there is a possible reporting error in the 1997 data, but are unable to validate this claim. We also do not speculate about the origin of any possible reporting error. However, we advise readers to consider the 1997 data cautiously.
12. Direct expenditures include spending for current operations and capitals outlays and exclude intergovernmental expenditures.
13. Former Moore County commissioner and metropolitan executive Billy H. Thomas confirmed that this spike was most likely due to a vehicle or equipment purchase similar to the one made for fire protection but did not have firsthand knowledge of such a purchase (Thomas 2007).

References

Knoxville News Sentinel. 2007. Unified County, City Back on Table. March 27.

Moore County News. 1987a. Metro Vote Count Official, 1375–95. November 26.

———. 1987b. 2668 Voters: County Metro Vote Is Set for Tuesday. November 12.

Thomas, Billy H. 2007. Former mayor and metropolitan executive for Lynchburg/Moore County. Telephone interviews by Mary Ellen Wiggins. Lynchburg, TN, April 4 and 16.

9

Unification Promises and Outcomes

The Case of Athens and Clarke County, Georgia

Dan Durning and Paula Sanford

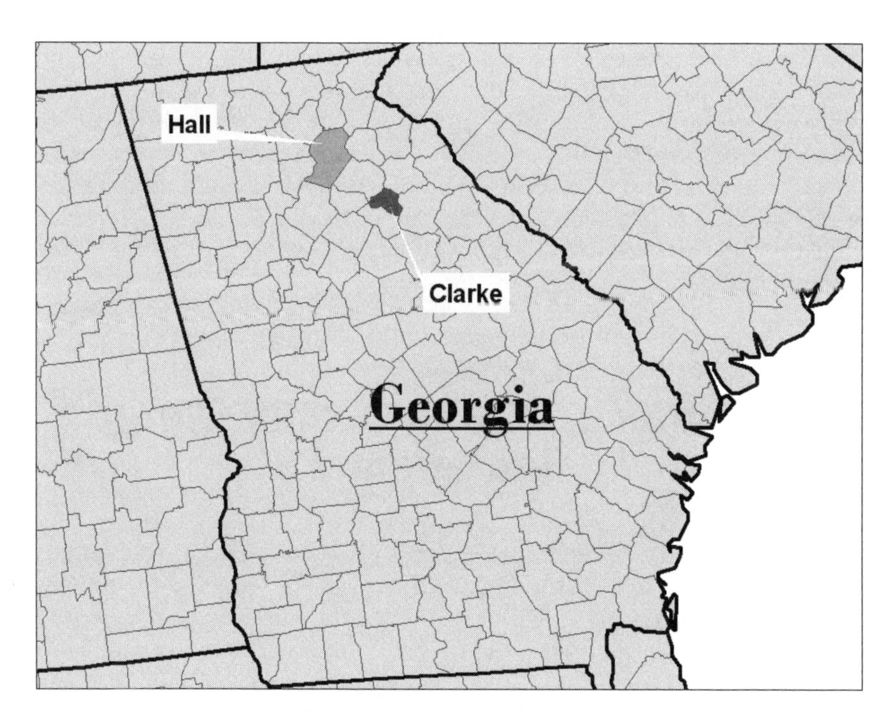

Map 9 Locations of Hall County and Clarke County, Georgia
Source: U.S. Bureau of the Census.

On August 7, 1990, the citizens of the city of Athens and Clarke County, Georgia, voted to merge their city and county governments to create a new "unified" government (map 9). This vote was the final act in a prolonged effort to consolidate the two governments. It followed voter rejection of consolidation proposals in 1969, 1972, and 1982.

The 1990 referendum differed from the earlier ones not only in its outcome but also in the strategy adopted by consolidation proponents. One important difference in strategy was that proponents labeled the proposed merger as "unification" rather than consolidation. Another key difference was that the merger effort was initiated and led by prominent citizens, not by elected city and county officials, and the merger process included extensive efforts to invite Clarke County residents to participate in writing and marketing the new charter. This strategy enabled supporters to frame the proposed merger as a citizen-initiated effort aimed at unifying the governments and to formulate a fresh narrative about the effects it would have.

This chapter examines the narrative constructed by unification advocates and seeks to determine to what extent it was accurate in forecasting the actual results of the government merger. After providing some background on the Athens/Clarke County consolidation, we look at how unification advocates talked about the issue to convince voters to support it. Through their advocacy, unification supporters framed the issue and created a narrative that included assertions about the problems caused by the existing structure of government and arguments about how unification would solve those problems to create a better future. Finally, we address the question of the extent to which unification has produced the future described in the proconsolidation narrative.

The Athens/Clarke County Merger: Background

As discussed by Durning, Gillespie, and Campbell (2004), the Athens/Clarke County merger can best be understood as the culmination of a process that lasted over twenty-five years. During that time, support for consolidation fluctuated but never disappeared. The defeat of consolidation proposals in 1969, 1972, and 1982 did not crush this support nor long deter supporters for three main reasons: (1) In each referendum, a majority of city voters supported consolidation; (2) with each referendum, a larger percentage of voters in unincorporated Clarke County voted for the proposal (29 percent in 1969, 42 percent in 1972, and 45 percent in 1981); and (3) in each referenda, the proposed merger received almost 50 percent of the total vote (in 1982, the total was 4,999 votes for consolidation and 5,003 against).

The odds for a successful merger referendum increased in 1983 when Georgia adopted a new Constitution that included a provision that made city–county consolidation easier. This provision eliminated the requirement that to be approved, a consolidation proposal must receive a majority of votes by voters living in unincorporated areas of the county. It states that a proposed consolidation is approved in a referendum if it receives a majority of all votes on the issue and if a majority of voters in each affected city votes to give up the city charter.

The fourth effort to merge Athens and Clarke County began in the late 1980s, triggered by a group of citizens appointed in 1987 by the Clarke County government to work for voter approval of a 1 percent special-purpose local-option sales tax (SPLOST). After the SPLOST referendum, a dozen or so members of the group—without a government mandate—continued to meet to discuss the future needs of Athens and Clarke County. The group renamed itself the Quality Growth Task Force (QGTF).

The QGTF, which was led jointly by the manager of one of the county's larger local manufacturing plants and by a highly regarded University of Georgia (UGA) vice president, examined issues related to the future of Athens and Clarke County. In the fall of 1988 it invited a diverse mixture of two hundred people from Northeast Georgia to meet to identify major concerns of the region. This group specified five areas of concern—water, public education, transportation, regional planning, and government—and the QGTF appointed committees to examine them.

As the study process proceeded, the QGTF's government issues committee proposed consolidation as a solution to many of the concerns identified by the other committees. It invited residents of Athens and unincorporated Clarke County to attend a town meeting to discuss the idea of consolidation. On July 10, 1989, about three hundred residents attended the meeting, and by a show of hands, they backed, almost unanimously, the appointment of a fifteen-person unification study commission.

Later in July, both the Athens City Council and the Clarke County Commission voted to create the "Athens/Clarke County Unification Commission," with fifteen members, five appointed by the city, five by the county, and five by the task force. The Unification Commission appointees consisted of four UGA administrators or faculty members, nine local business people, a retired principal, and a retired UGA administrator.[1] No appointees were local government elected officials or employees.

During September and October 1989, the Unification Commission convened nine well-attended town meetings throughout the county to collect citizen views on what should be in the new charter. In October the Unification Commission created five task forces, which met during a four-week period to study issues related to the proposed consolidated government. It invited every person in Clarke County to become a member of the task force of his or her choice.

The Unification Commission met for two days in November 1989 to write the charter. The commission reached a consensus on most charter provisions. It circulated the draft charter for review and later made some small changes in response to the suggestions it received.

In early March 1999, local legislation was enacted by the Georgia General Assembly to submit the proposed charter to voters for their decision. In late June, the charter was precleared by the U.S. Department of Justice under the Voting Rights Act.[2] The referendum was held on August 7, 1990.

The Consolidation Narrative and Counternarrative

Campaigns for and against consolidation usually are built around a narrative. In its most effective form, a narrative tells a creditable, coherent story, and in the case of consolidation, the advocate's story is usually about an imperfect present and an improved future. Elements of the prototypical consolidation narrative include a story of fragmented governments that create the problems of inefficiency, disunity (which disrupts economic development), and ineffectiveness, and typically the story describes a future in which a consolidated government will make these problems disappear.

In most cases, the proconsolidation narrative must confront a counternarrative created by consolidation opponents. Often the counternarrative is even more compelling than the consolidation narrative. Their story is often one in which a small group of power-grabbing elites wish to seize control of local government.[3] The story often includes warnings about higher taxes and fees, new restrictions on property use in rural areas, and, sometimes, such things as busing schoolchildren. The story presents consolidation as the grave threat to the status quo, and opponents often argue, "If it ain't broke, don't fix it."

Of course, consolidation narratives and counternarratives differ for each consolidation campaign. They are unique for each time and location, and they usually combine elements of the typical consolidation narrative with specific concerns and issues. In this case, the proconsolidation narrative was created and disseminated by the Athens–Clarke County Unification Commission and its successor, "Citizens for a Unified Government." They were aided by an Atlanta-based public relations firm that was hired to assist with the "education" campaign for unification.[4]

The Athens/Clarke County consolidation narrative was shaped—and aided—by the early decision to label the merger proposal as "unification" rather than "consolidation." By changing this label, supporters were able to disassociate themselves from previous voter rejection of consolidation proposals and to emphasize the idea that the proposals would "unify" governments.

The consolidation narrative stressed the benefits of "unification" and why citizens should choose "The Better Way" (the campaign slogan). From the beginning of the campaign for unification, the narrative emphasized a five-point program of benefits: (1) better public safety, (2) contained costs, (3) attraction of new businesses, (4) elimination of duplicated services, and (5) elimination of bickering between city and county governments (*Athens Banner-Herald,* April 4, 1990).

This narrative was communicated in the advertisements, speeches, and personal campaigning by consolidation advocates. It was also disseminated through brochures and numerous newspaper advertisements financed by $50,000 in contributions to the "Citizens for a United Government."

Unlike the opponents in previous consolidation referendum campaigns in Clarke County, the opposition in 1990 was not well organized, spent little money, and lacked a coherent counternarrative. Opponents included several local elected officials; five (out of ten) city council members, one county commissioner, and two former county commissioners spoke against the unification (*Athens Banner-Herald,* August 3, 1990). Also, some African American leaders publicly opposed the merger. Nevertheless, the only organized opposition was by the "Community Coalition Against Consolidation" (CCAC), whose existence was announced by a former county commissioner a few days before the referendum. He claimed that the CCAC had "hundreds" of members, but the group held no open meetings and provided no evidence of large-scale support. Although the activities of proponents were covered prominently in the local newspapers, the opponents either held no organized public campaign events or their events were not reported.

The CCAC purchased a few advertisements in the local newspapers (*Athens Banner-Herald,* August 7, 1990) and distributed a mimeographed flyer just before the election. This flyer asserted that the consolidation would potentially increase water and sewage rates, decrease police protection, and reduce solid waste pickup services. In addition to these criticisms, others writing and speaking against consolidation claimed that it would cause voters to lose representation, would reduce the number of elected minority council members, and would result in increased taxes.

Promises of Unification and Results

The major promises of unification were not made by elected officials or local government employees but by members of the Athens–Clarke County Unification Commission and its successor, "Citizens for a United Government." Through charter provisions and through the narrative they created and disseminated, these members made implicit promises about the outcomes of the unified government's future policymaking.

As mentioned above, five major outcomes were promised in the proconsolidation narrative presented in speeches, advertisements, and campaign materials. These outcomes can be divided into three major categories (the quotations in each category are from the main proconsolidation campaign brochure):

Increased governmental efficiency:

Taxes. "Other places—Columbus, Nashville, Lexington, Jacksonville—that have unified their governments have found that government costs are more easily contained when there is one government instead of two."

More efficient services. "The new plan will eliminate duplicate services, bring greater efficiency to local government and a better quality and delivery of services to all residents."

More effective economic development:

"A single government will enable us to attract healthy new businesses to the area, but—even more importantly—it will enable us to focus and coordinate growth and protect and enhance Athens and Clarke County's unique quality of life for *all* of its citizens."

More effective police department:

> "One coordinated police force means better response times for all of us. Everyone wants to live in a safer community, and this is one easy step we can take in that direction."

According to the proponent's narrative, another outcome would be that unification would eliminate bickering between city and county governments. By definition, merging the local governments would eliminate separate city and county governments, thus achieving this promise.

In addition to these major promises, consolidation supporters made other strategic promises, and tried to ensure that they would be carried out by including provisions in the charter to either restrict or mandate actions by the new unified government. These promises were made mainly to attract votes or deter opposition to the unification proposal. The provisions included:

- Addressing concerns about higher water rates charged to residents of unincorporated areas. The city of Athens owned the water system serving the county, and it charged residents outside of Athens almost double the rate charged to city residents. The unification charter required creation of a study commission to study this situation to recommend equitable rates (and implicitly, to do away with the differential).
- Insuring that the name "Athens" would continue to be used and prominently featured. Some longtime residents wanted to maintain the historic identity of the city even though it would become part of a unified government.
- Designing commission districts so that black residents would have, to the extent possible, the same percentage representation in the unified government legislative body as they had in the Athens City Council and Clarke County Commission.
- Requiring creation of a "Department of Human and Economic Development" to address the concerns of low-income residents.
- Protecting the jobs and benefits of city and county employees by limiting the discretion of the new government to reduce its workforce or decrease the benefits provided to employees.

In the following subsections, we examine to what extent unification provided the beneficial changes that were promised by unification supporters.

Unification and Governmental Efficiency

The prounification narrative asserted that unification would (1) contain the costs of providing services and (2) provide more efficient services. Thus the promise was that in the future the cost of a fixed amount of services would be less if provided by the unified government than it would be if provided by separately by the City of Athens and Clarke County governments.[5]

In a careful study of preunification and postunification expenditures in Athens and Clarke County, Selden and Campbell (2000) found that the consolidated government had reduced real expenditures and real per capita expenditures for some services. However, their study did not show conclusive evidence that the expenditure reductions were directly related to the unification. Also, their findings are tenuous because they examined expenditures during a limited time frame, with data for only two fiscal years before the consolidation took full effect and six years after.

Selden and Campbell collected line-item budget data from the city of Athens, Clarke County, and the Athens–Clarke County (A-CC) unified government budgets from fiscal year (FY) 1990 (July 1989 through June 1990) to FY 1997 (July 1996 through June 1997). The FY 1990 and FY 1991 budgets had been formulated separately by the City of Athens and Clarke County. The remaining budgets had been adopted by the unified government.[6]

The charter of the A-CC unified government limited its ability to reduce personnel expenditures by guaranteeing that no city or county employee would lose employment or benefits due to the unification. Thus the unified government was able to eliminate redundant employees only through retirements and voluntary separations. At the same time it had to equalize salaries and benefits so that employees in similar positions received similar compensation. It has spent an estimated $4.9 million annually to equalize salaries and another $130,000 a year on adjusted benefits. These additional costs have been incorporated into A-CC's annual operating budgets.

Despite the higher personnel costs following the unification, the inflation-adjusted expenditures in some functions and departments were reduced after the governments merged. The analysis by Selden and Campbell showed real expenditures on the finance function and on leisure services were less in FY 1997 than in FY 1992. However, the same reduction did not occur for all functions.

In addition to simply comparing preunification and postunification expenditures in A-CC, Selden and Campbell also compared the A-CC unified government's expenditures with those for three comparable city and county governments in Georgia. The comparison governments were the city of Albany and Dougherty County, the city of Gainesville and Hall County, and the city of Warner Robbins and Houston County. The counties in which these governments were located had populations similar to Clarke County in 1990 (table 9.1), and the counties had other characteristics in common (see table 9.2).[7]

In comparing the A-CC unified government's expenditures with those by comparable city and county governments, Selden and Campbell found that from FY 1992 to FY 1997, real per capita expenditures by the A-CC unified government declined for general fund functions, police services, and fire services, but some of the comparison city and county governments had similar or even greater reductions in expenditures. For example, A-CC's real per capita expenditures on police services fell by 10.29 percent from FY 1992 to FY 1997; during the same period, real per capita expenditures by Gainesville and Hall County on police services declined even more—by 18.97 percent—while spending by the other two city and county governments increased (Selden and Campbell 2000, 191). Because the declines in postunification real per capita expenditures occurred not only in A-CC but also in one or more of the comparison city and county locations, the evidence does not conclusively support the hypothesis that unification was the variable responsible for the A-CC unified government's lower real per capita expenditures.

Following the same general approach as Selden and Campbell, we examined preunification and postunification general fund expenditures, but with different data. These data came from the annual survey of local government finance conducted by the Carl Vinson Institute of Government for the Georgia Department of Community Affairs. This survey asks

Table 9.1 Population of Clarke County and Comparison Counties, 1980, 1990, 2000 Census

	Population			% Change	
County	1980	1990	2000	1980–90	1990–2000
Clarke	74,498	87,594	101,489	17.6	15.9
Dougherty	100,718	96,311	96,065	–4.4	–0.3
Hall	75,849	95,428	139,277	25.8	45.9
Houston	77,605	89,208	110,715	15.0	24.2
Georgia	5,462,982	6,487,216	8,186,453	18.7	26.2

Source: U.S. Bureau of the Census.

Table 9.2 Characteristics of Clarke County and Comparison Counties

County	Land Area (square miles)	1990 Median Age (years)	1989 Poverty Level (%)	1989 Median Household Income (dollars)	1990 Gross Appraised Property Value (billions of dollars)
Clarke	120	25.5	19.6	22,986	1.156
Dougherty	329	29.9	25.4	23,762	1.075
Hall	393	32.2	11.5	27,397	1.647
Houston	376	33.4	10.4	32,317	0.965

Sources: The 1990 median age is from the U.S. Census Bureau, reported at www.gadata.org/information_services/Census_Info/1990county_comparison.htm; poverty levels and median household income are from the U.S. Census Bureau, Small Area Income and Poverty Estimates, 1989 (www.census.gov/hhes/www/saipe/county.html); the 1990 gross appraised property value (called the tax digest) is from the Georgia Department of Community Affairs, as reported by the University of Georgia's Vinson Institute of Government.

each city and county government to report its expenditures by function. These data are available from the Georgia Department of Community Affairs (www.dca.georgia.gov).

We collected expenditure data for 1985, 1992, and 2002 for the A-CC unified government; for the three comparison city and county governments in Selden and Campbell's study; and, combined, for city and county governments located in nine counties with 2005 populations within 10 percent of Clarke County's population. These counties include Carroll (101,577), Columbia (100,589), Coweta (105,376), Dougherty (95,681), Douglas (107,217), Fayette (101,333), Floyd (94,009), Lowndes (95,787), and Paulding (105,936). We adjusted annual nominal expenditures by the Consumer Price Index for the Atlanta region to account for inflation. The base year of the index is 1983; the index for 1985 was 108.9, the index for 1992 was 138.5, and the index for 2002 was 177.3.

Although we include several comparison city and county governments to add greater depth to the data analysis, our primary comparison is with the Gainesville and Hall County governments. The Gainesville and Hall County governments are a good comparison for the A-CC unified government, for three main reasons. First, Hall County is located in the same part of Georgia as Clarke County and is subject to many of the same socioeconomic influences. Second, the *daytime* populations of the two counties are roughly comparable. Hall County and Clarke County had nearly the same *residential* populations in 1980, but since then, Hall County's residential population has grown much more rapidly than Clarke County's. Nevertheless, Clarke County's daytime population swells as residents of nearby counties commute to work for employers in Clarke County. Conversely, because parts of Hall County are located within commuting distance of Atlanta, it has a loss in daytime population.[8] The net result is that the daytime populations of the two countries are similar. Third, Clarke and Hall counties have several economic characteristics in common; both have a substantial number of higher-income households (attracted by Lake Lanier in Hall County and UGA in Clarke County), and both have a significant portion of their populations working in blue-collar and service jobs. Hall County is home to a large poultry industry that has attracted many migrant Latino workers. Clarke County also has a poultry processing plant, plus many other blue-collar and service jobs at UGA and local industries.

Before the A-CC unification, the city and county governments in Clarke County and in Hall County had combined some services through functional consolidation or interlocal agreements. As shown in table 9.3, six years before unification, several services were provided exclusively in the city of Athens and Clarke County by either the city government (water and sewer, parks and recreation, building inspections, code enforcement, and planning) or the county government (fire protection and public health), Similarly, Hall County and Gainesville had combined social services, planning, building inspections, and code enforcement; plus the city government exclusively provided water and sewer services and the county government provided public health services.

Ten years after the unification, all local government public services are provided by the unified government in A-CC. In Gainesville and Hall County, planning and building inspection/code enforcement are no longer combined services but are provided separately by the two governments. Social services remained functionally consolidated, and the city government is the sole provider of water and sewer services, whereas the county government is the provider of public health services.

As shown in table 9.4, using 1985, 1992, and 2002 expenditure data, we calculated changes in real per capita operating expenditures from 1985 to 1992 (preunification) and from 1992 to 2002 (postunification). Note that 1992 was the transition year, during which the first A-CC unified government budget was adopted and expenditures were constrained to equal those in the city of Athens and Clarke County during FY 1991, adjusted for inflation.

Table 9.4 shows the total operating expenditures in 1985, 1992, and 2002 by the A-CC unified government and by the comparison city and county governments. It also shows the calculations of nominal and real per

Table 9.3 Level of Functional Consolidation

Service	Six Years before Consolidation		One Year before Consolidation		Ten Years after Consolidation	
	Athens/ Clarke County	Gainesville/ Hall County	Athens/ Clarke County	Gainesville/ Hall County	Athens/ Clarke County	Gainesville/ Hall County
Fire protection	ILA-CO	S	ILA-CO	S	F	S
Social services	S	F	S	F	F	F
Law enforcement	S	S	S	S	F	S
Parks and recreation	ILA-CI	S	ILA-CI	S	F	S
Planning	F	F	F	F	F	S
Building inspection/ code enforcement	CI	F	CI	F	F	S
Economic development	P	P	P	P	P	P
Utilities (water/sewer)	CI	CI	F	CI	F	CI
Public works	S	S	F	S	F	S
Public health	CO	CO	CO	CO	F	CO

Key: CI = city function only; CO = county function only; F = functional consolidation (city and county operations combined into single department); ILA = interlocal agreement between city and county/government performing service; P = privatized (one or both governments may pay third party for service); S = separately provided by both city and county.

Table 9.4 Operating Expenditures by County, 1985, 1992, 2002

Year and County	Estimated Population	Expenditures (dollars) Total	Nominal Per Capita	Real Per Capita
1985				
Clarke County	80,822	29,167,411	360.88	331.39
Hall County	81,713	22,788,713	278.89	256.09
Dougherty County	103,059	36,558,301	354.73	325.74
Houston County	83,677	19,608,197	234.33	215.18
Comparable counties	761,485	138,417,993	181.77	166.92
1992				
Athens/Clarke County	88,334	48,278,941	546.55	394.62
Hall County	99,810	45,968,850	460.56	332.54
Dougherty County	97,659	73,269,927	750.26	541.71
Houston County	93,310	33,878,634	363.08	262.15
Comparable counties	883,352	273,559,257	309.68	223.60
2002				
Athens/Clarke County	103,881	74,643,733	718.55	405.27
Hall County	152,235	108,245,648	711.04	401.04
Dougherty County	95,875	105,925,430	1104.83	623.14
Houston County	116,768	58,572,301	501.61	282.92
Comparable counties	1,125,818	561,464,831	498.72	281.28
% change				
1985–92				
Athens/Clarke County	9.3	65.5	51.4	19.1
Hall County	22.1	100.4	65.1	29.8
Dougherty County	(5.2)	101.7	100.1	66.3
Houston County	11.5	72.8	54.9	21.8
Comparable counties	16.0	97.6	70.4	34.0
1992–2002				
Athens/Clarke County	17.6	54.6	31.5	2.7
Hall County	52.5	135.5	54.4	20.6
Dougherty County	(1.8)	44.6	47.3	15.0
Houston County	25.1	72.9	38.2	7.9
Comparable counties	27.4	105.2	61.0	25.8

Source: Georgia Department of Community Affairs.

Note: Expenditures are the sum of expenditures by the county government and all cities within each county. The comparable counties are those with a 2005 population within 10 percent of Athens/Clarke County, including Carroll (101,577), Columbia (100,589), Coweta (105,376), Dougherty (95,681), Douglas (107,217), Fayette (101,333), Floyd (94,009), Lowndes (95,787), and Paulding (105,936) counties.

capita expenditures for each year. The second part of the table shows preconsolidation changes (e.g., expenditures in 1992 compared with those in 1985) and postconsolidation changes (e.g., expenditures in FY 2002 compared with those in FY 1992).

If unification increased the efficiency of providing government services in Clarke County, we would expect to find the following: (1) The preconsolidation changes in real per capita expenditures by Athens and Clarke County would be roughly the same as the preconsolidation per capita expenditures by the comparison city and county governments, (2) the postconsolidation changes in real per capita expenditures by the A-CC unified government would increase less or decrease more than the preconsolidation changes in expenditures by Athens and Clarke County, and (3) the postconsolidation real per capita expenditures by the A-CC unified government would show smaller increases or larger decreases than changes in expenditures by the comparison city and county governments.

According to table 9.4, the percentage change in real per capita operating expenditures by the Athens and Clarke County governments from 1985 to 1992 was 19.1 percent, but expenditures by the A-CC unified government from 1992 to 2002 increased by only 2.7 percent. In contrast, real per capita operating expenditures by Gainesville and Hall County did not show such a large difference in the preconsolidation and postconsolidation periods; they increased by 29.8 percent from 1985 to 1992 and by 20.6 percent from 1992 to 2002.

With one exception, the percentage changes in real per capita expenditures by the other comparison city and county governments were more like those by Gainesville/Hall County than by the A-CC unified government; the percentage changes in real operating expenditures were less from 1992 to 2002 than from 1985 to 2002, but they were still in double digits. The exception was Warner Robbins and Houston County, whose real per capita operating expenditures increased by 21.8 percent from 1985 to 1992 and by 7.9 percent from 1992 to 2002. These changes in real per capita expenditures were more like those by the A-CC unified government than by the comparable city and counties; nevertheless, the percentage postconsolidation change in real expenditures was still substantially greater in Warner Robbins and Houston County than in Athens/Clarke County.

In summary, these comparisons showed a smaller increase in real per capita operating expenditures by the A-CC unified government from 1992 to 2002 than by the Gainesville and Hall County governments and by the other comparison governments. Also, they showed that this smaller postconsolidation increase came after a preconsolidation period (1985–2002), in which Athens and Clarke County expenditures rose at a much higher rate, one that was roughly comparable to that found in Gainesville and Hall County and in most of the comparison governments.

Table 9.5 provides information on the operating expenditures of police and sheriff departments during the preunification and postunification periods.[9] The differences in the changes in preconsolidation and postconsolidation expenditures are even more dramatic than those for total operating expenditures. During the preconsolidation period (1985–92), the percentage increase in the real per capita expenditures on law enforcement by the Athens and Clarke County governments was very close to the increase in expenditures by Gainesville and Hall County, 68.4 percent and 68.2 percent, respectively. However, after consolidation (1992–2002), A-CC's real per capita expenditures on law enforcement *declined* by 6.8 percent while Gainesville and Hall County's expenditures *increased* by 1.5 percent. The pattern of preconsolidation and postconsolidation changes in real per capita expenditures on law enforcement varied in the other comparison city and county governments, but none had a percentage decline in expenditures during the postconsolidation period. In fact, the increases in real per capita expenditures on law enforcement from 1992 to 2002 ranged from 16.2 to 51.9 percent.

Table 9.6 shows operating expenditures for fire service. In Athens/Clarke County, real per capita expenditures increased by 43.2 percent from 1985 to 1992, but they *declined* by 2.9 percent from 1985 to 1992. In contrast, real per capita expenditures *increased* by 28.1 percent in Gainesville and Hall County from 1985 to 1992 and by 20.1 percent from 1992 to 2001. The preconsolidation and postconsolidation changes in the other comparison city and county governments varied, but they resembled those in Gainesville and Hall County more than in A-CC. None of the comparison city and county governments had a percentage decline in real per capital expenditures on fire service from 1995 to 2002; the percentage increases ranged from 17.4 to 48.7.

The postconsolidation decline in real per capita expenditures on fire service is remarkable because the Athens and Clarke County fire departments had merged a decade before the unification. Thus when the unification took place, the Clarke County government had long been the sole provider of fire protection services in the county. Nevertheless, the expenditure comparisons show that the unified government was able to obtain efficiencies in fire service.

The last service we examine is public works, road maintenance, and drainage. We focus on expenditures for these public works functions rather than all public works expenditures to make sure that we are comparing expenditures on the same services across counties. Although governments consistently include road maintenance and drainage within the purview of

Table 9.5 Police and Sheriff Department Operating Expenditures, 1985, 1992, and 2002

Year and County	Population	Expenditures		
		Total	Nominal Per Capita	Real Per Capita
1985				
Clarke County	80,822	5,036,164	62.31	57.22
Hall County	81,713	3,263,276	39.94	36.67
Dougherty County	103,059	6,683,818	64.85	59.55
Houston County	83,677	3,814,553	45.59	41.86
Comparable counties	761,485	24,320,975	31.94	29.33
1992				
Athens/Clarke County	88,334	11,788,738	133.46	96.36
Hall County	99,810	8,525,049	85.41	61.67
Dougherty County	97,659	8,674,668	88.83	64.13
Houston County	93,310	7,340,580	78.67	56.80
Comparable counties	883,352	47,353,440	53.61	38.71
2002				
Athens/Clarke County	103,881	14,773,856	142.22	80.21
Hall County	152,235	16,902,654	111.03	62.62
Dougherty	95,875	16,565,296	172.78	97.45
Houston County	116,768	13,666,755	117.04	66.01
Comparable counties	1,125,818	108,054,852	95.98	54.13
% Change 1985–92				
Athens/Clarke County	9.3	134.1	114.2	68.4
Hall County	22.1	161.2	113.9	68.2
Dougherty County	–5.2	29.8	37.0	7.7
Houston County	11.5	92.4	72.6	35.7
Comparable counties	16.0	94.7	67.8	32.0
1992–2002				
Athens/Clarke County	17.6	25.3	6.6	–16.8
Hall County	52.5	98.3	30.0	1.5
Dougherty County	–1.8	91.0	94.5	51.9
Houston County	25.1	86.2	48.8	16.2
Comparable counties	27.4	128.2	79.0	39.9

Source: Georgia Department of Community Affairs.

Note: Includes expenditures by the county government and the city government within each county.

Table 9.6 Fire Department Operating Expenditures, 1985, 1992, and 2002

		Expenditures		
Year and County	Population	Total	Nominal Per Capita	Real Per Capita
1985				
Clarke County	80,822	2,725,714	33.72	30.97
Hall County	81,713	2,476,778	30.31	27.83
Dougherty County	103,059	4,116,162	39.94	36.68
Houston County	83,677	1,813,197	21.67	19.90
Comparable counties	761,485	17,190,874	22.58	20.73
1992				
Athens/Clarke County	88,334	5,424,965	61.41	44.34
Hall County	99,810	4,927,361	49.37	35.64
Dougherty County	97,659	5,336,842	54.65	39.46
Houston County	93,310	3,180,410	34.08	24.61
Comparable counties	883,352	28,536,944	32.31	23.33
2002				
Athens/Clarke County	103,881	7,930,568	76.34	43.06
Hall County	152,235	11,550,819	75.87	42.79
Dougherty County	95,875	9,976,690	104.06	58.69
Houston County	116,768	5,982,339	51.23	28.90
Comparable counties	1,125,818	55,811,859	49.57	27.96
% Change 1985–92				
Athens/Clarke County	9.3	99.0	82.1	43.2
Hall County	22.1	98.9	62.9	28.1
Dougherty County	–5.2	29.7	36.8	7.6
Houston County	11.5	75.4	57.3	23.7
Comparable counties	16.0	66.0	43.1	12.5
1992–2002				
Athens/Clarke County	17.6	46.2	24.3	–2.9
Hall County	52.5	134.4	53.7	20.1
Dougherty County	–1.8	86.9	90.4	48.7
Houston County	25.1	88.1	50.3	17.4
Comparable counties	27.4	95.6	53.5	19.9

Source: Georgia Department of Community Affairs.

Note: Includes expenditures by the county and city governments within each county.

public works, they may not be consistent in where they place other responsibilities. For example, some cities or counties may put park maintenance in the public works department while others put the function in their parks department.

A comparison of percentage changes in real per capita public works expenditures across the preconsolidation and postconsolidation periods showed a pattern similar to those for general operating, law enforcement, and fire protection expenditures (table 9.7). Both the A-CC unified government and the Gainesville and Hall County governments decreased real per capita expenditures from 1985 to 1992, but the Gainesville and Hall County governments increased real per capita expenditures by 39.1 percent from 1992 to 2002, while the A-CC unified government decreased these expenditures by 10.3 percent. None of the other comparison city and county governments decreased their real per capita expenditures from 1992 to 2002. The increased expenditures by the Gainesville and Hall County governments may be attributable to its urbanization, which required paving some gravel roads and upgrading or widening traditionally rural roads to accommodate increased traffic. Because Clarke County is much smaller and its residential population grew at a lower rate, it likely had less need to invest as much money in road improvement.

In summary, this analysis of expenditures has reinforced the findings of Selden and Campbell that showed that following unification, real per capita expenditures by the A-CC unified government decreased for some services and functions. Also, it provides much stronger evidence that unification was the cause of at least some of the decrease in expenditures.

According to this analysis, the efficiency improvements projected by unification advocates have been achieved for operating expenses, law enforcement, fire protection, and public works (street improvement and drainage). The postconsolidation changes in real per capita expenditures showed improvement compared with (1) changes in preconsolidation expenditures by the city of Athens and Clarke County and (2) changes in the expenditures of the comparison city and county governments, including Gainesville and Hall County. Real per capita operating expenditures by the A-CC unified government increased by only 2.1 percent from 1992 to 2002, and its real per capita expenditures on law enforcement, fire protection, and public works declined. In contrast, real per capita operating expenditures by comparison city and county governments increased by at least 7.8 percent (up to 25.8 percent), and none of the comparison city and county governments decreased their real per capita expenditures on law enforcement, fire protection, and public works during the postconsolidation period.

Table 9.7 Public Works Department (Roads and Drainage) Operating Expenditures, 1985, 1992, and 2002

Year and County	Population	Expenditures		
		Total	Nominal Per Capita	Real Per Capita
1985				
Clarke County	80,822	2,874,635	35.57	32.66
Hall County	81,713	3,594,680	43.99	40.39
Dougherty County	103,059	6,894,950	66.9	61.43
Houston County	83,677	3,044,080	36.38	33.41
Comparable counties	761,485	19,847,349	26.06	23.93
1992				
Athens/Clarke County	88,334	3,033,415	34.34	24.79
Hall County	99,810	2,866,231	28.72	20.74
Dougherty County	97,659	2,547,095	26.08	18.83
Houston County	93,310	3,509,494	37.61	27.16
Comparable counties	883,352	24,422,062	27.65	19.96
2002				
Athens/Clarke County	103,881	4,094,862	39.42	22.23
Hall County	152,235	7,783,401	51.13	28.84
Dougherty County	95,875	6,996,677	72.98	41.16
Houston County	116,768	6,407,891	54.88	30.95
Comparable counties	1,125,818	45,506,059	40.43	22.80
% changes 1985–92				
Athens/Clarke County	9.3	5.5	–3.5	–24.1
Hall County	22.1	–20.3	–34.7	–48.7
Dougherty County	–5.2	–63.1	–61.0	–69.3
Houston County	11.5	15.3	3.4	–18.7
Comparable counties	16.0	23.0	6.1	–16.6
1992–2002				
Athens/Clarke County	17.6	35.0	14.8	–10.3
Hall County	52.5	171.6	78.0	39.1
Dougherty County	–1.8	174.7	179.8	118.6
Houston County	25.1	82.6	45.9	14.0
Comparable counties	27.4	86.3	46.2	14.2

Source: Georgia Department of Community Affairs.

Note: Includes expenditures by the county and city governments within each county.

Unification and Economic Development

Proponents of unification argued that ''a single government would be better able to attract new businesses." This economic development argument is one of the newer and, perhaps, more persuasive justifications for city–county consolidation (see Feiock and Carr 1997).

To explore whether unification has had a beneficial impact on A-CC's economy, we examined preunification and postunification data on county income and employment. As shown in table 9.8, we compared different income data for 1982, 1992, and 2002, including (1) per capita income; (2) total income, including earned income; dividends, interest, and rent; and transfers of residents of the county; (3) earned income of residents of the county; and (4) earnings by place. The "earned income of residents of the county" includes income earned by A-CC residents who work in the county and those who commute to work outside the county. "Earnings by place" includes income earned within the county by residents and by nonresidents who commute to work in A-CC.

When comparing changes of income in A-CC with those of nearby Hall County and with changes in the state of Georgia, we find no improvements in A-CC's income measures in the postunification period. From 1992 to 2002, A-CC's per capita income continued to grow more slowly than the average per capita income of all state residents, and its growth in total income, earned income, and earnings by place lagged behind Hall County and the state. Thus we can find no evidence that unification had a positive impact on per capita income, total income, earned income, and earnings by place.

The data in table 9.9 measure changes in employment to determine differences in the preunification and postunification periods. Again, employment and employment changes in Clarke County are compared with those in Hall County and in the state of Georgia. Again, no clear improvements are found in the number of jobs, wage-paying and salaried jobs, or number of proprietors. Changes in the total number of jobs and number of wage-paying and salaried jobs were slightly lower from 1992 to 2002 than from 1982 to 1992. The differences closely tracked changes in the state; Hall County showed a faster growth in the number of jobs and wage-paying and salaried jobs from 1992 to 2002 than in the previous decade.

The A-CC's slower income and job growth was likely due, at least in part, to the impact of the University of Georgia, the county's largest employer, on its economy. In recent years, UGA has capped its student population, and as a result, its professional workforce has grown more slowly than in the past. Also, because of the presence of this large university, A-CC's employers have ready access to a large, well-educated workforce; for many jobs, the supply of workers

Table 9.8 Changes in Personal Income, 1982–92, 1992–2002

Year and Type of Income	Athens/Clarke County	Hall County	State of Georgia
1982			
Per capita income (dollars)	8,995	9,622	10,059
Total income (thousands of dollars)	698,714	758,518	56,833,911
Earned income (thousands of dollars)	486,305	539,306	–
Earnings by place (thousands of dollars)	759,622	567,491	–
1992			
Per capita income (dollars)	16,366	17,787	19,075
Total income (thousands of dollars)	1,482,107	1,817,546	130,040,771
Earned income (thousands of dollars)	976,709	1,255,924	–
Earnings by place (thousands of dollars)	1,580,340	1,375,918	–
2002			
Per capita income (dollars)	22,655	24,830	28,544
Total income (thousands of dollars)	2,315,299	3,771,554	244,957,039
Earned income (thousands of dollars)	1,437,801	2,572,200	–
Earnings by place (thousands of dollars)	2,615,893	2,874,180	–
% change 1982–92			
Per capita income	81.9	84.9	89.6
Total income	112.1	139.6	128.8
Earned income	100.8	132.9	–
Earnings by place	108.0	142.5	–
1992–2002			
Per capita income	38.4	39.6	49.6
Total income	56.2	107.5	88.4
Earned income	47.2	104.8	–
Earnings by place	65.5	108.9	–

Source: Regional Economic Information System, Bureau of Economic Analysis, U.S. Department of Commerce.

Note: Total income includes earned income; dividends, interest, and rent; and transfers. Earned income consists of income earned by residents of the county. Earnings by place includes income earned by both residents and nonresidents working in the county.

Table 9.9 Employment by Type, Athens/Clarke County, Hall County, and Georgia, 1982, 1992, and 2002

County and Employment Type	1982	1992	2002	% Change 1982–92	% Change 1992–2002
Clarke County					
Total jobs	49,311	61,552	76,345	24.8	24.0
Wage-paying and salaried jobs	44,853	55,532	66,791	23.8	20.3
Proprietors	4,458	6,020	9,554	35.0	58.7
Hall County					
Total jobs	40,861	56,768	82,427	38.9	45.2
Wage-paying and salaried jobs	34,514	48,558	69,100	40.7	42.3
Proprietors	6,347	8,210	13,327	29.4	62.3
Georgia					
Total jobs	2,801,776	3,722,082	4,893,363	32.8	31.5
Wage-paying and salaried jobs	2,424,560	3,210,818	4,110,267	32.4	28.0
Proprietors	377,216	511,264	783,096	35.5	53.2

Source: Regional Economic Information System, Bureau of Economic Analysis, U.S. Department of Commerce.

exceeds the demand, holding down growth in wages. In addition, the university attracts many ancillary businesses, such as restaurants and student-oriented retail establishments that serve the university population; such businesses provide mainly lower-paying service jobs.

Clarke County did experience an increase in the number of proprietors from 1992 to 2002 that was greater than from 1982 to 1992, and the increase was a few percentage points greater than the percentage increase in the state. However, it was less than the percentage increase in Hall County. This higher-than-state average increase in A-CC is the only evidence of a potentially beneficial impact of unification on employment.

Unification and Law Enforcement Effectiveness

A prominently featured promise of the prounification campaign was that the governmental merger would result in a more effective police department and, thus, a safer community. To determine the impact of unification on law enforcement, we examined the number of reported crimes and arrests in Athens/Clarke County and Hall County in 1982, 1992, and 2002. Also, we calculated changes in reported crimes and arrests during the pre-unification period (1982–92) and the postunification period (1992–2002).

The data on reported crimes and arrests are presented in table 9.10. An analysis of these data provides mixed evidence about the impact of unification on public safety. On one hand, the data show improvements in A-CC, with substantial reductions in reported part 1 crimes, part 1 arrests, and total arrests during the postconsolidation period (1992–2002).[10] In comparison, reported crimes and arrests in A-CC rose sharply during the preconsolidation period (1982–92). Thus, the preconsolidation and post-consolidation differences in changes in reported crime and arrests are striking. Crime declined in A-CC during the decade following unification, and it increased during the decade preceding unification.[11]

On the other hand, comparisons of arrests and reported crime in Clarke County with those in Hall County bring into question whether unification was the variable that caused the favorable changes in arrests and reported crime during the decade following consolidation. According to the data given in table 9.10, arrests per 1,000 persons for part 1 crimes increased in A-CC at a much higher rate from 1982 to 1992 (the preconsolidation period) than in Hall County (90.3 percent in A-CC, and 18.0 in Hall County) and decreased at a lower rate during the postconsolidation period, from 1992 to 2002 (–36.9 percent in A-CC, and –56.8 percent in Hall County). Thus, in both the decade before and the decade after A-CC's unification, the changes in Hall County's arrests per 1,000 persons for part 1 crimes were better (less of an increase and more of a decrease) than in A-CC.

The data on *total* arrests per 1,000 persons show a similar pattern as arrests per 1,000 persons for part 1 crimes; while Hall County had a decrease, A-CC had an increase in arrests during the decade before unification, and A-CC had a smaller decrease than Hall County from 1992 to 2002. Thus, the analysis of both part 1 and total arrests per 1,000 persons showed no improvement in arrests in Clarke County compared with Hall County following unification. These results do not support the hypothesis that unification improved law enforcement in Clarke County by decreasing the amount of crime.

A different result is found in the analysis of reported part 1 crimes per 1,000 persons. This analysis provides some evidence that unification may have had an impact on reported crime. In A-CC, reported part 1 crimes per 1,000 persons increased more in A-CC during the decade before consolidation than in Hall County (30.6 percent in A-CC and 10.6 percent in Hall County), but they *decreased* more during the postconsolidation decade (–29.2 percent in A-CC and –23.8 percent in Hall County). This postconsolidation difference may be attributable to unification.[12]

Table 9.10 Reported Crimes and Arrests, Athens/Clarke County and Hall County, 1982, 1992, and 2002

	Year			% Change	
Reported Crimes and Arrests, and County	**1982**	**1992**	**2002**	**1982–92**	**1992–2002**
Reported part 1 crimes					
Clarke County, total	5,969	8,853	7,264	48.3	–17.9
Clarke County, per 1,000 persons	76.8	100.4	71.1	30.6	–29.2
Hall County, total	3,228	4,527	5,242	40.2	15.8
Hall County, per 1,000 persons	40.9	45.3	34.5	10.6	–23.8
Arrests for part 1 crimes					
Clarke County, total	649	1,402	1,025	116.0	–26.9
Clarke County, per 1,000 persons	8.4	15.9	10.0	90.3	–36.9
Hall County, total	837	1,253	822	49.7	–34.4
Hall County, per 1,000 persons	10.6	12.5	5.4	18.0	–56.8
Part 1 arrests per reported part 1 crimes					
Clarke County	0.109	0.158	0.141		
Hall County	0.259	0.277	0.157		
Arrests for total offenses					
Clarke County, total	4,342	7,142	5,386	64.5	–24.6
Clarke County, per 1,000 persons	55.9	81.0	52.7	44.9	–34.9
Hall County, total	6,054	7,180	5,178	18.6	–27.9
Hall County, per 1,000 persons	76.8	71.8	34.1	–6.5	–52.5

Source: Federal Bureau of Investigation.

Note: Part 1 crimes are homicide, forcible rape, robbery, assault (aggravated, plus simple), burglary, larceny (and burglary vehicle), and vehicle theft.

The impact of unification on the effectiveness of law enforcement in A-CC is measured, though crudely, by the ratio of part 1 arrests to reported part 1 crimes (part 1 arrests/part 1 crimes). This ratio is the percentage of reported part 1 crimes that result in an arrest. The ratios, presented in table 9.10, show that, compared with A-CC, Hall County had *much* better ratios of arrests to reported crime in 1982 and 1992, but had only a *slightly* better ratio in 2002. In 1982, for each 100 reported part 1 crimes, Hall County had 25.9 arrests and A-CC had 10.9 arrests. In 1992, the ratios were 27.2 arrests per 100 reported part 1 crimes in Hall County and 15.80 arrests in A-CC. However, the A-CC ratio of arrests to reported crimes declined only slightly from 1992 to 2002, while it decreased greatly in Hall County; the ratio was 14.1 arrests per 100 reported part 1 crimes in Clarke County and 15.7 in Hall County. It seems noteworthy that A-CC's ratio was stable during a time it decreased real per capita expenditures on law enforcement, and Hall County's ratio fell by nearly half as it was increasing real per capital expenditures on law enforcement.

In summary, from these reported crime and arrest data, we can conclude that arrests and crime rates fell significantly in A-CC during the decade following unification, but it is not possible to determine conclusively that unification was the variable that caused (or contributed significantly to) those declines. The analysis does not show an improvement in total and part 1 arrests per 1,000 persons in A-CC after unification compared with those in Hall County during the same period. It does provide evidence of an improvement in reported part 1 crimes during this period in A-CC compared with Hall County, but the data are complicated by the large influx of undocumented workers into Hall County during this time.

The analysis does provide limited evidence that unification delivered on the promise of more effective law enforcement. A comparison of the ratio of part 1 arrests to part 2 reported crimes shows improvements in A-CC, compared with Hall County, during the postunification decade. The ratio declined much less in A-CC than in Hall County, indicating that A-CC maintained its effectiveness as it reduced its real per capita expenditures on law enforcement.

Because lowering crime and improving public safety include many elements beyond law enforcement (e.g., lowering poverty, reducing drug use, school attendance), it may have been unrealistic for unification proponents to promise enhanced public safety without a more comprehensive strategy. A-CC is currently undertaking a multifaceted antipoverty initiative, which may be more successful in improving public safety over the long term.

Unification and Other Strategic Promises

In addition to the major promises of greater governmental efficiency, higher levels of economic development, and a more effective police department, unification supporters also made several other less prominent promises to broaden support for, or at least minimize opposition to, unification, Most of these promises were fulfilled—no employees were fired or had their benefits reduced as a result of unification; within a year after unification, water rates were equalized, ending the differences in rates charged to residents of the city and residents of unincorporated areas; a Department of Human and Economic Development was created; and "Athens" has remained part of the name of the government.

The one promise that has not been strictly fulfilled concerns African American representation on the ten-person unified government commission. The charter created two (out of eight) single-member districts in which blacks had a majority of voters. It also created a super district (out of two, each made up of half of the electorate), in which blacks comprised about 30 percent of the voters. The expectation was that two African Americans would be elected to the commission in some elections and three would be elected in others. However, so far the unified government has always had two African Americans on the commission; no African American has been elected to the commission from a super district. As a result, Blacks have consistently made up 20 percent of the unified government commission. In comparison, in 1990, Athens had three blacks on its ten-person city council and Clarke County had one black on its five-person commission, a total of four African American in the fifteen elected positions (26.6 percent). African Americans make up about 27.4 percent of A-CC's population.

Conclusion

In this chapter we have identified the narrative used by consolidation supporters to help convince residents to vote in the 1990 referendum to "unify" Athens and Clarke County. The narrative included several implicit promises about the outcomes of unification. One type of promise was aimed narrowly at specific groups and interests to attract their support for the merger, or at least to discourage them from actively opposing it. Fulfillment of these promises was guaranteed, to the extent possible, by provisions in the charter. Other promises were intended generally to persuade voters to support the merger. These promises concerned major improvements in government efficiency, economic development, and public safety

We examined the extent to which the promised outcomes of unification were achieved in the decade following unification. We found evidence that one promise (more efficient government) has been fulfilled, another (more effective economic development) has not been fulfilled, and the third (more effective police department) may have been partly fulfilled (table 9.11).

Table 9.11 Summary of Athens/Clarke County Case

Overall Assessment of Evidence	H1: Efficiency	H2: Economic Development	H3: Other Promises
Not enough data available			
No evidence		☑	
Weak			
Moderate	☑		☑
Strong			

According to our analysis, unification resulted in efficiencies in unified local government, lowering the real per capita costs of some services from 1992 to 2002. During this period, comparable city and county governments did not have the same declines in expenditures.

Our analysis provides no convincing evidence that unification contributed to income and employment improvements in A-CC The evidence is clear that unification did not boost incomes or employment in Clarke County from 1992 to 2002, and without significantly diversifying the economic base of the county, these tasks may prove difficult to achieve.

Our analysis showed that A-CC had a significant reduction in arrests per 1,000 persons for total and for part 1 crimes from 1992 to 2002. Although these postconsolidation reductions were positive developments for A-CC, it is not possible to attribute them to unification because Hall County had even greater reductions in arrests per 1,000 persons during this period. However, a comparison of postconsolidation changes in reported part 1 crimes per 1,000 persons and trends in the ratio of part 1 arrests to part 1 reported crimes provides some weak evidence that unification had a beneficial impact on law enforcement in both comparisons, and A-CC had results during the postconsolidation period that were better than those of Hall County.

In sum, the record of achievement for the ambitious promises made by unification supporters has been mixed. The promises over which the A-CC unified government had the most control—such as improved government efficiency and equalizing water rates—were achieved. However, the other promises—enhanced economic development and law enforcement—were more complex and less subject to direct, immediate influence by the A-CC government, and evidence indicates that A-CC was much less successful or even unsuccessful in fulfilling these promises.

Notes

1. For the official history of the unification effort, see "Unification History," *A-CC Online*, www.athensclarkecounty.com/history/unify.htm.
2. Under the Voting Rights Act, the U.S. Department of Justice reviews major changes in state and local government laws in specified states, including Georgia, to determine if they would have a detrimental impact on the voting rights and representation of racial minorities. E.g., in 1998 the department rejected the merger of the city of Augusta and Richmond County, Georgia, that had been approved by voters; see Campbell, Gillespie, and Durning 2004.
3. Durning and Edwards (1992) compared the perspectives of consolidation held by proponents and opponents in two counties. They found that most proponents viewed consolidation proposals to be an effort to improve government efficiency and most opponents viewed the proposals as attempts to shift power from one group of people to another.
4. The A-CC Unification Commission led the education effort until the day after the Department of Justice precleared the unification proposal and the referendum date was set. At that time, the Athens–Clarke County Unification Committee transformed itself into the "Citizens for a Unified Government." It added nine prominent citizens to its membership.
5. Winterville, a small city in Clarke County, opted out of consolidation and it still has its separate city government and budget.
6. The unification occurred on January 1, 1991, but the separate city and county budgets for FY 1991 remained in effect until June 30, 1991. The FY 1992 budget (July 1991 through June 1992) was constrained by the charter to have expenditures that would be no more than the combined expenditures of the two former governments in FY 1991, adjusted for inflation.
7. These comparison counties, of course, do not perfectly match Clarke County, which has a smaller area (in square miles), lower median age, lower median income, and higher poverty rate than the other three counties, though its poverty levels and median incomes are near those in Dougherty County; see table 9.2. The differences are caused, to some extent, by the large student population—more than 32,000 enrolled in the University of Georgia—in Clarke County.
8. Evidence that Clarke and Hall counties have similar daytime populations can be seen in table 9.7, which shows that in 2002 income "earned by place" was similar for Clarke County and Hall County, but "earned income" differed substantially. Income "earned by place" consists of income earned within the county by both residents and

nonresidents. It was $2.6 billion in Clarke County and $2.9 billion in Hall County. "Earned income" is income earned by residents of a county who work inside or outside of the county. "Earned income" in 2002 was $1.4 billion in Clarke County and $3.8 billion in Hall County. This comparison shows that in Clark County a large portion of income "earned by place" was paid to nonresident commuters and that a large portion of "earned income" in Hall County consisted of income earned outside of Hall County.

9. It should be noted that as a result of A-CC's unification, the county and city police departments were merged, but the sheriff, as a state constitutional officer, and his office continue to function separately from the consolidated police department, carrying out limited law enforcement responsibilities.
10. Part 1 crimes are homicide, forcible rape, robbery, assault (aggravated, plus simple), burglary, larceny, and vehicle theft.
11. We assume that arrests and reported crime are closely correlated to the number of crimes that are committed. Thus, increases in arrests and reported crime indicate an increase in crime and decreases in arrests and reported crime are assumed to reflect a decrease in crime.
12. Calculating accurate changes in Hall County's reported crime rates is complicated by a rapid increase from 1992 to 2002 in the number of undocumented workers living there. To some extent, these workers and their families may not appear in the annual population estimates for the county. Also, crimes committed against them may not show up in reported crimes because they are hesitant to report crimes affecting them. Thus they have an unknown impact on both the numerator (reported crimes) and denominator (population) used to calculate reported crimes per 1,000 persons in 1992 and 2002.

References

Campbell, Richard W., William L. Gillespie, and Dan Durning. 2004. Financial Crisis, Racial Accommodation, and the Consolidation of August and Richmond, Georgia. In *Case Studies of City–County Consolidation: Reshaping the Local Government Landscape,* ed. Suzanne M. Leland and Kurt Thurmaier. Armonk, NY: M. E. Sharpe.

Durning, Dan, and David Edwards. 1992. The Attitudes of Consolidation Elites: An Empirical Assessment of Their Views of City–County Mergers. *Southeastern Political Review* 20, no. 2:355–83.

Durning, Dan, William L. Gillespie, and Richard W. Campbell. 2004. "The Better Way": The Unification of Athens–Clarke County, Georgia. In *Case Studies of City–County Consolidation: Reshaping the Local Government Landscape*, ed. Suzanne M. Leland and Kurt Thurmaier. Armonk, NY: M. E. Sharpe.

Feiock, Richard C., and Jered B. Carr. 1997. A Reassessment of City/County Consolidation: Economic Development Impacts. *State and Local Government Review* 2, no. 3:166–71.

Selden, Sally C., and Richard W. Campbell. 2000. The Expenditure Impacts of Unification on a Small Georgia County: A Contingency Perspective of City–County Consolidation. *Public Administration Quarterly* 24, no. 2:169–201.

→ 10 ←

Improving the Efficiency and Effectiveness of Service Delivery in Local Government

The Case of Wyandotte County and Kansas City, Kansas

Suzanne M. Leland and Curtis Wood

Map 10 Locations of Shawnee County and Wyandotte County, Kansas
Source: U.S. Bureau of the Census.

City–county consolidation is frequently discussed as a solution to the economic problems that plague American cities and counties. According to a *Wall Street Journal* article, with reductions in federal and state grants and rising health care and pension costs, more cities are considering mergers in order to slash expenses and attract revenue-generating economic development (Maher 2005). Cities that are facing financial problems are interested in consolidation as a way to stem population loss and as a solution to budgetary woes and economic frailty. Cities that are not facing such troubles are still angling toward the idea of consolidation to avoid a similar fate (Leland and Thurmaier 2006). Other growing cities—such as Athens, Georgia, and Jacksonville—have used consolidation to streamline government and improve land development and tax planning (Maher 2005). In this chapter, we are interested in the case of a city and county that faced severe economic decline, Wyandotte County/Kansas City, Kansas (map 10). In the face of declining population and businesses, large losses in revenue, skyrocketing taxes, and little hope for economic improvement, voters approved consolidation in April 1997.

The situation in Wyandotte County/Kansas City, is intriguing because city–county consolidation is such a rare event. It is an extreme local government reform. Despite a renewed interest in consolidation across the nation to solve the aforementioned problems plaguing local governments, the vast majority of modern consolidation efforts have failed (about 80 percent since 1970). It seems while many reformers urge city–county consolidation, the American people continually reject their advice (Leland and Thurmaier 2006). The history of proposals for metrowide governance in general has been one of universal rejection (Glendening and Atkins 1980). Many efforts are doomed before they even make the referendum ballot. Since 1970, at least 110 local government consolidation attempts have reached the referendum stage; however, only 21 of these attempts passed. Another 19 city–county consolidations occurred before 1970. Although the idea of reforming two local governments via a merger interests many citizens and politicians, the majority of these efforts fail, either during the process of drafting a charter or once they reach the ballot (Leland and Thurmaier 2006).

Currently, there are no systematic studies that empirically demonstrate that city–county consolidation cuts costs and leads to improved service delivery. This leaves many local government leaders to wonder if this innovation is right for them, and if it is, how they can convince voters to support consolidation when these arguments do not resonate with the average voter considering a local government merger. This chapter directly addresses this gap in the literature by studying two Kansas cases that are demographically and economically similar—one that has consolidated, and the other in which the city and county remain separate. Using a quasi-experimental design, we compare demographic, fiscal, and economic data from the consolidated Wyandotte County/Kansas City, Kansas, government to the fragmented jurisdictions of the City of Topeka and Shawnee County, Kansas, seven years before and seven years after the 1997 consolidation, to determine whether the promises made to voters about consolidation have been fulfilled and whether the consolidation has resulted in increased efficiency (economy).

The extant evidence is mixed as to whether fragmented or consolidated government leads to more technical efficiency. The issue is highly controversial and normative, making it difficult to sort out the true effects of each alternative. Consolidation entrepreneurs argue that a consolidated government will bring about technical efficiency by ridding governments of the duplication, patronage, and corruption that contribute to more expensive service delivery and limited transparency (Feiock and Carr 1999). Stephens and Wikstrom (2000) contend that citizens are generally better off when city–county consolidations are established because they result in more regional economic development, service efficiencies and cost savings, modernization, more uniform and better-quality services, and more orderly regional development and growth. Fisher (1996) contends that economies of scale are more possible when capital-intensive operations are centralized and consolidated.

Proponents of consolidation have also adopted the perspective that by improving efficiency, local governments can ultimately lower property taxes and compete with nearby suburbs that are gaining residents while they are experiencing population loss (Rusk 1994; Peirce, Johnson, and Hall 1993). David Rusk (2003) is among the leading analysts of American metropolitan areas who contends that elastic cities gain population, capture suburban growth, experience more racial and economic integration and equality, show greater real income gains, reduce poverty levels, have a more-educated workforce, and have better bond ratings than inelastic cities. Elastic cities are cities that expand their boundaries, and city–county consolidation is an important strategy for cities to become more elastic.

Reformers who advocate consolidation, however, typically overlook or discount the competing values of local democratic control and self-determination available through the formation of additional units of government, especially in metropolitan areas. For many American voters, retaining independent local governments and maximizing pluralistic grassroots control and perceptions of governmental responsiveness seem preferable to the centralization of local governments, despite claims of the economies and efficiencies promised by consolidation (Halter 1993). Voters seem to find the alternatives to consolidation more enticing; therefore they enjoy more support. Municipal expansions through annexation, interlocal government agreements, and contracting out services are often more politically feasible options for local governments seeking cost reductions, and therefore are a more common means for achieving the same objective (Carr and Sneed 2004; Thurmaier and Wood 2004).

Scholars have also empirically demonstrated that fragmented governments can be as technically efficient as or more so than consolidated governments. Hawkins and Ihrke (1999) examined twenty-five studies on the effects of concentration and thirty studies on the effects of fragmentation. What they found was that 64 percent of the studies showed that consolidation does not have the positive effects claimed by reformers; twenty-one fragmentation studies showed that fragmentation lowers the cost of public services or at least does not increase expenditures, whereas nine studies showed that fragmentation increases the costs of government. Schneider (1989) showed empirically that more fragmented metropolitan areas had slower expenditure growth than more consolidated areas. This is consistent with research by Eberts and Gronberg (1988), Dilorenzo (1983), and Wagner and Weber (1975). Feiock (2004) contends that the evidence available does not provide strong support for the contention that consolidated government can produce the promised fiscal and economic benefits.

The little evidence that does exist suggests that consolidated government costs will actually increase in the short term, a finding that is predicated on the notion that labor-intensive local governments will incur additional personnel costs when a consolidation occurs (Campbell and Selden 2000). Compensation and fringe benefit packages are usually leveled up, and employees are given guarantees that they will keep their existing positions. When unions are present, these matters are further complicated and costs may rise. The new government also often needs to combine information technology and communications systems to be compatible; build new buildings for the newly unified government; and change logos on stationary, vehicles, and uniforms. All these factors could initially lead to increased costs of service delivery. However, there is little if any empirical evidence as to the longer-term budgetary impact of consolidation.

In this analysis, we join the chorus of scholars seeking to answer the important question of whether city–county consolidation can deliver on the promises made and will result in longer-term technical efficiency by analyzing two nearby communities that have similar socioeconomic profiles: one where the city and county have consolidated, and the other where the city and county remain separate.

Background on the Wyandotte Merger and Promises Made to Voters

The idea of a city–county merger in Wyandotte County and Kansas City, has a long history. It can be traced as far back as 1968, when the Kansas House of Representatives formed a commission to study the merits of consolidating the two governments. The commission recommended structural consolidation (Citizens' Commission 1970). However, there was insufficient community support, and the issue never made it to the ballot (Kelley 2000). In 1987 the Wyandotte County commissioners formed a study group to address mounting concerns about fragmentation, duplication, and inefficiency in local governments (Leland 2004). A six-person commission contracted with a private consulting firm to produce a comprehensive study on consolidation. But hopes of a referendum were dashed when the commission disbanded due to a lack of citizen support (Scot Gard and Associates 1988).

The issue was revisited in 1994 by a Citizen's Task Force (CTF) concerned about corruption and the increasing costs of service delivery in the Kansas City, area. It was spearheaded by private citizens, led by local business executives, and backed by the Chamber of Commerce, the mayor, the city council, and the League Women of Voters. The CTF concluded that "consolidation will be a major step toward changing the many hardships this community faces. It will not eliminate our county or city governments. Rather, if properly structured, it will create an accountable and accessible government that citizens have confidence in" (Kelley 1994). Having been chartered and funded by both city and county governments, the CTF analyzed issues and alternatives pertaining to consolidation. It recommended consolidation and proposed a new structure for the unified government (DeWitt 1995). Unfortunately for the reformers, under Kansas law they did not have the authority to pursue consolidation beyond their own recommendations (Kelley 2000).

Finally, in the spring of 1996, the Kansas state legislature passed Bill 464, which created a five-member commission of Wyandotte County residents to determine if merging the two governments was a viable solution to a continuing decline in the quality of life in Wyandotte County.[1] Citizens expressed frustration with their current government structures, and the majority of citizens held a negative perception across the metropolitan area. The Consolidation Study Commission (1997) was charged with the task of recommending one of three options to the governor of Kansas. The first called for the full structural consolidation of the two entities, the city of Kansas City, and Wyandotte County. Under this plan, three small rural municipalities would be excluded from consolidation: Bonner Springs, Edwardsville, and part of Lake Quivira (with a combined total population of 6,000). This option would then go to the Kansas state legislature, and if not acted upon in thirty days, the voters residing in all the municipalities (including the three excluded communities) would cast their votes for or against consolidation on April 1, 1997 (Stockwell 2000). The second option was for functional consolidation. This proposal would be voted upon by the citizens of the entire county, if not rejected in thirty days by the Kansas state legislature. Finally, the third option was that no action be taken. The city and county would remain separate (Leland 2004).

The Consolidation Study Commission held thirty-two public hearings to deliberate each of the respective options and subsequently recommended the first option, the structural consolidation of the city of Kansas City, and Wyandotte County. After the endorsement of this option by the commission, the state legislature had thirty days to approve or disapprove, or the recommendation would go directly before the voters. On April 1, 1997, the residents of Wyandotte County voted 60 percent in favor of the commission's recommendation to form the Unified Government of Wyandotte County and Kansas City (Leland 2004).

The reformers in Wyandotte County advocated merging the city and county governments in order to modernize and professionalize the county government, which was run by three partisan full-time commissioners dominated by the local Democratic machine. Unlike the city, the county did not have a personnel classification system, a professional administrator, nonpartisan officials, a procurement code, or a professional programmatic budgeting system. In addition, neither the city nor the county had an ethics code or commission to investigate allegations of unethical behavior.

Wyandotte County/Kansas City, was plagued with economic and fiscal problems, including a declining population, an increase in the minority population, increasing poverty, urban blight, high unemployment, and the highest local property taxes in Kansas. David Rusk (1994) cited Kansas City, as among one of thirty-two cities "past the statistical point of no return." Rusk placed Kansas City, on his list because the city had experienced an 11 percent decline in population since the 1950s, an increase in the proportion of minority residents to 38 percent, and a widening city–suburb income gap with a ratio of 63 percent. Kansas City, was accompanied on the list by such cities as East Saint Louis; Gary, Indiana; and Buffalo.

In 1995, the Kansas City, Chamber of Commerce reported that Wyandotte County had the highest property tax in the state of Kansas and in the Kansas City metropolitan area, with a levy of 175.493 mills. Kansas City's, citizens paid 32 percent more in property taxes than the average of other cities in the region. The chamber blamed the high taxation rate for the loss of more than 2,000 residents a year since 1990 and a total of more than 12,225 residents in five years, once factoring in the area's most recent annexation of Piper Township (Chamber of Commerce 1995). The report concluded that "this community is facing an economic crisis and has lost its competitive edge to the point that families and businesses choose not to locate here and leave in alarming numbers" (Chamber of Commerce 1995).

In addition, Census data indicated that residents that continued to stay in Wyandotte County/Kansas City, were becoming poorer. According to the 1990 Census data, per capita income in Kansas City, was the lowest in the region and the state. Unemployment was the highest in the state, at 6.4 percent. More than 23,000 of the 151,000 residents were receiving food stamps, representing a 45 percent increase since 1990. Further, the chamber reported that the real estate market was also in a state of decline. From 1990 to 1995, only 718 new homes were built in Kansas City. During this same five-year period, 1,538 units were demolished. This means that while surrounding communities were experiencing rapid growth, Kansas City, was destroying twice as many homes as it built.

The business community and citizens started to demand change, and talk of consolidation to lower taxes began to surface. The head of the CTF believed that neither the city nor the county was responding appropriately to the crisis. Citizens called for urban renewal and improved economic development through consolidation. Reformers advocated consolidation in hopes that modernization and professionalization of the county would in turn help curb urban decline and fiscal stress by eliminating the negative portrayal of the community (Leland and Johnson 2000). As one newspaper reporter characterized the state of the county in 1997 (preconsolidation): "Backbreaking tax bills from past costly government decisions were driving out many longtime residents, many with the ability to create a better city and county. They give up; no longer do they want to pour their tax dollars down a rat hole of inefficient and patronage government. Nor do businesses want to invest in a polluted political climate" (Sigman 1997).

The issue of consolidation was propelled forward by the prospect of acquiring a new NASCAR racetrack. Both the city and county wished to land a NASCAR racetrack in the early spring of 1997, just before the vote. Both saw the track as a way to turn around the area's economic problems. However, the city was said to have too much debt to be able to successfully negotiate, and the county was said to not have enough leadership or accountability to successfully reach a deal. Proconsolidation forces emphasized that a new unified government would have the clout to pull off such a project (Kelley 2000; Stockwell 2000).

Reformers promised voters if they approved consolidation, they would reduce property taxes (approximately 2 percent a year), create an ethics commission, stem the loss of rooftops and population, and most important, land a new economic development project for their area—the NASCAR racetrack. On April 1, 1997, more than 60 percent of the voters of Kansas City, decided to consolidate the governments of Wyandotte County and Kansas City. The successful referendum marked the thirty-seventh time in the history of the United States that citizens had voted to consolidate their county and city governments.

Table 10.1 illustrates the resulting level of functional consolidation for the Unified Government of Wyandotte County/Kansas City, for nine functions and how that level of functional consolidation compared with the preconsolidated governments and the comparison case. It is important to note that law enforcement in Wyandotte County/Kansas City (albeit a major expenditure for the city), was the only functionally consolidated service before consolidation. Seven years after consolidation, all services were fully functionally consolidated.

Table 10.1 Level of Functional Consolidation of Services for the Experimental Case (E), Wyandotte County/Kansas City; and for the Comparison Case (C), Shawnee County/Topeka

	7 Years before Consolidation		1 Year before Consolidation		7 Years after Consolidation	
Service Function	**E**	**C**	**E**	**C**	**E**	**C**
Fire protection	CI	CI	CI	CI	F	CI
Social services	CU	CU	CU	CU	F	CU
Law enforcement	S	S	F	S	F	S
Parks and recreation	S	S	S	S	F	S
Planning	S	S	S	S	F	S
Economic development	S	S	S	S	F	S
Utilities (water/sewer)	CI	CI	CI	CI	F	CI
Public works	S	S	S	S	F	S
Public health	CU	CU	CU	CU	F	CU

Source: Provided by the City of Topeka Budget Office and the Unified Government Research Director and Budget Office.

Key: CI = city function only; CU = county function only; F = functional consolidation (city and county operations combined into single department); ILA = interlocal agreement/contract with the city or county; P = privatized; S = separately provided by both city and county.

Socioeconomic Comparison of the Two Kansas Cases

We selected Shawnee County, Kansas, and the City of Topeka, Kansas, as our comparison (control) case for this study for many reasons. First, they are both located in the same state and therefore are subject to the same state laws regulating local governments. Second, city–county consolidation has been heavily debated in Shawnee County and the City of Topeka and was defeated in the fall of 2006. Third, Wyandotte County and Kansas City, are more similar demographically and in population to Shawnee County and the City of Topeka than to other counties in the state. Fourth, Shawnee County and the City of Topeka form an industrial region located in the northeastern part of Kansas, near Wyandotte County and Kansas City.

Table 10.2 shows the socioeconomic similarities and dissimilarities between the experimental (Wyandotte County/Kansas City) and the control (Topeka/Shawnee County) cases in 1990.[2] The two cases are very close in median age, and in their relative ranking for crime index offenses, the number of housing units, and the number of persons receiving food stamps. However, the two cases are not close with regard to the unemployment rate or per capita income.

Table 10.2 Comparison of Counties in 1990, Before Consolidation

Measure	Shawnee County	Wyandotte County	Kansas (Statewide)
Median age (years)	33.8	31.7	32.9
Crime index offenses; rank	12,704; 4th	19,458; 2nd	129,188
Housing units; rank	68,991; 3rd	61,514; 4th	944,726
Persons receiving food stamps; rank	9,303; 3rd	16,485; 2nd	141,828
Unemployment rate; rank	5%; 17th	8.7%; 2nd	4.5%
Per capita income; rank	18,798; 19th	14,100; 92nd	18,085

Source: Kansas Center for Community Economic Development, Policy Research Institute, the University of Kansas.

Note: The rank is among all 105 counties in Kansas.

Hypotheses

We test the three main hypotheses within the framework of the overall research design, with some specific hypotheses in each category:

H1: The Efficiency Hypothesis: A consolidated government improves efficiency (economy) by a reduction in the rate of growth in expenditures per capita.

H2: The Economic Development Effectiveness Hypothesis

H2a: The consolidation was effective in the goal to stem the loss of population.

H2b: The consolidation was effective in the goal to improve the economy through the growth in retail sales.

H2c: The consolidation was effective in the goal to reverse the trend in the loss in rooftops.

H3: The Other Promises Hypothesis

H3a: The consolidation was effective in achieving the goals to reduce property taxes, bring in a NASCAR track, and create an ethics commission.

H3b: A consolidated government results in increased citizen trust and positive performance ratings toward local government performance.

We use a classic comparative case study design (figure 10.1) to assess these questions. We assess data on one consolidated government (Wyandotte County/Kansas City) and a comparable city/county (Shawnee County/Topeka) in the same state that did not consolidate. One of the greatest benefits of a comparative case design is that one gains valuable information from systematic analysis without losing the rich variation of data obtainable from a case analysis.

Experimental Group (unified government)	$\mathbf{Ob}_{t11}$	$\mathbf{C}^3$	$\mathbf{Ob}_{t12}$
Comparison Group (unconsolidated)	$\mathbf{Ob}_{t21}$		$\mathbf{Ob}_{t22}$

Figure 10.1 Research Design

To test these hypotheses (except for Hypothesis H1), we compare two sets of observations. The first observation is the pretest and posttest for each indicator in each case to determine what absolute change or progress has been made by each case (Ob_{t11} and Ob_{t12} and Ob_{t21} and Ob_{t22}). Next, for each indicator we compare the two cases against each other first before consolidation (Ob_{t11} and Ob_{t21}) and then after consolidation (Ob_{t12} and Ob_{t22}) to identify the relative change or improvement brought about by the consolidation. The results of our study will inform those in other communities who are interested in consolidation about the benefits and costs of consolidation, and thus will provide public administrators, elected officials, and citizens with further insights into consolidation as a local government structural and service delivery option.

Findings

Seven years after the consolidation, Wyandotte County/Kansas City were experiencing a fiscal, demographic, and economic renaissance, and the promises made by consolidation supporters had been kept. "While the move [consolidation] helped the combined governments cut their workforce and trim property taxes four years running, it also had a less tangible but no less crucial impact: The periodic scandals that had beset both county and city governments came to an end, and the unified government's relationship with state government in Topeka improved dramatically. That, in turn, helped it win perhaps the biggest boost to its economy in a generation: the immense Kansas Speedway, which now anchors a state 'tourism district' and budding retail center" (Gurwitt 2002, 2). The effort to "clean up" city and county government was provided with a boost soon after the consolidation when the unified government created an ethics commission, hired an ethics administrator, and developed ethics policies and related employee ethics training programs.

The selection of Wyandotte County as the site for the new NASCAR track and the surrounding development of Village West—a 400-acre retail and entertainment destination district that includes Cabella's Outfitters, Nebraska Furniture Mart, the Kansas City T-Bones minor league baseball park, a destination hotel, a family destination resort, and a shopping center—have contributed significantly to the revitalization of Kansas City. The NASCAR racetrack and Village West development have led to rising home values and a housing boom, increased sales and property tax revenue, and millions of tourists each year. "In 2003, Kansas City, tallied its highest single-year total of housing starts in the past forty years, with 433 new single-family housing permits issued," and the Homebuilders Association of Greater Kansas City ranked Kansas City, sixth out of sixty-eight metropolitan-area communities in the number of new housing starts (Marinovich 2004).

The evidence also supports the hypothesis that, as promised by the supporters of consolidation, the consolidation has made it possible to stabilize the loss of population, improve the economy through the growth of retail sales, and reduce the loss of rooftops. During the six years before the 1997 consolidation (1989–96), Wyandotte County and Kansas City, were losing 11 to 12 percent of their population; but during the seven years after consolidation, the population increased slightly—a remarkable turnaround (table 10.3). During the seven years before the consolidation, the Topeka and Shawnee County population increased 1.74 and 1.68 percent, respectively. During the seven years after consolidation, the rate of population growth in Topeka declined relative to the seven years before consolidation. Although the rate of population growth in Shawnee County after the consolidation was twice the rate of population growth during the seven years before consolidation, the Shawnee County rate of improvement cannot match the turnaround in Wyandotte County/Kansas City. The retail sales report data (table 10.4) shows that although Topeka continues to outpace Kansas City, in percentage increase in retail sales, the gap has been narrowing during the postconsolidation period. Retail sales increased in Kansas City, by 19 percent during the seven years before consolidation and 25 percent during the seven years after consolidation, an increase of about 32 percent in the rate of retail sales growth. InTopeka, retail sales increased

Table 10.3 Population Change Before and After Consolidation

Government	1989	1996	Change %	1997	2004	Change %
Wyandotte County	173,626	155,072	–10.69	—	—	—
Kansas City	162,070	142,630	–11.99	—	—	—
Unified	—	—	—	144,400	145,010	0.42
Topeka	118,580	120,646	1.74	120,645	121,886	1.03
Shawnee County	162,388	165,122	1.68	165,122	170,902	3.50

Sources: Population and housing data, U.S. Bureau of the Census; Kansas Secretary of State's Office; Kansas League of Municipalities; *Kansas Governmental Journal.*

Note: The data for Wyandotte County and the unified government do not include the minor municipalities that did not join the consolidation.

Table 10.4 Retail Sales in Millions of Dollars

Jurisdiction	1989 Retail Sales	1996 Retail Sales	1990–96 % Change	1997 Retail Sales	2004 Retail Sales	1997–2004 % Change
Kansas City	$993	$1,176	19			
Unified	—	—		$1,220	$1,520	25
Topeka	$1,468	$1,950	33	$1,999	$2,669	34
Ratio of Topeka to Kansas City			1.78			1.37

Sources: City of Topeka Budget Office; research director and Budget Office, Unified Government.

33 percent before consolidation and 34 percent after consolidation. During the seven years before consolidation, the percentage growth in retail sales in Topeka was 1.78 more than in Kansas City. However, the gap narrowed to 1.37 during the seven years after consolidation.

The evidence suggests that progress has also been made in stemming the loss of rooftops (table 10.5).[3] Although the number of net new single-family house building permits during the postconsolidation period has still declined in Kansas City, the rate of decline has been reduced by 59 percent relative to the preconsolidation period, and the rate of improvement in Kansas City, is about twice that of Topeka. Since 2002, the net number of new residential rooftops in Kansas City has been a positive number—36 in 2002, 199 in 2003, and 234 in 2004.

Table 10.5 Changes in Rooftops

City	1990–96	1997–2004	Change in Postconsolidation Period
Kansas City	–921	–377	544 (59%)
Topeka	+942	+1,221	279 (30%)

Sources: City of Topeka Budget Office; research director and Budget Office, Unified Government.

Efficiency and Economy

The data also show support for the hypothesis that the consolidated government has improved efficiency (economy) by a reduction in the rate of growth in expenditures per capita. Table 10.6 demonstrates that during the preconsolidation period, total expenditures per capita for Kansas City/Wyandotte County increased about 47 percent and increased 34 percent during the postconsolidation period, a decline in the growth rate of about 28 percent.[4] In the preconsolidation period, the growth in per capita expenditures was significantly higher in Wyandotte County/Kansas City than Topeka/Shawnee County, but during the postconsolidation period the opposite occurred. In Topeka/Shawnee County, expenditures per capita increased 32 percent during the preconsolidation era and 55 percent during the postconsolidation period, an increase in the growth rate of about 72 percent. Due to the fact that expenditures per capita grew significantly more slowly for the unified government than the City of Topeka/Shawnee County after consolidation, the ratio of expenditures growth per capita between Topeka/Shawnee County and Wyandotte County/Kansas City went from 0.68 (preconsolidation) to 1.62 (postconsolidation).

Figure 10.2 shows the combined expenditures per capita for Wyandotte County/Kansas City, Kansas, and Topeka/Shawnee County, Kansas, in 1989, 1996, 1997, and 2004. The combined per capita expenditures for Wyandotte County/Kansas City were 74 percent of the combined per capita expenditures for Topeka/Shawnee County in 1989, and that ratio climbed to 82 percent in 1996, indicating that the rate of per capita expenditure growth in Wyandotte County/Kansas City during the preconsolidation period was higher than that in Topeka/Shawnee County. However, in the postconsolidation period, the ratio of unified government per capita expenditures to Topeka/Shawnee County declined from 80 percent in 1997 to 69 percent in 2004, indicating that during the postconsolidation

Table 10.6 Combined Expenditures per Capita and Rate of Increase

Jurisdiction	1989	1996	1989–96 % Increase	1997	2004	1997–2004 % Increase
Wyandotte County/ Kansas City	$799	$1,171	47	$1,169	$1,561	34
Topeka/ Shawnee County	$1,078	$1,424	32	$1,457	$2,258	55
Ratio of Shawnee to Wyandotte			0.68			1.62

Sources: City of Topeka Budget Office; research director and Budget Office, Unified Government.

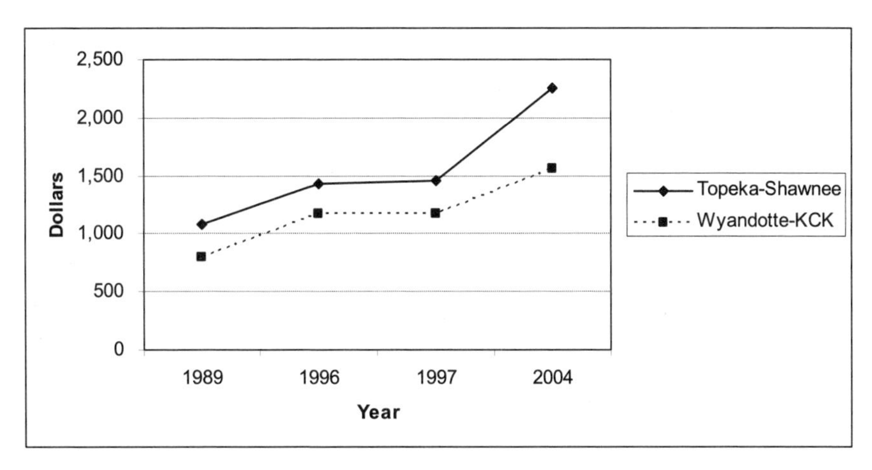

Figure 10.2 Expenditures per Capita
Sources: City of Topeka Budget Office; research director and Budget Office, Unified Government.

period per capita expenditures in Topeka/Shawnee County were growing faster than in the unified government.

Changes in expenditure priorities before and after consolidation for the jurisdictions can be determined by looking at the changes in expenditures per capita for various governmental functions. Tables 10.7 and 10.8 show the 1989, 1996, 1997, and 2004 combined expenditures per capita, the percentage changes in expenditures per capita, and the priority rankings of fifteen governmental functions in Topeka/Shawnee County and Wyandotte County/Kansas City, respectively.[5] When examining the five highest-priority functions (public safety, public utilities, public works, general government, and debt service) in Topeka/Shawnee County (table 10.7), during the postconsolidation period the percentage of total expenditures allocated to debt service increased substantially (from 10.9 percent of total expenditures in the base year, 1997, to 20.2 percent in 2004), while there was a decrease in the proportionate share of public safety and public works expenditures during the same period.

Debt service went from a number five ranking in 1989, 1996, and 1997 (the base year) to a number two ranking in 2004, as the debt per capita climbed from 37 percent during the seven preconsolidation years to a 187 percent increase during the postconsolidation years. In the base year (1997), debt service made up about 11 percent of all budgeted expenditures; however, by 2004 debt service made up more than 20 percent of all expenditures.

Table 10.7 Expenditures per Capita and Ranking by Function for Topeka/Shawnee County

Function	1989 $ / Rank / % of Total	1996 $ / Rank / % of Total	1989–96 % Change	1997 $ / Rank / % of Total	2004 $ / Rank / % of Total	1997–2004 % Increase
General	131 / 4 / 12.2	176 / 3 / 12.4	34.4	191 / 3 / 13.1	278 / 4 / 12.3	45.6
Public safety	265 / 1 / 24.6	365 / 1 / 25.6	37.7	381 / 1 / 26.1	528 / 1 / 23.4	38.6
Public works	138 / 3 / 12.8	173 / 4 / 12.1	25.4	172 / 4 / 11.8	177 / 5 / 7.8	2.9
Utilities	218 / 2 / 20.2	272 / 2 / 19.1	24.8	286 / 2 / 19.6	409 / 3 / 18.1	43
Parks and recreation	85 / 6 / 7.9	114 / 6 / 8	34.1	121 / 6 / 8.3	130 / 6 / 5.8	7.4
Debt service	119 / 5 / 11	163 / 5 / 11.4	37	159 / 5 / 10.9	456 / 2 / 20.2	187
Community / economic development and tourism	8 / 10 / 0.7	19 / 9 / 1.3	138	17 / 9 / 1.2	13 / 10 / 0.6	–23.5
Judicial	19 / 9 / 1.8	37 / 8 / 2.6	95	33 / 8 / 2.3	45 / 9 / 2	36.4
Culture	20 / 8 / 1.9	1 / 13 / 0.1	–35	1 / 12 / 0.1	2 / 13 / 0.1	100
Education	0 / 14 / 0	0 / 14 / 0	0	0 / 14 / 0	0 / 14 / 0	0
Social services	4 / 12 / 0.4	12 / 10 / 0.8	200	12 / 10 / 0.1	11 / 11 / 0.5	–8.3
Metro planning	6 / 11 / 0.6	5 / 11 / 0.4	–17	4 / 11 / 0.3	8 / 12 / 0.4	100
Public transit	0 / 14 / 0	0 / 14 / 0	0	0 / 14 / 0	0 / 14 / 0	0
Health	66 / 7 / 6.1	87 / 7 / 6.1	32	78 / 7 / 5.4	101 / 7 / 4.5	29.5
Other	1 / 13 / 0.1	2 / 12 / 0.1	100	1 / 12 / 0.1	100 / 8 / 4.4	9,900
Total	1,078	1,424	32.1	1,457	2,258	55

Sources: City of Topeka Budget Office; research director and Budget Office, Unified Government.

Table 10.8 Expenditures per Capita and Ranking by Function for Wyandotte County/Kansas City

Function	1989 $ / Rank/ % of Total	1996 $ / Rank / % of Total	1989–96 % Increase	1997 $ / Rank / % of Total	2004 $ / Rank / % of Total	1997–2004 % Increase
General	163 / 2 / 20.4	265 / 2 / 22.2	62.6	185 / 2 / 15.8	148 / 5 / 9.5	–20
Public safety	251 / 1 / 31.4	406 / 1 / 34	61.8	433 / 1 / 37	622 / 1 / 39.8	43.7
Public works	80 / 4 / 10	113 / 4 / 9.5	41.3	133 / 3 / 11.4	185 / 2 / 11.9	39.1
Utilities	96 / 3 / 12	118 / 3 / 9.9	22.9	126 / 4 / 10.8	162 / 3 / 10.4	28.6
Parks and recreation	33 / 7 / 4.1	32 / 8 / 2.7	–3	40 / 7 / 3.4	52 / 8 / 3.3	30
Debt service	58 / 6 / 7.3	95 / 5 / 8	63.8	123 / 5 / 10.5	162 / 3 / 10.4	31.7
Community/economic development and tourism	60 / 5 / 7.5	70 / 6 / 5.9	16.7	41 / 6 / 3.5	72 / 6 / 4.6	75.6
Judicial	12 / 10 / 1.5	27 / 9 / 2.3	125	34 / 8 / 2.9	53 / 7 / 3.4	55.9
Culture	2 / 13 / 0.3	4 / 11 / 0.3	100	4 / 12 / 0.3	8 / 11 / 0.5	100
Education	0 / 14 / 0	0 / 13 / 0	0	0 / 13 / 0	0 / 13 / 0	0
Social services	13 / 9 / 1.6	16 / 10 / 1.3	23.1	10 / 11 / 0.9	49 / 9 / 3.1	390
Metro planning	0 / 14 / 0	0 / 13 / 0	0	0 / 13 / 0	0 / 13 / 0	0
Public transit	10 / 11 / 1.3	0 / 13 / 0	–100	19 / 10 / 1.6	0 / 13 / 0	100
Health	15 / 8 / 1.9	43 / 7 / 3.6	187	20 / 9 / 1.7	47 / 10 / 3	135
Other	6 / 12 / 0.8	4 / 11 / 0.3	33.3	0 / 13 / 0	1 / 12 / 0.1	N.A.
Total	799	1,193	49.3	1,169	1,561	33.5

Sources: City of Topeka Budget Office; research director and Budget Office, Unified Government.

Note: N.A. - not available.

Another notable change in expenditures per capita (but in the opposite direction from debt service) occurred in the public works function, as public works expenditures per capita increased by 25.4 percent during the preconsolidation period but only 2.9 percent during the postconsolidation era. In the base year (1997), public works expenditures made up 11.8 percent of all budgeted expenditures, but only 7.8 percent of all expenditures in 2004.

It is interesting to note that although public safety, public works, utilities, debt service, and the general fund were also the five highest-priority functions in Wyandotte County (table 10.8), the trends in Wyandotte County are different than in Shawnee County. Although the proportionate share of public safety expenditures decreased during the postconsolidation period in Shawnee County, the opposite occurred in Wyandotte County.

By 2004, public safety expenditures made up almost 40 percent of all expenditures for the unified government (ranked first), up from 37 percent in the base year (1997). Also, the proportionate share of debt service expenditures did not explode in Wyandotte County as they did in Shawnee County. In Wyandotte County, debt service increased by only 31.7 percent during the postconsolidation period, down from the 63.8 percent increase during the preconsolidation era, and the proportion of total expenditures attributed to debt service remained at about 10 percent of total expenditures during the postconsolidation period. However, it is noticeable that the absolute amount and relative share of general fund expenditures declined in Wyandotte County during the postconsolidation period. By 2004, general fund expenditures per capita had declined to $148 (down from $185 in 1997), and general fund expenditures made up 9.5 percent of total expenditures (down from 15.8 percent in 1997).

Citizen Attitudes toward Local Government

A large amount of data on citizen satisfaction with local government performance exists for Wyandotte County before and after consolidation. There are even recent data on citizen satisfaction with the new consolidated government. However, there are limited data on citizen satisfaction in Shawnee County, with the exception of a recent 2006 survey of law enforcement (sheriff's office) service provision. There is no available sheriff's office survey during the preconsolidation period, so it is not possible to measure citizen attitudes before and after the consolidation. There are also data on citizen satisfaction for City of Topeka, but these data do not include the rest of the county or perceptions of the overall countywide government, and there is no preconsolidation period survey.

Wyandotte County Citizen Satisfaction

As part of the strategic planning process, the Wyandotte County Economic Development Council conducted a public opinion survey of Wyandotte County citizens in 1989, 1991, and 2000. The results of the three citizen surveys show a trend of deteriorating citizen perception of local government performance before the 1997 consolidation and improving citizen attitudes toward local government performance after the consolidation.

In the 1991 survey, a random sample of 400 Wyandotte County residents were interviewed by telephone. In the 2000 survey, 506 Wyandotte County citizens were surveyed by mail, with a response rate of 27.7 percent. The Information and Research Department of the City of Kansas City, prepared the summary of results and analysis of the 1991 survey, and where appropriate, compared the results with the 1989 survey. The unified government's Budget and Research Department prepared the summary results and analysis of the 2000 survey.

The average rating of overall local government conditions went down slightly, from 2.52 in 1989 to 2.5 in 1991, and then increased to 2.66 in the 2000 survey.[6] In 1989, 46.3 percent of the respondents (176 persons) rated local government conditions in the two lowest categories, and this increased slightly, to 47.6 percent (180 persons), in the 1991 survey. In 2000, three years after consolidation, 42.2 percent of the respondents (191 persons)rated local government conditions in the two lowest categories, a reduction of 5.4 percent. In 1989, 19.2 percent of the respondents (73 persons) rated local government conditions in the two highest categories as compared with 17.5 percent (66 persons) in the 1991 survey. In 2000, three years after consolidation, the proportion of respondents rating local government conditions in the two highest categories increased by 8.6 percent, to 26.1 percent (118 persons).

The same trend before and after consolidation is evident in the perceived change in local government performance over time. In the 1989 survey, 30.4 percent of the respondents (115) said that local government is getting worse, and this increased to 35 percent (133) in 1991. In 2000, however, only 26.7 percent of the respondents (119 persons) said that local government was getting worse. In 1989, 16.7 percent of the respondents (63) said that local government was getting better, whereas only 11.8 percent of the respondents said that local government was getting better in 1991. By 2000, three years after consolidation, 24 percent of the respondents (107) answered that local government was getting better.

In late 2000, three years after the city–county consolidation, the Mid-America Regional Council, the regional council of government, commissioned the ETC Institute of Olathe, Kansas, to perform a citizen survey in the eight-county Kansas City metropolitan region. The survey included questions pertaining to citizens' attitudes toward their local government. The results of the survey were published in the *Metro Outlook: Measuring the Progress of Metropolitan Kansas City* (Metro Outlook 2001). The survey included 1,675 randomly selected citizens. In the data set of 1,675 citizens, there were 146 citizens who resided in Wyandotte County and 1,529 who lived in the remainder of the metropolitan region.

Curtis Wood (2004) examined the results of the 2000 survey and determined that Wyandotte County citizens were as satisfied with the performance and responsiveness of the unified government and as trusting of their governmental leaders as were citizens in other jurisdictions in the eight-county Kansas City metropolitan area. Given the history of political corruption and citizen frustration and disappointment in Wyandotte County, the results of the analysis are encouraging (Frederickson, Johnson, and Wood 2002).

More recent survey data for Wyandotte County citizens reveal that consolidation is largely perceived as a success, particularly in the western part of the county. In August 2006, the University of Kansas conducted a random survey of 457 Wyandotte County residents regarding the performance of the consolidated government vis-à-vis local government before consolidation. About 73 percent of respondents believed that the consolidated government is more responsive to their needs than their previous governing structure; 91 percent indicated the consolidated government is more effective at promoting economic development; 74 percent thought the consolidated government is more responsive to their neighborhood needs, more ethical, and more efficient; and 80 percent felt that local government is more professional. When analyzed by zip code, it appears that residents located in the central part of the city (predominantly African American) are somewhat less satisfied with consolidation and are less likely to feel that the local government has improved in terms of responsiveness and professionalism (Keim 2006). This is interesting, because it was primarily the western part of the county that vocalized opposition to consolidation during the referendum campaign.

Shawnee County and Topeka Citizen Satisfaction

The only available countywide data is a Shawnee County survey conducted by the sheriff's office in 2006 to fulfill guidelines established by the Commission on Accreditation for Law Enforcement Agencies. The 2006 survey indicates that Shawnee County citizens seem fairly satisfied with the services provided by the sheriff's office; however, only 50 percent of the respondents gave the sheriff's office a grade of an "A" in terms of satisfaction with the overall handling of the responsibility to protect and serve the citizens of Shawnee County (Shawnee County Sheriff's Office 2006).

Citizen satisfaction data exist for only the City of Topeka after 1997; therefore it is not possible to compare citizen attitudes before and after the 1997 consolidation. In 2000, the University of Kansas conducted a citizen survey that included several questions about the overall quality of life in Topeka. In general, the results of the 2000 Topeka survey demonstrate that citizens have an unfavorable attitude toward the quality of government services, although citizens are satisfied with the performance of city employees (University of Kansas MPA Program 2001). In addition, the citizens of Topeka are not as optimistic about their economic prospects as are the citizens of Wyandotte County.

Topeka residents were most satisfied with fire protection (79.3 percent), ambulance service (73.6 percent) and parks (73.6 percent). The majority of Topeka residents gave a less than favorable rating for street repair (36.9 percent gave it a favorable rating), enforcement of house nuisance code (28 percent gave it a favorable rating), and downtown economic development. The last was given the lowest number of favorable ratings (with 14.4 percent giving it a favorable rating).

The survey results also indicated that in 2000, 65 percent of Topeka residents rated the overall neighborhood quality good or very good. Only 38.2 percent rated the employment opportunities in Topeka as good or very good, and only 18.2 percent rated the new business opportunities as good or very good.

On the basis of the postconsolidation citizen satisfaction data, it appears that the citizens of Wyandotte County are more satisfied with the performance of their local government than are the citizens of Shawnee County and Topeka.

Conclusion

The evidence provided in the quasi-experimental case study supports the hypotheses that the consolidated government has initially been able to deliver on the promises made and that the consolidated government is more efficient relative to the two similar fragmented governments in terms of expenditure growth per capita. We find that city–county consolidation has contributed to the reverse in population decline, has slowed the loss of rooftops, and has helped spur retail sales in Wyandotte County, thus making it possible to narrow the gap in retail sales growth with Shawnee County,

Table 10.9 Summary of Wyandotte County/Kansas City Case

Overall Assessment of Evidence	H1: Efficiency	H2: Economic Development	H3: Other Promises
Not enough data available			
No evidence			
Weak			
Moderate	☑	☑	☑
Strong			

and has resulted in increased levels of citizen satisfaction pertaining to economic development, efficiency, effectiveness, responsiveness, and professionalism (table 10.9).

Although this study demonstrates support that consolidation can overcome fiscal and economic distress, reverse urban decline, combat flight to the suburbs, and improve governmental efficiency and perceived governmental performance, we caution elected officials, public administrators, civic leaders, and citizens of other fragmented communities that the benefits of consolidation may not be broadly generalized to their communities, particularly if they are heavily unionized, vary substantially in geographic size, or partially consolidate selected functions. In addition, researchers should continue to monitor, record, and assess the demographic, fiscal, and economic trends over a longer period in Wyandotte County and Shawnee County to definitively determine if the absolute and relative progress made by the unified government can be sustained.

Notes

1. The consolidation study committee was originally to be placed on the ballot during the 1996 presidential primary. However, the presidential primary was canceled for budgetary reasons, so Republican governor Bill Graves appointed the five members: two Republicans and three Democrats.
2. The 1990 data are used for this comparison because some of these rankings are only conducted every ten years. The year 1990 is the closest data point before consolidation.

3. The number of net new rooftops is the net number of single-family home building permits (total building permits less demolition permits). The Topeka, Kansas, data were provided by the Topeka Shawnee County Metro Planning Department; and the Kansas City, data came from the unified government's Research Department.
4. The 1990, 1996, 1997, and 2004 actual expenditures for Shawnee County, Kansas, came from the budget forms submitted by the county to the State of Kansas for all budgeted funds. The 1990, 1996, 1997, and 2004 actual expenditures for the City of Topeka budgeted funds came from the operating budgets. The 1989 and 1996 Wyandotte County, Kansas, actual expenditures for all budgeted funds came from the budget forms submitted by the County to the State of Kansas. The 1989 and 1996 Kansas City's actual expenditures for all budgeted funds came from the 1989 and 1996 Comprehensive Annual Financial Report. The year 1997 is the first one when the unified government reported its actual expenditures. Therefore, 1997 is used as the base year. The 1997 actual expenditures for the Unified Government of Kansas City, Kansas, and Wyandotte County, Kansas, came from the 1997 Comprehensive Annual Financial Report and the 1999 unified government's budget document. The 2004 actual expenditures for the unified government came from the 2006 budget forms submitted to the State of Kansas provided by the director of the budget. All expenditures are non–Generally Accepted Accounting Principles and expenditure totals do not include interfund transfers (double budgeting).
5. The "general" government function includes all general fund expenditures not separately itemized, including facility management; "public safety" includes fire, police, 9-1-1, and ambulance; "public works" includes streets, bridges, traffic, and garage; "utilities" include water, sewer, stormwater, and sanitation; "parks and recreation" includes zoo, golf, extension services, and the county fair; "debt service" includes the principal and interest on general obligation debt; "CD/ED/Tourism" is the community development function, economic development, and tourism related activities and contracts; "judicial" includes the court services; "culture" includes the arts, historical society, and the library; "education" includes the community college; "social services" includes expenditures to social service agencies and for indigent citizens; "metro planning" includes expenditures to promote regional activities and initiatives; "public transit" is for public transportation services; "health" includes expenditures for mental and physical health services, animal control, and noxious weeds; and "other" includes unidentified expenditures.

6. The 1989, 1991, and 2000 surveys were on a 5-point scale, with a score of 1 indicating a poor rating and a score of 5 indicating an excellent rating.

References

Campbell, Richard, and Sally Selden. 2000. Does City–County Consolidation Save Money? The Unification of Athens–Clarke County Suggests It Might. *Policy Notes* 1, no. 1 (March):1–2.

Carr, Jered, and Bethany Sneed. 2004. The Politics of City–County Consolidation: Findings from a National Survey. In *City–County Consolidation and Its Alternatives: Reshaping the Local Government Landscape,* ed. Jered Carr and Richard Feiock. Armonk, NY: M. E. Sharpe.

Chamber of Commerce. 1995. Board of County Commissioner's Memorandum to Chamber of Commerce. September 8.

Citizens' Commission on Local Government of Wyandotte County, Kansas. 1970. Kansas Legislative Library. 352.0073, Wt, c2.

Consolidation Study Commission. 1997. *Final Report.* Kansas City, KS: Consolidation Study Commission.

DeWitt, John. 1995. Metropolitan Government Reform: A Case Study of Potential Governmental Consolidation within Wyandotte County. Master's thesis, University of Kansas.

Dilorenzo, T. 1983. Economic Competition and Political Competition: An Empirical Note. *Public Choice* 40 (2):203–9.

Eberts, Randall W., and Timothy J. Gronberg. 1988. Can Competition among Local Governments Constrain Government Spending? *Economic Review, Federal Reserve Bank of Cleveland,* First Quarter, 2–9.

Feiock, Richard. 2004a. Do Consolidation Entrepreneurs Make a Deal with the Devil? In *City–County Consolidation and Its Alternatives,* ed. J. B. Carr and Richard Feiock. Armonk, NY: M. E. Sharpe.

———. 2004b. Metropolitan Governance and Institutional Collective Action. *Urban Affairs Review* 44 (3): 356–77.

Feiock, Richard C., and Jered B. Carr. 1999. Private Incentives and Public Entrepreneurs: The Promotion of City/County Consolidation. *Public Administration Quarterly* 24, no. 2:223–45.

Fisher, R. C. 1996. *State and Local Public Finance.* Chicago: Irwin.

Frederickson, H. George, Gary A. Johnson, and Curtis Wood. 2002. Type III Cities. In *The Future of Local Government Administration: The Hansell*

Symposium, ed. H. George Frederickson and John Nalbandian. Washington, DC: International City/County Management Association.

———. 2004. *The Adapted City: Institutional Dynamics and Structural Change.* Armonk, NY: M. E. Sharpe.

Glendening, Parris N., and Patricia Atkins. 1980. City–County Consolidations: New Views for the Eighties. In *The Municipal Yearbook, 1980.* Washington, DC: International City/County Management Association.

Gurwitt, Rob. 2002. Governing's Public Officials of the Year. *Governing, City and State,* November.

Halter, Gary. 1993. City–City Consolidations in the United States. *National Civic Review* 82, no. 3 (Summer):282–88.

Hawkins, Brett W., and Douglas M. Ihrke. 1999. Research Note: Reexamining the Suburban Exploitation Thesis in American Metropolitan Areas. *Publius: The Journal of Federalism* 29, no. 3:109–22.

Keim, Susan. 2006. Citizen Satisfaction—WYCO/KCK Consolidation. Working paper.

Kelley, Kevin. 1994. Blueprints Ready for Change. *Kansas City, Kansan.* April 12.

———. 2000. Personal interview with the leader of Wyandotte Countians for Change and Consolidation Task Force. April 18.

Leland, Suzanne. 2004. Reforming Politics through Reorganization: City–County Consolidation in Wyandotte County/Kansas City, Kansas. In *Reshaping the Local Government Landscape: Case Studies of Local Government Consolidation,* ed. Suzanne Leland and Kurt Thurmaier. Armonk, NY: M. E. Sharpe.

Leland, Suzanne, and Gary Johnson. 2000. "Stealing Back Home: How One City and County Beat the Odds and Successfully Consolidated Their Governments." Paper presented at the April Midwest Political Science Association Meeting, Chicago, IL.

Leland, Suzanne, and Kurt Thurmaier. 2006. Lessons from 35 Years of City–County Consolidation Attempts. In *Municipal Yearbook.* Washington, DC: International City/County Management Association.

Maher, Kris. 2005. To Cut Costs, Cities Ponder Mergers with Counties. *Wall Street Journal,* February 22, A2.

Marinovich, Carol. 2004. State of the Government. Speech, January 27.

Metro Outlook. 2001. *Metro Outlook: Measuring the Progress of Metropolitan Kansas City.* Kansas City: Metro Outlook.

Peirce, Neal, Curtis Johnson, and John Stuart Hall. 1993. *Citi States: How Urban America Can Prosper in a Competitive World.* Washington, DC: Seven Locks Press.

Rusk, David. 1994. Bend or Die. *State Government News,* February, 6–10.

———. 2003. Cities without Suburbs: A Census 2000 Update. Washington, DC: Woodrow Wilson Center Press.

Schneider. Mark. 1989. *The Competitive City: The Political Economy of Suburbia.* Pittsburgh: University of Pittsburgh Press.

Scot Gard and Associates. 1988. *A Study of City–County Consolidation in Wyandotte County, Kansas City, Kansas.* Kansas City: Scot Gard and Associates.

Shawnee County Sheriff's Office. 2006. Citizen Survey, Summer, Conducted and Published by Shawnee County.

Sigman, Robert P. 1997. A Way Out of the Morass. *Kansas City Star,* January 19.

Stephens, Ross, and Nelson Wikstrom. 2000. *Metropolitan Government and Governance: Theoretical Perspectives, Empirical Analysis and the Future.* New York: Oxford University Press.

Stockwell, Robert. 2000. Interview with the former executive director of the Consolidation Study Commission. January.

Thurmaier, Kurt, and Curtis Wood. 2004. Interlocal Agreements as an Alternative to Consolidation. In *City–County Consolidation and Its Alternatives: Reshaping the Local Government Landscape,* ed. Jered Carr and Richard Feiock. Armonk, NY: M. E. Sharpe.

University of Kansas MPA Program. 2001. 2000 Topeka Citizen Survey. February.

Wagner, Richard E., and Warren E. Weber. 1975. Competition, Monopoly, and the Organization of Government in Metropolitan Areas. *Journal of Law and Economics* 18 (December):661–84.

Wood, Curtis. 2004. Executive Summary: Metropolitan Governance in Urban America: A Study of the Kansas City Region. *Kansas Governmental Journal* 90, no. 5:146–49.

11

Promises Made, Promises Kept

Kurt Thurmaier and Suzanne M. Leland

City–county consolidations have a long history in the United States, and the representative cases reviewed in this volume span more than forty years of this history. Our objective in this chapter is to scan these representative cases for patterns of effects that lead to the conclusions that consolidations have lived up to the promises made by their proponents in the referenda campaigns that gave them birth. In particular, we review these nine pairs of cases (a total of eighteen observations in our sample) for evidence that consolidations keep promises to increase local government efficiency, increase local government effectiveness in economic development, and also fulfill any other assorted promises made during consolidation campaigns.[1]

In chapter 1 we presented the research design that frames this comparative case study, and we acknowledged the challenges that our contributing authors faced in obtaining the data needed to make this design work. Again, we thank our research team and credit them with a vast reserve of determination and patience in finding the data, whether deep in the storage cellars of courthouses and public libraries or buried inside archived files from censuses of governments. This has truly been a monumental undertaking, and it is no wonder that it has not been attempted before.

This chapter systematically analyzes the three hypotheses presented in chapter 1, based on our research design (see figure 1.1):

H1: The consolidated governments operate more efficiently than unconsolidated governments, due to selective functional service consolidations.

H2: Consolidated governments will have higher economic growth rates than similar nonconsolidated communities due to structural effectiveness gains.

H3: The consolidated government delivered on its other promises made in the proconsolidation campaign.

We consider two types of observations. First, we compare the consolidation and comparison cases within each case chapter with respect to a particular hypothesis. Second, we synthesize these results and draw conclusions for each hypothesis based on an assessment of the sample of nine sets of cases. We draw our conclusions about the hypothesis based on the combination of data.

We first analyze the efficiency promise, then the economic development hypothesis, and then the other promises made by consolidation campaigns. The next section of the chapter synthesizes the findings from the three hypotheses to answer the question of whether consolidations, on balance, have lived up to their promises. We conclude the chapter with a discussion of our satisfaction with our research design, and of how researchers might pursue future studies about the efficiency and effectiveness of local governments in metropolitan areas.

The Efficiency Promise in Consolidation Referenda

There are now thirty-nine consolidated governments across the nation. Although a frequently discussed local government reform, city–county consolidation (where a major municipality and county have structurally merged to form a unified government) is unusual, and is even considered a revolutionary change (Rosenbaum and Kammerer 1974). Approximately 80 percent of consolidation efforts fail (Leland and Thurmaier 2006). But the discussion of consolidation is alive and well in the halls of local governments and state legislatures, especially during this time of economic crisis. Since the recession began in late 2008, reformers in states such as Texas, Indiana, Florida, New York, and Pennsylvania have been considering the consolidation of cities and counties as a solution to save money. Cities and counties such as Pittsburgh/Allegheny County and Charlotte/Mecklenburg County are also revisiting the issue.

Our efficiency hypothesis (H1) is based on the long-standing argument by consolidation proponents that consolidation will reduce the overall cost of government. Therefore, we define efficiency in their terms. There has been considerable discussion in the urban policy literature about the debate on the new regionalism versus fragmentation. Although the regionalists' perspective advocates consolidation to reduce governmental fragmentation and take advantage of economies of scale, several public choice theorists argue that this approach will fail to achieve any efficiency with regard to the use of scarce resources (Tiebout 1956; Ostrom, Tiebout, and Warren 1961). Indeed, from the public choice perspective, single-unit governments are more likely to behave as monopolists and reduce the quality of services while prices (taxes) rise (Leland and Rosentraub 2007). There have been few empirical studies examining whether consolidation produces more efficient and effective local government service delivery. The majority of studies involve single case studies (e.g., Benton and Gamble 1984; Selden and Campbell 2000; Carr, Bae, and Lu 2006; Durning 1995; Swanson 1996), as opposed to focusing on multiple cases and their longer-term results (Carr and Feiock 1999; Feiock and Carr 1997; Lyons and Lowery 1989; Reese 2004; Vojnovic 2000). Only Benton and Gamble (1984) systematically compare expenditure growth in the ten years before consolidation to the ten years following consolidation, although for only a single comparison case.[2] Our team of sixteen investigators followed a rigorous comparative case study design to test the efficiency hypothesis.

For city–county consolidation to be adopted, it is not unusual to have many departments of the city and county remain independent, even though they are governed by a unified elected body. This is because the process of adopting consolidation is politically charged and the end product is typically developed as a result of years of bargaining at both the state and local levels. This means that consolidated governments are not uniform when compared with one another. Each one varies greatly in the level of consolidation of services between the city and county.

To return to our discussion in chapter 1, table 11.1 again presents three groups of cases, based on the relative levels of functional consolidation, both premerger and postmerger. The only group where we would expect to see large efficiency gains from merging city and county governments is when there are completely separate city and county services before the merger and all the services are merged postconsolidation (group A). In group B, functional consolidation is already present before the adoption of the consolidated government, and few functions (if any) are left to be merged; that is, the efficiency gains are already achieved before the merger. The efficiency gains in group C are also small, but for a different reason; the city–county

Table 11.1 Variable Expectations of Efficiency Gains

	Premerger Level	
Postmerger Level	**Low Consolidation**	**High Consolidation**
High	Large Efficiency Gains A	Small Efficiency Gains B
Low	C Small Efficiency Gains	

consolidation that results still retains separated service jurisdictions, with small efficiency gains, if any.

This variation in consolidation premerger and postmerger is an important factor when assessing whether or not the consolidated government will become more efficient after the merger. In many cases, there is little or no opportunity to achieve economies of scale because services remain separate. In situations where the major services are already functionally consolidated, there is little duplication to eliminate. We would expect consolidating cities and counties to have the greatest opportunity to realize efficiencies when the major services (e.g., police, fire, public works) previously were operated separately by both the city and county but were merged after consolidation. In these cases, there are opportunities to streamline operations by ridding the governments of duplication and taking advantage of economies of scale. Our primary means of testing the efficiency hypothesis is to measure and compare the growth in expenditures in two periods: ten years before the consolidation, and ten years after the consolidation.[3] Our primary measures focus attention on total expenditures, and expenditures on highways (or public works), law enforcement, and fire protection. In some cases, the investigators use the measures from the census of governments, while other investigators use categories from city and county budgets. Thus, the expenditure measures are comparable within each case comparison and generally comparable across all consolidated and comparison cases as well. All the measures are reported on a per capita basis, adjusting for population changes during the twenty-year period.

Most of the data come from the Census of Governments, dating back to 1957 for counties and 1951 for cities. Some of the data come from cases that involved researchers scrounging in courthouse basements because the census did not collect data from small municipalities or the data are missing from the census tables. Many of these states did not have open records acts during this period (pre-1970s). This makes rigorous quantitative time-series analysis (e.g., ARIMA) impossible across all cases. Hence, the definition of total expenditures is not always exactly the same *across* cases. However, to preserve internal validity, the exact same total expenditures definition is used *within* each pair of cases.[4] Because the key analysis is of the relative increase or decrease in expenditures, comparing the consolidated county and the combined (city + county) expenditures of the comparison county, the slight differences in total expenditure definitions are immaterial to our analysis.[5]

Efficiency Expectations from Consolidations

The nine consolidated cases reviewed in this study present decidedly mixed results regarding the proponents' efficiency promise. About half the comparative case analyses present substantial evidence of improved efficiency following consolidation. Conversely, about half suggest that the expenditures in the comparison counties grew at slower rates than in the consolidation counties. Table 11.2 summarizes the expenditure analysis from the nine cases in the project.

Three cases fall into group A, where we would expect significant efficiency gains from consolidation: Jacksonville/Duval County, Butte/Silver Bow County, and Lexington/Fayette County. As seen in table 11.2, in the years before consolidation, two-thirds of the consolidation cases were growing more slowly than the comparison cases. But in the ten years following consolidation, only one of the consolidation cases was still growing more slowly than the comparison case. This does not provide prima facie support for Hypothesis 1a. However, the in-depth analysis of each case reveals that there is more complexity to the story.

In the Jacksonville/Duval County consolidation, all the major services (fire, social services, law enforcement, and parks and recreation) were functionally separate before consolidation and were then merged under consolidation. Although table 11.2 reveals that overall expenditure growth was somewhat higher (15 points) than in Tampa/Hillsborough County, the analysis also reveals that Jacksonville/Duval County actually made efficiency gains in the three specific services areas of public works, public safety, and fire protection. The consolidated government had substantially lower growth in all three of these areas. This suggests that the growth in expenditures was elsewhere, although it is clear that the total expenditures grew faster in Jacksonville/Duval County than in Tampa/Hillsborough County.

In the Butte/Silver Bow County case, social services, planning, economic development, and public health were all largely county functions and did not need to be merged during consolidation. Water was supplied to the city and county privately by the copper mine, leaving no water utilities to consolidate. Consolidation, however, forced the merger of fire, law enforcement, parks and recreation, and public works. As with many other consolidation cases, pay rates for sheriff's deputies were brought up to the level of police officers dding an immediate increase to

Table 11.2 Expenditure Analysis of the Efficiency Hypothesis

		Expenditure Growth per Capita 10 Years Before Consolidation (% Change)							
		Total Expenditures		Public Works Expenditures		Public Safety Expenditures		Fire Expenditures (Other than Public Safety)	
Jurisdiction	C^3 Year	C^3 Case	Comparison Case	C^3 Case	Comparison Case	C^3 Case	Comparison Case	C^3 Case	Comparison Case
Butte/Silver Bow County, MT	1976	76	99	28	84	107	57		
Jacksonville/Duval County, FL	1967	43	39	32	–23	27	29	52	34
Lexington/Fayette County, KY	1972	38	42	–9	58	115	275	43	64
Athens/Clarke County, GA	1990	19	30	–24	–49	68	68	43	28
Carson City/Ormsby County, NV	1969	61	44	33	30	44	30	171	59
Wyandotte County/Kansas City, KS	1997	63	34	41	25	62	38		
Virginia Beach/Princess Anne County, VA	1963	33	31	608	36	264	0		
Lynchburg/Moore County, TN	1988	–12	–25	10	–24	227	5	409	45
Nashville/Davidson County, TN	1963	54	45	45	–9	13	16	98	55

Table 11.2 (Continued)

Butte/Silver Bow County, MT	1976	–39	–22	–68	–60	9	34		
Jacksonville/Duval County, FL	1967	186	171	23	96	141	233	103	251
Lexington/Fayette County, KY	1972	294	135	320	69	234	140	278	172
Athens/Clarke County, GA	1990	3	21	–10	39	–17	2	–3	20
Carson City/Ormsby County, NV	1969	13	6	–24	4	–8	58	–1	60
Wyandotte County/Kansas City, KS	1997	–20	46	39	3	48	39		
Virginia Beach/Princess Anne County, VA	1963	181	78	118	27	88	74		
Lynchburg/Moore County, TN	1988	50	41	–81	–10	317	–10	41	–17
Nashville/Davidson County, TN	1963	113	156	70	68	97	108	–4	171

Sources: Data compiled from the chapters in this volume, with various sources (with matching source within each case comparison).

Note: C^3 = City–County Consolidation.

law enforcement spending, which stabilized over time. Still, as seen in table 11.2, expenditures in Butte/Silver Bow County grew more slowly in the postconsolidation years than in Bozeman/Gallatin County. Although it is true that overall expenditures in Butte/Silver Bow County grew more slowly in the years before merger, that was not the case with public safety expenditures, where Butte/Silver Bow County grew 107 percent compared with only 57 percent in Bozeman/Gallatin County. After merger, however, and despite the increased spending for deputies, public safety expenditures in Butte/Silver Bow County grew only 9 percent, compared with 34 percent in the comparison case. Butte/Silver Bow County offers support for Hypothesis 1a.

The case of Lexington/Fayette County does not conform to efficiency expectations, even though it follows the pattern of low consolidation premerger and high consolidation postmerger. This is because consolidation was initiated to increase services to outlying areas. It was not to increase efficiency by eliminating duplication. Services were not functionally consolidated before consolidation; the levels of services expanded dramatically when they were merged during consolidation, substantially raising the costs of government service delivery and precluding efficiency gains in this case. Across the board, spending in Lexington/Fayette County in the postmerger years was higher than in the comparison case of Louisville/Jefferson County, offering no support for Hypothesis 1a.

The cases in group B had a substantial level of services that were already functionally merged before the political consolidation, leaving few services to consolidate after the political merger. The cases in our sample that fall into this group include Athens/Clarke County, Carson City/Ormsby County, Wyandotte County/Kansas City, and, to a lesser extent, Virginia Beach/Princess Anne County. These cases offer mixed support for Hypothesis 1b, because half the consolidation cases produced efficiency gains but the other half did not.

Before the Athens/Clarke County consolidation, several of the major city and county services were already functionally merged. Fire protection and parks and recreation had interlocal government agreements (ILAs) in place, and the planning, utilities, and public works services were functionally consolidated. Postconsolidation, this left only two major services to combine: social services and law enforcement. Clarke County had already created a county police department several years before consolidation, leaving the sheriff to maintain court security and run the jail; merging the city and county police departments still remained as a postconsolidation task. Still in all, Athens/Clarke County's expenditures grew more slowly postconsolidation than the comparison case, whether measured by total expenditures or our three focus services. Table 11.2 indicates that police and fire expenditures actually decreased in Athens/Clarke County following consolidation, compared with increases in the comparison case.

In the Carson City/Ormsby County consolidation, the city and county already shared fire and engineering departments, as well as a city–county manager and clerk, among other positions. Although the rationale for the consolidation included efficiency improvements, so much functional consolidation had already occurred that the political consolidation was a capstone event to a longer consolidation process. Thus the data given in table 11.2 indicate that Carson City/Ormsby County's expenditures were growing more slowly before consolidation than the comparison group. After final consolidation, total expenditures in Carson City/Ormsby County grew somewhat (7 percent) faster than in the comparison group, but table 11.2 also reveals that Carson City/Ormsby County's expenditures in public works, public safety, and fire services actually decreased following consolidation, while those expenditures increased in the comparison group. Despite substantial functional consolidation before the actual political merger, the analysis indicates substantial counterfactual evidence regarding Hypothesis 1b.

In Wyandotte County/Kansas City, law enforcement was already functionally consolidated before consolidation. It was established through an ILA when Kansas City's jails were shut down by the court system. In exchange for housing prisoners in the county jail, the city assumed road patrol for the county. This was the only functionally consolidated service before consolidation. After the consolidation, all major city and county services—such as planning, parks and recreation, roads, sewer and water, and fire protection—were combined. Efficiency gains were enhanced by the fact that the city and county had almost contiguous and overlapping boundaries. The analysis presented in table 11.2 indicates that Wyandotte County/Kansas City's expenditures were growing substantially faster than those of Topeka/Shawnee County in the years before consolidation. After consolidation, however, overall expenditures actually fell in Wyandotte County/Kansas City, compared with a 46 percent increase in Topeka/Shawnee County. Conversely, expenditures in public works and public safety continued to grow faster in Wyandotte County/Kansas City than in Topeka/Shawnee County following the merger, providing mixed support overall for Hypothesis 1b.

Four services in Virginia Beach (culture, public health, public welfare, and education) were functionally consolidated before the merger. But the major services where we would likely find duplication—law enforcement, economic development, planning, fire, law enforcement, and parks and recreation—were all still separate. After the consolidation, all these services were merged. Table 11.2 suggests that efficiency gains were not evident.

However, a more nuanced analysis by Swartz indicates that efficiency gains were actually realized (chapter 3, this volume). The Virginia Beach consolidation requires a second-level analysis of the data before one can conclude whether or not efficiency has increased or decreased. The rapid rise in population in Virginia Beach / Princess Anne County seriously skews the expenditure data, relative to the moderate population growth of Richmond and Henrico County. As Swartz notes in chapter 3 of the present volume,

> This quasi-experimental case study supports the hypotheses that the consolidated government of Virginia Beach is more efficient and delivered on its campaign promises. Comparing only per capita expenditure data between Richmond and Virginia Beach, however, does not yield findings that bode well for reform advocates. We must take into consideration Virginia Beach's extensive population growth during the years under review. This is taken into account by examining marginal increases, which calculates changes in expenditures per capita by population changes. When this calculation is considered, the efficiency argument associated with economies of scale appears to be true in this instance. Although Virginia Beach's per capita expenditures nearly doubled immediately following consolidation (as a result of expanding services), there was a decrease in per capita expenditures in the last three years of review that hints at possible cost savings in the long run.

Group C represents the scenario in which the majority of services were separate before consolidation, and they remained so after, or were broken into different service jurisdictions mirroring the old city and county boundaries. Unigov (Indianapolis) is notorious for this scenario. Only after thirty years of consolidation were services such as police and fire consolidated (Leland and Rosentraub 2007).Two of the cases in our study also fit into this category, and both cases are located in Tennessee: Lynchburg/Moore County and Nashville/Davidson County. In both cases, the consolidation technically merged all departments, but it kept two different levels of services. In Nashville/Davidson County, where only public health services were functionally consolidated before the merger, two separate service districts were created postmerger. The General Services District (GSD) and the Urban Services District (USD) were created to provide for differential tax and service levels. Residents of the USD had a full range of city services. The areas that made up the GSD had a lower tax rate until services were provided. Still, table 11.2 suggests that expenditures grew more slowly in Nashville/Davidson County than in Louisville/Jefferson County in the ten years following the Nashville/Davidson County consolidation. Moreover, fire expenditures actually fell in this period in Nashville/Davidson County, while they increased substantially in Louisville/Jefferson County.

The Lynchburg/Moore County consolidation provides less surprising results. This merger basically transformed the county government into a GSD, and the City of Lynchburg from a municipal government into the Lynchburg USD. The Lynchburg USD was structured as a municipal corporation and remained an independent taxing district under the authority of the Urban Council, which comprised the three members of the Metropolitan Council representing the Lynchburg USD. The Lynchburg USD was established as a tax district to provide funding for services available only to residents of the Lynchburg area and not the remainder of the GSD. Therefore, the potential efficiency gains from eliminating duplicate services through consolidation were most likely in Lynchburg, where the three positions of mayor, recorder, and treasurer could be eliminated and absorbed into the new merged government.

When the consolidation occurred, the former Lynchburg mayor's duties were assigned to the new metropolitan executive, and the county trustee (renamed metropolitan trustee) assumed responsibilities formerly held by the Lynchburg treasurer. The office of county clerk assumed responsibility for duties of the Lynchburg recorder, under the new title of metropolitan secretary. Likewise, fire and police responsibilities were consolidated into single merged departments. The small size of Lynchburg's city government—the city employed a single police officer, and the fire department was staffed by volunteer firefighters—simplified the consolidation process and generated little concern over job attrition; but it also precluded significant efficiency gains from the merger. Table 11.2 reveals that with only one exception (public works, postmerger), the Lynchburg/Moore County's expenditures grew faster than those of the Decatur/Meigs County comparison case.

The analysis from table 11.2 reaffirms the mixed findings of the individual case studies. Overall, we cannot find sustained support for our efficiency hypothesis. We do not find consistent efficiency gains in group A cases, as expected. Yet we find substantial efficiency gains when we did not expect them in groups B and C. In light of the mixed evidence, what are we to conclude about the efficiency promises made for consolidation cases?

In the specific expenditure categories where we would expect increased efficiency from consolidation, public works and public safety (police and fire), only a bare majority of the consolidation cases present slower growth in expenditures than their comparison counties. Carson City/Ormsby

County, Butte/Silver Bow County, and Athens/Clarke County all present greater efficiency in the ten years after consolidation than their comparisons. Nashville/Davidson County had slower expenditure growth in public safety (including fire) than its comparison case; Lynchburg/Moore County had greater efficiency only in the public works category.

There also are no discernible patterns of increased or decreased efficiency based on the decade of the consolidation. The only subtle distinction, perhaps, is that most of the consolidations in the 1960s increased efficiency in public safety (75 percent of them) and fire expenditures (100 percent of them). That compares to only 55 percent of all cases in public safety, and 66 percent of all cases in fire services. Of the consolidations after 1970, about 60 percent were more efficient than their comparison cases in total expenditures (Butte/Silver Bow County, Athens/Clarke County, and Wyandotte County/Kansas City) and in public works expenditures (Butte/Silver Bow County, Lynchburg/Moore County, and Athens/Clarke County).

Analyzing the data based on the population size of the consolidated communities also reveals no difference between large-population communities and smaller communities. If we divide the cases between those with consolidated counties under 100,000 residents and those with counties of more than 100,000, there is no pattern of difference in growth rates in the ten years following consolidation. About half the cases in each group were more efficient than the comparison county (i.e., had lower growth rates in the ten years after consolidation).

The quantitative and qualitative analyses of the nine cases found evidence for increased efficiency in six consolidated counties: Butte/Silver Bow County, Jacksonville/Duval County, Nashville/Davidson County, Athens/Clarke County, Wyandotte County/Kansas City, and Virginia Beach/Princess Anne County. The investigators of each case use multiple measures to analyze the efficiency gains (or losses) from consolidation.

Accept the Null Hypothesis for Efficiency Gains

Overall, we are hard-pressed to conclude that the consolidations improved efficiency of operations, as measured by growth in expenditures. Our research design enables us to compare growth in expenditures in comparable periods, with comparable governments, using the same measures in each pair (consolidated and comparison cases), both overall and in specific service areas. Given the relatively small sample size and the imprecision in measurements, a notable increase in efficiency should be evident from more than a bare majority of cases. Coupled with the more detailed and subtle analysis from each case study, we must conclude that there is no support for the hypothesis that consolidations predictably lead to increased efficiency in local government. It can—and does—happen, but increased efficiency is not a predictable outcome of consolidating city and county governments.

The Economic Development Promise in Consolidation Referenda

In our previous study of city–county consolidation (Leland and Thurmaier 2004), we found that voters were more likely to support consolidation campaigns that promised increased economic development effectiveness than those that promised increased efficiency in local government operations. Our current research team has tested Hypothesis H2—that consolidated governments are actually more successful at economic development than their comparison case.

We have measured economic development effectiveness directly and indirectly. Measuring relative population growth preconsolidation and postconsolidation, and between the consolidation case and its comparison case, indirectly measures economic development success. Simply put, we expect a community with a thriving economy to attract more people and retain more residents because they will be satisfied with the community's employment opportunities, wage levels, and overall economic health. Thus, we expect consolidated governments (1) to have higher population growth in the ten years after consolidation compared with the ten years before, and (2) to have higher population growth in the ten years after consolidation relative to the comparison counties.

Economic development success can also be measured with a set of economic indicators, including total employment, numbers of manufacturing establishments, numbers of retail establishments, and housing data. One of the severe limitations of this set of measures, however, is that the U.S. Bureau of the Census does not collect and report this information from small municipalities, which represent half of our study population. Moreover, many municipalities—especially smaller, rural ones—do not keep or retain these data themselves, especially for long periods. Hence, getting data for small cities for decades ago is virtually an impossible task.[3] Nevertheless, our research team was anything if not persistent, and most chapters have assembled some set of economic indicators to test this hypothesis. In many cases, they have tried proxy variables to measure different kinds of economic activity, even if indirectly.

The Data

We first assess population data across all nine chapters to establish the context of the case assessment, and we then examine the selected economic indicators reported by the chapter authors. We then review the conclusions from the individual chapters.

Data on Population Changes

Table 11.3 presents a consolidated statement of population changes in the nine comparative case studies. The analysis is based on county populations, because these incorporate municipal populations as well.[6] Unfortunately, this aggregated analysis cannot analyze the unconsolidated city populations relative to either the consolidation year or the comparison city. We can note at the outset that only two of the consolidated counties had larger populations than the comparison counties at the time of consolidation (Nashville/Davidson County and Jacksonville/Duval County). In all the other cases, the consolidating counties had smaller populations; this is an artifact of choosing comparison cases and not an attribute of the consolidations themselves.

The data given in table 11.3 present very mixed results regarding economic development in the postconsolidation period. In five of the cases (55 percent), the comparison county has higher population growth than the consolidated county. Three of the four cases (Butte/Silver Bow County, Lynchburg/Moore County, and Wyandotte County/Kansas City) require a more nuanced analysis. Each of these cases had declining populations in the ten years preceding consolidation. Table 11.3 shows that the consolidated governments have stemmed the severe population losses the counties were facing before consolidation. Although they had slower population growth, the gap between them and their comparison counties diminished over the period. Lynchburg/Moore County even recorded positive population growth in the postconsolidation period, although it was less than the comparison county's growth.

In both the Athens/Clarke County and Jacksonville/Duval County cases, the consolidated counties continue to lag in population growth relative to their comparison counties, as they did before consolidation. In the other four cases, the consolidated governments recorded higher population growth than their comparison counties both before and after consolidation. Of the four cases where the consolidated county's growth exceeded that of the comparison county, only in the Nashville/Davidson County case has the comparison county (Louisville's Jefferson County) narrowed the gap in population growth.

Overall, one could argue that in six of nine cases, the relative strength of the population growth in the consolidated counties is stronger than in the comparison counties. This is significant in light of the fact that in all but two cases, the consolidated counties were smaller to begin with. Given urbanization trends in the United States in the last thirty years, one would expect, ceteris paribus, that the larger counties would grow faster than the smaller counties.

Data on Economic Measures

Table 11.4 summarizes the economic development data presented in the case chapters. Although it is difficult to discern a pattern of more effective economic development by the consolidated governments in the ten years following consolidation, there are slightly more indicators favoring consolidated governments. Overall, there are twelve measures that indicate the consolidated governments performed better than their comparison counties, and nine that indicate the contrary situation. The pattern is more pronounced when one divides the sample into large and small populations, at 100,000 residents. Across the seven measures in table 11.4, there are seven instances where the small consolidated government (under 100,000 population) performed better than their small counterparts, though the small comparison government performed better in economic development in five instances over the period. Similarly, large consolidated governments performed better than their comparison cases in economic development measures in five instances, though there were four instances of the contrary case. The small consolidation cases tended to outperform their comparison cases in retail sales, although the larger comparison cases tended to outperform their consolidation cases in this area (table 11.4). Larger consolidations tended to outperform their comparison cases in housing growth, although there is no difference for small consolidations and their counterparts.

This is certainly not overwhelming evidence that consolidated governments are performing better than their comparison cases. However, the case studies that delved into the nuances of the cases provide supporting evidence and analysis for the conclusion that consolidated governments have achieved somewhat better economic development performance than their counterparts. Six chapters concluded the consolidated governments had stronger performances in the ten years following their consolidations.

Case Conclusions Summary for Economic Development

The Athens/Clarke County analysis provides "no convincing evidence that unification contributed to income and employment improvements . . . . The evidence is clear that unification did not boost incomes or employment in Clarke County from 1992 to 2002, and without significantly diversifying the

Table 11.3 Demographic Characteristics of Experimental and Comparison Cases

	10 Years before Consolidation		Year of Consolidation		10 Years after Consolidation	
Total Population	C^3 Case	Comparison Case	C^3 Case	Comparison Case	C^3 Case	Comparison Case
Lynchburg/Moore County, TN	5,178	8,500	4,696	9,394	5,740	12,481
Carson City/Ormsby County, NV	8,063	35,069	15,468	48,513	34,324	80,814
Butte/Silver Bow County, MT	41,981	32,505	38,092	42,865	33,941	50,463
Virginia Beach/Princess Anne County, VA	42,277	287,650	84,215	337,297	188,500	401,200
Athens/Clarke County, GA	74,498	75,849	87,594	95,428	101,489	139,277
Wyandotte County/Kansas City, KS	173,626	162,388	155,072	165,122	145,010	170,902
Lexington/Fayette County, KY	131,906	610,947	174,323	695,055	210,150	682,706
Nashville/Davidson County, TN	321,758	223,007	399,743	250,523	448,003	276,293
Jacksonville/Duval County, FL	455,411	397,788	528,865	490,265	571,003	646,960

Table 11.3 (Continued)

Lynchburg/Moore County, TN	–9	11	–20	–11	22	33
Carson City/Ormsby County, NV	92	38	54	55	122	67
Butte/Silver Bow County, MT	–9	32	–41	–29	–11	18
Virginia Beach/Princess Anne County, VA	99	17	82	105	124	19
Athens/Clarke County, GA	18	26	–8	–30	16	46
Wyandotte County/Kansas City, KS	–11	2	–12	–10	–6	4
Lexington/Fayette County, KY	32	14	18	22	21	–2
Nashville/Davidson County, TN	24	12	12	2	12	10
Jacksonville/Duval County, FL	16	23	–7	–24	8	32

Sources: Data compiled from the chapters in this volume, with various sources (with matching source within each case comparison).

Note: C^3 = City–County Consolidation. Based on comparable county data, nearest population census.

Table 11.4 Economic Growth of Experimental and Comparison Cases, Percent Change Ten Years After Consolidation

	Retail Sales		Manufacturing		Total Employment		Unemployment	
Jurisdiction	C^3 Case	Comparison Case	C^3 Case	Comparison Case	C^3 Case	Comparison Case	C^3 Case	Comparison Case
Lynchburg/Moore County, TN	–0.4[a]	–2[a]					–5	16[b]
Carson City/Ormsby County, NV	81	16[d]						
Butte/Silver Bow County, MT					–6	47		
Virginia Beach/Princess Anne County, VA	59[e]	–3[e]	59[f]	1[f]				
Athens/Clarke County, GA					24	45		
Wyandotte County/Kansas City, KS	25	34						
Lexington/Fayette County, KY	17	5	9	9				
Nashville/Davidson County, TN	378	428						
Jacksonville/Duval County, FL	635[i]	962[i]	–17	–28				

Table 11.4 (Continued)

Jurisdiction	Personal Income		Taxable Value		Housing	
	C^3 Case	Comparison Case	C^3 Case	Comparison Case	C^3 Case	Comparison Case
Lynchburg/Moore County, TN					28[c]	39[c]
Carson City/Ormsby County, NV			108	78		
Butte/Silver Bow County, MT			–49	–28		
Virginia Beach/Princess Anne County, VA						
Athens/Clarke County, GA	38	40				
Wyandotte County/Kansas City, KS					–377[g]	1,221[g]
Lexington/Fayette County, KY					37[h]	17[h]
Nashville/Davidson County, TN					35	36
Jacksonville/Duval County, FL	172	182				

Sources: Data compiled from chapters in this volume, with various sources (with matching source within each case comparison).

Note: C^3 = City–County–Consolidation.

[a]Change in sales and gross receipts tax revenues, 1987–97.
[b]County unemployment rates, 1989–98.
[c]Change in number of households, 1990–2000.
[d]Based on 3 comparison county average.
[e]Change in number of retail establishments, not jobs, 1972–82.
[f]Change in number of manufacturing establishments, not jobs, 1972–82.
[g]Change in number of rooftops.
[h]Change in number of households, 1972–82.
[i]Based on 1982 data.

economic base of the county, these tasks may difficult to achieve." In fact, the case study reveals that Athens/Clarke County had lower employment and personal income growth than the comparison county (or counties). The differences are discussed by the chapter authors, who note that the lower growth may be due, in part, to the closer proximity of the comparison county to the Atlanta metropolitan region, and the more stable economy of Athens/Clarke County, anchored by the University of Georgia. "Stable" in this case means slower growth relative to the comparison county.

The Butte/Silver Bow County area has not faired well economically, either in the ten years before or the ten years after consolidation, an artifact of being tied to the mining industry. Keim and Marlowe find little evidence of economic gains. "The consolidation arguably kept Butte/Silver Bow [County] solvent during a difficult fiscal period," they note, buying "the jurisdiction enough time to capitalize on the growth in population and capital investment that Montana would soon experience. Consolidation may be one of the reasons the Butte/Silver Bow [County] community has mitigated severe erosion of its economic base over the years and has begun to see some recent population and economic development growth in recent years." Still, Butte/Silver Bow County had lower employment and lower taxable value growth than its comparison case. Although it had slightly better retention of home value than its comparison case, it was still negative for the period ten years following consolidation.

There is no evidence that the Nashville/Davidson County consolidation resulted in more effective economic development than in its comparison case. The analysis by Nownes, Houston, and Schwerdt of population and retail sales data provides little evidence that Nashville/Davidson County "became a beacon for citizens and businesses after consolidation." There is little evidence that Nashville/Davidson County has become a model community "that would draw residents and businesses as consolidation supporters had hoped." They find that the number of housing units is about the same in both cases, but retail sales rose substantially less (378 percent) than in the comparison case of Knoxville/Knox County (428 percent).

Stronger retail sales and stronger growth in the number of households are two indicators of superior economic development performance in Lexington/Fayette County compared with Louisville/Jefferson County. They both had comparable growth in manufacturing in the postconsolidation period, indicating that Lexington/Fayette County matched its comparison case in basic economic infrastructure and outperformed it in the growing retail sector.

The Carson City/Ormsby County case presents one with a difficult challenge to test the economic development hypothesis. Lukemeyer tackles the challenge by comparing growth in Carson City/Ormsby County with three other counties in Nevada. The challenge is the limited economic development data available for the small communities in the state. Given the limitations, she finds evidence that consolidation resulted in stronger increases in retail sales than in the three comparison counties. Before consolidation, the average retail sales growth in the three counties was 36 percent, compared with only 24 percent in Carson City/Ormsby County. But as seen in table 11.4, the average retail sales growth in the three counties was only 16 percent in the postconsolidation period, compared with an 81 percent increase in Carson City/Ormsby County. In addition, she reports that the indirect economic development measure of growth in taxable value was stronger for Carson City/Ormsby County than for the average of the three comparison counties. Hence, there is some weak evidence to support the economic development hypothesis.

The Jacksonville/Duval County case is a tale of two cities with different economies, according to Dluhy. Both have economic development accomplishments; Jacksonville has grown in the manufacturing area and downtown, whereas Tampa's growth has been in the wholesale and retail sectors. He notes that both have also had aggressive and well-thought-out downtown and economic development strategies. He questions, however, whether consolidated government stands out in facilitating the development of these strategies, because cities throughout the South were pursuing a similar agenda. Overall, he concludes that Jacksonville/Duval County has had more effective economic development than Tampa/Hillsborough County; it has kept property taxes low and has been able to attract high-value-added manufacturing. Jacksonville/Duval County also has "invested considerable amounts of resources into infrastructure development and largely as a result of this investment; they have been able to maintain a steady and significant growth in the value added by manufacturing over time in their local economy."

The Wyandotte County/Kansas City case is one of an economic turnaround story. Wood and Leland find that consolidation "has contributed to the reverse in population decline, slowed the loss of rooftops, has helped spur retail sales in Wyandotte County," narrowing the gap in retail sales growth with Shawnee County. They also find evidence that the consolidation has resulted in increased levels of citizen satisfaction pertaining to economic development. The evidence supporting stronger economic development performance for Wyandotte County/Kansas City includes stronger retail growth and a reduction in the number of rooftops in the county. That said, we also note that these indicators still point to stronger retail sales growth in Topeka/Shawnee County, and that housing growth is positive during the period in Topeka/Shawnee County and still negative in Wyandotte County/Kansas City. The authors base their positive conclusion on the reversal of fortune for the consolidated government and anticipate that economic performance indicators will soon turn to positive territory following the investments by the consolidated government in new infrastructure to boost economic development, including massive development at the intersection of Interstate 70 and Interstate 435.

The Kellam organization promised that the Virginia Beach/Princess Anne County merger would result in long-term economic progress and improvements in metropolitan possibilities. Swartz concludes that these promises were kept. Virginia Beach/Princess Anne County recorded much stronger growth in retail and manufacturing sectors than Richmond/Henrico County in the postconsolidation period. This was no doubt bolstered by the substantial population growth in Virginia Beach due to expanded activities at the nearby naval bases. The Richmond/Henrico County economy had no such stimulus in the postconsolidation period.

Although Lynchburg/Moore County had stronger retails sales and a lower unemployment rate than its comparison case in the postconsolidation period, it also had slower growth in the number households. Carroll, Wagers, and Wiggins observe that the consolidation did not prevent losses in the sales tax base within the Lynchburg/Moore County metropolitan area, but one also observes that the comparison case had even weaker retail sales, losing 1.7 percent in the postconsolidation period, compared with a mere 0.4 percent loss in Lynchburg/Moore County. More important, perhaps, this case is about the distillery being saved from annexation, which would have led to a huge loss for the city. This is key evidence in analyzing whether consolidation improved economic development in this community, because it prevented substantial economic losses in the eyes of the consolidation proponents.

Consolidation supporters may argue that the support for Hypothesis 2 is stronger than we present. If one includes the "stop-loss" or "turnaround" cases, one can argue that consolidated governments have performed much better than had they not been consolidated. Consider the cases of Wyandotte County/Kansas City, Lynchburg/Moore County, and Butte/Silver Bow County, for example. The case authors argue that consolidation was essential to the economic performance of these communities, even if they underperform in the measures we use to compare with the matching case. Lynchburg would not have been able to keep the distillery in their tax base without consolidation. Without the value added from that industry, what would the economic performance of the county be today relative to the matching case? Leland and Wood argue that landing NASCAR was not an option for either the city or Wyandotte County, given the troubled politics between them; the prosperity from that initiative emanated from the consolidation and was very unlikely to happen without it. Butte/Silver Bow County is also viewed as a turnaround story by Keim and Marlowe.

The Jacksonville/Duval County and Virginia Beach/Princess Anne County cases demonstrate that hewing to a strict quantitative analysis with a comparison case has definite limits. Dluhy shows that Jacksonville/Duval County and Tampa/Hillsborough County have essentially followed different economic development strategies, and how does one reckon that manufacturing is a better strategy than retail, or vice versa? Virginia Beach exploded in population after consolidation, and Richmond has followed its own development path. Swartz argues that the growth realized in the consolidated community would have been unlikely without consolidation.

This leads us to consider a revision to our definition of economic development performance and appropriate benchmarks. If we use a broader definition and include turnaround and stop-loss cases, then this sample suggests there is substantial evidence that city–county consolidation can lead to better economic development performance than if the city and county remained separate entities. Conversely, opponents of consolidation can suggest that ILAs and other means of functional consolidation (e.g., special districts) might also achieve many of the economic development goals touted by consolidation reformers. Still, it is fairly clear to us that the performance of Lynchburg/Moore County could not have been achieved through an ILA because retaining the distillery required consolidation of jurisdiction, not shared services. Nor would an ILA between Kansas City, Kansas, and Wyandotte County resolve the political problems that stood as an obstacle to the development of the NASCAR track and subsequent benefits.

Taken together, the chapter analyses and the aggregated presentation of the population data and economic indicators suggest that the consolidated governments have performed better in terms of economic development than the comparison cases. The evidence is not overwhelming by any means. Still, difficulties in using exactly the same indicators notwithstanding, the multiple measures used for this analysis compel us to accept the hypothesis that *consolidated governments will have higher economic growth rates than similar nonconsolidated communities due to structural effectiveness gains.* This finding will bolster the case of those consolidation advocates who argue that the purpose of consolidation is the long-term economic development of the community, not increasing local government efficiency.

Other Promises in Consolidation Referenda

This section examines the degree to which the consolidations live up to the specific promises made in the referenda campaign beyond the issues of increasing efficiency and effectiveness. With few exceptions, these promises are evaluated without reference to the comparison city/county case. That is because the nature of most promises is very specific and requires no validity control. For example, several cases promised to avoid annexation from a neighboring city; the consolidations unambiguously accomplished this promise, and no reference to the comparison county is required to see that is so. In other cases, proponents promised that no employees would be laid off, or salaries would be equalized, or water services would be extended. In the next section, we summarize the conclusions from each case chapter, itemizing the promises and whether the consolidation delivered on the promises.

The Data

We first examine a group of cases where an annexation battle was the primary impetus for a consolidation effort. We then note a wide variety of other issues that were less important than either efficiency or economic development—but still bedeviled citizens and required attention in a consolidation campaign.

Annexation Cases

Three of the consolidation cases in our sample had annexation battles at the heart of the merger debate. In these three cases, improving efficiency and effectiveness were not central issues for the discussions. By virtue of unification, the central promises in these cases were met; each of the cities in these cases avoided annexation by a neighboring city or county, thereby preserving their sense of "community" and achieving related goals.

Lynchburg/Moore County

Carroll, Wagers, and Wiggins note that "the annexation issue had both emotional and economic implications for Lynchburg and Moore County and represented the central justification for consolidation." The next annexations would have engulfed Moore County High School, Motlow State Community College, and the Jack Daniel's Distillery, all of which were important to Moore County's identity and economic vitality. Jack Daniel's was a source of local pride as well as revenue streams from property taxes, local option sales taxes, and alcohol taxes. The consolidation fended off annexation and encroachment by surrounding governments and preserved the property tax base, making the consolidation of Lynchburg/Moore County "an automatic success." The consolidation was not as strong to deliver on promises of increased federal aid, the Carroll team notes; "although highway-related expenditures appeared to suffer due to fluctuation and decline in federal intergovernmental revenue, these vacillations had no apparent effect on education spending."

Lexington/Fayette County

Gillen argues that political and social factors were more important than efficiencies and good government in the Lexington/Fayette County case. The annexation of developed areas on the fringes of the city boundary was bound to a critical tax-benefit argument; the threat of increased taxes without increased services led residents to favor merger over annexation. With the merger, additional taxation would only result when additional services were added. This was the central issue. Moreover, proponents promised that consolidation would bring with it representation chosen by district elections rather than the previous at-large system, all but guaranteeing minority control of two or three seats on the governing council. The Lexington/Fayette County case is judged a success apart from the issues of increased efficiency and economic development because it kept the central promise in the consolidation campaign, fending off annexation and creating taxation with representation.

Virginia Beach/Princess Anne County

The Kellam Organization, Swartz notes, "promised that the merger would result in long-term economic progress, protection from annexation from Norfolk, appeals to local pride, and improvements in the metropolitan possibilities. Every promise was certainly kept." The consolidated government appealed to the local pride of Virginia Beach and precluded annexation from Norfolk, as well as improved metropolitan possibilities. Preserving independence from Norfolk was the central issue in this consolidation debate, and the merger is deemed to have successfully kept the primary promises; the efficiency and economic development improvements of concern to most mergers were of secondary importance.

Other Cases

The other cases in our sample tended to have economic development or efficiency at the heart of the promises made in the consolidation campaigns. The other promises we are examining in this section were of tertiary importance. Many of the promises relate to specific issues that bedeviled the city and the county governments, and their disaffected residents.

Wyandotte County/Kansas City

One of the most visible signs of the economic turnaround in the unified government of Wyandotte County/Kansas City is the immense Kansas Speedway that now anchors a state "tourism district" and exploding retail center at the intersections of Interstate 70 and Interstate 435. The development was a specific promise of the Wyandotte County/Kansas City reformers that had implications beyond increased economic development; the racetrack symbolizes a new government that has the professional capacity to lure such a development to an ailing economy. The reformers promised voters that the consolidation would result in increased responsiveness and professionalism in local government administration; most specifically, they promised that the reform would reduce property taxes (approximately 2 percent a year), spur the creation of an ethics commission to clean up perceived corruption, stem the loss of rooftops and population, and, most important, land a new economic development project for their area—the NASCAR racetrack.

Leland and Wood find that the combined governments delivered on those promises; the unified government cut the municipal workforce and trimmed property taxes four years running: The periodic scandals from county and city governments ended, and the unified government's relationship with state government in Topeka improved dramatically. In addition, the unified government created an ethics commission, hired an ethics administrator, and developed ethics policies and related employee ethics training programs. Overall, Leland and Wood find that the Wyandotte County/Kansas City consolidation lived up to the specific promises made to the voters, and the unified government continues to make progress on achieving the specific, longer-term economic goals.

Nashville/Davidson County

The list of promises made for the Nashville/Davidson County consolidation included professionalizing government services, eliminating financial inequities, equalizing services, and eliminating buck-passing. Nownes, Houston, and Schwerdt conclude that the Nashville/Davidson County consolidation kept most of these promises and did so early on. For example, citizen satisfaction surveys revealed increased clarity for accountability. In addition, the unified government quickly and successfully eliminated city–county financial inequities, including free riding by out-of-city residents who used city facilities without paying taxes for them, and the problem of double taxation, in which people paid taxes to both the city and the county when they received some services only from the city. Countywide equalization of services was begun in earnest, shifting several services formerly financed entirely or mostly by city taxpayers to a countywide tax base, especially schools and parks. The Metro government also kept promises to improve professionalization and specialization, including hiring an out-of-state consultant to run the fire department, a successful nationwide search for a new director of schools, and engaging a team from the International Association of Chiefs of Police to help clean up the image of the old city police department and county sheriff's patrol. Keeping this range of specific promises contributed much to the general satisfaction of citizens with the merger in subsequent years.

Jacksonville/Duval County

The Jacksonville/Duval County consolidation campaign included promises to eradicate political corruption and patronage, correct serious environmental problems, and employ professional management in government. The proponents promoted the good government image as integral to a new economic vision for the community. Dluhy observes that there have been no movements to disband the government since 1967, and that the citizens of Jacksonville have continued to support their unified government's sales tax increases on a number of occasions to clean up the Saint Johns River and complete other public facility and public works projects.

On a less positive note, Dluhy remarks that the consolidation of governments has denied the election of a black majority on the council and/or a black mayor, unlike other cities in the South that did not consolidate; and this was true despite the fact that the charter uses a combination of district and at-large representatives that at least guaranteed blacks four out nineteen district council members in 1968 when the new government was formed.

Athens/Clarke County

The consolidation narrative identified by Durning and Sanford incorporated several implicit promises aimed narrowly at specific groups and interests, including avoiding layoffs, equalizing water rates, improving waste services, and a more effective police department. They observe that fulfilling most of these promises was guaranteed, to the extent possible, by provisions in the charter. The evidence is weakest with respect to the improvements in public safety. Their comparison of postconsolidation changes in reported part 1 crimes per 1,000 persons and trends in the ratio of part 1 arrests to part 1 reported crimes provides weak evidence that unification had a beneficial impact on law enforcement. Still, in both comparisons, Athens/Clarke County "had results during the postconsolidation period that were better than those of Hall County."

Carson City/Ormsby County

Lukemeyer argues that the Carson City/Ormsby County consolidation was largely a "ho-hum" affair, with proponents presenting consolidation as a fairly minor change in government structure: "The promised benefits were limited to those that could be fairly ensured by structure of the charter." According to her analysis, the consolidation was relatively uncontroversial and successful for several reasons, including "Carson City's unique situation as a geographically small, densely populated county in a state of geographically large, sparsely populated counties; the dominance of Carson City in Ormsby County; the fact that formal consolidation followed—as was presented as primarily formalizing—a series of functional consolidations; and the fact that expectations and promises of benefits were fairly limited. The Carson City/Ormsby County case is an interesting example of an incremental approach to consolidation, one that is judged by internal observers by how well it simplifies local government. Although the efficiency hypothesis would seem to be central to this case, it would also seem that it was an unchallenged assumption that was taken for granted by the constituent parties in the merger.

Butte/Silver Bow County

The Butte/Silver Bow County case has the weakest record for meeting consolidation promises beyond increased efficiency and economic development. The promise of a unified governmental administration to provide effective leadership for area wide policy and development was related to the promise of a council of part-time commissioners for legislation and a full-time chief executive for administration. Keim and Marlowe find that "while the promise of unified governmental administration was kept, there is little evidence of consistent areawide policy and development." Their analysis suggests that "the number of partisan elected positions could be one of the most significant reasons for why there is no areawide policy planning and development." The chief executive officer is selected in a partisan election and has no requirement of professional public management credentials. They find little evidence of the professionalization outcomes one expects from a professional executive; the jurisdiction lacks a comprehensive strategic plan, a county mission, and a county vision statement, and there is no evidence of major economic development projects that would suggest the presence of strong and cohesive leadership. Although the consolidation kept the main efficiency promise of curbing property tax growth, the superficial way in which the leadership promises were kept provides weak evidence to support this hypothesis.

Summary for Other Promises

The consolidation cases in our sample were overwhelmingly effective in keeping the promises to voters that went beyond increasing efficiency or improving economic development. The notable exception is the Butte/Silver Bow County case, where the structural reform has not resulted in fundamental changes in policy leadership. Although the Carson City/Ormsby County case was uneventful and the promises made were uninspiring, Lukemeyer's analysis indicates that the consolidation has fulfilled the expectations of the residents. In the rest of the cases we have examined, the evidence is quite strong that the particular promises made to voters were kept, with very few exceptions.

Having now reviewed the evidence to support the three major hypotheses in our research design, the next section considers the evidence as a whole: Did the consolidations keep the promises made with respect to improved economic development, increased efficiency, and other promises particular to each situation?

Promises Kept?

When we consider the evidence regarding the nine cases in our sample, we conclude that the consolidations have largely lived up to their other promises made in the merger debates. Moreover, we are not surprised to find that the economic development promises have largely been kept, whereas the implicit (and sometimes explicit) promises of increased efficiency have not. These results conform to our previous work (Leland and Thurmaier 2004), demonstrating that consolidation referenda campaigns are more likely to be successful when they promise improved economic development for the community and more likely to fail if they promise increased efficiency of government performance. If there is a surprise in the findings, it is how annexation fights can render the efficiency and economic development arguments moot; they are not central to the campaigns in some cases, and are ironically replaced by the primary concern of community identity.

Accept the Null Hypothesis for Efficiency Gains

Increased government efficiency is a tempting promise to make in a consolidation campaign, and it is frequently made. As we found in our previous work (Leland and Thurmaier 2004), voters do not believe such promises and routinely vote against consolidations based on this promise. Our latest evidence gives the opponents to such consolidation campaigns strong evidence to support their votes. We do not find a discernible pattern of increased efficiency in consolidated governments relative to their comparison cases. There are a number of reasons why this is probably true.

First, the probability of increased government efficiency is often lowered by the compromising nature of consolidation campaigns. To neutralize powerful voting blocs, proponents often must sacrifice some of the easiest ways to economize. Thus, proponents often promise that there will be no layoffs of city and county employees; savings will accrue over the long run from attrition. This promise assumes that vacant positions will not be filled; however, these positions can—and often are—reallocated to other uses, presumably to make government more effective or to increase allocative efficiency within the organization. But the promise is to increase technical efficiency—to economize and reduce spending—not to increase allocative efficiency within the government organization.

Opportunities for economizing are further weakened when consolidation proponents need to promise to raise salaries in comparable positions to attain equity; the alternative of lowering salaries is not generally on the table—for example, one would not expect proponents to argue that they will lower the salaries of the police department's officers to the level of the deputies in the sheriff's office.

Second, promised economies of scale in service delivery (e.g., water, sanitation, policing) can be dwarfed by the new capital investments to raise rural service levels. Although debt financing can obviate the need for immediate and large capital spending, the debt still must be repaid with higher revenues, and for some time. In small jurisdictions, such as in Lynchburg/Moore County, where debt financing is not as easy to get as in larger jurisdictions, the spike in spending related to buying new fire engines, new police cars, and such can quickly obviate the expected economies of scale.

Although this was not an issue in the early consolidations, current efforts to merge governments can expect to spend more on merging information technology systems than any hypothesized savings that might come from fewer information technology staff. Savings from merging systems are far from obvious; our study suggests quite the contrary.

Finally, the presumed savings from blending the finance and budgeting administrations is illusory. These functions do not overlap much at all in a city and a county. The county's finance department is largely oriented toward collecting taxes on behalf of the constituent governments and the state, involving property assessments and billings that the cities do not perform. In addition, the expanded social service and other state-mandated functions of county government require attention at the budget office level that is not required in a city budget office.

It is not surprising, then, that there is little systematic evidence that consolidated governments operate more efficiently than their comparison communities. Although about half of the cases in our sample seem to have lower rates of expenditure growth, especially in some core local government functions, the other half of the sample does not produce the same data. Telling voters that there is a fifty/fifty chance of increasing government efficiency with a consolidated government does not seem to be a compelling argument for voting to support consolidation. Yet that is what our evidence in this study suggests is the probability.

Reject the Null Hypothesis for Economic Development Promises

Economic development in a community is subject to a wide variety of external factors. The overall national and regional economies have powerful effects on a community. In 2008, one also must acknowledge the increasing effects of the globalized economy, which was not a significant concern to most of our cases, especially those consolidations in the 1960s and 1970s.

Finding a discernible pattern of stronger economic development growth in a pair of counties, therefore, is not expected. Our research design carefully considered how to isolate key indicators from among many to measure economic growth in our pairs of communities. The key to finding a pattern has been using multiple measures consistently across the set of cases in our sample. One could pick a positive measure in county B that was ignored in county A because it was negative—if one's goal were to *demonstrate* economic performance rather than *test* for its presence. Although we do not have exactly consistent measures across all cases, we created a set of acceptable measures to use before our research team started mining for data in the basements of courthouses and the archives of the U.S. Bureau of the Census. If the data have been available, we have reported them. We did not discard any data that we could find to test our economic development performance. The truth is, such data are hard to come by for older cases; the Census data are getting better and more accessible, but that has not been true for several of our cases.

Nevertheless, all things considered, we find consistent evidence in our sample that the consolidated governments have performed more effectively in economic development than their comparison counties. We are not arguing that consolidation is either a necessary or a sufficient condition for economic development. We make no such claim. Whether a merger of city and county governments can yield a marginal increase in economic performance will be dependent on a host of factors pertaining to each community.

We also can make no claim from these data about the quality of economic growth in the consolidated governments relative to the comparison counties. A good example is the Tampa/Jacksonville County study. Jacksonville/Duval County has been more effective in retaining its manufacturing employment than Tampa/Hillsborough County, but the latter has had much stronger growth in the retail sector. How much influence has the structure of government had on the type and quality of economic development in these communities? Probably not much, because exogenous economic forces no doubt exert the largest influence.

That said, future research could examine how well consolidated governments are able to respond to economic development opportunities relative to comparable counties. Other research could compare our pairs of cases on these economic development measures in a more current period. Our design was specifically crafted to capture the more immediate affects of consolidation, if any, on economic performance. In this regard, the consolidated governments had stronger performances than the comparable counties.

Reject the Null Hypothesis for Other Promises

We can reject the null hypothesis regarding the specific promises made in consolidation campaigns other than the efficiency and economic development arguments. Only one case, Butte/Silver Bow County, fails the test. What is notable in this body of evidence is how annexation as a central driver for consolidation renders efficiency and economic development arguments moot. Whether or not the consolidated government is more efficient or performs better economically is unimportant to the voters; their focus is preserving their community identity. The paradox is interesting. Consolidation is approved by voters who want to preserve their community identity against aggressive annexation by a neighboring jurisdiction; yet in the very act of consolidating the governments, they vote to blend the identity of the city and the county into a new entity that did not exist previously and that will assume its own persona over time. And we find no evidence that the residents of Virginia Beach/Princess Anne County, Lexington/Fayette County, and Lynchburg/Moore County regret their actions. None of the consolidated communities in the study, for that matter, have discussed reverting back to their previous unconsolidated structures.

The Power of a Rigorous Research Design

We are confident in these results because we believe in the power of our rigorous research design. We trust the results because our design has high internal validity, despite data access problems. The measures we have used were set a priori, and the research team worked arduously to find the data demanded by the research design. When the specific measure was not possible, we used good proxies instead. The inconsistencies in the data stem from the availability of information, not from a convenient selection of variables to rationalize the bias of chapter authors.

In fact, the authors invited to participate in this project were decidedly agnostic with respect to the benefits of consolidation. As a team, we really had no bias one way or the other regarding the purported benefits promised by consolidation advocates. The benefits of the combined qualitative and quantitative design were especially pronounced in our analysis of the economic development performance hypothesis. A strict adherence to a quantitative analysis such as ARIMA, even if the data had been available (and they were not), would not have provided the reader with sufficient insights to make judgments about the performance of these governments. Readers may disagree with the conclusions of the chapter authors or the editors, but they now have a much richer understanding of the nuances of consolidations drawn from a systematic study.

Consolidation proponents and opponents alike owe a huge debt to the authors of this volume who struggled to adhere to the research design and find the data we needed. It was not easy at all to find most of the data. This was especially true for the smaller cities; they are excluded from the regular Census of Governments, and they also seem to lack professional data-archiving policies. In many cases, the "old" budgets and other reports have simply been tossed in the trash, with no remaining record. In cases where there might have been a record "somewhere," our research teams often faced indifferent or uncooperative officials who would not take the time to assist with our data requests. Conversely, we are very grateful to the countless officials who went out of their way and bent over backwards to help us find the budgets and reports needed to analyze our case studies. Without their help, this study would not have been successful.

Thinking Ahead

These results will likely give community leaders who are interested in improving the efficiency of their local governments some pause. If consolidation of city and county government does not necessarily yield increased technical efficiency, what are the alternatives to improving metropolitan efficiency?

Improving Metropolitan Efficiency

We distinguish here between the standard allocative efficiency arguments for fragmented metropolitan government and the desire by many consolidation advocates, especially in the business community, for economizing. There are two avenues that can be fruitful routes to more economical government services: targeted functional consolidation of promising services, and ILAs to share the costs and risks of providing government services.

Targeted Functional Consolidation

As the Carson City/Ormsby County case illustrates, cities and counties can decide to consolidate specific services to gain economies of scale. Although Carson City and Ormsby County eventually opted for full-scale political consolidation, that need not be the case. There are two areas that provide ready opportunities for functional consolidation.

Consolidating planning functions at the county level is not the same as giving the county absolute planning authority. For example, the City of Lawrence, Kansas, has shared planning functions with Douglas County in a partnership. Half of the planning board is appointed by the city, and the county appoints the other half. The planning director is jointly approved by both bodies.

There are several advantages to consolidating planning functions. First, joint planning can avoid annexation wars that consume valuable staff time and political capital; they also diminish respect for government by residents who see "turf battles" as inefficient government and counterproductive (Pluckhan 2006). As we can see in a few of our sample cases, an annexation war or the threat of annexation actually was the central issue spurring a city–county consolidation.

Consolidated planning can also increase the return on investment made by communities in economic development infrastructure. Creating a shared vision of economic development planning can more efficiently and effectively manage infrastructure improvements to avoid leapfrog developments and focus expensive capital projects where they are most likely to lead to capital investments and job creation by firms looking for new business locations.

Policing offers another promising avenue for functional consolidation. The simplest and most direct approach used by several communities has been to specialize the operations of the sheriff and the police. The sheriff's office is focused on protecting the county courthouse, serving the courts, and managing the county jail; the police department assumes responsibility for all other public safety functions, including patrols, detectives, and forensic science services.

This specialization achieves economies of scale without inheriting the political problems that often dog consolidation efforts. Because the sheriff's office and police departments are not merged, there is no need to integrate and rationalize the different pay scales often found in the two services. The jail staff will usually continue to have lower salary scales than the police officers, for example. Meanwhile, the patrolling and detective work for the county can be handled by a single agency (the police department), and there is not confusion over who is responsible for answering a 911 call based on the caller's location.

Interlocal Agreements Can Economize with Flexibility

A second and related avenue for economizing on service delivery is to create an interlocal agreement to share costs, risks, and benefits of providing public services. ILAs have a long history in American governments, but they have not been studied extensively until recently. A recent study of ILAs in Iowa (Chen and Thurmaier 2008) suggests that ILAs are created to increase the effectiveness, as well as efficiency, of local services. The impetus for ILAs provides a focusing effect. Moreover, equitable sharing of benefits is important for the success of ILAs, and the population and type of service also matter.

A common form of economizing ILA is a mutual aid agreement between fire departments, or between police departments. These agreements reduce the need for expensive capital investments for police and fire equipment. For example, in the Kansas City metropolitan area, only one municipality had an armored vehicle for riot duty, but it was available to most all of the other local governments if they needed it. Similarly, an expensive extended ladder truck was placed strategically near the edge of a city so that it could also respond to a mutual aid request of a neighboring jurisdiction that could have need if a certain building were on fire (Thurmaier and Wood 2002).

Other ILAs obviate the need for high-cost public works equipment by creating flexible lending policies between neighboring jurisdictions. These agreements can be informal understandings between departments in neighboring communities, but increasingly they are codified in a memorandum of understanding or other contract to specify liability issues for equipment damages, personal injury, and depreciation reimbursement.

One area for economizing ILAs that does not seem to have become popular is back office support. For example, a small municipality could contract with a neighboring town for budgeting and financial management, or purchasing, and so on. Many municipalities are members of risk management pools and investment pools, which are essentially agreements to let some other entity manage the risk issues of the organization, or manage its investments. Extending this concept to basic office processing operations may provide economies of scale that cannot be realized without managers thinking (and operating) outside the jurisdictional box.

Improving Metropolitan Economic Development

Even though we find evidence that consolidated governments have performed better in economic development than their comparison cases, there are other options to improving economic development performance besides the politically difficult process of consolidation. Even consolidated governments can explore these options to further increase economic development performance.

Councils of government (COGs) have a mixed reputation for being valuable tools for local economic development (Weaver 2007). Having been originally created for regional planning, especially transportation, COGs now have a wide range of competencies and profiles. For instance, the Mid-America Regional Council (MARC) consists of thirty-three locally elected leaders representing the 9 counties and 120 cities in the bistate (Kansas and Missouri) metropolitan Kansas City region (see MARC 2009). MARC is a voluntary association with a mission to foster better understanding and cooperation on transjurisdictional issues, including transportation, child care, aging, emergency services, public safety and 911 calls, and environmental issues. It was instrumental in creating a joint purchasing program that has been very successful in helping member jurisdictions economize in quite a few service areas (Thurmaier and Wood 2002).

Area chambers of commerce are nongovernmental organizations that often include public- and private-member organizations. Transjurisdictional chambers mimic the transjurisdictional character of local and regional economies, which are indifferent to political boundaries unless they become barriers to market efficiency. Cities and counties can support and encourage metropolitan or area chambers as a framework for overcoming interjurisdictional competition.

Ultimately, metropolitan economic development can succeed when elected and appointed government officials think regionally and act locally to create a regional approach. This requires them to share sovereignty with other jurisdictions in the delivery of specific public services. Sharing accountability for service delivery can lead to finger pointing and confusion from residents when problems arise. But pooling resources from a number of jurisdictions can provide more effective service delivery. There are numerous success stories, including three communities in the Des Moines metropolitan area that created and manage a joint dispatch center, among other cooperative activities (Westcom 2009). The three cities have succeeded because the elected officials and city managers know that success depends on overcoming "tribalistic tendencies" that are barriers to mutual benefits (Thurmaier 2006, 145).

The Overall Validity of Our Study

Overall, we are pleased to present the results of this study to our academic colleagues and to practitioners. A major weakness of our study is that we were unable to measure the service effectiveness levels of the consolidations and comparison cases. The major barrier to such findings is the lack of performance measurement data, and in particular, data on citizen satisfaction. A few authors were able to find some citizen satisfaction data, but even then we do not have continuous and comparable data before and after consolidations, nor were we able to acquire matching data from the comparison cases. Future studies could create a research design to compare uniform performance measures, including citizen satisfaction, with selected services in the consolidated governments relative to the comparison cases. An ideal design would identify communities in consolidation discussions, survey citizens about service satisfaction, and then resurvey postconsolidation audiences (if voters agree, of course). Practitioners engaged in consolidation debates, even those thinking about initiating a consolidation effort, now have a more realistic perspective of what outcomes can be expected from a successful consolidation. Arguments that promise increased efficiency are unlikely to be successful, and opponents will no doubt seize upon the results of this study as evidence to cast doubts on such promises. Conversely, proponents who argue that the consolidation can improve economic development performance now have some credible evidence to support their point of view.

Scholars who study the relative merits of fragmented and consolidated governments will find much to consider in this study. There is a good reason that such a study has not been attempted previously: It is incredibly difficult to meet the high standards for scholarly evidence. We are confident that our rigorous research design, and the tremendous effort of our chapter research teams, has provided scholars with the first comprehensive analysis of consolidated governments in the United States. Although it may not be perfect, and there is some degree of measurement error in our measures and data, we are confident that the better economic development performance patterns we find in these case analyses are real, and that these promises can be made—and kept—by other consolidation proponents.

The Next Study

Local government consolidations are not just a U.S. phenomenon. In other countries, legislatures decree the consolidations of large and small communities, and also of equivalent municipal and county levels. A comparative study to analyze whether these consolidations provide economizing or increased economic development performance would perhaps help isolate the factors that matter most to achieving these objectives. In countries where consolidations are voluntary, a comparison of electoral campaigns and whether consolidations deliver on the promises would also provide a broader context to contribute to the debate on consolidation versus fragmentation among scholars in economics, political science, and public administration.

Beyond a comparative study of consolidated governments, we need a national comparative study to measure the value added in efficiency and effectiveness of ILAs and functional consolidations of selected public services. Such a study would enable us to create a benefit/cost analysis of consolidations relative to ILAs and the functional consolidation of selected services. Any volunteers?

Notes

1. There are actually a few more total observations, because the Nevada consolidation case is compared with the average of three other counties in Nevada, and the Georgia case is also compared with more than one comparison county.
2. Feiock and Carr (1997) also conduct a pre- and post-time series analysis for economic development measures.
3. The one exception is the KCK/Wyandotte case. At the time of conducting this research only 7 years of data were available.
4. The most difficult inconsistency in reported census data is whether there are entries for *direct general expenditures* and/or *general expenditures.* Thus, when the census tables fail to include intergovernmental expenditures (because they were not reported to the census bureau), one must use *general expenditures,* even if it is (potentially) an incomplete total of expenditures for that city or county for that year.
5. In most case analyses, the investigators adjusted the data for inflation using implicit price deflators; this dampens the size of growth over ten years. Although a few investigators did not take that step, it is not a threat to our internal validity because the treatment is the same for the experimental case and the comparison county. In addition, it is the *relative* growth of the experimental case in relation to the comparison case that we are analyzing, not the absolute size of the growth; though some consolidation cases thus show larger expenditure growth than other consolidation cases, such a comparison is inappropriate within our research design.
6. Proper adjustments were made for the Virginia case, because those populations are reported separately by the Census Bureau data.

References

Benton, Ed, and Darwin Gamble. 1984. City–County Consolidation and Economies of Scale: Evidence from a Time-Series Analysis in Jacksonville, Florida. *Social Science Quarterly*, March, 190–98.

Carr, J., S. Bae, and W. Lu. 2006. City–County Governments: A Tale of Two Cities. *State and Local Government Review* 38:259–69.

Carr, J., and R. Feiock. 1999. Metropolitan Government and Economic Development. *Urban Affairs Review* 34, no. 3:476–89.

Chen, Yu-Che, and Kurt Thurmaier. 2008. Interlocal Agreements as Collaborations: An Empirical Investigation of Impetuses, Norms, and Success. *American Review of Public Administration* 68, no. 3:537–48.

———. 2009. Interlocal Agreements as Collaborations: An Empirical Investigation of Impetuses, Norms, and Success, in *The American Review of Public Administration* 39 (5):536–52.

Durning, D. 1995. The Effects of City–County Government Consolidation: The Perspectives of Unified Government. *Public Administration Quarterly* 19, no. 3:272–98.

Feiock, R. C., and J. Carr. 1997. A Reassessment of City/County Consolidation: Economic Development Impacts. *State and Local Government Review* 29, no. 3:166–71.

Leland, S., and M. Rosentraub. 2007. Consolidated and Fragmented Governments and Regional Cooperation: Surprising Lessons from Charlotte, Cleveland, Indianapolis, and Wyandotte County/Kansas City, Kansas. Paper presented at 2008 Urban Affairs Association Conference, Baltimore.

Leland, Suzanne, and Kurt Thurmaier, eds. 2004. *Reshaping the Local Government Landscape: Case Studies of Local Government Consolidation.* Armonk, NY: M. E. Sharpe.

———. 2006. Lessons from 35 Years of City–County Consolidation Attempts. In *Municipal Yearbook.* Washington, DC: International City/County Management Association.

Lyons, W. E., and David Lowery. 1989. Governmental Fragmentation versus Consolidation: Five Public-Choice Myths about How to Create Informed, Involved, and Happy Citizens. *Public Administration Review* 49, no. 6:533–43.

MARC (Mid-America Regional Council). 2009. About MARC: Advancing Regional Progress through Leadership, Planning, Action. www.marc.org/aboutmarc.htm.

Ostrom, V., C. Tiebout, and R. Warren. 1961. The Organization of Government in Metropolitan Areas: A Theoretical Inquiry. *American Political Science Review* 55:831–42.

Pluckhan, Lon. 2006. Annexation Evolution: Do Social Networks Impact the Effectiveness and Efficiency of Annexation Agreements in Iowa? 28E Management Report prepared in cooperation with IowAccess Council and Information Technology Enterprise, Iowa Department of Administrative Services. Public Policy and Administration Program, Iowa State University, Ames.

Reese, L. 2004. Same Governance, Different Day: Does Metropolitan Reorganization Make a Difference? *Review of Policy Research* 21, no. 4:595–611.

Rosenbaum, W. A., and Gladys Kammerer. 1974. *Against Long Odds: The Theory and Practice of Successful Governmental Consolidation.* Administrative and Policy Studies Series 03-022, vol. 2. Beverly Hills, CA: Sage.

Seldon, S., and R. Campbell. 2000. The Expenditure Impacts of Unification in a Small Georgia County: A Contingency Perspective of City. *Public Administration Quarterly* 24, no. 2:169–201.

Swanson, B. 1996. Jacksonville, Consolidation and Regional Governance. In *Regional Politics and the Post-City Age,* ed. H. V. Slavic and R. Vogel. Thousand Oaks, CA: Sage.

Thurmaier, Kurt. 2006. High-Intensity Interlocal Collaboration in Three Iowa Cities. *Public Administration Review* 66 (Supplement 1): 144–46.

Thurmaier, Kurt, and Curtis Wood. 2002. Interlocal Agreements as Overlapping Social Networks: Pitcket-Fence Federalism in Metropolitan Kansas City. *Public Administration Review* 62 (5) (Sept.–Oct.): 585–98.

Tiebout, C. 1956. A Pure Theory of Local Government Expenditures. *Journal of Political Economy* 44:416–24.

Vojnovic, I. 2000. The Transitional Impacts of Municipal Consolidations. *Journal of Urban Affairs* 22:385–417.

Weaver, Chad. 2007. The Impact of Councils of Government on Community Networks in the State of Iowa. 28E Management Report prepared in cooperation with IowAccess Council and Information Technology Enterprise, Iowa Department of Administrative Services. Public Policy and Administration Program, Iowa State University, Ames.

Westcom. 2009. Westcom Dispatch, City of West Des Moines. www.wdm-ia.com/Index.aspx?page=312.

Contributors

Deborah A. Carroll is an associate professor in the Department of Public Administration and Policy of the School of Public and International Affairs at the University of Georgia. Her research focuses on financial management and fiscal policy issues pertaining to state and local governments with an emphasis on taxation, revenue diversification, and urban economic development.

Milan J. Dluhy is a professor of public administration in the Department of Public and International Affairs at the University of North Carolina at Wilmington. He is the author of several books, including *Solving Urban Problems in Metropolitan Areas* and *The Miami Fiscal Crisis: Can a Poor City Reclaim Fiscal Prosperity?*

Dan Durning recently retired from the Carl Vinson Institute of Government at the University of Georgia, where he was director of the International Center for Democratic Governance, which worked with partner institutions in Albania, China, Georgia, Kazakhstan, Russia, Ukraine, and other countries. During his seventeen years at the Vinson Institute, his research included evaluations of the Athens/Clarke County unification and fiscal impact analyses of two proposed city–county consolidations in Georgia. He also advised groups considering consolidation efforts in three other states.

Shawn Gillen received his PhD in public administration from the University of Kentucky. He is currently the city administrator of Grand Rapids, Minnesota, and adjunct professor of management at the College of St. Scholastica. His research interests include budget theory, public policy, and intergovernmental finance.

David J. Houston is an associate professor at the University of Tennessee, Knoxville. His teaching interests include public administration theory, public policy, policy analysis, and research methods. Previously, he spent five years as a member of the Department of Political Science at the University of Mississippi.

Susan Keim is a doctoral candidate in public administration at the University of Kansas. Her area of specialization is urban policy. Her research interests include civic engagement, leadership, and local government.

Suzanne M. Leland is currently an associate professor in the Political Science Department at the University of North Carolina, Charlotte. Her expertise includes state and local politics, intergovernmental relations, and urban policy. She is the coeditor of the book *Reshaping the Local Government Landscape: Cases in City–County Consolidation.*

Anna Lukemeyer is an associate professor of public administration at the University of Nevada, Las Vegas. Her research interests include education policy and finance, and public law policy and finance. She is the author of the book *Courts as Policymakers: School Finance Reform Litigation.*

Justin Marlowe is an assistant professor at the Evans School of Public Affairs at the University of Washington. His research interests include public financial management and municipal management.

Anthony J. Nownes is a professor of political science at the University of Tennessee, Knoxville. His research interests include interest groups, voting behavior, and public policy. He is the author of the book *Total Lobbying: What Lobbyists Want (and How They Try to Get It).*

Paula Sanford is a faculty member at the University of Georgia's Carl Vinson Institute of Government. Her work includes doing applied research and providing technical assistance for local governments in a variety of areas, such as incorporation, annexation, consolidation, and organizational improvements.

Marc Schwerdt is an assistant professor in the Department of History, Politics, and Philosophy at Lipscomb University in Nashville. He conducts research in a variety of fields, including local politics, international relations, and political behavior.

Nicholas J. Swartz is an assistant professor of public policy and administration at James Madison University in Harrisonburg, Virginia. His area of specialization is urban policy. His research interests include regionalism, public budgeting, quality-of-life frameworks, and economic effects.

Kurt Thurmaier is professor and director of the Division of Public Administration at Northern Illinois University. His career includes four years in the Wisconsin State Budget Office as a budget and management analyst, a Fulbright Scholarship at Jagiellonian University in Kraków, serving as a consultant to Polish local governments through the International City/County Management Association, and consulting on U.S. city–county consolidation efforts. His books include *Policy and Politics in State Budgeting* and *Case Studies of City–County Consolidations: Reshaping the Local Government Landscape*.

Kristin A. Wagers is a doctoral student in political science at the University of Tennessee specializing in judicial politics, public law, and public administration. Her research interests include criminal justice and the administration of state and local government. She has published articles in *Public Works, Management & Policy, The Justice System Journal,* and *Police Practice & Research.*

Mary Ellen Wiggins graduated from the University of Georgia with an MPA and from Wellesley College with a BA in urban studies. Her work in local government includes a Mayoral Fellowship with the City of Chicago. She currently works as a program examiner for the Office of Management and Budget in Washington.

Curtis Wood is an associate professor at Northern Illinois University. His research interests include budgeting and finance, local government structure, and interlocal government agreements. Previously, he served twenty years in city government, three years in city management, and seventeen years as a finance director.

Index

NOTE: *f* indicates a figure; *t* indicates a table.

F